AN INTRODUCTION

TO THE

MAITHILI DIALECT

OF

THE BIHARI LANGUAGE

AS SPOKEN IN

NORTH BIHAR

AN INTRODUCTION

TO THE

MAITHILI DIALECT

OF

THE BIHARI LANGUAGE

AS SPOKEN IN

NORTH BIHAR

GEORGE A. GRIERSON, C.I.E., Ph.D., D. Litt.

GYAN

Published by

GYAN

Gyan Publishing House
5, Ansari Road
Daryaganj, New Delhi-110002
Phone: 011-47034999, 9811692060
E-mail: books@gyanbooks.com

Distribution Network
gyanbooks.com
India, USA, Canada, UK, Australia, France

ISBN: 978-81-212-8963-4 (PB)
First Published, 1909

2nd Impression 2023

Printed at: Gyan Press, Delhi.

AN INTRODUCTION TO THE MAITHILI DIALECT OF THE BIHARI LANGUAGE AS SPOKEN IN NORTH BIHAR

AUTHOR: GEORGE A. GRIERSON

AN INTRODUCTION

TO THE

MAITHILĪ DIALECT

OF

THE BIHĀRĪ LANGUAGE

AS SPOKEN IN

NORTH BIHĀR

BY

GEORGE A. GRIERSON, C.I.E., Ph.D., D.Litt.,

Honorary Member of the Asiatic Society of Bengal, of the American Oriental Society, of the Nāgarī Pracāriṇī Sabhā, and of the Société Finno-Ougrienne; Foreign Associate Member of the Société Asiatique de Paris; Corresponding Member of the Königliche Gesellschaft der Wissenschaften zu Göttingen, formerly of His Majesty's Indian Civil Service.

SECOND EDITION.

PART I.

GRAMMAR.

Calcutta:

PRINTED AT THE BAPTIST MISSION PRESS AND PUBLISHED BY THE ASIATIC SOCIETY, 57, PARK STREET.

1909.

PREFACE TO THE SECOND EDITION.

When I undertook the preparation of this second edition of my Maithilī Grammar, my intention was to do little more than to arrange a corrected reprint of the first edition published in 1881. I soon found that the necessary corrections were so heavy and so important that the whole work had to be recast. It has, in fact, been rewritten.

When the first edition was prepared, the only specimens of literary Maithilī available were those then in my possession, and subsequently published in my Maithilī Chrestomathy. Since then more literary materials have been discovered and have been made available to students. These have all been carefully worked through by me, and, as a result, I have been able to give in the present edition of the Grammar a fairly complete set of examples of the manner in which the various forms are employed. The examples are not absolutely complete, for I have rigidly confined myself to passages taken from actually existing literature. With the exception of a few reproduced from the first edition, not a single example has been made up for the purpose of illustration.

The second edition has been prepared in England, and I have not had the advantage of further native assistance; but, on the other hand, I have fully utilized my notes which have been accumulating during the past twenty-five years. As compared with the former edition, the book represents a quarter of a century's progress in the study of an interesting and by no means easy dialect.

GEORGE A. GRIERSON.

CAMBERLEY,
June 11*th*, 1906.

CONTENTS.

PART I.

Alphabet and Vocabulary.

PART II.

Declension.

PART III.

CONJUGATION.

PART IV.

INDECLINABLES.

INTRODUCTION.

In submitting the following somewhat full grammar of the Maithili dialect to the Asiatic Society of Bengal, I wish to explain the sources of my information.

They may be divided into two classes—

1st—Forms obtained by translating into Maithili.

2nd—Forms obtained by translating from Maithili.

The first I obtained as follows: I printed paradigms of all the forms in Hindī and Sanskrit Grammar and circulated them as widely as possible amongst the paṇḍits, village school masters, and educated native gentlemen of Northern Mithilā, with directions to give the exact translation of each of these forms in their own native language.

I was enabled, in this way, to collect some fifty most useful books of forms, supplied by representatives of all classes of society, from the village *guru*, who knew little more than the herd-boys he taught, to the most learned paṇḍits of Mithilā. I am glad to say that the utmost interest was taken in my design, for the people are proud of their language and were pleased at the idea of its being made a polite one by obtaining the honour of print. These books of paradigms formed the basis of this grammar. They were compared with each other; and where one was found wanting, another supplied the deficiency. At the same time, it must not be imagined that they showed many mutual discrepancies: on the contrary, considering the many varied sources from which they were derived, their unanimity was wonderful and justifies me in hoping that what I here publish will be found fairly accurate.

With regard to the forms obtained by translating from Maithili, they were obtained in various ways. In cutcherry I collected myself a large number of words from the mouths of the witnesses who came in from a distance. These I found very useful in checking the books of forms above referred to. I also collected a number of country songs, which afforded invaluable materials when properly sifted.

From these two sources, aided by the practical knowledge possessed by myself and one or two native friends, the following grammar has been compiled. I wish I could believe that it is thoroughly accurate; all I can say is that we have done our best to make it as accurate as possible.

The above was what I said about the first edition. During the twenty-five years which have since elapsed, I have had frequent opportunities of checking my statements on the spot, and, when necessary, of correcting them. A large mass of notes on the language has also accumulated, and the results of all these have been incorporated in the present edition.

The *Chrestomathy*, published in Part II of the first edition, contained all the Maithilī literature then known to me. Its most important contents were the *Song of Salhēs*, the *Song of the Famine*, a collection of poems attributed to Vidyāpati Ṭhakkura, and another of poems by Harṣa Nātha. Since then the following Maithilī works have been published: *Twenty-one Vaishṇava Hymns*, Manbōdh's *Haribans*, the *Gīt Dinā Bhadrīk* and the *Gīt Nebārak*, all edited by the present writer. An excellent *Rāmāyaṇa* and a translation into Maithilī of Vidyāpati's Sanskrit *Puruṣa Parīkṣā* have also been composed by Paṇḍit Chandra Jhā, and have been printed and published in Darbhanga. All these have been carefully worked through by me, and have furnished innumerable examples of the various forms given in the grammar.

Maithilī is one of the three dialects,—Maithilī, Magahī, and Bhojpurī—of the Bihārī language. Roughly speaking, we may say that Maithilī occupies North Bihār, east of the river Gaṇḍak, although towards the east it has crossed the Ganges and is spoken in parts of South Bihār. Magahi occupies South Bihār, east of the Sōn, and the northern of the two plateaux of Chota Nagpur. Bhojpurī occupies the southern plateau of Chota Nagpur and the the country north and south of the Ganges as far west as, say, Benares. Maithilī and Magahī are much more closely related to each other than either is to Bhojpurī. Indeed, the last named might almost be called a separate language. The approximate number of the speakers of each, each in its own habitat, are:—

Maithilī	...	...	...	10,000,000
Magahī	...	...	...	6,240,000
Bhojpurī	...	...	...	20,000,000
		Total	...	36,240,000

Besides these there are speakers of the various Bihārī dialects scattered all over Northern India and even in the Deccan.

Turning more specially to Maithilī, the standard form of the language is that spoken in the Madhubani subdivision of the Darbhanga district, and in the adjoining portion of the district of Bhagalpur. It is this form which is described in the present grammar. The other forms of the dialect are described in the present writer's *Seven Grammars* quoted below.

The following account of the Maithilī dialect, as a whole, is taken from the Vol. V[2] of the Linguistic Survey of India :—

Maithilī or Tir^a^hutiyā is, properly speaking, the language of Mithilā or Tairabhukti (the ancient name of Tirhut). According to the Mithilā-māhātmya, a Sanskrit work of considerable repute in the territory which it describes, Mithilā is the country bounded on the north by the Himālaya, on the south by the Ganges, on the west by the river Gandak, and on the east by the river Kosi. It thus includes the British districts of Champaran, Muzaffarpur and Darbhanga, as well as the strip of the Nepal Tarai, which runs between these districts and the lower ranges of the Himālaya. The districts of Muzaffarpur and Darbhanga originally formed one district called Tirhut, and that name is still used as a convenient appellation for the country included in these two districts. At the present day, the language of the greater portion of Champaran is a form of Bhojpurī and not Maithilī, but, with that exception, Maithilī is spoken over the whole of this tract. It has also extended east of the river Kosī, and occupies the greater part of the district of Purnea. It has moreover crossed the Ganges, and is now spoken over the whole of the South-Gangetic portion of the Bhagalpur District, over the eastern portion of the South-Gangetic portion of the Monghyr District, and in the north and west of the Sonthal Parganas.

Maithilī is spoken in its greatest purity by the Brāhmaṇas of the north of the Darbhanga and Bhagalpur districts, and by those of western Purnea. These men have a literature and traditions that retarded the corruption of the dialect. It is also spoken with some purity, but with more signs of the wearing away of inflexions, in the south of the Darbhanga District, and in those portions of the Monghyr and Bhagalpur Districts which lie on the northern bank of the Ganges. This may be called Southern Standard Maithili. To the east, in Purnea, it becomes more and more infected with Bengali, till, in the east of that District it is superseded by the Siripuriā dialect of that language which is a border form of speech, Bengali in the main, but containing expressions borrowed from Maithilī, and written, not in the Bengali character, but in the Kaithī of Bihār. The Maithilī spoken in Purnea may be called Eastern Maithilī.

South of the Ganges, Maithilī is influenced more or less by the Magahī spoken to its west, and, partly also by Bengali. The result is a well-marked dialect, locally known as *Chikā-chikī bōlī*, from its frequent use of the syllable '*chik*,' the base on which the Verb Substantive is conjugated.

The Maithilī spoken in the Muzaffarpur District, and in a strip of country on the western side of Darbhanga, is strongly infected by the neighbouring Bhojpuri spoken in various forms in the adjacent district of Saran and in the greater part of Champaran. So much is this the case, that, as spoken by some people, it is difficult to say whether the dialect is Maithilī or Bhojpurī. It may be called Western Maithilī.

The Musalmāns of Mithilā do not all speak Maithilī. In Muzaffarpur and Champaran, they speak an altogether different dialect, closely allied to the language of Oudh. It is locally known as Shēkhai or as Musalmānī, and is sometimes called Jolahā Bōlī, after the caste which forms one of the most numerous Musulmān tribes, according to popular opinion, of the locality. The true Jolahā Bōlī, however, is the language spoken by the Musalmāns of Darbhanga, which is a form of Maithilī, though somewhat corrupted by the admission of Persian and Arabic words to its vocabulary.

The number of people who speak each form of Maithilī is as follows:—

Number of Sub-dialect.				Number of Speakers.
Standard	...	...	...	1,946,800
Southern Standard		...	...	2,300,000
Eastern	...	...	...	1,302,300
Chikā-chikī	...	...	...	1,719,781
Western	...	...	...	1,783,495
Jolahā	...	...	...	337,000
Total number of speakers of Maithilī in Maithilī-speaking districts ...				9,389,376

These figures do not include the speakers of Maithilī in the Nepal Tarai, concerning whom no figures are available. Under any circumstances, therefore, we shall be justified in assuming that at least ten million people speak Maithilī in the country of which it is the vernacular.

The number of persons who speak Maithilī in other parts is unknown. All that we can say is that, in Bengal and Assam, they have been estimated as amounting to about 275,000 people. They are not so numerous in other provinces.

Maithilī is the only one of the Bihārī dialects which has a literary history. For centuries the paṇḍits of Mithilā have been famous for their learning, and more than one Sanskrit work of authority has been written by them. One of the few learned women of India whose name has come down to us was Lakhimā Ṭhakkurāṇī, who, according to tradition, lived at the end of the 14th century A.D. Nor was the field of vernacular literature neglected by them. The earliest vernacular writer, of whom we have any record, was the celebrated Vidyāpati Ṭhakkura or Ṭhākur, who graced the court of Mahārājā S'iva Siṁha of Sugāonā, and who flourished in the middle of the 15th century. As a writer of Sanskrit works he was an author of considerable repute, and one of his works, translated into Bengali, is familiar as a text-book, under the name of the *Puruṣa-parīkṣā*, to every student of that language. But it is upon his dainty songs in the vernacular that his fame chiefly rests. He was the first of the old master-singers whose short religious poems, dealing principally with Rādhā and Kriṣṇa, exercised such an important influence on the religious history of Eastern India. His songs were adopted and enthusiastically recited by the celebrated Hindu reformer Caitanya, who flourished at the beginning of the sixteenth century, and, through him, became the house-poetry of the Lower Provinces. Numbers of imitators sprung up, many of whom wrote in Vidyāpati's name, so that it is now difficult to separate the genuine from the imitations, especially as in the great collection of these Vaiṣṇava songs, the *Pada-kalpa-taru*, which is the accepted authority in Bengal, the former have been altered in the course of generations to suit the Bengali idiom and metre. The *Pada-kalpa-taru* was the only record that we had of the poet's vernacular works, till, in the first edition of the *Maithilī Chrestomathy*, the present writer was enabled to publish a collection of songs attributed to Vidyāpati, which he collected in Mithilā itself, partly from the mouths of itinerant singers and partly from manuscript collections in the possession of local paṇḍits. That all the songs in this collection are genuine is not a matter capable of proof, but there can be little doubt that most of them are so, although the language has been greatly modernised in the course of transition from mouth to mouth during the past five centuries. A larger collection of these songs has been made by Babu Nagēndra Nāth Gupta, and will, it is believed, shortly be published.

Vidyāpati Ṭhakkura or, as he is called in the vernacular, Bidyāpat[i] Ṭhākur, had many imitators in Mithilā itself, of whom we know nothing except the names of the most popular, and a few stray verses. Amongst them may be mentioned Umāpati, Nandīpati, Mōda-narāyaṇa, Ramāpati, Mahīpati, Jayānanda, Caturbhuja, Sarasa-rāma, Jayadēva, Kēśava, Bhañjana, Cakrapāṇi, Bhānunātha, and Harṣanātha or, in the vernacular, Harkh-nāth. The last two were alive when the present writer was in Darbhanga thirty years ago.

Amongst other writers in Maithilī may be mentioned Manbōdh Jhā, who died about the year 1788 A.D. He composed a *Haribans*, or poetical life of Kṛṣṇa, of which ten cantos are still extant, and enjoy great popularity.

The drama has had several authors in Mithilā. The local custom has been to write the body of a play in Sanskrit, but the songs in the vernacular. The best known of these plays are as follows. None of them has been published.

The *Pārijāta-haraṇa*, and the *Rukmiṇī-pariṇaya*, both by Vidyāpati Ṭhakkura.

The *Gaurī-pariṇaya* by Kavi-lāla.

The *Uṣā-haraṇa* by Harṣanātha above mentioned.

The *Prabhāvatī-haraṇa* by Bhānunātha above mentioned.

Under the enlightened guidance of the late Mahārāja of Darbhanga, there has been a remarkable revival of Maithilī literature during the past few years. At least one author deserving of special note has come to the front, Candra Jhā, who has shown remarkable literary powers. He has written a *Mithilā-bhāshā Rāmāyaṇa*, and a translation, with an edition of the original Sanskrit text, of the *Puruṣa-parīkṣā* of Vidyāpati Ṭhakkura, both of which will well repay the student by their perusal.

No translation of any part of the Bible into Maithilī has been issued by the Bible Society, nor is that language included amongst those into which the Serampore missionaries translated the Scriptures. At the same time, if an article in the *Calcutta Review* is to be believed, the first translation of any portion of the Bible into any language of Northern India was that of the Gospels and Acts, made into the Chikā-chikī dialect of Maithilī, by Father Antonio, at the end of the eighteenth century. The only other translations with which I am acqnainted are versions of the Sermon on the Mount, and other short portions of Scripture, made about thirty years ago by Mr. John Christian, and published at Monghyr.

Authorities—

I.—Early References.—The earliest reference which I can find to Maithilī or Tirhutiyā is in Amaduzzi's preface to Beligatti's *Alphabetum Brammhanicum*, published in 1771. This contains a list of Indian languages amongst which is 'Tourutiana.'

Colebrooke in his famous essay on the Sanskrit and Prakrit languages written in the year 1801, is the first to describe Maithilī[1] as a distinct dialect. He points out its affinity with Bengali, discusses the written character used by the Brāhmaṇs, and adds, 'as the dialect of Mithilā has no extensive use, and does not appear

1 *Asiatic Researches*, Vol. VII (1801), pp. 199 ff. Reprinted in his *Essays*. Ed. 1873, p. 26.

to have been at any time cultivated by elegant poets, it is unnecessary to notice it any further in this place.' Since then,[1] like the other dialects of Bihār, Maithilī remained unnoticed and forgotten, till Mr. Fallon gave a few specimens of it in the *Indian Antiquary*[2] in the year 1875. In the preceding year, it is true, some examples of the dialect were given in Sir George Campbell's *Specimens*,[3] but they are there classed as some of many dialects of Hindī spoken in Bihār. Indeed, at this time it was the general belief that, all over Bihār, the language spoken was a corrupt form of Hindī, whereas, as Colebrooke had long previously pointed out, it was much more nearly allied to Bengali than to the Hindī of the North-Western Provinces. Matters remained in this state, till the first edition of the present Maithilī grammar appeared in the year 1880-81.

II.—GRAMMARS—

Beside the present work, reference may be made to the following:—

HOERNLE, A. F. R.,—*A Grammar of the Eastern Hindī compared with the other Gaudian Languages.* London, 1880. In this Grammar, Dr. Hoernle recognized Maithilī as a dialect distinct from Hindī. He was able to give some specimens of its grammatical forms, but no published materials were then available.

GRIERSON, G. A.,—*Seven Grammars of the Dialects and Sub-Dialects of the Bihárí Language.* Part I, *Introductory*, Calcutta, 1883; Part IV, *Maithil-Bhojpúrí Dialect of Central and South Muzaffarpur*, 1884; Part V, *South Maithilí Dialect of South Darbhangá, North Munger, and the Mudhepúrá Subdivision of Bhagalpúr;* Part VI, *South Maithil-Mágadhí Dialect of South*

---

[1] Note, however, Aimé-Martin's *Lettres édifiantes et curieuses*, Paris, 1840. In Vol. II, p. 295, when describing the languages of India, he says, 'le *Marthila* (sic) se retrouve dans Neypal.'

[2] Vol. IV (1875), p. 340.

[3] *Specimens of Languages of India, including those of the Aboriginal Tribes of Bengal, the Central Provinces and the Eastern Frontier*, Calcutta, 1874. The specimens given are headed, 'Vernacular of West Tirhoot,' 'Vernacular of East Tirhoot,' and 'Vernacular of West Purneah (Hindee),' respectively. They will be found on pp. 60 ff.

Munger and Bárh Subdivision of Patna; Part VII, *South Maithili-Bengálí Dialect of South Bhagulpúr;* Part VIII, *Maithil-Bangálí Dialect of Central and Western Puraniyá.*

KELLOGG, The Rev. S. H.,—*A Grammar of the Hindī Language in which are treated . . . . the colloquial dialects of Maithila* (sic), *etc., with copious philological notes.* Second Edition, Revised and Enlarged. London, 1893. (The first edition does not deal with Maithili).

The Maithilī portion of Dr. Kellogg's work is confessedly based on the grammars of the present writer.

III.—DICTIONARIES—

GRIERSON, G. A.,—Besides the vocabulary attached to the Maithilī Chrestomathy, there is one in the edition of Manbōdh's Haribans mentioned below.

HOERNLE, A. F. R., and GRIERSON, G. A.,—*A Comparative Dictionary of the Bihārī Language.* Part I, Calcutta, 1885; Part II, 1889. Only two parts issued.

IV.—GENERAL LITERATURE—

Regarding Vidyāpati, see Beames, *The Early Vaishnava Poets of Bengal, Indian Antiquary* ii, 1873, p. 37, and the same author's *On the Age and Country of Bidyāpati, ibid.* iv, 1875, p. 299. See also the Bengali Magazine entitled the *Baṅga-darśana*, Vol. iv, for Jaishṭha, 1282, Bg. san, pp. 75 and ff. Also the present writer's *Vidyāpati and his Contemporaries*, in *Indian Antiquary*, Vol. xiv, 1885, p. 182; Eggeling, *Catalogue* of Sanskrit MSS. in the India Office Library, Part iv, No. 2864; and the present writer in the *Proceedings* of the Asiatic Society of Bengal, for August, 1895. Also the present writer *On Some Mediæval Kings of Mithilā*, in *Indian Antiquary*, Vol. xxviii, 1899, p. 57. Also Nagēndra Nāth Gupta, *Vidyāpati Ṭhākur* in J.A.S.B., Vol. lxxiii, Pt. I, Extra No. 1904, pp. 20 ff., and the present writer in J.A.S.B. [N. S.], Vol. i (1905), p. 228. The following contain editions of the Bengali recension of the poet's works. *Vidyāpati-krita-padāvali*, edited by Akshaya Chandra Sarkār. Chinsurah, 1285, Bg. s. *Vidyāpatir Padāvali*, Edited with an Introduction by S'āradā Charaṇ Maitra. Second Edition, Calcutta, 1285, Bg. s. *Prāchīna Kāvya Saṁgraha*, Part I, Edited by Akshaya Chandra

Sarkār. Calcutta, 1291, Bg. s. Up to the date of writing the only edition of the Mithilā recension is that in the Maithilī Chrestomathy.

For the benefit of those who wish to study Maithilī, the following is a list of the principal works that have been published in the language.

Besides the text in the Maithilī Chrestomathy we have :—

Twenty-one Vaishṇava Hymns. Edited and translated by the present writer. *Journal* of the Asiatic Society of Bengal, Vol. liii, 1884, Special Number, pp. 76 and ff.

Manbodh's Haribans, Edited and translated by the same. *Ibid.* Vol. li, 1882, pp. 129 and ff., and Vol. liii, 1884, Special Number, pp. 1 and ff.

Selected Specimens of the Bihārī Language, Part I, The Maithilī Dialect. The Gīt Dīnā Bhadrik, and the Gīt Nebārak. Edited and translated by the same. *Zeitschrift der Deutschen Morgenländischen Gesellschaft,* Vol. xxxix, 1885, pp. 617 and ff.

Vidyāpati's *Puruṣa-parīkṣā,* Edited, and translated in prose and verse into Maithilī, by Candra Jhā. Darbhangā, Rāj Press. Śākē 1810.

Mithilā-Bhāṣā Rāmāyaṇa, by Candra Jhā. A version of the story of the Rāmāyaṇa in Maithilī verse. Darbhangā, Union Press. San 1299 Faslī.

MAITHILĪ GRAMMAR.

PART I.

ALPHABET AND VOCABULARY.

CHAPTER I.

The Alphabet.

1. The Alphabets in use in Mithilā are three—The Dēva-nāgarī, the Maithilī, and the Kaithī. The first is familiar to every reader of this, and need not be described here. In Mithilā it is not much used in common life, and seldom even in manuscripts.

2. The Maithilī is the character used by the Maithil Brāhmaṇs, both in the affairs of common life, and in their sacred books. Few of the Brāhmaṇs, who are not professed paṇḍits, can read the Dēva-nāgarī character. The Maithilī character is also affected by Maithil Kāyasthas, who pretend to be better educated than their fellows. The Maithilī character is nearly the same as that of Bengali, differing only in one or two letters.

3. The Kaithī character is that in general use throughout Mithilā by all educated persons who are not Brāhmaṇs. It is a corruption of the Dēva-nāgarī, and can be written much faster than the latter, even as fast as *shikasta* Urdū. There was a clerk in my office in Madhubanī, who could write excellent Kaithī more quickly than even the most practised of the old "Persian" muharrirs. Besides the speed with which it can be written, it has the advantage of thorough legibility. It is the official character employed in Government offices throughout Bihār and Chutiā Nāgpur.

4. A lithographed comparative table, giving specimens of these three alphabets, will be found at the end of this Grammar.

Pronunciation.

(*a*) *Vowels.*

5. The vowels should be pronounced as in Sanskrit, with the following exceptions:—

6. The vowel *a* has four distinct sounds, not two, as in Sanskrit. In Sanskrit we have अ *a* and आ *ā*. In Maithilī each of these has developed into a pair, a short and a long. The sound of short अ *a* is peculiar. It is not so broad as that of the corresponding vowel in Bengali, but on the other hand it is broader than the neutral vowel in Hindī. We may describe it as something between the *o* in 'cob,' and the *u* in 'cub,' or as the short sound corresponding to the long *a* in the word 'all.' From this has developed a long sound almost exactly like that of the *å* in 'all.' This long sound is nearly confined to the termination of the second person in verbs, and is due to the influence of a *u* which once followed it, but has now disappeared. Thus, the termination अऽह *åh* is derived from an older अहु *ahu*. The sound is not usually represented in native writing but is commonly written merely as अ *a*. When it is desired to show it in writing it is sometimes represented by the mark of length ऽ above the line, and sometimes by the *visarga* ः. Thus देखबऽह or देखबःह. I shall in these pages employ the former sign, and in transliteration, I shall adopt the sign *å*, which is the character used for this sound in the publications of the Assam Government, and has been borrowed from Swedish.

7. Just as a long अऽ *å* sound has been developed from अ, so a secondary short *a*-sound has been developed from आ *ā*. Ordinarily speaking, this letter is pronounced as the *a* in 'far.' Sometimes, according to the rule of the short antepenultimate to be described below (*see* § 32 and ff.), it has to be shortened, and is then pronounced like the *a* in 'farrier.' In native writing it is not customary to indicate this sound, an ordinary आ *ā* being usually written in its place. Some writers, however, use ॳ *a* for this sound, instead of आ. In the following pages, I shall indicate it, in the

Dēva-nāgarī character, by the short mark ˈ written above the line. Thus मांरलै, I killed. In transliteration I shall indicate it by the sign *ă*. Native scribes would write this word either मारलै or मरलै. This short आ *ă* has a great tendency to be weakened to अ *a*, and it may be taken as a general rule that, unless ambiguity would ensue it does usually become अ *a*. Thus the long form of पानि *pānī*, water, is properly पांनिया *păniyā*, but is usually पनिया *paniyā*. On the other hand, 'I killed,' is always pronounced मांरलै *mărᵃlai*, and never मरलै *marᵃlai*, however it is written, because the latter pronunciation would lead to ambiguity, मरलै *marᵃlai* properly meaning 'he died.'

8. The rule for the pronunciation of a final *a* is the same as in Hindī. As a general rule, it is silent in prose as in गुण pronounced *guṇ*. not *guṇa*; फल *phal*, not *phala*. In other terms these words are practically monosyllables, and the final silent *a* is not counted as a syllable in applying phonetic rules depending on the number of syllables in a word (*see* §§ 28 and ff., 32 and ff.). Similarly सफल *saphal* must be treated as a dissyllable. not as a trisyllable. and so on. In transliteration this final silent *a* will be omitted in the following pages in writing prose. In poetry it is pronounced and will therefore be represented in transliteration.

In a few cases a final *a* is pronounced even in prose. When there is any doubt, I shall indicate it in the Dēva-nāgarī character by the sign ०, and in transliteration I shall. when so pronounced. always write it in full. The most important cases in which it is pronounced are :—

(i) Original monosyllables. such as न *na*. not.

(ii) Words in which the final *a* is necessary for enunciation. as in शास्त्र० *śāstra*. a holy book; प्रिय० *priya*, dear; ग्राह्य० *grāhya*. acceptable (see § 26).

(iii) A few verbal forms, in which it is really *ǎ*, as in देखिहˈ *dekhihǎ*. be pleased to see; देखि कˈ *dēkhⁱ-kǎ*, having seen.

9. When two words are compounded, the final *a* of the first member reappears and is pronounced very lightly. Thus फलदायक

(फल *phal* + दायक *dāyak*) is pronounced *phal^{a}dāyak*, in which the ^{a} is hardly audible, very like the Hebrew *sh^{a}wā mobile.*

The same imperfect *a* also occurs in many polysyllabic words in the syllable after the accent, when not final. Thus हमरा *hám^{a}rā*, me; देखबंह *dékh^{a}bāh*, you will see (but देखब *dḗkhab* with the *a* fully pronounced as it is in the final syllable); देखल *dḗkhal* or देखलिऐ *dékh^{a}liai*, I saw. As above shown, I represent this imperfect vowel in transliteration by a small ^{a} above the line. I have not thought it necessary to indicate it in the Dēva-nāgarī character. Natives never do so.

In poetry, the final silent *a*, and this imperfect ^{a} are always fully pronounced. We thus have, in poetry, *guṇa*, *phala*, *saphala*, *phaladāyaka*, *hamarā*, *dekhabāh* (or, more usually, the older form *dekhabahu*), *dēkhaba*, *dēkhala* and *dekhaliai*.

10. The short vowels इ *i* and उ *u*, when final in prose are also, as a rule, only half-pronounced. They may then be compared, in this respect, to the 'compound *sh^{a}wās*' of Hebrew, which, however, occur at the beginning, not at the end, of a syllable. They are not absolutely silent, but (as in Sindhī, Kāśmīrī, and Dravidian languages) are barely audible. Natives make no attempt to indicate in writing the extreme shortness of these vowels. As the matter is of some importance, I shall in the following pages indicate the fact by the sign for *virāma* (्) placed under the vowel-sign. In transliteration I shall indicate it by small letters above the line. Thus, अछि् *ach^i*, he is; देखथु् *dēkhath^u*, let him see. As in the case of the final absolutely silent *a*, these imperfect ^{i} and ^{u} are not counted as forming syllables in applying the rule of the short antepenultimate (§ 32). For the purposes of that rule देखथु् *dēkhath^u* is a word of two syllables.

There are exceptions in which a final *i* is pronounced as a full vowel. These are:—

(i) The final *i* of the plural termination अनि *^{a}ni*, as in लोकनि *lok^{a}ni* (not लोकनि् *lōkan^i*) people, the plural of लोक *lōk*, a person.

(ii) The final *i* of masculine nouns, as in पानि *pāni*, water; मानि *māni*, proud (not पानि् *pān^i*, मानि् *mān^i*).

(iii) A final *i* preceded by a vowel, as in हलुकाइ *halukāi*, lightness (not हलुकाइ् *halukā*^{i}).

These imperfect vowels are frequently nasalised by *anunāsika*. Thus देखितहिँ *dekhitah*$^{\tilde{i}}$, immediately on seeing; देखलहुँ *dekh*^{a}*lah*$^{\tilde{u}}$, I saw.

In poetry these imperfect ^{i} and ^{u} are fully pronounced. thus *achi*, *dēkhathu*.

11. As in the case of आ *ā*, the vowel ए *ē* has two sounds, a short and a long. The long sound is the one with which we are familiar in Sanskrit, something like that of the *a* in 'mate.' The other is the corresponding short sound, something like that of the *e* in 'met.' Natives make no distinction between these two sounds in writing. In the following pages, the long sound will be represented by ए or, when non-initial, by ॆ, and the short sound by ऎ or, when non-initial, by ॅ. In transliteration I shall represent them by *ē* and *e* respectively.

It should be noted that ऎ *e* and इ *i* are freely interchangeable. Thus, we may either have पऎताह *paĕtăh* or पइताह *païtăh*, he will see. Northern Maithili, as a rule, prefers to use ऎ *e*.

12. In an exactly similar way, there is a pair of long and short *o* sounds. The long is the Sanskrit ओ *ō*, and is sounded like the second *o* in 'promote.' The short has the sound of the first *o* in the same word, and will be represented in the following pages by ऒ or, when non-initial, by ॊ. The corresponding transliteration will be *ō* and *o*, respectively. Native writers make no distinction between these two sounds, representing both by ओ. As in the case of ऎ *e* and इ *i*, ऒ *o* and उ *u* are freely interchangeable, ऒ *o* being usually preferred in the north and उ *u* in the south. Thus, we have either पऒलहुँ *paŏlah*$^{\tilde{u}}$ or पउलहुँ *paülah*$^{\tilde{u}}$, I obtained.

13. In Sanskrit the vowels ऐ *ai* and औ *au* are really diphthongs made up of आ + इ *ā* + *i* and आ + उ *ā* + *u*, respectively. Their origin is therefore *āi* and *āu*, and the pronunciation is distinctly long. We may compare the pronunciation of the *ai* in the English word *aisle*, and of the *ou* in the English word 'our.' In Maithilī these sounds only occur in words directly borrowed

from Sanskrit as in कैकेयी *Kaĩkēyī*, औषध *aũṣadh*. In Maithilī these letters invariably represent an older अ + इ (or ए) *a* (not *ā*) + *i* (or *e*) and अ + उ (or ओ) *a* (not *ā*) + *u* (or *o*) respectively. In fact, at the present day native writers sometimes write ऐ and औ and sometimes अइ or अए, अउ or अओ. Thus they write the present participle of the root देख *dēkh*, see, sometimes देखैत (or in this book दॆखैत *dekhait*) and sometimes देखइत (or in this book दॆखइत *dekhaït*). I have even, on occasions, seen the word spelt देखयित, in which the य is merely a fulcrum for carrying the ि much as *alif* is employed in Hindōstānī. Again 'I shall obtain' is written पइबै (or in this book पइबै *païbai*), पएबै (or in this book पएबै *paëbai*), or पैबै (or in this book पैबै *paibai*). Similarly they indicate 'he will obtain,' by पउताह (or in this book पउताह *paütăh*), पओताह (or in this book पओताह *paötăh*) or पौताह (or in this book पौताह *pautăh*). Native writers make no distinction between the Sanskrit and Maithilī *ai* and *au*. Both *ai* sounds they represent, in the Sanskrit fashion by ऐ, and both *au* sounds by औ. As, however, the Maithilī sounds are shorter both by origin and in pronunciation, I represent the short sounds by ऐ (or, when non-initial, by ै), and by औ (or, when non-initial by ौ), respectively. In transliteration, I represent the long sounds by *aĩ* and *aũ*, and the short sounds by *ai* and *au*.

It is important to note that the Maithilī ऐ *ai* and औ *au* are merely alternative graphic representations of अइ *aï* or अए *aë* and अउ *aü* or अओ *aö*, respectively. This rule must be borne in mind in counting syllables for applying the rule of the short antepenultimate (§ 33, ii) in which both ऐ *ai* and औ count each as *two* syllables. Thus, the word दॆखैत *dekhait*, seeing, must be considered as a word of three syllables, *viz.*, दॆ *de* + ख *kha* + इत *it*, and not as one of two.

As, whatever the method of writing employed may be, the

pronunciation of अइ and ऐ and of अउ and औ is in each case identical, I shall in future make no distinction in transliteration.[1] I shall represent both अइ and ऐ by *ai*, and both अउ and औ by *au*. अए will be represented by *ae* (pronounced, however, the same as *ai*), and अओ will be represented by *ao* (pronounced as *au*).

14. Native scribes are by no means uniform in their methods of representing vowel-sounds in writing. In the table below I give the system of spelling adopted for this grammar, and also the more usual scribal variations.

System of spelling adopted in this Grammar.	*Variations often employed by native scribes.*
इ initial (इच्छा, a wish, देखइत, seeing).	यि (यिच्छा), यी (यीच्छा), ए (देखएत)
इ medial (लिखित, written).	ई (लीखीत) (very common).
ई initial (ईंटा, a brick).	यी (यींटा).
उ initial (उक्का, a torch).	वु (वुक्का), or वू (वूक्का).
ऊ initial (ऊँच, high).	वू (वूँच), or वु (वुँच).
ऊ medial (झूठ, false).	ु (झुठ) (very common).
ए / ए } initial (एक, one).	ये (येक).
ऐ / ऐ } initial (ऐंठ, twist).	यै (यैंठ).
ओ / ओ } initial (ओर, direction).	वो (वोर).

NOTE.—All the above are only varieties of spelling, and have nothing to do with pronunciation.

[1] Whether the sound is really dipthongal, or whether the two elements are separately pronounced, it is difficult to say. Pronunciation varies in different months. In old Maithili the sound was certainly not dipthongal, and it seems to me that at the present day the vowels are beginning to coalesce, but that the custom has not yet been established.

15. The vowels ऋ *ṛ* ॠ *ṝ* and ऌ *ḷ* only occur in words borrowed direct from Sanskrit. When so met, they are pronounced like *ri*, *rī*, and *li*, respectively. They are never found in pure Maithilī words.

16. The following is therefore a complete conspectus of all the Maithilī vowels. Those which are only found in Sanskrit words are marked with the letter S.

Short.	Long.
अ *a*	अ॑ *å*
आ *ă*	आ *ā*
इ *i*	ई *ī*
उ *u*	ऊ *ū*
ऋ *ṛ* (S.)	ॠ *ṝ* (S.)
ऌ *ḷ* (S.)	
ए *e*	ए *ē*
ऐ *ai*	ऐ *āi* (S.)
ओ *o*	ओ *ō*.
औ *au*	औ *āu* (S.)

17. The Sanskrit *Visarga* (:) no longer exists in Maithilī except in a few borrowed words. The character is, however, as stated above, sometimes, but rarely, employed to indicate the sound of the letter *å*.

18. *Anusvāra* (˙), when immutable, is also retained in a few words borrowed from Sanskrit. It is very commonly employed (like the changeable *anusvāra* of Sanskrit) as a *compendium scripturae* for ङ् *ṅ*, ञ् *ñ*, ण् *ṇ*, न् *n*, or म् *m* before another consonant of the same class. Thus बुंदा instead बुन्दा *bundā*. It will hence be represented in transliteration by *ṅ*, *ñ*, *ṇ*, *n*, or *m*, according to circumstances. Native writers very commonly employ it instead of *anunāsika*.

19. *Anunāsika* (˙) is met extremely frequently. It indicates the nasal sound which we hear in the French word 'bon.'

It will be represented in transliteration by the mark ˜ placed over the nasalised vowel. Thus अँखिया *ãkhiyā*, an eye. मैं *mai͂* or मँ *mẽ* in; बाँहि *bā̃hⁱ*, an arm; देखलऊँ *dekhᵃlahũ*, I saw.

20. *Consonants.*

क् *k*, ख् *kh*, ग् *g*, घ् *gh*, ङ् *ṅ*, च् *c*, छ् *ch*, ज् *j*, झ् *jh*, ञ् *ñ*, ट् *ṭ*, ठ् *ṭh*, ड् *ḍ*, ढ् *ḍh*, त्, *t*, थ् *th*, द् *d*, ध् *dh*, न् *n*, प् *p*, फ् *ph*, ब् *b*, भ् *bh*, म् *m*, य् *y*, र् *r*, ल् *l*, व् *w*, श् *ś*, स् *s*, and ह् *h* are usually pronounced as in Sanskrit.

21. When ड् *ḍ* and ढ *ḍh* are not initial they become ड़् *ṛ* and ढ़ *ṛh*. These cerebral *ṛ*-sounds, are not so definitely cerebral as in Western Hindī. They are very frequently interchanged with र् *r* and र्ह् *rh* respectively, and, indeed the latter dental sounds more nearly approach the correct pronunciation. Thus, 'a horse' is either घोड़ *ghōṛ* or घोर *ghōr*, of which two the latter is the preferable spelling. Native custom as to writing these sounds fluctuates.

22. The pronunciation of ण *ṇ* is peculiar. The cerebral nature of its sound is much more marked than in the Sanskrit of Eastern India. It has more the sound of a muffled cerebral *r* followed by a cerebral *ṇ*; e.g., रावण is pronounced almost like *Rābarṇ*. the *r* in *rṇ* having a peculiar muffled sound, impossible to describe in writing. न *n* is occasionally substituted for ण *ṇ* and is then pronounced as *n*.

23. Original य् *y* and व् *w* always become ज् *j* and ब् *b* respectively, although the letters य् and व् are often retained in writing. In the following pages the spelling will strictly follow the pronunciation. Thus I shall write जौबन *jaūban*, not यौवन *yaūvan*, and बात *bāt*, not वात *wāt*. The only cases in which we find य् *y* and व् *w* with their proper pronunciations are when they are used euphonically,—like the *ya-śruti* of the Prakrit Grammarians,—as described in the following sections.

24. When two vowels, of which the latter is short or long *ă* come together, a euphonic य् *y* or व् *w* is often inserted to prevent

a hiatus. The insertion is generally optional, and is merely intended to facilitate utterance. This euphonic insertion takes place between *ă* and *ā*, between *ī* and *ā*, between *ē* and *ā*, between *ū* and *ā*, and between *ŏ* and *ā*.

(i) Between *ă* and *ā* the semi-vowel which is inserted is always *w*.[1] नेनआ *nen*ᵃ-*ā* becomes नेनवा *nen*ᵃ*wā*, a boy. In this case the insertion is not optional, but is compulsory.

(ii) Between *i* or *e* and *ā*, the inserted letter is *y*. Thus मालिआ *mălia* or मालिया *măliyā*, a gardener. In this case the insertion of the *y* is quite optional, but careful writers generally insert it.

(iii) Between *ī* or *ē* and *ā* it is always *w* which is inserted, and the insertion is compulsory. Thus मालीवा *mălīwā* for मालीआ *mălīā*, a gardener. Here it must be explained, that the *w* was originally really between *a* and *ā*. Almost the only case in which *ī* immediately precedes *ā* is in the redundant form of nouns (§ 41). This form properly ends in इयवा *iy*ᵃ*wā*, thus—मालियवा *măliy*ᵃ*wā* —and the इय *iy*ᵃ is liable to be contracted to ई *ī*, so that we get लीवा *mălīwā*.

(iv) Between *ū* or *ŏ* and *ā*, the inserted vowel is always *w*. The insertion is quite optional, not compulsory, but careful writers usually omit it. We thus get आँसुआ *ãsuā* or आँसुवा *ãsuwā*, a tear.

In the following pages, I shall follow the usage of the most careful writers, and shall spell upon the principles indicated by the forms नेनवा *nen*ᵃ*wā*, मालिया *măliyā*, मालीवा *mălīwā*, and आँसुआ *ãsuā*.

The above are the only instances in which य् *y* and व् *w* really occur in Maithilī, and it will be seen that, as they are euphonic additions and only appear between contiguous vowels, they can never occur at the beginning of a word, except in the case of the incorrect native spellings indicated in § 14.

---

[1] In Western India, on the contrary, it is usually *y*.

It must, however, be mentioned that the diphthongs ऐ *ai* and औ *āū* are often written अय *ayᵃ* and अव *awᵃ* by some writers. This is only a question of spelling. Again the vowel ए *e* is often written य *ya*, and the vowel ओ *o* is often written व *wa*. Thus we find होएब *hōeb*, to be, written होयब ; केओ *keō*, any one, written क्यो *kyō;* and पाओल *pāōl*, I got, written पावल *pāwal.* This again is a mere matter of spelling. The pronunciation is not affected.

25. The sibilants श् *ś* and ष् *ṣ* only appear in words borrowed from Sanskrit. The only sibilant which Maithilī has of its own is the dental स् *s*. श् *ś* is pronounced as in Sanskrit; but ष् *ṣ* when standing alone, and not compounded with another consonant is always pronounced like ख *kh*. Thus षष्ठ *ṣaṣṭh*, sixth, pronounced *khaṣṭh*. This pronunciation is universal: the vulgar even write such a ष *ṣ* phonetically ख *kh*. In the compound consonant र्ष *rṣ* ष *ṣ* is also always pronounced as ख *kh*; e.g. आकर्षण *ākarṣaṇ* is pronounced *ākarkhaṇ* By some this ख *kh* sound of ष *ṣ* is pronounced as a guttural breathing, and not as a guttural check,—something, but not quite, like the Persian خ *kh*, or the *ch* in 'loch.' The compound letter क्ष *kṣ* is pronounced like च्छ *cch*, which is occasionally written for it by the vulgar; *e.g.* लक्ष्मी is so written, and is pronounced as *Lakṣmī* by purists, but is commonly written and pronounced लच्छमी *Lacchᵃmī.* The compound ष्प *ṣp* is peculiar. It is pronounced something like *hfp;* e.g., पुष्प *puṣp*, a flower, is pronounced *puhfp*. This seems to be a relic of the old Sanskrit *upadhmānīya*.

Native scribes regularly write श *ś* for स *s;* thus, they write शागर *śāgar*, instead of सागर *sāgar*, the sea. The pronunciation is, however, always that of a dental स् *s*. In Māgadhī Prakrit every स् *s* was pronounced as श् *ś*. This pronunciation has long ceased to exist in Bihār, but the mode of writing has survived.

26. The letter ह *h*, when compound with य *y*, becomes ह्य *hy*, which, in words borrowed from Sanskrit, is pronounced in a

peculiar way. If *zh* be taken to represent the Persian ژ *zh*, the pronunciation of this compound can best be represented by *zhjy*; e.g., ग्राह्य॰, *fit to be accepted*, is pronounced *grăzhjya*, the final य *a* being retained in pronunciation, though usually inert, for the sake of euphony (§ 8).

27. The mute letters are divided into surds and sonants. Surds and sonants may each be aspirated or unaspirated. Thus—

Surds.		Sonants.	
Unaspirated.	Aspirated.	Unaspirated.	Aspirated.
क् *k.*	ख् *kh.*	ग् *g.*	घ् *gh.*
च् *c.*	छ् *ch.*	ज् *j.*	झ् *jh.*
ट् *ṭ.*	ठ् *ṭh.*	ड् *ḍ*, ड़् *ṛ*	ढ् *ḍh*, ढ़् *ṛh.*
त् *t.*	थ् *th.*	द् *d.*	ध् *dh.*
प् *p.*	फ् *ph.*	ब् *b.*	भ् *bh.*

In connexion with the sonants, there is an important rule.

(i) When any unaspirated sonant is preceded by *anunāsika*,[1] the nasal of the corresponding class may be substituted for the two.

(ii) When an aspirated sonant is preceded by *anunāsika*, the nasal of the corresponding class aspirated by the addition of *h* may be substituted for the two.

Thus—

(i) ँग् ~ *g* may become ङ् *ṅ*. Thus. आँग *ā̃g* or आङ *āṅ* a limb.

ँज् ~ *j* may become ञ् *ñ*. This is, however, of very rare occurrence. Example, आँजू *ā̃jū* or आञू *āñū*. a tear.

---

[1] Traces of a somewhat similar change have been noted on Māgadhī Prakrit, e.g. *aññali* for *añjali*.

ँड़् ~ *ṛ* may become ण् *ṇ*. Thus, भाँड़ *bhā̃ṛ* or भाण *bhāṇ*, an earthen pot.

ँद् ~ *d* may become न् *n*. Thus, नीँद *nī̃d* or नीन *nīn*, sleep.

ँब् ~ *b* may become म्. *m*. Thus. नीँब *nī̃b* or नीम *nīm*, a *nīm*-tree.

(ii) ँघ् ~ *gh* may become ङ्ह् *ṅh*. Thus. सीँघ *sī̃gh* or सीङ्ह *sīṅh*, a lion.

ँझ् ~ *jh* may become ञ्ह् *ñh*. This, as in the case of ँज् ~ *j*, is very rare. Example माँझ *mā̃jh* or माञ्ह *māñh*, middle.

ँढ़् ~ *ṛh* may become ण्ह् *ṇh*. Thus, कोँढ़ *kõṛh* or कोण्ह *kõṇh*, a pumpkin.

ँध् ~ *dh* may become न्ह् *nh*. Thus बाँध *bā̃dh* or बान्ह *bānh*, bind. Compare as a reverse example कान्ह *kānh* or काँध *kā̃dh*, a name of *Kṛṣṇa*.

ँभ् ~ *bh* may become म्ह् *mh*. Thus खाँभ *bhā̃bh* or खाम्ह *khāmh*. a pillar.

All the above changes are quite optional. Those of ँड़् ~ *ṛ*. ँढ़् ~ *ṛh*. ँद् ~ *d*, ँध् ~ *dh*, ँब् ~ *b*. ँभ् ~ *bh*, are very common. The others, especially those of ँज् ~ *j* and ँझ् ~ *jh*, are more rare.

There is one point to be noted. The aspirated nasals ङ्ह् *ṅh*. ञ्ह् *ñh*, ण्ह् *ṇh*, न्ह् *nh*, and म्ह् *mh*. are never treated as compound letters. and do *not* make a preceding vowel long by position. They are treated exactly like aspirated mutes ख् *kh*, घ् *gh*, छ् *ch*, झ् *jh*, and so on. They might indeed be added as single letters to the alphabet. Thus :—

Gutturals. क् *k*, ख् *kh*. ग् *g*, घ् *gh*, ङ् *ṅ*, ङ्ह् *ṅh*.

Palatals. च् *c*, छ् *ch*, ज् *j*. झ् *jh*, ञ् *ñ*, ञ्ह् *ñh*.

Cerebrals, ट् *ṭ*, ठ् *ṭh*, ड् *ḍ*, ड़् *ṛ*, ढ् *ḍh*, ढ़् *ṛh*, ण् *ṇ*, ण्ह् *ṇh*.

Dentals, त् *t*, थ् *th*. द् *d*, ध् *dh*, न् *n*, न्ह् *nh*.

Labials प् *p*, फ् *ph*, ब् *b*, भ् *bh*, म् *m*, म्ह् *mh*.

ACCENTUATION.

28. The stress accent exists in Maithilī, but is not strongly pronounced. In counting syllables for fixing the place of an accent, the final silent *a* of words ending in a consonant, and a final imperfect *ⁱ* and *ᵘ* are not considered. On the other hand, the imperfect *ᵃ* in the middle of a word, corresponding to the Hebrew *shᵃwā mobile*, is counted as a syllable. For instance, in the word देखलहुँ *dékhᵃlàhᵘ*, there are for our present purposes three syllables, *viz.*, दे *dé* + ख *khᵃ* + लहुँ *làhᵘ*.

(i) If a word ends in a consonant (whether followed by imperfect *ⁱ* or *ᵘ* or not) preceded by a long vowel or a diphthong, the main accent is on the last syllable. Thus किसान *kisā́n*, a cultivator: देखलहुँन्हि *dèkhᵃlahū́nhⁱ*, you saw; देखलिऐन्हि *dèkhᵃliáinhⁱ*, I saw.

(ii) If a word ends in a fully pronounced vowel, and if the penultimate is long, the accent falls on the penultimate. Thus पानि *pā́ni*, water; छोटक्का *chòṭákkā*, small.

(iii) In other cases (except in the case of words borrowed from Sanskrit) the accent falls on the antepenultimate. Thus हमरा *hámᵃrā*, me; लोकनि *lókᵃni*, people: खोपड़ी *khópᵃṛī* a hut: देखलहुँ *dékhᵃlàhᵘ*, I saw; तितलिया *titáliyā*, a butterfly.

If a word, which has the accent on the antepenultimate, takes a suffix, the antepenultimate becomes the syllable before the antepenultimate, and may optionally retain the accent. Thus, the word तितली *títᵃlī*, a butterfly, has the accent on *tí*, the antepenultimate. The long form of तितली *titᵃlī* is made by suffixing *ā*, and we get तितलिया *titaliyā*. This ordinarily has the accent on *tá*, the new antepenultimate, according to the above rule; thus *titáliyā*, but some people retain the accent on the *tí*, and say *títaliyā*. Pronunciation in this respect fluctuates much.

(iv) In words borrowed from Sanskrit, the accent may be thrown back as far as the syllable before the antepenultimate, provided the antepenultimate and the penultimate are both short. Here again pronunciation varies. कुटिलता, deceitfulness, may be either *kúṭilatā* or *kùṭilᵃtā*.

29. If the accent does not fall on the first syllable of a word, that syllable has a secondary accent, which I indicate by the sign ̀, as in *kìsā́n*, *dèkh*[a]*lahū́nh*[i], *dèkh*[a]*liáinh*[i], *chòṭákkā̃*, *tìtáliyā* and *kùṭil*[a]*tā* given above.

30. If a word ends in imperfect [i] or [u] and if the last syllable has not the main accent of the word, then that syllable has a secondary accent, as in देखथि *dékhàth*[i], he may see ; ककरहुँ *kák*[a]*ràh*[u], any one (accusative) ; देखलहुँ *dékh*[a]*làh*[u], I saw.

31. In compound words, the first member retains its own stress-accent as a secondary accent, the stress-accent of the second member being the stress-accent of the word. Thus मुख-चंद *mùkh*[a]*cánd*, the moon of a girl's face. Compound words borrowed directly from Sanskrit are often treated as simple words. Thus विद्यापति *bidyā-pat*[i], which, according to the above rule, should be pronounced *bìdyā-pát*[i] is always pronounced *bìdyā́pàt*[i]. The word is the name of a famous poet of Mithilā.

Rule of the Short Antepenultimate.

32. The following rules are most important. They are applied rigorously throughout the whole system of Maithilī Grammar, and unless they are fully grasped, much of what is in the following pages will be found obscure.

(i) *The rules here given apply only to Maithilī words. They do not apply to words borrowed direct from Sanskrit, which are not subject to change.*

(ii) *The genius of the whole Maithilī language is adverse to the existence of a long vowel in a Maithilī word, when it would occupy a position removed more than two syllables from the end of a word.*

Note.—In counting syllables neither the final silent *a*, nor a final imperfect [i] or [u] counts as a syllable; but the medial imperfect [a], corresponding to the Hebrew *sh*[a]*wā mobile* does so count. Thus घर *ghar*, a house, is a word of one syllable; देखब *dēkhab*, I shall see, आओरि *āor*[i], and, सूतथु *sūtath*[u] let him sleep, are words of two syllables; while सुतिहँ *sutihå*, sleep thou, and देखबें *dekh*[a]*bẽ*, you will see, are words of three syllables.

33. The practice of shortening a vowel is subject to the following rules:—

(i) Whenever the vowel आ *a* finds itself in the antepenultimate syllable, *i.e.*, in the third from the end of the word, it is shortened to आ॑ *ă*. Thus, ना॑उआ *năuā* (or, contracted, नौआ *nauā*) long form of नाउ *nāū*, a barber; आ॑गिया *ăgiyā*, long form of आगि *āg*[i], fire; पा॑ओलह *păolăh* (or, contracted, पौलह *paulăh*), 2nd plur. past of पाएब *pāeb*, to obtain; मा॑रलक *măr°lak*, he struck, from मारब *mārab*, to strike; बा॑तिया *bătiyā*, long form of बात *bāt*, a word.

There is a tendency to pronounce and write this shortened आ॑ *ă* as if it were अ *a*, so that we sometimes hear, instead of the above; नउआ *naüā*; अगिया *agiyā*; बतिया *batiyā*. But this is only in the case of nouns. आ॑ *ă* does not often become अ a in verbs, as this would tend to give rise to ambiguity. Thus, the verb *mār*, means 'strike,' while, if we shortened it to *mar*, the root would mean 'die.' Sometimes, however, we find आ *ā* shortened to अ *a*, even in verbs. In this respect, the rule is that we may have अ *a* if no ambiguity occurs. Compare § 7.

(ii) Similarly, any other vowel finding itself in the antepenultimate, is shortened, provided a consonant which is not euphonic य *y* or व *w* follows it. Thus, सिखलक *sikh°lak*, he learnt, from √ सीख *sīkh*, learn; देखइत *dekhaït* (or, contracted) देखैत *dekhait*), seeing. On the other hand, चूअलाह *cū°lăh* or चूवलाह *cūw°lăh*, he dripped; सीअलक *sī°lak* or सीयलक *sīy°lak*, he sewed; from roots चू *cū* and सी *sī*; in which the long *ī* and the long *ū* are retained as they are followed by vowels or by euphonic *y* or *w*.

From the above it will be noted that the contraction of *a* and *i* to *ai* does not affect the shortening. In other words ऐ *ai* and औ *au*, for the purposes of these rules, count as two syllables each.

(iii) Any vowel whatever, finding itself removed more than three syllables from the end of the word is shortened, whether it is followed by a consonant or not. Thus चुअतथीन्हि *cuit°thīnh'* (if) he had dripped, from root चू *cū* ; होइअइ *hoiaï* (or, contracted होइऐ *hoiai*), (if) I becomė, from root हो *hō*, become ; देखितिअउ *dekhitiaü* (or, contracted देखितिऔ *dekhitiau*) (if) I had seen you, from root देख *dēkh*.

34. Amongst native writers of Maithili no fixed usage has as yet established itself regarding the graphic representation of the short antepenultimate. Though it is always pronounced short, it is often *written* long. Thus we find the words given above sometimes written भाउजा, बाभिया, पाथोलक (or पौलक) मारलक, बातिया, सौबलक, and चूअतथीन्हि, and sometimes भउजा (or भौजा), बभिया, पथोलक, मरलक, बतिया, सिबलक, and चुअतथीन्हि देखइत and होइऐ are, of course always written देखइत and होइऐ as the writers have no character for short *e*, *o*, or *ai*.

35. All the above examples have exhibited the shortening of vowels long by nature. Exactly the same principle is followed in the case of vowels long by position. When such vowels precede a compound consonant (usually a nasal plus a mute, or a double mute), the nasal is weakened to *anunāsika*, and the double consonant is simplified. Thus from the root बन्ध *bandh*, to bind we have बँधुआ *bãdhuā* or बन्हुआ *banhuā* (see § 27, ii) not बन्धुआ *bandhuā*, a prisoner; and from the long form (see § 41) छोटक्का *choṭakkā*, small, we have the redundant form छोटकवा *choṭak°wā*.

———o———

CHAPTER II.

VOCABULARY.

36. In the preceding pages I have more than once made a distinction between Maithili words and Sanskrit words.

37. Maithili is an Indo-Aryan language, and though the statement is not strictly accurate, it may conveniently be said to be descended from Sanskrit. According to native belief it *is* so

descended.[1] In the course of its development it passed through various stages, the latest of which (before the birth of Maithilī) was that known as Māgadhī Prakrit, the colloquial language of the whole of Bihār, in various stages of development from, say, the time of Buddha (550 B.C.) down to about A.D. 1000.[2] From this Māgadhī Prakrit are directly descended not only Maithilī and the other languages of Bihār, but also Bengali, Assamese, and Oṛiyā. For our present purposes it is sufficient to remember that the Maithilī Vocabulary is descended from Sanskrit through Māgadhī Prakrit.

38. In order to supply real or fancied deficiencies in this vocabulary, writers have borrowed words from other languages,—English, Persian, Arabic, and Sanskrit. The English, Persian, and Arabic importations are very few in number, but the case is different with Sanskrit. In the vocabulary compiled for this work, out of the first hundred words, about twenty-seven may claim to be more or less distorted forms of words borrowed direct from Sanskrit, without having passed through Māgadhī Prakrit. These borrowed Sanskrit words are just as foreign to the language as are Latin words borrowed at the present day by French or Italian. Natives are quite aware of the existence of these two classes of words, and have given each class a name. They call the words borrowed from Sanskrit *Tatsamas*, *i.e.*, 'the same as It' ('It' being Sanskrit), while the true Maithilī words, which have developed naturally through Māgadhī Prakrit they call '*Tadbhavas*' *i.e.*, 'sprung from It.'

39. The distinction between these two classes of words is of importance, for *Tatsamas*, like all borrowed words in all languages, are treated as foreigners and are not subject to the phonetic rules which govern *Tadbhavas*. For instance, the rule of the short antepenultimate does not apply to *Tatsamas*. Again *Tatsamas* cannot be conjugated (with one or two rare exceptions) as verbs. For instance दर्शन *darśan* is a *Tatsama* meaning 'seeing,' but we cannot

---

[1] Accurately speaking, it is descended from an ancient form of Indo-Aryan speech akin to, but not the same as, that which became fixed by ancient literary use in the form of Sanskrit.

[2] It must be understood that these limits are only approximate.

say दर्शने-अछि *darśanai-ach*[i], he sees. If we want to use the word we must compound it with another *Tadbhava* verb and say दर्शन करै-अछि *darśan karai-ach*[i], he does seeing. From this it follows that the class of *Tatsama* words is confined to nouns substantive or nouns adjective, and that, as a broad rule, no verb can be a *Tatsama.*

For the future, on the following pages, I shall employ these two words, *tatsama* and *tadbhava*, in the sense explained above.

PART II.

DECLENSION.

CHAPTER I.

FORMATION OF NOUNS.

40. Space will not permit us to go at any length into the question of the formation of Maithilī nouns. It must suffice to say that, with few exceptions, nouns are formed on the same principles as in Western Hindī, and in other Indo-Aryan languages. I shall first deal with—

EQUIVALENT FORMS OF NOUNS.

41. All nouns, whether substantives or adjectives, admit of various equivalent forms, *i.e.*, of various forms which do not differ appreciably in meaning. These forms are the *short*, the *long*, and the *redundant*. The *short* form may be either *weak* or *strong*. In practice every noun does not take all these four forms, only experience can teach which of the short forms (the weak or strong) is employed in the case of any particular noun ; but theoretically all nouns, and in reality some few nouns, do take both. All nouns can, at option, take the long and redundant forms.

42. The *short* form is the primary form by which the word is generally known. It is also, in most cases, the only one admissible in good and literary language.

43. Of its two varieties, the *weak* form is the shortest form of the noun, generally ending in a consonant, a short *i*, or an imperfect

ⁱ. Thus घोड़ *ghōṛ*, a horse; लोह *lōh*, iron; पानि *pāni*, water; मारि a beating; छोट *chōṭ*, small (masc.); छोटि *chōṭⁱ*, small (fem.).

44. The *strong* form is simply the weak form (when such exists) strengthened by the addition of आ *ā*, or by the lengthening of the final vowel. When there is no weak form, the strong form always ends in a long vowel. Thus, घोड़ा *ghōṛa*, a horse; लोहा *lōhā*, iron; मारी *mārī*, a beating; छोटा *chōṭā*, small (masc.); छोटी *chōṭī*, small (fem.); आँसू *ā̃sū* (no weak form), a tear; पोथी *pōthī* (no weak form), a book.

45. The *long* forms of *substantives* are made by adding one of the suffixes आ *ā*, या *yā* or वा *wā* (sometimes vulgarly आँ *ā̃* or एँ *ẽ*, याँ *yā̃* or येँ *yẽ*, वाँ *wā̃* or *wẽ*) to the short form, the final vowels of which, if long, are shortened. Thus घोड़वा *ghorᵃwā* (or -ᵃ*wā̃*,-ᵃ*wẽ*), a horse; मॅरिया *măriyā* or मॅरिआ *măriā*, a beating, पोथिया *pothiyā* or पोथिआ *pothiā*, a book; आँसुवा *ā̃suwā* or आँसुआ *ā̃suā*, a tear.

46. The *long* forms of *adjectives* are similarly made by adding one of the suffixes का *kā* or क्का *kkā* (fem. की *kī* or क्की *kkī*) to the short forms. Thus, from बड़ *baṛ* or बड़ा *baṛā* (short forms), great, we have as long form बड़का *baṛᵃkā*. So from छोट *chōṭ* or छोटा *chōṭā*, small, we have छोटका *choṭᵃkā* or छोटक्का *choṭakkā*, and from भारि *bhāri* or भारी *bhārī*, heavy, भॅरिका *bhărikā* or भॅरिक्का *bhărikka*. For the long form of the feminine छोटि *chōṭⁱ*, however, we must go back to the masculine छोट *chōṭ*, and form a new feminine from the long form. Thus, छोटकी *choṭᵃkī* or छोटक्की *choṭakkī*. There is no such form as छोटिका *choṭikā* or छोटिक्का *choṭikkā* derived directly from छोटि *chōṭⁱ*.

47. The *redundant* forms of substantives and adjectives are formed from their long forms precisely as long forms of substantives are formed from their short forms, *viz.*, by adding आ *ā*, या *yā*, or वा *wā*, to the long forms; but, once these additions are made

there are frequent contractions. We thus get the following table exhibiting all the forms at one view.

Short form.		Long form.	Redundant form.
Weak.	Strong.		
घोड़ *ghōṛ*, a horse	घोड़ा *ghōṛā*	घोड़वा *ghoṛ*ᵃ*wā*	घोड़ौवा *ghoṛauwā* (contracted from घोड़ववा *ghor*ᵃ*w*ᵃ*wā*.
घर *ghar*, a house (masc.)	none	घरवा *ghar*ᵃ*wā*	घरौवा *gharauwā* (similarly contracted).
None	सभा *sabhā*, an assembly (fem.)	सभवा *sabh*ᵃ*wā*	सभौवा *sabhauwā*.
बात *bāt*, a word (fem.) (So all feminines ending in a consonant.)	none	बातिया *bătiyā*	बातियवा *bătiy*ᵃ*wā* (or contracted) बातीवा *bătīwā*.
मारि *mār*ⁱ, a beating. (So any noun ending in ⁱ.)	मारी *mārī*	मारिया *măriyā*	मारियवा *măriy*ᵃ*wā* or मारीवा *marīwā*.
पानि *pāni*, water. (So any noun in *i*.)	none	पानिया *păniyā*	पानियवा *păniy*ᵃ*wā* or पानीवा *pănīwā*.
None.	पोथी *pōthī*, a book. (So any noun in ī.)	पोथिया *pothiyā*	पोथियवा *pothiy*ᵃ*wā* or पोथीवा *pothīwā*.

SHORT FORM.		Long form.	Redundant form.
Weak.	Strong.		
None	आँसू *ãsū*, a tear. So any noun in *ū*.	आँसुआ *ăsuā*	आँसुअवा *ăsuªwā* or आँसूआ *ăsūā*.
छोट *chōṭ*, small So any masculine adjective.	छोटा *chōṭā*	{ छोटका *choṭªkā* { छोटक्का *choṭákkā*	छोटकवा *choṭªkawā*. छोटकवा *choṭákªwā*.
छोटि *chōṭi*, small. So any feminine adjective.	छोटी *chōṭī*	{ छोटकी *choṭªkī* { छोटक्की *choṭákkī*	छोटकिया *choṭªkiyā*. छोटकिया *choṭákiyā*.

48. With reference to the above table, attention must be called to the remarks in § 24 concerning the optional insertion or omission of euphonic य् *y* and व् *w*. For instance, instead of बाँतिया *bătiyā*, we may have बतिआ *batiā*, and instead of आँसुआ *ăsuā*, we may have आँसुवा *ăsuwā*. Attention is also to be called to the fact that natives very frequently substitute अ *a* for आँ *ă* in writing (this does not affect the pronunciation). So that, in native books, we should usually find forms like बतिया *batiyā*, बतीवा *batīwā*, पनिया *paniyā*, अँसुआ *ãsuā*, and so on. It will be noticed that the rule of the short antepenultimate (§§ 32 and ff.) comes into full force in these forms.

49. All these forms, the short weak, the short strong, the long, and the redundant, have, in theory, exactly the same meaning. The long form is, however, generally used in a non-honorific sense or to give definiteness. Thus नेनवा *nenªwā*, the boy (familiarly or contemptuously); घोड़वा *ghoṛªwā*, *the* horse. The long form in the feminine is frequently employed in the sense of a

diminutive. Thus नेनी *nēnī*, a girl, नेनिया *neniyā*, a little girl; खाट *khāṭ*, a bed, खटिया *khaṭiyā*, a cot.

50. The redundant form is used in much the same sense as the long form, but only by the vulgar or in familiar language. The vulgar, indeed, employ both the long and the redundant forms as caprice dictates, in the sense of the short form. The use of the redundant form in this way is still more vulgar or familiar than that of the long form.

Nominal Suffixes.

51. In the following examples, as my object is here purely practical, I shall not attempt to distinguish between primary and secondary suffixes. It must be understood that अइ *ai* or अए *ae* and ऐ *ai* are always absolutely interchangeable, and so also अउ *au* or अओ *ao* and औ *au*. I have written, in each case, the forms which I have seen most frequently.

52. आ *ā* **(Masculine).** The strong short forms in आ *ā* correspond to the large class of Hindi nouns which end in आ *ā*, such as Hindi घोड़ा *ghōṛā*, a horse; but many nouns, which in Hindi are only used in the strong form, in Maithili prefer the weak form. Thus :—

Maithilī.	*Hindī.*
आन्ह *ānh*, blind	आँधा *ā̃dhā*
ऊँच *ū̃c*, high	ऊँचा *ū̃cā*
कान *kān*, one-eyed	काना *kanā*
कान्ह *kānh*, the shoulder	काँधा *kā̃dhā*
गहीर *gahīr*, deep	गहिरा *gahirā*
गोर *gōr*, pale	गोरा *gōrā*
घोड़ *ghōṛ*, a horse	घोड़ा *ghōṛā*
चून *cūn*, lime	चूना *cūnā*
छूर *chūr*, a knife	छूरा *chūrā*
दहिन *dahin*, right (not left)	दहिना *dahinā*
बहीर *bahīr*, deaf	बहिरा *bahirā*

Maithilī.	*Hindī.*
मूस *mūs*, a rat	मूसा *mūsā*
लोह *lōh*, iron	लोहा *lōhā*
सार *sār*, a brother-in-law	साला *sālā*
सोन *sōn*, gold	सोना *sōnā*
So (weak form in ⁱ)	
मारि *mārⁱ*, a beating	मारी *mārī*

In some cases Maithilī has the strong, as well as the weak form. Thus, घोड़ा *ghōṛā* as well as घोड़ *ghōṛ*, लोहा *lōhā* as well as लोह *lōh*, but in all the above, the weak form is the one customarily heard.

Weak nouns are of course very common in Hindī. But I think it is safe to say that they are much more common, both in the case of masculine and in that of feminine nouns, in Maithilī.

53. आ *ā* **(Feminine).** Nearly all the feminine words in आ *ā* are *tatsamas* borrowed directly from Sanskrit, such as सभा *sabhā*, an assembly. The only Maithilī *tadbhavas* which I have noted as ending in this letter are बुन्द *bund* or बुन्दा *bundā*, a drop, and the connected बुना *bunā*, zero, the figure 0.

54. आस *ās*, वास *wās*. These usually form desideratives as in Hindī, but are not so common as in that language. The only forms which I have met in Maithilī are:—

पिआस *piās*, thirst; hence पिआसल *piāsal*, thirsty.

तरास *tarās*, thirst; hence तरासल *tarāsal*, thirsty.

(This word is not to be confounded with तरास *tarās*, fear).

मुतवास *mutᵃwās*, desire to make water (Hindī मुतास *mutās*).

हगवास *hagᵒwās*, desire to stool (Hindī हगास *hagās*).

Other words with (in form) the same suffix, but not desideratives, are such as:—

झपास *jhapās*, a violent burst of rain (so Hindī for *jhapavāsā*, sudden rain).

गड़ाँस *gaṛā̃s*, a pole-axe (Hindī गँड़ासा *gā̃ṛāsā*).

The derivation of the suffix in the last two words is obscure.

55. आह *āh*, (*Fem.* आहि *ahⁱ*), weak form; आहा *āhā* (*Fem.*

āhī), **strong form.** This is a common adjectival termination in Maithilī. Thus :—

अधलाह *adh*°*lāh*, bad.

पिछड़ाह *pich*°*ṛāh*, slippery.

बताह *batāh* or बउराह *baurāh*, mad.

बलुआह *baluāh*, sandy.

The strong form is specially used in the following three cases :—

पछिमाहा *pachimāhā*, a man of the west.

दछिनाहा *dachināhā*, a man of the south.

उतराहा *ut*°*rāhā*, a man of the north.

But पूबा *pūbā*, a man of the east.

56. As probably connected with these forms we may quote घोड़हिया *ghoṛahiyā*, a horse-dealer, which is the long form of घोड़ाही *ghoṛāhī*, a masculine noun which I have not met in the short form. Compare also बटोही *baṭōhī*, a wayfarer, from बाट *bāṭ*, a road.

57. इ *i*, **weak short form ;** ई *ī*,* **strong short form ;** इया *iyā*, **long form.**

The weak short form is mainly employed to make feminines from masculine weak short forms ending in a consonant ; as गोर *gōr*, fair, fem. गोरि *gōr*ⁱ. It also forms feminine nouns generally, as in गोहि *gōh*ⁱ, an iguana ; डाँरि *ḍā̃r*ⁱ, a line ; भुँइ *bhũi* (the final vowel fully pronounced being preceded by a vowel, see § 10) ; or भुइयाँ *bhuiyā̃* (long form), the ground ; लग्गति *laggat*ⁱ, an assessment ; बाँहि *bā̃h*ⁱ, an arm ; करुआरि *karuār*ⁱ, an oar ; दूरि *dūr*ⁱ, distance ; आगि *āg*ⁱ, fire.

An important class falling under this head consists of feminine verbal nouns formed by adding इ ⁱ to the root, as in मारि *mār*ⁱ, a beating ; भूलि *bhūl*ⁱ, an error.

In Hindī most of the above end in long ई *ī*, as in गोरी *gōrī*, गोही *gōhī*. Sometimes in that language the final vowel is dropped, as in बाँह *bā̃h* (fem.), an arm ; दूर *dūr* (fem.), distance ; and in the case of Hindī verbal nouns the इ ^{i} may be either dropped or the strong form is used, as मार *mār* (fem.) or मारी *mārī*, a beating.

Masculine nouns of this class (when in the weak form) end in a fully pronounced इ *i*, not in इ ^{i}. They generally represent Sanskrit words ending in ऋ *ṛ* (or ऋक *ṛka*) इक *ika*, ईय *īya*, or इन् *in*. Such are नाति *nāti*, a grandson; दूबि *dūbi* (masculine, not feminine), *dūb* grass; पानि *pāni*, water; केहरि *keh*^{a}*ri*, a lion; डाँड़ि *ḍā̃ṛi*, a rower सूँड़ि *sū̃ṛi*, a distiller; तेलि *tēli*, an oil-man; तमोलि *tamōli*, a betel-seller; कोढ़ि *kōṛhi*, a leper; मानि *māni*, proud.

Many of these words are also pronounced with a long ई *ī*, or, in other words, have strong forms in use as well as the weak ones. Thus, we have also नाती *nātī*, केहरी *keh*^{a}*rī*, तमोली *tamōlī*, and so on, but the forms with short इ *i* are the more usual. So, for feminine nouns, we have माटि *māṭ*^{i} or माटी *maṭī*, earth; काँकरि *kā̃kar*^{i} or काँकरी *kā̃k*^{a}*rī*, a cucumber; कूँजि *kū̃j*^{i} or कूँजी *kū̃jī*, a key; दहि *dah*^{i} or दही *dahī*, curdled milk (this word is feminine, not masculine).

The strong form in ई *ī* also sometimes occurs as the only form for feminine nouns as in माँछी *mā̃chī*, a fly; खरी *kharī*, chalk; लगारी *lagarī*, inquisitiveness (and other similar abstract nouns, instead of with the more usual termination आई *āī*). We sometimes meet this feminine long ई *ī* in diminutives, as दाढ़ *dāṛh*, a long beard, दाढ़ी *daṛhī*, a beard. पुजेरी *pujērī*, a priest, and मोती *motī*, a pearl, are examples of masculine words in ई *ī*, which do not also optionally end in इ *i*.

The long form is used, *quâ* long form, in the case of any of the foregoing nouns, and then usually has a meaning either familiar, contemptuous, or diminutive, as in माली *mālī*, a gardener, long form मालिया *māliyā* or मलिया *maliyā*, the gardener (familiarly), or (contemptuously) the wretched gardener; पोथी *pōthī*, a book, पोथिया *pothiyā*, a small book. कोढ़ी *kōṛhī*, leprous, कोढ़िया *koṛhiyā*, a poor unfortunate leper.

The same long termination is employed to indicate (*a*) a man, country, and (*b*) his profession.

Thus :—

(*a*) सेन्हिया *senhiyā*, a man of Sindh ; मगहिया *magahiyā*, a man of Magah or Magadha ; तिरहुतिया *tirᵒhutiyā*, a man of Tirhut or Tīrabhukti ; मथुरिया *mathuriyā*, a man of Mathurā ; नेपालिया *nepăliyā*, a man of Nēpāl ; पहाड़िया *pahăṛiyā*, a man of the *pahāṛ* or mountain, a mountaineer.

(*b*) अढ़तिया *aṛhatiyā*, a broker ; कमरिया *kamariyā*, a blanket-wearer, a labourer ; घटिया *ghaṭiyā*, a brāhmaṇ who attends ghāṭs.

Exhibiting character more generally are फुसिया *phusiyā*, a flatterer ; चिकनिया *cikaniyā*, one who is always shining and clean (from चिक्कन *cikkan*, smooth) ; and दुखिया *dukhiyā*, one who is miserable, poverty-stricken.

58. Connected with these इ *i*-suffixes is आई *āī* or आइ *āi*, **long form** अइया *aiyā*. As in Hindī, this forms abstract nouns. Thus :—भलाई *bhalāī*, goodness ; खटाई *khaṭāī*, acidity ; छोटाई *choṭāī*, smallness, and hundreds of others.

It is also employed to signify the wages or price of any operation, as in चराई *carāī*, the wages of a herdsman ; पिसाई *pisāī*, wages of grinding ; खेवाई *khēwāī*, ferry hire ; ढोलाई *ḍholāī*, the cost of carriage. Connected with this are words like धोआई *dhōāī*, the art of washing (as well as the cost of it) ; बटनाई *baṭᵒnāī*, the art of twisting ropes ; पटकनाई *paṭᵒkanāī*, a task of winnowing.

The long form in अइया *aiyā* is employed to form masculine adjectives, such as घरइया *gharaiyā*, domesticated (Hindī घरेला *gharēlā*) ; बनइया *banaiyā*, wild ; गमइया *gamaiyā*, rustic. It also forms feminine diminutives, such as मढ़इया *maṛhaiyā*, a small hut. Compare (the short form) तलाई *talāī*, a small pond (from ताल *tāl*, a pond). In Hindī, the long form तलइया *talaiyā* is preferred.

59. इम *im* **(weak form),** इमा *imā* **(strong form).**—This suffix also occurs in Bengali and Marāṭhī. In Maithilī it is found in the word लालिम *lālim* or ललिमा *lalimā*, redness.

60. **उ** ^{u}**, weak short form ; ऊ *ū*, strong short form ; उआ *uā*, long form.**—Where we have weak forms in Maithilī, Hindī has strong forms. Thus:—

भालु *bhāl*^{u}, a bear; but Hindī भालू *bhālū*.

नाउ *nāu* § 10, iii), a barber ; ,, नाऊ *nāū*.

बहु *bah*^{u}, a son's wife ; ,, बहू *bahū*.

In some cases the imperfect उ ^{u} has altogether disappeared, so that we have—

बालु *bāl*^{u} or बाल *bāl* (fem.) sand, but Hindī बालू *bālū*.

माम *mām* or even मामा *māmā*, a maternal uncle, H. मामू *māmū*.

In all these cases, the existence of the उ ^{u} as a termination is due to an accident of origin, and the termination does not necessarily indicate any special shade of meaning. Most उ *u*-suffixes can be referred to the Sanskrit termination उक *uka*, which has also survived without change, and will be found under the क *k*-suffixes.

The suffix ऊ *ū* of the strong form often has the force of the agent. Thus, उजाड़ू *ujāṛū*, a destroyer; खाऊ or (long form) खौआ *khauā*, an eater; डाकू *ḍākū*, a shouter, hence, a robber; बिगाड़ू *bigāṛū*, a spoiler; झाड़ू *jhāṛū*, a sweeper, a broom. Less distinctively nouns of agency are सहरू *sah*^{a}*rū*, a citizen (from شهر *shahr*, a city), and पहरू *pah*^{a}*rū*, a watchman (from पहर *pahar*, a watch, a guard). In गमारू *gamārū*, rustic; दुलारू *dulārū* or (long form) दुलरुआ *dularuā*, a darling; मेहरारू *meh*^{a}*rārū*, a woman; and भगेड़ू *bhagēṛū*, a runaway, the ऊ *ū*-suffix is simply pleonastic, as explained below, under the head of ल *l*- र *r*- ड़ *ṛ*-suffixes. The suffix implies quality in भक्कू *bhakkū*, a fool (Hindī भकुआ *bhakuā*); नक्कू *nakkū*, long-nosed (Hindī, the same).

As usual, the long form उआ *uā* is commonly employed contemptuously as in भड़ुआ *bhaṛuā*, a pimp, but not so always. In दुलरुआ *dularuā*, quoted above, it is an affectionate diminutive, while the meaning is unchanged in खौआ *khauā* and in गेरुआ *geruā*, a large kind of pillow.

Parallel to the आई *āī*-suffix we have also an आऊ *āū*-suffix, with a long form अउआ or औआ *auā*. It forms adjectives, as in झगड़ाऊ *jhag^a^rāū* or झगड़उआ *jhag^a^rauā*, quarrelsome; रहाऊ *rahāū*, abiding, a dweller, an old inhabitant. The long form of बिगाड़ू *bigāṛū*, quoted above, is not the regular बिगड़ुआ *bigaṛuā*, as we might expect, but is बिगड़ौआ *big^a^ṛauā*, as if formed from * बिगड़ाऊ *big^a^ṛāū*.

Most causal verbs have their roots ending in आव *āw*, and from these a number of similar words are framed, such as जड़ाऊ *jaṛāū*, studded (with gems), jewelled. The termination आव *āw* is often written आओ *āo*, and this gives verbal-nouns, such as अटकाओ *aṭ^o^kāo*, the act of stopping, which should be distinguished from the आऊ *āū*-suffix.

61. औन्ह *aunh* or औन *aun* (fem. औन्हि *aunh^i^* or औनि *aun^i^*). This termination forms adjectives generally implying a moderate degree of the quality referred to. The final consonant in every case may be either न्ह *nh* or न *n*. It agrees in sense with the Hindī termination एला *ēlā*. Just as in Hindī we have गोरा *gōrā*, fair, light-coloured, and गोरेला *gorēlā*, fairish, rather light-coloured, so we have Maithilī गोर *gōr*, fair, गोरौन्ह *goraunh* or गोरौन *goraun*, fairish. Other examples are :—

अन्हरौन्ह *anh^a^raunh*, darkish.

अमिलौन्ह *amilaunh*, acidish.

उजरौन्ह *uj^a^raunh*, whitish (उज्जर *ujjar*, white).

उसरौन्ह *us^a^raunh*, saline (ऊसर *ūsar*, salt land).

कचौन्ह *kacaunh*, rawish.

करिऔन्ह *kariaunh*, blackish (कारि *kāri*, black).

कसौन्ह *kasaunh*, rather astringent.

गोबरौन्ह *gob^{a}raunh*, brown land (the colour of गोबर *gōbar* or cow-dung).

गोलौन्ह *golaunh*, globular (गोल *gōl*, round).

तितौन्ह *titaunh*, bitterish.

दुधौन्ह *dudhaunh*, milky.

धुरौन्ह *dhuraunh*, dusty (धूरि *dhūr^{i}*, dust).

नेनौन्ह *nenaunh*, youthful (नेना *nēnā*, a lad).

पिरौन्ह *piraunh*, yellowish (पीअर *piar*, yellow).

फटौन्ह *phaṭaunh*, cracked (of milk).

बुढ़ौन्ह *buṛhaunh*, oldish (बूढ़ *būṛh*, old).

मठौन्ह *maṭhaunh*, sour (मट्ठा *maṭṭhā*, buttermilk).

मेघौन्ह *meghaunh*, cloudy.

ललौन्ह *lalaunh*, reddish (लाल *lāl*, red).

In all the above न *n* may be substituted for न्ह *nh*.

62. क *k*.—A number of nouns are formed by the addition of the letter क *k* preceded by a vowel.

With अक *ak*, we have common words like सरक *sarak* or सड़क *saṛak*, a road; फाटक *phāṭak*, a gate; बइठक *baiṭhak*, a seat.

Many are primary nouns,—formed from verbs whose roots end in क *k*. They are the same in form as the roots. Such are[1] अटक *aṭak*, stoppage; कड़क *kaṛak*, a crash; कचक *kacak*, a sprain; खड़क *khaṛak*, a clang; खटक *khaṭak*, 'pit-a-pat'; गहक *gahak*, reeling in drink; चउँक *caũk*, starting; चिलक *cilak*, चमक *camak*, झलक *jhalak*, झमक *jhamak*, दलक *dalak*, दमक *damak*, glitter; चटक *caṭak*, a crack, snap; and many others.

With आक *āk* or आँक *ā̃k*, are उड़ाँक *uṛā̃k*, one who flies (not

---

[1] See Mr. Beames' Comparative Grammar, Vol. II, p. 31. My list has been prepared by going through Mr. Beames' list with a native of Mithilā.

causal, one who causes to fly); पिआक *piāk*, a drinker; चढ़ाक *caṛhāk*, a rider. Adverbs are also made with this suffix, as झटाक *jhaṭāk*, suddenly; फटाक *phaṭāk*, unawares; तड़ाक *taṛāk*, immediately; पटाक *paṭāk*, immediately; खटाक *khaṭāk*, immediately.

With उक *uk*, we have मारुक *māruk*, quarrelsome, one disposed to fight.

With अइक *aik*, we have सेबइक *sebaik* (Hindī सेवाइत *sēwāit*), a worshipper.

63. गर *gar*. This suffix implies agency. Thus काँटगर *kāṭ*^{a}*gar* thorny; हथगर *hath*^{a}*gar*, able to use the hands; गोड़गर *goṛ*^{a}*gar*, able to use the feet. The last two examples occur in a poem describing the babyhood of *Kṛṣṇa*. As he grew big he began to be able to use his hands and his feet. I have not met the suffix elsewhere in literature, but it is very common in the colloquial language, and can be employed with almost any word in the above sense. In ordinary conversation हथगर *hath*^{a}*gar* means 'dexterous.'

64. त *t* is mostly employed as the suffix of the present participle, usually with अइ *ai* prefixed, as in देखइत *dekhait*, seeing. When verbal roots end in vowels, the termination is lightened, as in जाइत *jāit*, going; सिउत *siut*, sewing; होअइत *hōait* or होइत *hōit*, becoming. The suffix अइत *ait*, also occurs in words like चढ़इत *caṛhait*, a mounted man; डकइत *ḍakait*, a robber (these two are really present participles); and नतइत *natait*, a relation (from नाता *nātā*, relationship). There are several words similarly formed from nouns in Hindī, but नतइत *natait* is the only one which I have noted in Maithilī.

65. Of a quite different origin is a group of words ending in आहटि *āhaṭ*^{i}, अउटी *auṭī*, or अउती *autī*. These generally form abstract nouns. Thus: गड़बड़ाहटि *gaṛ*^{a}*baṛāhaṭ*^{i}, confusion; गजबजाहटि *gaj*^{a}*bajāhaṭ*^{i}, confusion; गुलगुलाहटि *gul*^{a}*gulāhaṭ*^{i}, whispering

घनघनाहटि *ghan^{a}ghanāhaṭ^i*, a great noise; चनचनाहटि *can^a-canāhaṭ^i*, speaking loudly; फरफराहटि *phar^{a}pharāhaṭ^i*, throbbing; सनसनाहटि *san^{a}sanāhaṭ^i*, humming in the ear, and many other similar forms. It will be observed that all these words contain reduplications, and are more or less onomatopœic. Maithilī reserves the termination आहटि *āhaṭ^i*, for this class of words, and has no words corresponding to (*e.g.*) the Hindī खिसियाहट *khisiyāhaṭ*, fretfulness: खुजलाहट *khuj^{a}lāhaṭ*, itching. In Maithilī these ideas are represented by खिसियाएब *khisiyāeb* and कुड़ियाएब *kuṛiy^{e}eb*, respectively, the termination आएब *āeb* (of the infinitive or verbal noun) being usually employed in the place of the Hindī आहट *āhaṭ*. Cf. § 67.

The termination अउटी *auṭī* or अउती *autī* which is connected with the above, is not so common as in Hindī. It forms an abstract noun in सिधउटी *sidhauṭī*, uprightness (from सिद्ध *siddh*, upright). It expresses property in words like जेठउती *jeṭhautī*, the share of an eldest son, and बपउटी *bapauṭī*, the share of a father. Connected with this idea is छोड़उती *choṛautī*, ransom; while mere relationship is indicated in words like हरउती *harautī*, a particular kind of bamboo with a narrow pipe (cf. Hindī हरौटी *harauṭī*, a staff, derivation doubtful); सिकउती *sikautī*, a reed basket, from सीक *sīk*, a reed; चुनउटी *cunauṭī*, a box for holding lime; कजरउटी *kajarauṭī*, a box for holding collyrium.

66. न *n* (fem. नि *n^i*,) weak form; ना *nā* (fem. नी *nī*) strong form.

Suffixes of which न् *n* is the characteristic letter, are common in Maithilī (even if we exclude the numerous *tatsama* words in *ana* borrowed from Sanskrit). Such suffixes are not employed to make infinitives as they are in Hindī.

Both weak and strong forms are frequently employed to make nouns of the instrument. Such are:—

(*a*) Masc. weak forms—

चपकन *capᵃkan*, a close-fitting coat (√चपक *capak*, compress).

छट्टन *chaṭṭan*, a gold-washer's pan.

ड़ाँसन *ḍā̃san*, a washerman's mallet.

दतुअन *datuan*, a tooth-brush (दाँत *dā̃t*, a tooth).

पटकन *paṭᵃkan*, an instrument for teasing cotton.

बाढ़न *bāṛhan*, a broom.

मथन *mahan*, an oil-mill pestle.

लोपन *lōpan*, a poker.

From causal roots we have—

घेरान *gherān*, a fence.

अतरावन *atᵃrāwan*, the reeds of a loom for keeping the threads apart (cf. Skr. अन्तर *antara*).

चपरावन *capᵃrāwan*, a perforated block of iron for shaping nailheads.

लगावन *lagāwan*, a stuffed calf-skin shown to a cow to make its milk flow, literally, 'an appliance,' hence 'an imposture.'

(*b*) Fem. weak forms—

चालनि *cālanⁱ*, a sieve.

छाओनि *chāonⁱ*, an encampment (छाव *chāw*, thatch).

पीअनि *pīanⁱ*, tobacco for smoking (as distinct from snuff).

लाड़नि *lāṛanⁱ*, a grain-parcher's broom.

(*c*) Masc. strong forms—

अखैना *akhainā*, a threshing rake.

अँचना *ā̃cᵃnā*, a poker.

खिखोरना *khikhorᵃnā*, a weaver's scraper.

करना *karᵃnā*, a curd-vessel.

झपना *jhapᵃnā*, ढकना *ḍhakᵃnā*, or ढपना *ḍhapᵃnā*, a cover.

झरना *jharᵃnā*, a broom.

पिटना *piṭ*ᵃ*nā*, a cobbler's mallet.

भरना *bhar*ᵃ*nā*, the stuffing of a quilt.

मोचना *moc*ᵃ*nā*, a barber's tweezers (मोंछ *mōch*, a moustache).

From causal roots, we have—

खेलाओन *khelāon* or खेलौना *khelaunā*, a toy.

छोरौना *chorauna*, a door-key.

बिछाओन *bichāon* or बिछओना *bichaonā* or बिछौना *bichaunā*, bedding.

मिलौना *milaunā*, a potter's smoother.

हथौना *hathaunā*, a toddy-vessel.

(*d*) Fem. strong forms. These are the most common of all—

खुरचनी *khurac*ᵃ*nī*, a pot-scraper.

उबहनी *ubah*ᵃ*nī*, a well-rope.

कटरनी *kaṭar*ᵃ*nī*, a cobbler's awl.

घिरनी *ghir*ᵃ*nī*, a pulley.

छिटकनी *chiṭ*ᵃ*kanī*, a door-bolt.

छेंवनी *chēw*ᵃ*nī*, a potter's cutting string.

छेनी *chēnī*, a chisel.

ठेकनी *ṭhek*ᵃ*nī*, a prop.

नथुनी *nathunī*, a nose-ring.

नहरनी *nahar*ᵃ*nī*, a nail parer, a gouge.

बटनी *baṭ*ᵃ*nī*, a silk-reel.

बैसनी *bais*ᵃ*nī*, a seat.

मथनी *math*ᵃ*nī*, a kind of hammer.

महनी *mah*ᵃ*nī*, a churn-dasher.

From causal bases—

चलौनी *calaunī*, a windlass handle.

छलौनी *chalaunī*, the cover of an ass's pad.

तरौनी *taraunī*, a sweetmeat-stand.

The same suffixes are also employed to indicate an occupation, trade, or profession. Thus:—

कोड़न *kōran*, hoeing.

पिसान *pisān*, the trade of corn-grinding.

लेन देन *lēn dēn*, taking (and) giving, trade, traffic.

पटावन *paṭāwan*, irrigation.

उछटनी *uch*^{a}*ṭanī*, weeding.

कटनी *kaṭ*^{a}*nī*, reaping.

कमैनी *kamainī*, weeding.

केरौनी *keraunī*, weeding.

टिपनी *ṭip*^{a}*nī*, superficial weeding.

टुँगनी *ṭũg*^{a}*nī*, a special method of reaping.

फरनी *phar*^{a}*nī*, the application of the ploughshare (फर *phar*), the first ploughing of the season.

डेँगौनी *ḍẽgaunī*, separating grain from the ears by beating on the ground.

I have not noted any strong masculine forms in ना *nā* in this sense.

The same suffixes are further extended to imply the *result* of any occupation, or even a more indefinite connection with the root. Thus:—

छारन *chāran*, a grass thatch.

धोअन *dhōan*, opium-washings.

बहारन *bahāran*, sweepings.

चटनी *caṭ*^{a}*nī* (√ चाट *cāṭ*, lick), a relish with food, 'chutnee.'

छितनी *chit*^{a}*nī*, a broken basket.

Causal bases sometimes take the suffixes to indicate a ceremonial observance. Thus we have:—

चुमावन *cumāwan*, the kissing ceremony in a marriage.

छेकौनी *chekaunī*, the stopping at the door, part of a marriage ceremony.

मुदेखौनी *mudekhaunī*, presents given to a bride on showing her face.

Compare मँगनी *mãgᵃnī*, a betrothal.

A few nouns of agency are formed with the strong form of this suffix. Those which I have noted are all vulgar and indecent abusive terms, such as हगना *hagᵃnā*, मुतना *mutᵃnā*, or पदना *padᵃnā*. They all imply that the action indicated is done to excess.

67. ब *b*, अब *ab*, एब *eb*.—This forms infinitives and verbal nouns, as in देखब *dēkhab*, to see, the act of seeing. When a verbal root ends in आ *ā* or ओ *ō*, the suffix is एब *eb*, not अब *ab*. Thus पाएब *pāeb*, to obtain; जाएब *jāeb*, to go; होएब *hōeb*, to become. In देब *dēb*, to give, and लेब *lēb*, to take, the junction vowel is dropped.

When this suffix is added to intransitive roots in आ *ā*, it also forms abstract nouns, as in खिसियाएब *khisiyāeb*, fretfulness (from √ खिसिया *khisiyā*, to be fretful), कुड़ियाएब *kuṛiyāeb*, to be angry. Cf. § 65.

68. ल *l*- र *r*- ड़ *ṛ*-**suffixes.**—The letter ल *l* is characteristic of many noun forms.

The simplest is अल *al*, (fem. अलि *alⁱ*), or (strong form) अला *ᵃlā* (fem. अली *ᵃlī*).

अल *al* forms past participles, such as देखल *dēkhal* (fem. देखलि *dēkhalⁱ*), seen. In the case of verbs ending in vowels, it is sometimes उल *ul*, इल *il*, एल *el* or ओल *ol*. Thus सिअल *sial* or सिउल *siul*, sewn; मुइल *muil*, dead; आएल *āel*, come: पाओल *pāol*, obtained.

It also forms adjectives on the same lines, such as दुखाएल *dukhāel*, grieved (also a past participle); निनाएल *nināel*, drowsy; डेराएल *ḍerāel*, fearful; घमाएल *ghamāel*, perspiring; अउँघाएल *aũghāel*, sleepy; सरमाएल *sarᵃmāel* (from شرم *sharm*, shame) bashful; and many others. All these may be looked upon as participles of neuter verbs, whose roots end in आ *ā*.

The same termination is employed to make verbal nouns or

infinitives, with an oblique form in आ *ā*, as देखल *dēkhal*, the act of seeing; देखला सँ *dekh^alā sa͂*, from seeing.

The strong form अला *^alā* is generally employed to make diminutives, and its feminine अली *^alī* is used for things of a still smaller size. Thus चकला *cak^alā*, a paste-board (from चाक *cāk*, a wheel); टिकुली *ṭikulī*, a wafer: कोठली *koṭh^alī*, a small room: तसला *tas^alā*, a brass vessel, तसली *tas^alī*, a small one.

Another connected suffix is इल *il*, strong form इला *ilā*, which is not so common in Maithilī as elsewhere. It forms possessive adjectives from substantives. The only true Maithilī examples which I have noted with certainty are मांझिला *mā̃jhilā*, the middle of three brothers, or the second of four brothers: and साँझिल *sā̃jhil*, the third son of a family of four or more.

Of much more frequent occurrence is the closely related अइल *ail*, with the same meaning. It is often found where literary Hindī has other suffixes. Thus:—

Maithilī.	*Hindī*
तोनइल *tonail*, pot-bellied	तोंदइल *tõdail*.
धोधइल *dhodhail*, pot-bellied	धोंधाला *dhõdhālā*.
दंगइल *dãgail*, a brawler	दंगइत *dãgait*.
बोझइल *bojhail*, load-bearing	बुझइल *bujhail*.

In बँसइला *bā̃sailā*, a young bamboo, the strong form, like अला *^alā* forms a diminutive.

Another form of अइला *ailā* is एला *ēlā*, which we have in सउतेला *sautēlā*, of or belonging to a co-wife, and (feminine diminutive) खम्हेली *khamhēlī*, a small pillar.

Parallel to इल *il*, we have उल *ul* in काजुल *kājul*, a worker, bread-winner. Its strong form उला *ulā*, fem. उली *ulī*, is more common, and, like the other strong forms, the feminine usually is a diminutive. Thus:—

टिकुली *ṭikulī*, a wafer.

गछुली *gachulī*, a young tree.

कठुली *kaṭhulī*, a small wooden bowl.

खटुली *khaṭulī*, a small bamboo litter.

गेड़ुली *geṛulī*, a small pillow (गेड़ुआ *geṛuā*, a large pillow).

अंठुली *ãṭhulī*, a small आंठी *ā̃ṭhī* or fruit-stone.

बातुल *bātul*, a stammerer; बतुली *batulī*, a pitiful, stammering woman.

And many others. Occasionally the उ *u* is strengthened to ओ *ō* (cf. एला *ēlā* above), as in टिकोला *ṭikōlā*, a young mango.

69. Cognate to the ल *l*-suffixes are those whose characteristic letter is ड़ *ṛ* or र *r*.

The suffix अड़ा *ᵃṛā* (fem. अड़ी *ᵃṛī*) is as pleonastic as the long form in अवा *ᵃwā*, which every noun can take. Perhaps in the masculine it adds a shade of contempt. In the feminine it gives a diminutive meaning. This suffix is not so common in Maithili in the west, अरा *ᵃrā* (fem. अरी *ᵃrī*) being more usual. An example is झोँपड़ा *jhõpᵃṛā* or खोँपड़ा *khõpᵃṛā*, a hut; feminine झोँपड़ी *jhõpᵃṛī* or खोँपड़ी *khõpᵃṛī*, a small hut. So, from मटुका *maṭukā*, a large vessel, we have मटकुड़ी *maṭᵃkuṛī*, a milk-pail; टुकड़ा *ṭukᵃṛā* or टुकरा *ṭukᵃrā*, a piece; टुकड़ी *ṭukᵃṛī* or टुकरी *ṭukᵃrī*, a small piece.

The suffix is sometimes strengthened to एड़ू *ēṛū*, as in भगेड़ू *bhagēṛū*, a runaway, fugitive.

The connected अरा *ᵃrā*, (fem. अरी *ᵃrī*) is used with similar meaning, and is more often met with in Maithilī. Examples are चक्की *cakkī* or चकरी *cakᵃrī*, a mill-stone; गेठरी *geṭhᵃrī*, a bundle; मुँगरी *mũgᵃrī*, a small grain-mallet; टुकरा *ṭukᵃrā*, -री-*rī*, as above.

Parallel to the suffix ओला *ōlā*. we have औरी *aurī* in घमौरी *ghamaurī*, small heat-spots, prickly-heat, from घाम *ghām*, heat.

70. There is another pair of ल *l*- and र *r*-suffixes preceded the letter आ *ā*.—Some of the examples are merely deformed

tatsamas like किरपाल *kir°pāl*, Sanskrit कृपालुः *kṛpāluḥ*. But others are *tadbhavas*. The termination is आल *āl* (fem. आलि *āl*ⁱ) or आर *ār* (fem. आरि *ār*ⁱ). Strong forms are आला *ālā* (fem. आली *ālī*) or आरा *ārā* (fem. आरी *ārī*). This has several derivations, according to the particular words with which it is used.[1] In putting them here together, no attempt is made to consider derivation. All words formed with these suffixes are of a very similar nature, and for practical purposes they can all be considered at the same time. The ल *l*-suffix is the less common of the pair. We have दढ़ियाल *daṛhiyāl*, bearded, from दाढ़ी *daṛhī*. a beard. With the र *r*-suffix we have दुधारि *dudhār*ⁱ or दुधारी *dudhārī* (feminine), milch (of a cow); पियार *piyār* (fem. पियारि *piyār*ⁱ), a beloved one, as against the Hindī प्यारा *pyārā* (fem. -री-*rī*). पेटारा *peṭārā*, a basket-box, fem. पेटारी *peṭārī*, used in a diminutive sense: गमार *gamār*, rustic; दुलार *dullār*, a darling (Skr. दुर्लभः *durlabhaḥ*). The last two words often take an additional final *ū*-suffix. Thus गमारू *gamārū*, दुलारू *dulārū* (or long form employed affectionately. दुलरुआ *dularuā*), without change of meaning. So also the Sanskrit-Prakrit महिला *mahilā* becomes मेहरारू *meh°rārū*. a woman.

71. The suffix पन *pan* प्पन *ppan*, आपन *āpan*, is as common in Maithilī as in other Indo-Aryan vernaculars. It forms abstract nouns from adjectives or substantives. Thus:—.

चुगलपन *cugal°pan*, backbiting.

छुधरपन *chudhar°pan*, meanness (छूधर *chūdhar* = शूद्र *śūdra*).

छोटपन *choṭ°pan*. smallness.

ठगपन *ṭhag°pan*. cheating.

दृढ़पन *dṛṛh°pan*. firmness.

धूर्तपन *dhūrt°pan*. knavery.

[1] Cf. Dr. Hoernle's Gaudian Grammar, pp. 118, 129, 135. 150.

नेनपन *nen^apan*, childhood.

बलेलपन *balel^apan*, foolishness.

बहेड़पन *baheṛ^apan*, ne'erdoweelness.

बुड़िपन *buṛipan*, foolishness (बूड़ि *būṛi*, a fool).

बुढ़पन *buṛh^apan* or बुढ़प्पन *buṛhappan*, old age.

भलापन *bhalāpan* or भलपन *bhal^apan*, honesty.

भँड़पन *bhā̃ṛ^apan* or भँड़प्पन *bhā̃ṛappan*, roguery.

रँड़पन *rā̃ṛ^apan*, widowhood (राँड़ *rā̃ṛ*, a widow).

लँगटपन *lā̃gaṭ^apan* or नँगटपन *nā̃gaṭ^apan*, blackguardliness (लंगट *langaṭ*, नंगट *nangaṭ* or नँगटा *nā̃g^aṭā*, naked).

लगरपन *lagar^apan*, inquisitiveness (लगार *lagār*=' Paul Pry ').

लड़िकपन *laṛik^apan*, boyhood.

सेयानपन *seăn^apan*, full-ageness (when a young lady has, as we should say in England, 'her hair up,' she is सेयानि *seănⁱ*).

It will be observed that the suffix is added even to *tatsama* words.

72. वाह *wāh* (fem. वाहि *wāhⁱ*).—This is the regular termination of nouns of agency and is the equivalent in meaning of the Hindi वाला *wālā*. Thus :—

अनवाह *an^awāh*, the man in charge of the other (अन्य *anya*) or spare pair of bullocks, when ploughing is going on.

कतरवाह *katar^awāh*, one who cuts sugarcane for feeding a sugarcane press.

करिनवाह *karin^awāh*, a man who works a करीन *karīn* or irrigation lever.

कोदरिवाह *kodariwāh*, a worker with a कोदारि *kodārⁱ* or mattock.

गछवाह *gach^awāh*, one who climbs trees (गाछ *gāch*, a tree).

गँजवाह *gā̃j^awāh*, one who uses a गाँज *gā̃j*, or fish trap.

गड़िवाह *gaṛiwāh*, a cart-driver.

गुनवाह *gun^awāh*, the man who tows a boat (गुन *gun*, a rope).

गैवाह *gaiwāh*, a tender of cows.

घोड़वाह *ghor^{a}wāh*, a groom.

चरवाह *car^{a}wāh*, one who grazes cattle.

झलिवाह *jhaliwāh*, a cymbal-player (झाली *jhālī*. cymbals).

टोकवाह *ṭok^{a}wāh*, an asker (टोक *ṭōk*, ask).

पैनवाह *pen^{a}wāh*, a cattle-driver (पैना *painā*, a cattle-whip).

बधवाह *badh^{a}wāh*, a field watchman (बाध *bādh*, village lands).

मोँरवाह *mõr^{a}wāh*, one who drives cattle round and round in a mill (मोँर *mõr*, a turn).

लठिवाह *laṭhiwāh*, a wielder of cudgels.

सुनवाह *sun^{a}wāh*, one who hears complaints.

हथिवाह *hathiwāh*, an elephant-keeper.

हरवाह *har^{a}wāh*, a ploughman.

The suffix is optionally spelt and pronounced बाह *bāh*, so that we may have अनबाह *an^{a}bāh*, कतरबाह *katar^{a}bāh*, and so on. Further, an abstract noun can be formed from these nouns of agency by adding the fem. suffix इ ^{i}. Thus गड़िवाहि *gaṛiwāh^{i}*, the profession of a cart-driver. So from the √ चार *cār*, graze (active), we have चरबाह *car^{a}bāh*, a cattle-grazer, and thence चरबाहि *car^{a}bāh^{i}*, cattle-grazing.

73. सार *sār*.—This is not a proper suffix, being simply a derivative form of शाला *śālā*, a house. In Maithilī it is used as a suffix, and not as a member of a compound word. The whole compound is treated as if it were one word, with the usual shortening of the antepenultimate vowel. Thus, from—

हाथी *hāthī*, an elephant, we have हथिसार *hathisār*. an elephant-stable.

घोड़ *ghōr*, a horse, we have घोड़सार *ghor^{a}sār*, a horse-stable.

छाटि *chāṭi*, a pupil (Skr. छात्र *chātra*), छटिसार *chaṭisār*, a school.

Similarly, कनिसार *kanisār*, a furnace for parching grain, and बनिसार *banisār*, a prison.

CHAPTER II.

Gender, Number and Case.

74. The noun has two Genders.—Masculine and Feminine. Words derived direct from the Sanskrit, which were originally neuter, generally become masculine in Maithilī.

The most important exceptions to this last rule are आँखि *ākh*^{i}, an eye; दहि *dah*^{i} or दही *dahī*, curdled milk; दूरि *dūr*^{i}, distance; and पुस्तक *pustak*, a book: which are feminine. आगि *āg*^{i}, fire, though derived from a masculine Sanskrit word, is feminine in Maithilī.

75. There are two numbers, the singular and plural.

The plural number of nouns in Maithilī is simply formed by the addition of a noun signifying multitude. Those most commonly used are सभ *sabh* and सबहि *sabah*^{i} [1] meaning 'all,' and लोकनि *lok*^{a}*ni* meaning 'people.' The last is only used with animate objects. सभ *sabh* and सबहि *sabah*^{i} can be used indifferently either before or after the qualified noun. Thus नेना सभक *nēnā sabhak* नेना सबहिक *nēnā sab*^{a}*hik*, सभ नेनाक *sabh nēnāk*, सबहि नेनाक *sabah nēnāk* and नेना लोकनिक *nēnā lok*^{a}*nik* are all possible forms of the genitive plural of नेना *nēnā*, a boy. लोकनि *lok*^{a}*ni*, be it observed, can only be used *after* the qualified noun. In all circumstances, whatever be the order of the words, the postposition deciding the case comes last.

76. The same rules partially apply to pronouns: but, in addition to the word signifying plurality, many of them have entirely new bases for their plural forms.

77. Throughout the following Paradigms, I shall generally use only the word सभ *sabh* to designate the plural; but it must always be understood that, unless specially forbidden, सबहि *sabah*^{i} and लोकनि *lok*^{a}*ni* can also be used.

---

[1] The old Maithili poet Vidyāpati sometimes has सबहु *sabah*^{u}, instead of सबहि *sabah*^{i}. Compare song I. 6.

78. *Organic cases.*—There was a case-termination हि *hi* or हिँ *hĩ* and another हु *hu* or हुँ *hũ* in Apabhraṁśa Māgadhī Prakrit. These have survived in Maithili in the forms हि h^i, हिँ $h^{\tilde{i}}$, हु h^u and हुँ $h^{\tilde{u}}$, which can be used for practically any oblique case. They are not often heard nowadays, except in poetry and proverbial sayings, but they are common in these. They are also frequently met in the old poetry of Vidyāpati.

Examples of the use of हि h^i and हिँ $h^{\tilde{i}}$ in the various cases are as follows :—

Accusative—सत्रुहि आन *satruh*^{i} *ān*, he brings an enemy.

पड़रुहिँ मार *par*^{a}*ruh*$^{\tilde{i}}$ *mār*, beat the buffalo calves.

Instrumental—बलहि *balah*^{i}, by force, violently.

अचरहिँ झारि झुरि दितहुँ *acarah*$^{\tilde{i}}$ *jhār*^{i} *jhur*^{i} *ditah*$^{\tilde{u}}$, I would have swept it with my body-cloth.

Ablative—नेँदहि सिख चरबाहि अहीर *nẽdah*^{i} *sikh carabāh*^{i} *ahīr*, from boyhood cowherds learn cattle-tending.

Locative—जमुना हरदहि *jamunā haradah*^{i}, in the Jamunā-pool.

अदँकहिँ सिंदुर मेट गेल *adãkah*$^{\tilde{i}}$ *sindur mēṭ gēl*, in her astonishment, the vermilion was rubbed off.

गदरौ खेतहि सुखाएल *gad*^{a}*rī khētah*^{i} *sukhāel*, the unripe crop has dried up in the fields.

The following are examples of हु h^u and हुँ $h^{\tilde{u}}$:—

Dative—सबहु जथोचित कैल परनाम *sabah*^{u} *jathōcit kail par*^{a}*nām*, to all he made meet reverence.

Ablative—ओतहु *otah*^{u}, from there.

किछु नहिँ ततहुँ भेल *kich*^{u} *nah*$^{\tilde{i}}$ *tatah*$^{\tilde{u}}$ *bhēl*, nothing came to pass from there.

Genitive.—अकरूरहु चलएक डौल *ak*^{a}*rūrah*^{u} *calaek ḍaul*, an opportunity for the coming of Akrūr.

Locative.—पकड़हु परम निपुन *pacharah*^{u} *param nipun*, exceedingly skilled in wrestling.

कोपहुँ कटु नहिँ भाखथि कबहु *kōpahu kaṭu nahĩ bhākhathi kabahu*, even at any time he speaketh not harshly in anger.

Most of the above examples come from poetry, in which a final इ *i* or उ *u* is fully pronounced, but I have written them as if they were prose, so as to illustrate the grammatical forms.

In modern prose Maithilī the form हिँ *hĩ* is contracted to एँ *ẽ* and is reserved for the termination of the Instrumental while हि *hi* is contracted to ए *ē*, and is reserved for the termination of the Locative. Examples will be found below, in dealing with the separate cases.

79. *Inorganic cases.*—In Maithilī (except in the organic Instrumental formed by adding एँ *ẽ*, and the organic Locative formed by adding ए *ē*) cases are formed by suffixing postpositions. In Hindōstānī these postpositions are added directly to the noun without any change of the latter. Thus, फल का *phal kā*, of fruit, नारी को *nārī kō*, to the woman. But, when a *tadbhava* noun (which is not a noun of relationship) ends in आ *ā*, that आ *ā* is changed to ए *ē* before a postposition. Thus, from घोड़ा *ghōṛā*, a horse, we have घोड़े का *ghoṛe kā*, of a horse. In Maithilī the position is almost exactly reversed. *Tadbhava* nouns in आ *ā* are never changed, while certain other nouns do change before postpositions. In other words, the oblique form in Maithilī is always the same as the direct form except in the case of certain nouns in इ *i*, ड़ *ṛ*, न *n*, ब *b*, ल *l* and र *r*. For instance घोड़ा *ghōṛā*, a horse, has its genitive घोड़ा केर *ghōṛā kēr*, not घोड़े केर *ghōṛē kēr*.

80. The following are the rules for ascertaining the oblique form *in the singular* of those nouns which take it :—

(*i*) All verbs form a feminine verbal noun by adding इ *i* to the root (see § 57). Thus देखब *dekhab*, to see; root देख *dēkh*; verbal noun देखि *dēkhi*, seeing, in the sense of 'the act of seeing.' All these verbal nouns in इ *i* have an oblique form in ऐ *ai*, as in देखै कँ

dēkhai kē, for seeing. The oblique form itself is often used as a dative of purpose, as in ओकरा देखै गेल छलहुँ *okᵃrā dēkhai gēl chalahᵘ*, I had gone for seeing him, *i.e.*, to see him. Other examples of the use of this oblique form are:—

हम चरैक (*i.e.*. चरै+क) लेल ओकरा छाड़लेँ रहैत छी, *ham caraik* (*i.e.*, *carai+k*) *lēl okᵃrā chāṛᵃlē̃ rahait chī*, I have let it (a goat) loose for the sake of grazing (*i.e.*, to graze).

दौड़ल सलहेस केँ पकड़ै *dauṛal salᵃhēs kē̃ pakᵃṛai*, they ran to catch Salhēs.

चललीह हरवा बेचै *calᵃlīh harᵃwā bēcai*, she went to sell strings of beads.

अपना चढ़ैक घोड़ी देलक *apᵃnā caṛhaik ghōṛī dēlak*, he gave the mare of his own riding (*i.e.*, his own riding mare).

In the case of the roots दे *dē*, give, and ले *lē*, an म *m* (or sometimes ब *b*) is inserted in the oblique form. Thus, देइ *dēi*, the act of giving, oblique देमै *dēmai*. Verbs whose roots end in इ *i* insert a *a* ब *b* throughout. Thus √ पि *pi*, drink, verbal noun, पिबि *pibⁱ*, oblique पिबै *pibai*. Examples of these forms are:—

हमरा एक बकरी लेमैक अछि *hamᵃrā ek bakᵃrī lēmaik achⁱ*, to me of taking one she-goat there is (necessity), *i.e.*, I must get a she-goat.

In the following we have also the direct verbal noun भरि *bharⁱ*, the filling:—

नेना सभ केँ पिबैक भरि भै जाइत छैक *nēnā sabh kē̃ pibaik bharⁱ bhai jāit chaik*, there becomes the filling of the drinking for the children, *i.e.*, we get enough for the children's drinking.

Note that some people write and pronounce the final ऐ *ai* of this oblique form as if it were अ *ǎ*, thus चरअक *carǎk*, बेचअ *bēcǎ*, etc.

This oblique form of verbal nouns is very frequently employed in the construction of compound verbs, under the head of which several more examples will be found.

81. (*ii*) There are two other verbal nouns ending in ब *b* (§ 67) and ल *l* (§ 68), which have the same meaning. Thus देखब *dēkhab*. the act of seeing, to see; देखल *dēkhal*, the act of seeing. The former is commonly employed as an infinitive, but both are true nouns, and are thus declined :—

Nominative Singular	देखब *dēkhab*	देखल *dēkhal*
Oblique Singular	देखबा *dekhᵃbā*	देखला *dekhᵃlā*
Organic Instrumental Singular.	देखबें *dekhᵃbē̃*	देखलें *dekhᵃlē̃*
Organic Locative Singular.	देखबे *dekhᵃbē*, sometimes written देखबै *dekhᵃbai*.	देखले *dekhᵃlē*, sometimes written देखलै *dekhᵃlai*.

In the second noun न *n* is sometimes written for ल. We thus have the compound लेलें जाएब *lēlē̃ jāeb* or लेनें जाएब *lēnē̃ jāeb*, to go by means of taking, to take away.

Examples of the employment of these two verbal nouns are :—

(*a*) 1. Direct forms—

हुनक कानब सुनि *hunak kānab sunⁱ*, having heard his weeping.

छाड़ब की रहौ *chāṛab kī rahau*, what letting go was there to you, why did you let go ?

पछताएब *pachᵃtāeb*, the act of regretting. The oblique form is पछतैबा *pachᵃtaibā*, see below.

2. Oblique cases—

एकरा मारबा में *ekᵃra mārᵃbā mē̃*, in killing it.

ओकरा तकबा में in searching for it (√ ताक *tāk*, direct verbal noun ताकब *tākab*).

पछतैबाक *pachᵃtaibāk*, of regretting.

रातुक चलबे दिन में पहुँचल *rātuk calᵃbē̃ din mē̃ pahũcal*, by travelling by night, he arrived in the daytime.

(*b*) 1. Direct forms—

ओ कहल करैअछि *ō kahal karaiach*ⁱ, he does speaking, *i.e.*, he speaks frequently.

पछताओल *pach*ᵃ*tāol* (obl. पछतौला *pach*ᵃ*taulā*), the act of regretting.

कैल *kail* or करल *karal*, the act of doing.

2. Oblique cases—

पानि बरिसला बिना *pāni baris*ᵃ*lā binā*, without water raining, *i.e.*, (owing to) the want of rain.

चरी नहिं भेटला सँ *carī nah*ⁱ *bheṭ*ᵃ*lā sa͂*, from not getting fodder.

घुमला सँ की लाभ अछि *ghum*ᵃ*lā sa͂ kī lābh ach*ⁱ, what profit is there from wandering about.

दौर धूप कैला सँ किछु नहिं हैत *daur dhūp kailā sa͂ kicch*ᵘ *nah*ⁱ *hait*, nothing will result (*lit.* be) from running and fussing.

पछतौला सँ की भै सकैअछि *pach*ᵃ*taulā sa͂ kī bhai sakaiach*ⁱ what (good) can result from lamenting?

लगले *lag*ᵃ*lē*, on the attaching, *i.e.*, immediately.

82. Besides the above, several other nouns (including adjectives) ending in ड़ *ṛ*, ढ़ *ṛh*, न *n*, र *r*, ल *l*, and occasionally other letters also, have oblique forms in आ *ā*. I have noted the following as certain instances:—

बड़ *baṛ*, great	Oblique form	बड़ा *baṛā*.
अखाढ़ *akhāṛh*, an arena	..	अखाढ़ा *akhāṛhā*.
आँगन *ā̃gan*, a courtyard	..	आँगना *ā̃g*ᵃ*nā*.
नैन *nain*, an eye	..	नैना *nainā*.
दोसर *dōsar*, second	..	दोसरा *dos*ᵃ*rā*.
तेसर *tēsar*, third	..	तेसरा *tes*ᵃ*rā*.
पहर *pahar*, a watch	..	पहरा *pah*ᵃ*rā*.

आँचर *ã car* or आचर *ācar*, a body cloth.	Oblique form	अँचरा *ãc^{a}rā* or अचरा *ac^{a}rā*.
आन्हर *ānhar*, blind	,,	अन्हरा *anh^{a}rā*.
इँगुर *ĩgur*, red lead	,,	इँगुरा *ĩgurā*.
कोर *kōr*, a lap	,,	कोरा *kōrā*.
दिबार *dibār*, a wall	,,	दिबरा *dib^{a}rā*.
दुआर *duār*, a doorway	,,	दुअरा *duarā*.
पल्लर *pallar*, a plank	,,	पलरा *pal^{a}rā*.
बहीर *bahīr*, deaf	,,	बहिरा *bahirā*.
लिलार *lilār*, the forehead	,,	लिलरा *lil^{a}rā*.
पहिल *pahil*, first	,,	पहिला *pahilā*.
बदल *badal*, exchange	,,	बदला *bad^{a}lā*.

To these may be added :—

अगूँ *agū̃* or आगूँ *āgū̃*, front	,,	अगाँ *agā̃*, आगाँ *āgā̃*.
पछूँ *pachū̃* or पाछूँ *pāchū̃*, rear	,,	पछाँ *pachā̃*, पाछाँ *pāchā̃*.
ठाँइँ *ṭhā̃ī̃*, place	,,	ठैयाँ *ṭhaīyā̃*.
डीह *ḍīh*, a village-site	,,	डीहा *ḍīhā*.
दिस *dis*, a direction	,,	दिसा *disā*.
धनुख *dhanukh*, a bow	,,	धनुखा *dhanukhā*.

It is necessary to remark that these oblique forms are not invariably employed. We often find the direct form employed instead of the oblique one.

83. Examples are :—

(1) Direct forms—

बड़ अनुरोध बड़ा पय राख *baṛ* (direct) *anurōdh baṛā* (oblique) *pay rākh*, lay (the burden of) a great favour upon the great.

आँगन सुन देखि *ā̃gan sun dēkh^{i}*, seeing the courtyard empty.

नअन (*i.e.*, नैन) नोराएल *naen* (*i.e. nain*) *norāel*, (her) eye filled with tears.

दोसर रोये चन्ना *dōsar rōyē cannā*, the second one who weeps is Cannā.

तीनिक तेसर *tīnik tēsar*, the third after three.

जे परि पहर सूति गेल *jē par*^{i} *pahar sūt*^{i} *gēl*, how the watch went to sleep.

छाड़ु कन्हैया मोर आँचर *chāṛ*^{u} *kanhaiā mōr ā̃car*, let go, O Kṛṣṇa, my body-cloth.

आन्हर कुकुर बसातें भूखे *ānhar kukur basātē̃ bhūkhē*, a blind dog barks at the wind.

पहिल खंड हम लेब *pahil khaṇḍ ham lēb*, I shall take the first portion.

आगूँ थलथल *āgū̃ thal*^{a}*thal*, a pendulous front.

पाछूँ भारी *pāchū̃ bhārī*, a heavy behind.

(2) Oblique forms—

एक सै एकैस दण्ड खेलाइत अछि अखाड़ा पर *ek sai ekais daṇḍ khelāit ach*^{i} *akhāṛhā par*, he performs one hundred and twenty-one exercises upon the arena.

बड़ा पय राख *baṛā pay rākh*, as above.

कटगर तरु आँगना केओ राख *kaṭ*^{a}*gar taru āg*^{a}*nā keo rākh*, does anyone keep a thorn-tree in his courtyard ?

नैना काजर पेन्हि लेलि (for लेलन्हि *lēlanh*^{i}) *nainā kājar pēnh*^{i} *lel*^{i}, on her eyes she applied collyrium.

तेसराक अंत *tes*^{a}*rāk ant*, the end of the third.

सलहेसक पहरा सँ *sal*^{a}*hēsak pah*^{a}*rā sã*, from Salhēs's watch.

आँचरा डगरिया बहारितहुँ *ãc*^{a}*rā ḍagariyā bahăritah*^{u}, I would have swept the road with my body-cloth.

बहिराक सुतलहिँ की अन्हराक जगलहिँ की *bahirāk sut*^{a}*lah*^{ĩ} *kī, anh*^{a}*rāk jagalah*^{ĩ} *kī*, what of a deaf man by sleeping, what of a blind man by waking (*i.e.*, what do they respectively lose by sleeping or waking ?).

लिलरा सोभैअछि इँगुराक रोरिया *lil*^{a}*rā sobhaiach*^{i} *ĩgurāk roriyā*, on the forehead the fragments of red lead are beautiful.

हम सूतब तोहरा कोरा ददा सूतब बबाक कोरा *ham sūtab toh^{a}rā kōrā, dadā sūtab babāk kōrā*, I will sleep in your bosom, (my) brother will sleep in (my) father's bosom.

भद्रिक एहुनी-केहुनी दिबरा सटि गेल *bhadrik ehunī-kehunī dib^{a}rā saṭ^{i} gēl*, Bhadri's elbow, etc., (*i.e.*, elbows and knees) stuck against the wall.

दुअरा में *duarā mē̃*, in the doorway.

बगहा धिया पुता पलरा बैठल *bag^{a}hā dhiyā putā pal^{a}rā baiṭhal*, the girls and boys of Bag^{a}hā were seated on a plank.

पहिला पानि भरि गेल ताड़ *pahilā pāni bhar^{i} gēl tāṛ*, the tank is filled by the first (fall of) rain.

ओकरा बदला में *ok^{a}rā bad^{a}lā mē̃*, in exchange for that.

आगाँ पछाँ बिदा भेल *agā̃ pachā̃ bidā bhēl*, they departed one behind the other.

बिचे ठैयाँ बरहो बियोगवा *bicē ṭhaīyā̃ bar^{a}ho biyog^{a}wā*, in the middle place (write) the separation of the twelve (months).

फोटरा बरा डीहा में गाइ भड़कबैत अछि *phoṭ^{a}rā barā ḍīhā mē̃ gāi bhar^{a}kabait ach^{i}*. Phoṭ^{a}rā is scaring the cattle in Barā village (or Barā Ḍīh).

कोन दिसा के अबैत होइ कहहु बुझाय *kōn disā kē abait hōai kahah^{u} bujhāy*, tell clearly towards what direction he is coming.

मारब धनुखा देब खँसाय *mārab dhanukhā dēb khãsāy*, I will strike him with my bow (*i.e.*, with an arrow from my bow) and fell him.

It will be seen subsequently that these oblique forms in *ā* are much more frequently employed in the case of pronouns than in the case of nouns substantive.

84. As there is no organic plural in Maithilī, the question of a plural oblique form does not arise. The nouns of multitude, सभ *sabh*, सबहि *sabah^{i}*, and लोकनि *lok^{a}ni*, are treated exactly like singular

nouns. Thus, the organic instrumental plural of नेना *nēnā*, a boy. may (amongst other forms) be नेना सभें *nēnā sabhẽ* or सभ नेनें *sabh nēnẽ*.

85. There are (counting the vocative) eight cases,—*viz.*, Nominative. Accusative, Instrumental. Dative, Ablative, Genitive, Locative and Vocative.

86. The NOMINATIVE is used before all kinds and before al tenses of verbs. There is no case of the Agent as in Hindōstānī.

87. The ACCUSATIVE is the same in form as the nominative. When a noun has an oblique form this is sometimes employed instead of the accusative by the vulgar. Thus, in the Song of Salᵃhēs, Mālin says बालपन अचरा बान्हलि *bālᵃpan acᵃrā* (not आचर *ācar*) *bāṅhalⁱ*, (from my) girlhood I have kept my body-cloth tied (over my body), *i.e.*, have kept my bosom covered.

In cases in which Hindōstānī would employ the postposition को *kō*. Maithilī employs the dative postposition के *kē*, कें *kẽ*, कैं *kaĩ*, or काँ *kā̃*. as in बनौधिआ दौड़ल सलहेस कें पकड़ै *banaudhiā daural Salᵃhēs kẽ pakᵃṛai*, the Banaudhiās ran to seize Salᵃhēs.

Note that in old Maithili, the nominative and accusative often ends in ए *ē*. which is also an old Māgadhī Prakrit termination of the nominative case. Thus, Vidyāpati (i, 1) says, कामिनि करए सिनाने *kāminⁱ karae sinānē*, the fair one does bathing.

88. The INSTRUMENTAL denotes the instrument, means, cause, or agent, by which a thing is done. It in no way corresponds to the 'agent case' of Hindōstānī of which the suffix is ने *nē*. It is usually formed by the suffix सँ *sā̃* or सैं *saĩ* of which सउँ *saũ* and सोँ *sõ* are occasional varieties, which are more common in the older language.

The Organic Instrumental referred to above is formed by adding एँ *ẽ*, which is sometimes (especially in old poetry) written अइँ *aĩ*. It is added as follows :—

(*a*) When the noun ends in आ *ā*, the एँ *ẽ* is substituted for the final vowel. If the noun has an oblique form ending in आ *ā*, t is added to the oblique form in the same way. Thus कथा *kathā* a story, instrumental कथें *kathē*, by a story; नेना *nēnā*, a boy, नेनें *nēnē*, by a boy; आँचर *ā̃car*, a body-cloth, oblique form अँचरा *ā̃c*ᵃ*rā*, instrumental अँचरें *ā̃c*ᵃ*rē*.

(*b*) In the case of all other nouns, the एं *ē* is added without elision of the final vowel, but if the latter is long, it is shortened, and if it is one of the imperfect vowels इ ⁱ and उ ᵘ, it is fully pronounced. Thus फल *phal*, a fruit, फलें *phalē*, by a fruit; पानि *pāni*, water, instrumental पानिएं *pănīē*; बेटी *bēṭī*, a daughter, instrumental बेटिएं *beṭiē* (not बेटीएं *beṭīē*); सबहि *sabah*ⁱ, all, instrumental सबहिएं *sab*ᵃ*hiē*; भालु *bhāl*ᵘ, a bear, instrumental भालुएं *bhăluē*. The following are examples of the use of this organic instrumental:—

> कमर बाँधे छुरिएं कटारें *kamar bā̃dhē churiē kaṭārē*, he binds his waist with knife and dagger.
>
> गोरि माग़ु गौरबें आन्हरि *gōr*ⁱ *māg*ᵘ *gāūr*ᵃ*bē ānhar*ⁱ, a fair woman is blinded by pride.
>
> एं कथें ई भेल *ē kathē ī bhēl*, owing to this, it happened by conversation (*i.e.*, owing to the conversation). एं कथें *ē kathē* is not 'by this conversation, which would be एहि कथें *eh*ⁱ *kathē*.
>
> जें कानें स्रीमद्भागवत सूनल कोरान नहिं सुनि सकैछी *jē kānē srī-madbhāgavat sūnal korān nah*ⁱ *sūn*ⁱ *sakaichī*, I cannot hear the Qur'ān by the ear with which I have heard the S'rīmad Bhāgavata.

89. The Dative is formed by suffixing the postposition के *kē*, कें *kē*, कै *kaī*, or काँ *kā̃*.

90. The Ablative is formed by suffixing the postposition सँ *sā̃* or सैं *saī*, of which सउँ *saū̃* and सोँ *sō̃* (more common in the older language) are varieties. Verbs of speaking and asking govern the ablative of the person addressed as in Hindōstānī.

91. The sign of the Genitive is क *k*, which, at the present day, is no longer a postposition, but is a suffix attached to, and forming

one word with the base. Thus नेनाक *nēnāk*, of a boy; पानिक *pānik*, of water; नेना लोकनिक *nēnā lok^a^nik* of boys. When the base ends in an imperfect इ *i* or उ *u*, this vowel is pronounced fully in the genitive. Thus सबहिक *sab^a^hik*, of all: भालुक *bhāluk*, of a bear. When the base ends in a consonant, the vowel अ *a* is inserted before the क *k*. Thus, फलक *phalak*, of a fruit. When a noun has a separate oblique form, the क *k* is added to this. Thus बड़ *baṛ*, great, oblique form बड़ा *baṛā*, genitive बड़ाक *baṛāk*, of a great man; अपना चढ़ैक घोड़ा *ap^a^nā caṛhaik ghōṛā*, the horse of his own riding, his own riding horse.

In Southern Maithili, a long vowel is shortened before this क *k*. Thus नेनक *nēnak*, not नेनाक *nēnāk*, of a boy.

The postposition केर *kēr* is also employed to form the genitive. This is more common in poetry and in the older language. Examples are नेना केर *nēnā kēr*, of a boy; फल केर *phal kēr*, of fruit. In the case of personal pronouns, the के *kē* of केर *kēr* is dropped, and the remaining र *r* becomes a suffix, as in हमर *hamar*, my.

The suffixes क *k* and केर *kēr* of the genitive are by origin adjectival, like the Hindōstānī का *kā*, के *kē*, की *kī*, but when added to nouns substantives they are in modern Maithilī immutable, just as in the case of Bengali. They do not change either for gender or for case. Thus we have नेनाक बाप *nēnāk bāp*, the boy's father; नेनाक बाप केर *nēnāk bāp kēr*, of the boy's father: नेनाक माई *nēnāk māī*, the boy's mother; नेनाक भाए सभ *nēnāk bhāi sabh*, the boy's brothers. *This rule does not hold good in the case of pronouns, the genitives of which have an oblique form.*

92. The LOCATIVE indicates the place in, or the time at, which a thing is done. It is usually formed by the postposition मेँ *mē̃*, of which मेँ *mạ̃* and मोँ *mō̃* are optional forms. Of these three मोँ *mō̃* is the oldest, and is generally found in poetry. The organic form of the Locative ends in ए *ē*, as explained above. It is not much used in modern prose Maithili, though it is frequent in

poetry, where it is sometimes written ऍ or घर *ai*. In the modern colloquial dialect it is, however, often heard in phrases such as घरे घरे *ghurē ghurē*, in every house; गामे गामे *gāmē gāmē*, in every village, and so on. As an example from classical poetry we may quote Vidyāpati (v. 3) जाएब औघट घाटे *jāeb aughaṭ ghāṭē*, I shall go on the rugged river bank.

The following examples are all taken from one folk-song,—that of *Dīnā Bhadrī.*

घड़ि एक चलबे पहर बिति गेल *ghaṛi ek calᵒbē pahar biti gēl*, in (*i.e.*, after) going for one (or two) half-hours, a watch of the day passed.

चलैह जौरे मिलि *calāh jaurē mili*, having joined in company (with us), come along.

एहि ठामे *ehi ṭhāmē*, in this place.

बेना बरा डीहे रहथि अनेर *bēnā barā ḍīhē rahathi anēr*, Bēnā is wandering loose in Barā Ḍīh.

मुसाहुक दोकाने मना परि गेल *musāhuk dokānē manā pari gēl*, there was a prohibition (*i.e.*, they were stopped) at the shop o Musāhu.

एक जुम तमाकू मोरा नामे नहिं चढ़ाबै *ek jum tamākū mōrā nāmē nahĩ carhābai*, they do not offer a single chew of tobacco in my name.

सात नींदे सूतलि छलैक फेकुनी *sāt nīdē sūtali chalaik phekunī*. Phekunī was sleeping in seven sleeps (*i.e.*, was sound asleep).

बोझे बोझे बोरे बोरे नोन तमाकू तौलै *bōjhē bōjhē bōrē bōrē nōn tamākū taulai*, bundle after bundle and sack after sack (*lit.* in bundle in bundle, in sack in sack) does he weigh salt and tobacco.

बड़ भोरे छेंकल दुआर *baṛ bhōrē chēkul duār*, in the early morning you have obstructed my door.

93. The VOCATIVE usually takes the same form as the nominative. In speaking to a person of lower rank or age, the long form of the noun is preferred. Thus, नेना *nēnā*, a boy, becomes रौ

नेनवा *rau nenᵃwā.* नेनी *nēnī*, a girl, becomes गै नेनिया *gai neniyā.* रघू *Raghū*, a proper name, becomes रौ रघुआ *rau Raghuā.*

The following interjections are used with the vocative:—

(*a*) With masculine inferiors,—or familiarly, रौ *rau*, रे *rē.*

(*b*) With masculine equals or superiors, औ *au*, हौ *hau*, हे *hē.*

(*c*) With feminine inferiors,—or familiarly, गै *gai.*

(*d*) With feminine equals or superiors, है *hai.*

CHAPTER III.

Declension of Nouns.

94. There is in Maithilī really only one declension, but as the forms of some classes of nouns vary slightly from each other before some of the postpositions, it will be convenient to consider nouns in three classes.

95. I. The first class will consist of all nouns ending in आ *ā* or आँ *ā̃*.

II. The second class will consist of all nouns ending in a consonant.

III. The third class will consist of all other nouns.

The difference between these three classes will be noticed on comparison of the Instrumental and Vocative singular.

96. It will be remembered that every noun has three forms, a short, a long, and a redundant (see §§ 41 ff.). In the following pages I shall only deal with the short form. As every long and redundant form ends in आ *ā* or आँ *ā̃*, they all belong to the first class. Thus, फल *phal*, a fruit, belongs to the second class. Its long form is फलवा *phalᵃwā*, which belongs to the first class, its instrumental singular being फलवें *phalᵃwē̃.*

CLASS I.

All nouns ending in आ *ā* or आँ *ā̃*.

97. (1) Example of a Masculine noun ending in आ *ā*.

नेना *nēnā*, a boy.

Singular.

Nom.	नेना *nēnā*, a boy.	
Acc.	नेना *nēnā*, नेना कँ *nēnā kē̃*,	a boy.
Inst.	नेनें *nēnē̃*, नेना सँ *nēnā sā̃*,	by a boy.
Dat.	नेना कँ *nēnā kē̃*, to a boy.	
Abl.	नेना सँ *nēnā sā̃*, from a boy.	
Gen.	नेनाक *nēnāk*, नेना केर *nēnā kēr*,	of a boy.
Loc.	नेना में *nēnā mē̃*, in a boy.	
Voc.	रौ नेनवा *rau nenᵃwā*, O boy, (*or respectfully*) औ नेना *au nēnā*.	

Plural.

Nom.	नेना सभ[1] *nēnā sabh*, boys.	
Acc.	नेना सभ[1] *nēnā sabh*, नेना सभ कैं[2] *nēnā sabh kẽ*,	boys.
Inst.	नेना सभैं[3] *nēnā sabhẽ*, नेना सभ सँ *nēnā sabh sã*,	by boys.
Dat.	नेना सभ कैं[4] *nēnā sabh kẽ*, to boys.	
Abl.	नेना सभ सँ[5] *nēnā sabh sã*, from boys.	
Gen.	नेना सभक[6] *nēnā sabhak*, नेना सभ केर *nēnā sabh kēr*,	of boys.
Loc.	नेना सभ मैं[7] *nēnā sabh mẽ*, in boys.	
Voc.	रौ नेनवा सभ[8] *rau nen^{a}wā sabh*, औ नेना सभ *au nēnā sabh*,	O boys.

---

1 Other forms are सभ नेना *sabh nēnā*, नेना सबहि *nēnā sabah^{i}*, सबहि नेना *sabah^{i} nēnā* and नेना लोकनि *nēnā lok^{a}ni*.

2 Other forms are नेना सबहि कैं *nēnā sabah^{i} kẽ*, and नेना लोकनि कैं *nēnā lok^{a}ni kẽ*.

3 Other forms are नेना सबहिएँ *nēnā sab^{a}hiẽ*, नेना सबहि सँ *nēnā sabah^{i} sã*, नेना लोकनिएँ *nēnā lok^{a}niẽ* and नेना लोकनि सँ *nēnā lok^{a}ni sã*.

4 Other forms are नेना सबहि कैं *nēnā sabah^{i} kẽ* and नेना लोकनि कैं *nēnā lok^{a}ni kẽ*.

5 Other forms are नेना सबहि सँ *nēnā sabah^{i} sã* and नेना लोकनि सँ *nēnā lok^{a}ni sã*.

6 Other forms are नेना सबहिक *nēnā sabahik*, नेना लोकनिक *nēnā lok^{a}nik*.

7 Other forms are नेना सबहि मैं *nēnā sabah^{i} mẽ* and नेना लोकनि मैं *nēnā lok^{a}ni mẽ*.

8 Other forms are रौ नेना सबहि *rau nēnā sabah^{i}*, औ नेना लोकनि *au nēnā lok^{a}ni*.

98. (2) Example of a feminine noun, ending in आ *ā*.

कथा *kathā*. a story.

Singular.

Nom.	कथा *kathā*, a story.	
Acc.	कथा *kathā*. कथा कें *kathā kẽ*.	a story.
Inst.	कथें *kathẽ*, कथा सँ *kathā sã*.	by a story.
Dat.	कथा कें *kathā kẽ*, to a story.	
Abl.	कथा सँ *kathā sã*, from a story.	
Gen.	कथाक *kathāk*, कथा केर *kathā kēr*.	of a story.
Loc.	कथा में *kathā mẽ*, in a story.	
Voc.	हे कथा *hē kathā*. O story.	

Plural.

Nom.	कथा सभ *kathā sabh*, stories.	
Acc.	कथा सभ *kathā sabh*. कथा सभ कें *kathā sabh kẽ*,	stories.
Inst.	कथा सभें *kathā sabhẽ*. कथा सभ सँ *kathā sabh sã*,	by stories.
Dat.	कथा सभ कें *kathā sabh kẽ*, to stories.	
Abl.	कथा सभ सँ *kathā sabh sã*, from stories.	
Gen.	कथा सभक *kathā sabhak*, कथा सभ केर *kathā sabh kēr*.	of stories.
Loc.	कथा सभ म *kathā sabh mẽ*. in stories.	
Voc.	हे कथा सभ *hē kathā sabh*. O stories.	

CLASS II.

99. All nouns ending in a silent consonant.

फल *phal*, a fruit.

Singular.

Nom.	फल *phal*, a fruit.	
Acc.	फल *phal*, फल कें *phal kẽ*.	a fruit.
Inst.	फलें *phalẽ*. फल सँ *phal sã*.	by a fruit.
Dat.	फल कें *phal kẽ*, to a fruit.	
Abl.	फल सँ *phal sã*, from a fruit.	
Gen.	फलक *phalak*, फल केर *phal kēr*.	of a fruit.
Loc.	फल में *phal mẽ*, in a fruit.	
Voc.	हे फल *hē phal*, O fruit.	

Plural.

Nom.	फल सभ *phal sabh*, fruit.	
Acc.	फल सभ *phal sabh*. फल सभ कें *phal sabh kẽ*.	fruit.
Inst.	फल सभें *phal sabhẽ*, फल सभ सँ *phal sabh sã*,	by fruit.
Dat.	फल सभ कें *phal sabh kẽ*, to fruit.	
Abl.	फल सभ सँ *phal sabh sã*, from fruit.	
Gen.	फल सभक *phal sabhak*. फल सभ केर *phal sabh kēr*.	of fruit.
Loc.	फल सभ में *phal sabh mẽ*, in fruit.	
Voc.	हे फल सभ *hē phal sabh*, O fruit.	

As an example of a noun with an oblique form, we may take पहर *pahar*, a watch; Acc. पहर *pahar* or पहरा कें *pahᵃrā kẽ*; Inst.

पहरें *pah°rē̃* or पहरा सँ *pah°rā sã̄*, and so on. The plural is पहर सभ *pahar sabh*, etc., like फल सभ *phal sabh*.

CLASS III.

All nouns not ending in आ *ā* or in a consonant.

100. (1) Example of a masculine noun, ending in इ *i*.

पानि *pāni*, water.

Singular.

Nom.	पानि *pāni*. water.	
Acc.	पानि *pāni*. पानि कें *pāni kē̃*.	water.
Inst.	पानिएँ *pănie͂*. पानि सँ *pāni sã̄*,	by water.
Dat.	पानि कें *pāni kē̃*, to water.	
Abl.	पानि सँ *pani sã̄*. from water.	
Gen.	पानिक *pānik*. पानि केर *pāni kēr*.	of water.
Loc.	पानि में *pāni mē̃*. in water.	
Voc.	हे पानि *hē pāni*. O water.	

Plural.

Nom.	पानि सभ *pāni sabh*. waters.	
Acc.	पानि सभ *pāni sabh*. पानि सभ कें *pāni sabh kē̃*.	waters.
Inst.	पानि सभें *pāni sabhē̃*. पानि सभ सँ *pāni sabh sã̄*.	by waters
Dat.	पानि सभ कें *pāni sabh kē̃*, to waters.	
Abl.	पानि सभ सँ *pāni sabh sã̄*. from waters.	
Gen.	पानि सभक *pāni sabhak*. पानि सभ केर *pāni sabh kēr*.	of waters.
Loc.	पानि सभ में *pāni sabh mē̃*, in waters.	
Voc.	हे पानि सभ *hē pāni sabh*, O waters.	

101. (2) Example of a feminine noun ending in ई *ī*.

नेनी *nēnī*, a girl.

Singular.

Nom.	नेनी *nēnī*, a girl.	
Acc.	नेनी *nēnī*, नेनी कें *nēnī kẽ*,	a girl.
Inst.	नेनिएँ *neniẽ*, नेनी सँ *nēnī sã*,	by a girl.
Dat.	नेनी कें *nēnī kẽ*, to a girl.	
Abl.	नेनी सँ *nēnī sã*, from a girl.	
Gen.	नेनीक *nēnīk*, नेनी केर *nēnī kēr*,	of a girl.
Loc.	नेनी में *nēnī mẽ*, in a girl.	
Voc.	गै नेनिया *gai neniyā*, O girl.	

Plural.

Nom.	नेनी सभ *nēnī sabh*, girls.	
Acc.	नेनी सभ *nēnī sabh*, नेनी सभ कें *nēnī sabh kẽ*,	girls.
Inst.	नेनी सभें *nēnī sabhẽ*, नेनी सभ सँ *nēnī sabh sã*,	by girls.
Dat.	नेनी सभ कें *nēnī sabh kẽ*. to girls.	
Abl.	नेनी सभ सँ *nēnī sabh sã*. from girls.	
Gen.	नेनी सभक *nēnī sabhak*. नेनी सभ केर *nēnī sabh kēr*.	of girls.
Loc.	नेनी सभ में *nēnī sabh mẽ*. in girls.	
Voc.	गै नेनिया सभ *gai neniyā sabh*. O girls.	

102. (3) Example of a masculine proper noun ending ऊ *ū*.

रघू* *Raghū*, a proper noun.

Nom. रघू *Raghū*, Raghū.

Acc. रघू कें *Raghū kẽ*, Raghū.

Inst. { रघुएँ *Raghuẽ*, / रघू सँ *Raghū sã̆*. } by Raghū.

Dat. रघू कें *Raghū kẽ*, to Raghū.

Abl. रघू सँ *Raghū sã̆*, from Raghū.

Gen. रघुक *Raghūk*. of Raghū.

Loc. रघू में *Raghū mẽ*. in Raghū.

Voc. रौ रघुआ *rau Raghuā*, O Raghū, (*or respectfully*) हौ रघू *hau Raghū*.

103. As an example of a verbal noun in इ ^{i}, with an oblique form in ऐ *ai*, we may take चढ़ि *caṛh*^{i}, mounting; acc. चढ़ि *carh*^{i} or चढ़ै कें *caṛhai kẽ*; Instr. चढ़ै सँ *caṛhai sã̆* (चढ़ैएँ *caṛhaiẽ* is not used); and so on. Instead of चढ़ै *caṛhai*, we may have चढ़ँ *caṛhå̃* throughout.

CHAPTER IV.

Adjectives and Gender generally.

104. As the rules for the formation of the feminine of adjectives are the same as those for the formation of the feminine of substantives, it will be convenient to treat the whole subject of gender at the present opportunity.

105. Adjectives are liable to change for gender. That is to say, when agreeing with a feminine noun they are put in the feminine. Thus, the word ऐसन *aisan* means 'such,' and its feminine is ऐसनि *aisan*^{i}. The word झपट *jhapaṭ*, a pounce, is feminine, and

---

* Usually spelt thus in Maithilī.

hence we have in the story of Salᵃhēs the phrase ऐसनि झपट मारै *aisanⁱ jhapaṭ mārai*, (the parrot) makes such a pounce (that—). I have said that adjectives are *liable* to change for gender, but in practice the change very rarely takes place. In ordinary conversation the masculine gender is quite commonly used instead of the feminine, and, indeed, except to paṇḍits grammatical gender is almost unknown; that is to say, adjectives only become feminine when applied to female living creatures. The following rules as to gender apply to substantives, as well as adjectives.

106. It is a well-known fact that in Hindōstānī the adjectives which are *tadbhavas*, and which end in आ *ā* are in reality the only ones in that language which are affected by gender. *Tatsama* adjectives imported direct from the Sanskrit, and forming their feminines after the model of that language, do not form part of the living spoken stock of the Hindī dialect, but belong rather to the dead language of the books. The same is only partly true in Maithilī. In this language we find not only *tadbhava* but even some *tatsama* adjectives forming feminines distinctly the property of the language in which they have been adopted.

107. Rule I.—The first rule to be observed is that in Maithilī, *tadbhava words ending in a consonant form their feminine in short* इ *ⁱ*.

Examples:—

Masculine.	*Feminine.*
गोर *gōr*, fair	गोरि *gōrⁱ*.
बड़ *baṛ*, great	बड़ि *baṛⁱ*.
बुधियार *budhiyār*, wise	बुधियारि *budhiyārⁱ*.
अधलाह *adhᵒlāh*, bad	अधलाहि *adhᵒlāhⁱ*.
गमार *gamār*, rustic	गमारि *gamārⁱ*.
टेढ़ *ṭēṛh*, crooked	टेढ़ि *ṭēṛhⁱ*.

108. Rule II.—The second rule is peculiar to Maithilī, and is as follows: *Many Tatsama words ending in a consonant form their feminines in* इ *ⁱ*; *and that, whether in Sanskrit these words form their feminines in long* ई *ī or not.*

Examples: —

Masculine.		*Feminine.*
सुन्दर *sundar*, beautiful	Sanskrit,	सुन्दरी *sundarī*.
	Maithilī,	सुन्दरि *sundari*.
धूसर *dhūsar* dusty	S.	धूसरा *dhūsarā* or धूसरी *dhūsarī*.
	M.	धूसरि *dhūsar*ⁱ.
अत्यंत *atyant*, excessive	S.	अत्यन्ता *atyantā*.
	M.	अत्यंति *atyant*ⁱ.

The following may here be noted as irregular:—

Masculine.		*Feminine.*
सुबोध *subōdh*, wise	S.	सुबोधा *subōdhā*.
	M.	सुबुधि *subudh*ⁱ.

109. Rule III.—*Tadbhava words ending in* आ *ā, form their feminines in* ई *ī.*

Examples :—

Masculine.	*Feminine.*
बेटा *bōṭā*, a son	बेटी *bēṭī*, a daughter.
नेना *nēnā*, a boy	नेनी *nēnī*, a girl.

110. Rule IV.—Long forms of nouns substantive and redundant forms of adjectives in अवा ᵃ*wā* form their feminines in इया *iyā* or इआ *iā*. Redundant forms of nouns substantive in औवा *auwā* or औआ *auā*, form their feminines in इयवा *iy*ᵃ*wā*, इअवा *iawā*, or ईवा *īwā*. Thus :—

Masculine.	*Feminine.*
घोड़वा *ghoṛ*ᵃ*wā*, a horse	घोड़िया *ghoṛiyā* or घोड़िआ *ghoṛiā*, a mare.
छोटकवा *choṭ*ᵃ*kawā* or *choṭak*ᵃ*wā* } small	छोटकिया *choṭ*ᵃ*kiyā* or *choṭakiyā*, or छोटकिआ *choṭ*ᵃ*kiā* or *choṭakiā*.

Masculine.		*Feminine.*
घोरौआ *ghoraua* or घोरौवा *ghorauwā*	a horse	घोड़ियवा *ghoriy°wā*, घोड़िअवा *ghori-awā* or घोड़ीवा *ghoṛīwā*.

It is necessary to give further examples, as the subject has been already discussed in §§ 41 ff.

111. RULE V.—*Tadbhava words signifying colour form their feminines as follows* :—

Masculine.		*Feminine.*
उजर *ujar* or उजरा *uj°rā* or उजरका *ujar°kā*	white	उजरी *uj°rī*. or उजरकी *ujar°kī*.
कारी *kārī* or करिआ *kariā* or करिक्का *karikkā*	black	करिक्की *karikkī*.
पीरा *pīrā* or पीअर *pīar* or पिअरका *piar°kā*	yellow	पिअरकी *piar°kī*.
हरिअर *hariar* or हरिअरका *hariar°kā*	green	हरिअरकी *hariar°kī*.
लाल *lāl* or ललका *lal°kā*	red	ललकी *lal°kī*.

EXCEPTION.—गोर *gōr* fair, which makes गोरि *gōr*^{i}, or गोरिया *goriyā*. It will be observed that, in the feminine, all these adjectives prefer the long form.

Note also that नील *nīl*, dark blue, which also occurs in Sanskrit and which in that language forms its feminine नीला *nīlā*, or नीली *nīlī*, in Maithilī adopts नीली *nīlī* as its feminine form.

112. RULE VI.—The following classes of *Tatsama* words form their feminines generally as in Sanskrit :—

(*a*) Verbal adjectives in इ *i*, and ई *ī*, corresponding to Sanskrit adjectives in इन् *in*, nominative, ई *ī*.

Examples :—

	Masculine.		Feminine in Maithilī.
Sanskrit	मानी *mānī*	proud	मानिनी *māninī*
Maithilī	मानि *māni*		or मानिनि *mānin*^{i}.
S.	भावी *bhāvī*	future	भाविनी *bhāvinī*
M.	भावी *bhāvī*		or भाविनि *bhāvin*^{i}.
S.	हारी *hārī*	seizing	हारिणी *hāriṇī*
M.	हारी *hārī*		or हारिनि *hārin*^{i}.
S.	धारी *dhārī*	bearing	धारिणी *dhāriṇī*.
M.	धारी *dhārī*		or धारिनि *dhārin*^{i}.
S.	कारी *kārī*	doing	कारिणी *kāriṇī*
M.	कारी *kārī*		or कारिनि *kārin*^{i}.
S.	चिरंजीवी *chirañjīvī*	long-lived	चिरंजीविनी *chirañjībinī*
M.	चिरंजीबी *chirañjībī*		or चिरंजीबिनि *chirañjībin*^{i}
or	चिरंजिब *chirañjib*		or चिरंजीबि *chirañjīb*^{i}.

As an irregular under this head falls—

	Masculine.		Feminine in Maithilī.
S.	सुधर्मा *sudharmā*	virtuous	सुधर्मिणी *sudharmiṇī*.
M.	सुधर्मा *sudharmā*		

113. (*b*) Participles of the reduplicated perfect in वस् *vas*, and comparatives in ईयस् *īyas*.

Examples :—

	Masculine.		Feminine.
S.	विद्वान् *vidvān*	wise	बिदुषी *biduṣī* (pronounced —*khī*, see § 25.)
M.	बिद्वान *bidbān*		
S.	गरीयान् *garīyān*	heavier	गरीयसी *garīyasī*.
M.	गरीआन *garīān*		
S.	लघीयान् *laghīyān*	lighter	लघीयसी *laghīyasī*.
M.	लघीआन *laghīān*		

114. (*c*) *Nomina agentis* terminating in अक *ak*.

Examples :—

Masculine.		*Feminine.*
कारक *kārak*	a doer	कारिका *kārikā*.
पालक *pālak*	a protector	पालिका *pālikā*.
रक्षक *rakṣak*	a guardian	रक्षिका *rakṣikā*.
पाचक *pācak*	a cook	पाचिका *pācikā*.
सहायक *sahāyak*	a helper	सहायका *sahāy*^{a}*kā*.

115. (*d*) Gerundials and past participles passive.

Examples :—

Masculine.		*Feminine.*
मंतव्य *mantaby*^{a}	to be remarked	मंतव्या *mantabyā*.
वंदनीय *bandanīy*^{a}	praiseworthy	वंदनीया *bandanīyā*
जोग्य *jōgy*^{a}	worthy	जोग्या *jōgyā*.
मान्य *māny*^{a}	reverend	मान्या *mānyā*.
साध्य *sādhy*^{a}	easy	साध्या *sādhyā*.
जुक्त *jukt*	joined	जुक्ता *juktā*.
सुद्ध *suddh*	pure	सुद्धा *suddhā*.
आर्त *ārt*	pained	आर्ता *ārtā*.
खिन्न *khinn*	broken	खिन्ना *khinnā*.

116. (*e*) Other nouns and adjectives as :—

Masculine.		*Feminine.*
धूर्त *dhūrt*	a knave	धूर्ता *dhūrtā*.
स्याम *syām*	dark	स्यामा *syāmā*.
गरिष्ठ *gariṣṭh*	heaviest (venerable)	गरिष्ठा *gariṣṭhā*.
श्रेष्ठ *śrēṣṭh*	excellent	श्रेष्ठा *śrēṣṭhā*.
ब्रिंद *brind*	numerous	ब्रिंदा *brindā*.
आर्य्य॰ *ārjy*^{a}	respectable	आर्य्या *ārjyā*.

117. Rule VII.—The following anomalous forms should be noticed :—

(*a*) राजा *rājā*, a king, makes रानी *rānī*, a queen.

(*b*) Forms borrowed from Sanskrit *nomina agentis* in ऋ *tṛ*, have the following feminines :—

Examples :—

	Masculine.		*Feminine.*
S.	धाता *dhātā*	creator	धात्री *dhātrī*.
M.	धाता *dhātā*		धात्रि *dhātrⁱ*.
S.	ज्ञाता *jñātā*	knower	ज्ञात्री *jñātrī*.
M.	ग्यांता *gyā̃tā*		ग्यांत्रि *gyā̃trⁱ*.
S.	पाता *pātā*	protector	पात्री *pātrī*.
M.	पाता *pātā*		पात्रि *pātrⁱ*.

118. Adjectives do not generally change for case. In other words, like substantives, they do not usually possess oblique forms.

119. Certain adjectives ending in ड़ *ṛ*, न *n*, र *r* and ल *l* have, however, an oblique form in आ *ā*, which is employed when the noun with which they are in agreement is in an oblique case. In other words such adjectives follow the example of substantives. Examples of such adjectives are :—

बड़ *baṛ*, great.

ऐसन *aisan* or एहन *ehan*, such, and other pronominal adjectives ending in न *n*.

दोसर *dōsar*, second.

तेसर *tēsar*, third.

बहीर *bahīr*, deaf.

पहिल *pahil*, first.

Examples of these oblique forms will be found in §§ 82 and ff. The oblique forms are not often employed attributively except in the cases of ordinal numbers as in तेसरा पहरा में *tesᵉrā pahᵉrā mē̃*, in the third watch, and of pronominal adjectives. The latter will be discussed under the head of pronouns.

Comparison of Adjectives.

120. (*a*) *Comparative.* As in Hindōstānī, the comparative is formed, not by any change in the adjective, but by putting the word for the thing with which the comparison is made in the ablative case. Example, इ गाछी ओहि गाछी सँ सुंदरि छैक *i gāchī oh*^{i} *gāchī sa̐ sundar*^{i} *chaik*, this grove is more beautiful than that.

121. (*b*) *Superlative.* This is formed either by prefixing सभ सँ *sabh sa̐*, the ablative case of सभ *sabh*, all, or the adjective बड़ *baṛ* (which is liable to inflection according to gender) to the principal adjective. Examples: इ गाछी सभ सँ सुंदरि छैक *i gāchī sabh sa̐ sundar*^{i} *chaik*, this is the most beautiful grove; or इ गाछी बड़ि सुंदरि छैक *i gāchī baṛ*^{i} *sundar*^{i} *chaik*, this grove is very beautiful. Usually, in such sentences, gender is neglected when the adjective is employed predicatively, so that we generally meet these expressions in the following forms: इ गाछी ओहि गाछी सँ सुन्दर छैक *i gāchī oh*^{i} *gāchī sa̐ sundar chaik*; इ गाछी सभ सँ सुन्दर छैक *i gāchī sabh sa̐ sundar chaik*; इ गाछी बड़ सुन्दर छैक *i gāchī baṛ sundar chaik*.

122. Certain comparatives and superlatives are also borrowed direct from the Sanskrit, which need not be noted here.

Numerals.

Cardinals.

123. The following are the Cardinals up to 100. It will be observed that they differ from those in use in Hindī:—

१ एक *ek*.
२ दुइ *dui*.
३ तीनि *tīn*^{i}.
४ चारि *cār*^{i}.
५ पाँच *pā̃c*.
६ छौ *chau*.
७ सात *sāt*.
८ आठ *āṭh*.
९ नौ *nau*.
१० दश *daś*.
११ एगारह *egārah*.
१२ बारह *bārah*.
१३ तेरह *tērah*.
१४ चौदह *caudah*.

१५ पन्द्रह *pandrah.*
१६ सोलह *sōlah* or सोड़ह *sōṛah.*
१७ सत्रह *satrah.*
१८ अठारह *aṭhārah.*
१९ उनैस *unais.*
२० बीस *bīs.*
२१ एकैस *ekais.*
२२ बाइस *bāis.*
२३ तैस *tais.*
२४ चौबीस *caubīs.*
२५ पचीस *pacīs.*
२६ छब्बीस *chabbīs.*
२७ सत्ताइस *sattāis.*
२८ अठाइस *aṭhāis.*
२९ उनतीस *un^{a}tīs.*
३० तीस *tīs.*
३१ एकतीस *ek^{a}tīs.*
३२ बत्तीस *battīs.*
३३ तैंतीस *tẽtīs.*
३४ चौंतीस *caũtīs.*
३५ पैंतीस *paĩtīs.*
३६ छत्तीस *chattīs.*
३७ सैंतीस *saĩtīs.*
३८ अठतीस *aṭh^{a}tīs.*
३९ उनचालीस *un^{a}cālīs* or उननचालीस *unan^{a}cālīs.*
४० चालीस *cālīs.*
४१ एकतालीस *ek^{a}tālīs.*
४२ बेआलीस *beālīs.*
४३ तैंतालीस *taĩtālīs.*
४४ चौआलीस *cauālīs.*
४५ पैंतालीस *paĩtālīs.*
४६ छेआलीस *cheālīs.*
४७ सैंतालीस *saĩtālīs.*
४८ अठतालीस *aṭh^{a}tālīs.*
४९ उनचास *un^{a}cās* or उननचास *unan^{a}cās.*
५० पचास *pacās.*
५१ एकावन *ekāwan.*
५२ बावन *bāwan.*
५३ तिरपन *tir^{a}pan.*
५४ चौवन *cauwan.*
५५ पचपन *pac^{a}pan.*
५६ छप्पन *chappan.*
५७ सतावन *satāwan.*
५८ अठावन *aṭhāwan.*
५९ उनसठि *un^{a}saṭh^{i}.*
६० साठि *sāṭh^{i}.*
६१ एकसठि *ek^{a}saṭh^{i}* or एकसट्ठि *ek^{a}saṭṭh^{i}.*
६२ बासठि *bāsaṭh^{i}* or बासट्ठि *bāsaṭṭh^{i}.*
६३ तिरसठि *tir^{a}saṭh^{i}* or तिरसट्ठि *tir^{a}saṭṭh^{i}.*
६४ चौंसठि *caũsaṭh^{i}* or चौंसट्ठि *caũsaṭṭh^{i}.*
६५ पैंसठि *paĩsaṭh^{i}* or पैंसट्ठि *paĩsaṭṭh^{i}.*
६६ छेआसठि *cheāsaṭh^{i}* or छेआसट्ठि *cheāsaṭṭh^{i}.*
६७ सतसठि *sat^{a}saṭh^{i}* or सतसट्ठि *sat^{a}saṭṭh^{i}.*

६८ अठसठि *aṭh^{a}saṭh^{i}* or अड़सठि *aṛ^{a}saṭh^{i}* or अठसट्ठि *aṭh^{a}-saṭṭh^{i}*.

६९ उनहत्तरि *un^{a}hattar^{i}*.

७० सत्तरि *sattar^{i}*.

७१ अकहत्तरि *ak^{a}hattar^{i}*.

७२ बहत्तरि *bahattar^{i}*.

७३ तेहत्तरि *tehattar^{i}*.

७४ चौहत्तरि *cauhattar^{i}*.

७५ पचहत्तरि *pac^{a}hattar^{i}*.

७६ छेहत्तरि *chehattar^{i}*.

७७ सतहत्तरि *sat^{a}hattar^{i}*.

७८ अठहत्तरि *aṭh^{a}hattar^{i}*.

७९ उनासी *unāsī*.

८० अस्सी *assī*.

८१ एकासी *ekāsī*.

८२ बेरासी *berāsī* or बेआसी *beāsī*.

८३ तेरासी *terāsī*.

८४ चौरासी *caurāsī*.

८५ पचासी *pacāsī*.

८६ छेआसी *cheāsī*.

८७ सतासी *satāsī*.

८८ अठासी *aṭhāsī*.

८९ नवासी *nawāsī*.

९० नब्बै *nabbai*.

९१ एकानबे *ekān^{a}bē*.

९२ बरानबे *barān^{a}bē* or बेआनबे *beān^{a}bē*.

९३ तेरानबे *terān^{a}bē*.

९४ चौरानबे *caurān^{a}bē*.

९५ पँचानबे *pãcān^{a}bē*.

९६ छेआनबे *cheān^{a}bē*.

९७ सनतानबे *san^{a}tān^{a}bē*.

९८ अँठानबे *ãṭhān^{a}bē*.

९९ निनानबे *ninān^{a}bē*.

१०० सै *sai*.

Ordinals.

124. Ordinals are simple in their formation and run as follows :—

पहिल *pahil*, first.

दोसर *dōsar*, second.

तेसर *tēsar*, third.

चौठ *cauṭh*, or चारिम *cārim*, fourth.

पाँचम *pā̃cam*, fifth.

छठम *chaṭham*, sixth.

सातम *sātam*, seventh.

आठम *āṭham*, eighth.

नौम *naum*, ninth.

दशम *daśam*, tenth.

एगारहम *egār^{a}ham*, eleventh.

Etcetera ; the ordinals of the remaining numbers being formed by adding म *m* as a termination.

FRACTIONAL NUMBERS.

125. The following are useful:—

पाओ *pāo*, a quarter.

आध *ādh*, a half.

पौन *paun*, three-quarters; or, less by a quarter.

सवैयाँ *sawaiyā̃*, one and-a-quarter; or, plus a quarter.

डेओढ़ा *deōṛhā*, one-and-a-half; or, plus a half.

AGGREGATE NUMBERS.

126. Note the form दुनु *dunᵘ*, both.

CHAPTER V.

PRONOUNS.

127. The declension of Pronouns presents some important points of difference from that of nouns, which should be carefully noted.

128. While most nouns remain unchanged before postpositions, almost all pronouns have an oblique form. This oblique form falls under two heads.

129. (1) The old oblique form. This, in the case of the personal pronouns, is only found in poetry. In the case of other pronouns it is, at the present day, rarely used except when it refers to inanimate objects, or when the pronoun is employed as an adjective. Thus, the old oblique form of ई *ī*, this, is एहि *ehⁱ*, and

एहि कें *eh^{i} kẽ*, to this, is only found when 'this' is something inanimate. एहि कें *eh^{i} kẽ* could not be used if 'this' was a boy. But we can say एहि नेना कें *eh^{i} nēnā kẽ*, to this boy, because here एहि *eh^{i}* is used as an adjective.

The following is a list of these old oblique forms :—

Direct Form.	*Old Oblique Form.*
मेँ *mẽ*, (old poetic form), I	मोहि *moh^{i}*.
तू *tū*, thou	तोहि *toh^{i}*.
ई *ī*, this (non-honorific)	एहि *eh^{i}*, एह *eh*. or ऐह *aih*.
ई *ī*, this (honorific)	हिनि *hin^{i}* or हिन *hin*.
ओ *ō*, that (non-honorific)	ओहि *oh^{i}*, ओह *oh*, or औह *auh*.
ओ *ō*, that (honorific)	हुनि *hun^{i}* or हुन *hun*.
जे *jē*, who (non-honorific)	जाहि *jāh^{i}*.
जे *jē*, who (honorific)	जनि *jan^{i}*.
से *sē*, he (non-honorific)	ताहि *tāh^{i}*.
से *sē*, he (honorific)	तनि *tan^{i}*.
के *kē*, who ? (non-honorific)	काहि *kāh^{i}* (not used as an adjective).
के *kē*, who ? (honorific)	कनि *kan^{i}*.
की *kī*, what ? (substantive)	कथी *kathī*.
केओ *keo*, anyone	काहु *kāh^{u}*.

130. (2) The modern oblique form.—This is never used as an adjective. It is almost always the only form employed when the pronoun is used as a substantive and refers to an animate object. It is hence the only form used at the present day for personal pronouns. It is identical with the oblique form of the genitive, which is obtained by adding आ *ā* to the direct form of that case. Thus :—

Pronoun.	Genitive.	
	Direct.	Oblique.
मैं *mẽ*, I	मोर *mōr*	मोरा *mōrā*.
हम *ham*, I	हमर *hamar* or हमार *hamār*	हमरा *ham*^{a}*rā*.
तू *tū*, thou	तोर *tōr*	तोरा *tōrā*.
तोँह *tōh̃* or तोँ *tō̃*, thou	तोहर *tōhar* or तोहार *tohār*	तोहरा *toh*^{a}*rā*.
अपनहिँ *ap*^{a}*nah*$^{\tilde{i}}$, self	अप्पन *appan* or अपन *apan*	अपना *ap*^{a}*nā*
ई *ī*, this (non-honorific)	एकर *ēkar*	एकरा *ek*^{a}*rā*.
ई *ī*, this (honorific)	हिनक *hinak*	हिनका *hin*^{a}*kā*.
ओ *ō*, that (non-honorific)	ओकर *ōkar*	ओकरा *ok*^{a}*rā*.
ओ *ō*, that (honorific)	हुनक *hunak*	हुनका *hun*^{a}*kā*.
जे *jē*, who (non-honorific)	जकर *jakar*	जकरा *jak*^{a}*rā*.
जे *jē*, who (honorific)	जनिक *janik*	जनिका *janikā*.
से *sē*, he (non-honorific)	तकर *takar*	तकरा *tak*^{a}*rā*.
से *sē*, he (honorific)	तनिक *tanik*	तनिका *tanikā*.
के *kē*, who ? (non-honorific)	ककर *kakar*	ककरा *kak*^{a}*rā*.
के *kē*, who ? (honorific)	कनिक *kanik*	कनिका *kanikā*.

To the remaining pronouns these observations do not apply. It will be observed that in the honorific forms the genitive ends in क *k*, while all the other genitives end in र *r*.

131. We have observed (see §§ 75, 76) that nouns substantive have no proper organic plural. When the idea of plurality has to be expressed it is done by adding new words indicating plurality, such as सभ *sabh* or सबहि *sabah*^{i}, all ; लोकनि *lok*^{a}*ni*, people. The same is the case with pronouns. Their plurals are formed in the same way. In the ancient Māgadhī Prakrit from which Maithilī is descended there were distinct organic plural forms, and (except in the case of the pronouns of the first and second persons) these old plural forms have survived in the shape of the honorific singulars, the old singulars being relegated to a non-honorific meaning. With regard to the pronouns of the first and second persons the case is somewhat different. In ordinary Maithili, the old singulars (मैं *mẽ*, I and तू *tū*, thou) have fallen into disuse and are now only found in poetry. The old plural forms are now employed in the sense of the singular, and the plurals are now formed by the addition of सभ *sabh*, etc. (as is also the case with the honorific pronouns mentioned above) and are really by origin double plurals.

132. It may be mentioned here that the pronoun of the second person has also an honorific form अहाँ *ahā̃*, अहैं *ahaĩ* or अपने *ap*e*ne* which will be described later on.

133. The employment of the old oblique form varies, and the different methods of employment will be described under each pronoun.

134. The genitives of the pronouns are freely used as possessive pronouns, and, when agreeing with a noun in an oblique case they are put into the modern oblique form described above. It will be convenient to give examples of this once for all here.

(*a*) Direct Possessive Pronouns agreeing with nouns in the Nominative Form:—

हमर रोज हरज होइत *hamar rōj haraj hōit*, my means of livelihood will be spoiled.

त्रिया कारन मुदै तोर जुमल *triyā kāran mudai tōr jumal*, for the sake of a woman your enemy has come.

अप्पन सभ धन उड़ाय भिखारि भै गेल *appan sabh dhan uṛāy bhikhār*i *bhai gēl*, having wasted all his substance he became a beggar.

हुनक कानब सुनि *hunak kānab sun*i, having heard her lamentations.

जकर बेदुली लाएल, तकर केहन सुरखी *jakar bedulī lāel, takar kehan sur^{a}khī*, how wonderful must be the beauty of her whose *bedulī* you have brought.

जकर खेत तकर धान *jakar khēt, takar dhān*, whose is the field, his is the paddy-crop.

तकर अकरार लिखि दाखिल करह *takar akrār likh^{i} dākhil karah*, write and file a bond to that effect (*lit.* of that).

ककर घोड़ छैक *kakar ghōṛ chaik*, whose is the horse ?

(*b*) Oblique Possessive Pronouns agreeing with nouns in the Oblique Cases :—

हमरा सिरकी में *ham^{a}rā sir^{a}kī mẽ*, in my hut.

तोहरा घर में *toh^{a}rā ghar mẽ*, in your house.

गिरहस्थ अपना मन में कहलक *girhasth ap^{a}nā man mẽ kah^{a}lak*, the farmer said in his own heart.

अपना चढ़ैक घोड़ी देल *ap^{a}nā caṛhaik ghōṛī dēl*, he gave the mare of his own riding (*i.e.*, his own riding mare).

संग समाज सखी आइलि हुनका फुलवाड़ी *saṅg samāj sakhī āil^{i} hun^{a}kā phul^{a}wāṛī*, (her) companions and friends came (into) her garden.

हुनका कारन *hun^{a}kā kāran*, for his sake.

These oblique forms are not always employed. The direct form is often used instead of the oblique form, but not *vice-versa*. The oblique form is never used instead of the direct form.

The following pairs are therefore both correct; though the second is the more usual :—

हमर सिरकी में *hamar sir^{a}kī mẽ*, and
हमरा सिरकी में *ham^{a}rā sir^{a}kī mẽ*.

अप्पन चढ़ैक घोड़ी *appan caṛhaik ghōṛī*, and
अपना चढ़ैक घोड़ी *ap^{a}nā caṛhaik ghōṛī*.

And so for the other examples. But the following examples, in which an oblique form is used instead of a direct form, are wrong :—

> हुनका कानब सुनि *hun*^{a}*kā kānab sun*^{i}.
>
> जकरा खेत तकरा धान *jak*^{a}*rā khēt tak*^{a}*rā dhān*, this would mean 'to whom there is a field, to him there is a paddy-crop,' conveying an altogether different meaning.
>
> तकरा अकरार लिखि *tak*^{a}*rā ak*^{a}*rār likh*^{i}.

In phrases like हमरा सक नहिँ *ham*^{a}*rā sak nah*$^{\tilde{i}}$, I have no power (to do so and so), हमरा *ham*^{a}*rā* is not a genitive. It is a dative, and the sentence literally translated is 'to me power is not.'

The above possessive pronouns do not change for gender in the modern language. 'My mother' is हमर माई *hamar māī*, not हमरि माई *hamar*^{i} *māī*. In the old language, however, we now and then come across instances of the feminine.

135. Given the oblique form, the declension of pronouns closely follows that of nouns substantive. The principal points of difference are :—

(1) The Accusative singular is rarely the same as the nominative, but is in the oblique form either by itself or with the postposition कँ *kẽ*, added. Thus हम *ham*, I ; हमरा *ham*^{a}*rā* or हमरा कँ *ham*^{a}*rā kẽ*, me. The honorific pronoun of the second person, अपने *ap*^{a}*ne* or अहाँ *ahā̃*, and the interrogative pronoun की *kī*, what? are the only exceptions to this general statement.

(2) The Genitives are formed according to a different series of rules, as above explained.

(3) The Dative often drops the postposition कँ *kẽ*, an idiom which is not allowable in the case of nouns substantive. Thus हमरा कँ *ham*^{a}*rā kẽ* or हमरा *ham*^{a}*rā*, to me.

(4) Pronouns have the same form whether referring to masculine or feminine nouns.

(5) With the exception of the pronouns of the second person, they all want the vocative case.

PERSONAL PRONOUNS.

136. There are three sets of personal pronouns, the first set referring to the first person, the second to the second person, and the third to the third. Each of the two last sets consists of two divisions—an honorific, and a non-honorific division. In other words, the pronouns of the second and third persons have each two forms, an honorific and a non-honorific. To people accustomed to deal with eastern languages, I need do no more than point out the fact, except to notice *en passant*, that in no Eastern Indo-Aryan language is this distinction carried to a greater length* than in Maithilī. The pronouns of the third person are identical with the Remote Demonstrative Pronouns, and will be dealt with under that head.

137. In order to clear the way, I commence with the two old singular forms of the pronouns of the first and second persons which at the present day are only used in poetry. These are मैं *mẽ*, I, and तू *tū*, thou, and are declined as follows :—

Nom.	मैं *mẽ*, I.	तू *tū*, thou.
Acc.	मोहि *moh*^{i}, me.	तोहि *toh*^{i}, thee.
Instr.	मोहि सौं *moh*^{i} *sõ*, by me.	तोहि सौं *toh*^{i} *sõ*, by thee.
Dat.	मोहि *moh*^{i}, to me.	तोहि *toh*^{i}, to thee.
Abl.	मोहि सौं *moh*^{i} *sõ*, from me.	तोहि सौं *toh*^{i} *sõ*, from thee.
Gen.	मोर *mōr*, my, of me.	तुअ *tua*, or तोर *tōr*, thy, of thee.
Loc.	मोहि मौं *moh*^{i} *mõ*, in me.	तोहि मौं *toh*^{i} *mõ*, in thee.

The oblique forms of the genitive are मोरा *mōrā* and तोरा *tōrā*. In Vidyāpati, lxxix. 13, मोरा *mōrā* is employed as a dative of possession. नहिं मोरा टका अछि *nah*^{i} *mōrā* (scanned as if it were मोर *moru*) *ṭakā ach*^{i}, there is not a rupee to me. I have no money.

---

* It will be seen further on, that some verbs have not only a honorific and a non-honorific form depending on the subject, but have also another pair of honorific and non-honorific forms depending on the object.

The plural forms are not used. When necessary, the modern plurals are said to be employed instead, but I have never met an example of this.

138. It will be observed how closely the declensions of the pronouns of the first and second persons agree in the above paradigm. The same is the case in the modern pronouns, which are as follows :—

Singular.

Case	First person		Second person	
Nom.	हम *ham*, I.		तोँह *tõh*, or तोँ *tõ*. thou.	
Acc.	हमरा *ham^{a}rā*. हमरा केँ *ham^{a}rā kẽ*.	me.	तोहरा *toh^{a}rā*. तोहरा केँ *toh^{a}rā kẽ*.	thee.
Instr.	हमरेँ *ham^{a}rẽ*, हमरा सँ *ham^{a}rā sã*.	by me.	तोहरेँ *toh^{a}rẽ*, तोहरा सँ *toh^{a}rā sã*.	by thee.
Dat.	हमरा *ham^{a}rā*. हमरा केँ *ham^{a}rā kẽ*.	to me.	तोहरा *toh^{a}rā*. तोहरा केँ *toh^{a}rā kẽ*,	to thee.
Abl.	हमरा सँ *ham^{a}rā sã*. from me.		तोहरा सँ *toh^{a}rā sã*, from thee.	
Gen.	हमर *hamar*, or हमार *hamār*. my, of me.		तोहर *tōhar*, or तोहार *tohār*. thy, of thee.	
Loc.	हमरा मेँ *ham^{a}rā mẽ*, in me.		तोहरा मेँ *toh^{a}rā mẽ*, in thee.	
Voc.	... ...		हौ तोँह *hau tõh*, O thou.	

Plural.

Case	First person		Second person	
Nom.	हम सभ *ham sabh*, हमरा सभ *hamᵃrā sabh*,	we.	तोँह सभ *tõh sabh*, तोँ सभ *tõ sabh*, तोहरा सभ *tohᵃrā sabh*,	ye.
Acc.	हमरा सभ *hamᵃrā sabh*, हमरा सभ केँ *hamᵃrā sabh kẽ*,	us.	तोहरा सभ *tohᵃrā sabh*, तोहरा सभ केँ *tohᵃrā sabh kẽ*,	you.
Instr.	हमरा सभेँ *hamᵃrā sabhẽ*, हमरा सभ सँ *hamᵃrā sabh sã*,	by us.	तोहरा सभेँ *tohᵃrā sabhẽ*, तोहरा सभ सँ *tohᵃrā sabh sã*,	by you.
Dat.	हमरा सभ *hamᵃrā sabh*, हमरा सभ केँ *hamᵃrā sabh kẽ*,	to us.	तोहरा सभ *tohᵃrā sabh*, तोहरा सभ केँ *tohᵃrā sabh kẽ*,	to you.
Abl.	हमरा सभ सँ *hamᵃrā sabh sã*,	from us.	तोहरा सभ सँ *tohᵃrā sabh sã*,	from you.
Gen.	हमरा सभक *hamᵃrā sabhak*,	our, of us.	तोहरा सभक *tohᵃrā sabhak*,	your, of you.
Loc.	हमरा सभ मेँ *hamᵃrā sabh mẽ*,	in us.	तोहरा सभ मेँ *tohᵃrā sabh mẽ*,	in you.
Voc.	... ...		हौ तोँह सभ *hau tõh sabh*, हौ तोहरा सभ *hau tohᵃrā sabh*.	O ye.

Instead of सभ *sabh* we may as usual employ सबहि *sabah*^{i} or लोकनि *lok*^{a}*ni* throughout, except that it is not customary to use them with the direct forms हम *ham*, and तोँह *tõh* or तोँ *tõ*. Thus we do not hear हम सबहि *ham sabah*^{i}, or तोँह लोकनि *tõh lok*^{a}*ni*. In the genitive plural we can, as usual, have सभ केर *sabh kēr*, instead of सभक *sabhak*.

The terminations हिँ *h*^{ĩ} and हुँ *h*^{ũ} are often added to these pronouns. The former gives emphasis, and the second means 'also.'

Thus हमहिँ *hamah*^{ĩ}, I (emphatic), I alone, as distinguished from other people; हमहुँ *hamah*^{ũ}, I also; तोँहुँ *tõh*^{ũ}, thou also: हमरहुँ *ham*^{a}*rah*^{ũ} (with shortening of the final vowel of हमरा *ham*^{a}*rā*), to me also.

139. तोँह *tõh* and तोँ *tõ* are non-honorific pronouns of the second person. There are two honorific pronouns of this person. अहाँ *ahā̃* or अहैँ *ahaĩ*, and अपने *ap*^{a}*ne*.

These are declined exactly like substantives, and have no oblique form. Thus, genitive अहाँक *ahā̃k*, or अहैँक *ahaĩk*, and अपनेक *ap*^{a}*nek*, your. The only irregularity is the instrumental singular, the various forms of which are:—

अहैँ *ahaĩ*, अहाँ सँ *ahā̃ sã*, or अहैँ सँ *ahaĩ sã*, and अपने सँ *ap*^{a}*ne sã*, } by you.

The plural is, as usual:—

अहाँ (or अहैँ) सभ *ahā̃* (or *ahaĩ*) *sabh*, सबहि *sabah*^{i}, or लोकनि *lok*^{a}*ni*,

अपने सभ *ap*^{a}*ne sabh*, etc.

अपने *ap*^{a}*ne* is more honorific than अहाँ *ahā̃*. The latter is sometimes even used when talking to inferiors. अहाँ *ahā̃*, in fact, is *polite*; while तोँह *tõh* is *rude* or *vulgar*.

In Hindōstānī आप *āp*, your honour, is construed with the verb in the third person plural, as in आप कहाँ जाते हैं *āp kahā̃ jāte haī*, where is your honour going? In Maithilī, on the contrary, अहाँ *ahā̃* and अपने *apᵃne*, are construed with the second person honorific of the verb, as in अपने बड़त नीक कथा कहल *apᵃne bahut nīk kathā kahal*, your honour made a very excellent remark.

THE REFLEXIVE PRONOUN.

140. Closely connected with the foregoing is the Reflexive Pronoun अपनहिं *apᵃnahⁱ* or अपने *apᵃne*, self, which is employed exactly like the Hindōstānī आप *āp*, genitive अपना *apᵃnā*, always referring to the person of the subject of the sentence.

The genitive of अपनहिं *apᵃnahⁱ* is अपन *apan*, or अप्पन *appan*, own, with an oblique form अपना *apᵃnā*, which is also used as an oblique base. Thus, Acc. Dat. अपना *apᵃnā*, or अपना कें *apᵃnā kẽ*, to oneself.

The nominative plural is अपनहिं (or अपने) सभ *apᵃnahⁱ* (or *apᵃne*) *sabh*, सबहि *sabahⁱ*, or लोकनि *lokᵃni*. The oblique cases of the plural are formed from the base अपना सभ *apᵃnā sabh*, etc. Thus Gen. plural अपना सभक *apᵃnā sabhak*, अपना सबहिक *apᵃnā sabᵃhik*, अपना लोकनिक *apᵃnā lokᵃnik*, of selves.

The Locative plural, अपना सभ में *apᵃnā sabh mẽ*, or (as frequently happens) with the plural suffix dropped, अपना में *apᵃnā mẽ* means 'amongst themselves,' like the Hindōstānī आपस में *āpas mẽ*.

The following are examples of the use of this pronoun :—

अपनहिं बिलास सँ गेल सरलोगवा *apᵃnahⁱ bilās sã gēl sarᵃlogᵃwā*, he himself, after enjoyment (of this life), went to heaven.

अपने ब्राह्मनीक रूप धै कँगनिश्रा चढ़लि *apᵃne brahᵃmanīk rūp dhai kãganiā caṛhalⁱ*, she herself, taking the form of a Brāhmaṇ woman, ascended the bank.

अपन मरौटी अपने गाय गबैत चलू जोगिया गाम, *apan marauṭī*

upᵃne gāy yabait calū jogiyā gām, having sung our own death-song let us go singing to the village of Jogiyā.

अपन बहु बेटी रखलन्हि घर सुताय *apan bahᵘ bēṭī rakhᵃlanhⁱ ghar sutāy*, he has put his own daughter-in-law and daughter to sleep at home.

बैरी अपना बस में आबि जाय् *bairī apᵃnā bas mē ābⁱ jāy*, (if) an enemy come into one's own power.

अपना में मेलि कै कँ रहबँह *apᵃnā mē mēlⁱ kai kā̃ rahᵃbāh*, you will remain at peace amongst yourselves. *i.e.*, with each other.

THE DEMONSTRATIVE PRONOUNS, AND PRONOUN OF THE THIRD PERSON.

141. There are two Demonstrative Pronouns,—a Proximate, इ *i* or ई *ī*, this, and a Remote, ओ *ō*, that. The Remote Demonstrative Pronoun is also used as a Pronoun of the third person, with the meaning of 'he,' 'she,' or 'it.'

142. Each of these pronouns has two forms, a non-honorific and an honorific. Each of these latter, again, has two oblique forms, the old, and the modern.

143. These pronouns may be either substantives or adjectives. When used as substantives they are declined throughout. When used as adjectives they are unchanged when the substantive with which they are in agreement is in the form of the nominative, and are put in the old oblique form when the substantive is not in that form. Thus, ई नेना *ī nēnā*, this boy; ओ नेना *ō nēnā*, that boy; ई सभ नेना *ī sabh nēnā*, or ई नेना सभ *ī nēnā sabh*, these boys; ओ सभ नेना *ō sabh nēnā*, or ओ नेना सभ *ō nēnā sabh*, those boys; but एहि नेनाक *ehⁱ nēnāk*, of this boy; ओहि नेनाक *ohⁱ nēnāk*, of that boy; एहि सभ नेनाक *ehⁱ sabh nēnāk*, or एहि नेना सभक *ehⁱ nēnā sabhak*, of these boys; ओहि सभ नेनाक *ohⁱ sabh nēnāk*, or ओहि

नेना सभक *ohⁱ nĕnā sabhak*, of those boys. The modern oblique forms are never used in this way.

Other examples of the adjectival use of these pronouns are:—

एहि बेकूफ कें कहाँ तक नीक अकिल हैतैक, *ehⁱ bĕkūph kĕ kahā̃ tak nīk akil haitaik*, how far will wisdom come to this fool.

एहि फसिलक की रंग अछि *ehⁱ phasilak kī raṅg achⁱ*, what is the prospect of this harvest.

ओहि राति कँ कतहुँ चलैत गेल *ohⁱ rātⁱ kẵ katahŭ calait gĕl*, that night he went away somewhere.

ओहि रसायनीक ठेकान नहिं लागल *ohⁱ rasāyᵃnīk ṭhĕkān nahⁱ lāgal*, no trace was found of that alchemist.

144. When used as substantives, the non-honorific pronouns have two forms,—one referring to inanimate objects and using the old oblique form, while the other refers only to animate objects and uses the modern oblique form. Thus एहि में *ehⁱ mĕ*, in this (thing); एकरा में *ekᵃrā mĕ*, in this (living creature); ओहि में *ohⁱ mĕ*, in that (thing), in it: ओकरा में *okᵃrā mĕ*, in that (living creature), in him, in her.

There are thus three declensions of Demonstrative Pronouns when used as substantives, *viz*:—

(*a*) Non-honorific inanimate.

(*b*) Non-honorific animate.

(*b*) Honorific animate.

It stands to reason that an honorific inanimate declension is not likely to occur. The following is the declension of Demonstrative Pronouns.

145. (*a*) Non-Honorific Inanimate.

Singular.

	इ *i* or ई *ī*, this.	ओ *ō*. that.
Nom.	इ *i* or ई *ī*, this	ओ *ō*. that.
Acc.	इ *i*, ई *ī*, एहि *eh*^{i}. एहि कँ *eh*^{i} *kẽ*, this.	ओ *ō*, ओहि *oh*^{i}. ओहि कँ *oh*^{i} *kẽ*, that.
Instr.	एँ *ẽ*, एहि सँ *eh*^{i} *sã*, by this.	ओहि सँ *oh*^{i} *sã*, by that.
Dat.	एहि *eh*^{i}. एहि कँ *eh*^{i} *kẽ*, to this.	ओहि *oh*^{i}. ओहि कँ *oh*^{i} *kẽ*, to that.
Abl.	एहि सँ *eh*^{i} *sã*, from this.	ओहि सँ *oh*^{i} *sã*, from that.
Gen.	एकर *ēkar*, of this.	ओकर *ōkar*, of that.
Loc.	एहि मेँ *eh*^{i} *mẽ*, in this.	ओहि मेँ *oh*^{i} *mẽ*, in that.

Plural.

Nom.	इ सभ *i sabh*, or ई सभ *ī sabh*. these.	ओ सभ *ō sabh*, those.
Acc.	एहि सभ (कँ) *eh*^{i} *sabh* (*kẽ*). these.	ओहि सभ (कँ) *oh*^{i} *sabh* (*kẽ*), those.
Instr.	{ एँ सभ *ẽ sabh*, एहि सभ सँ *eh*^{i} *sabh sã*, } by these.	ओहि सभ सँ *oh*^{i} *sabh sã*, by those.
Dat.	एहि सभ (कँ) *eh*^{i} *sabh* (*kẽ*), to these.	ओहि सभ (कँ) *oh*^{i} *sabh* (*kẽ*). to those.
Abl.	एहि सभ सँ *eh*^{i} *sabh sã*. from these.	ओहि सभ सँ *oh*^{i} *sabh sã*, from those.
Gen.	एहि सभक *eh*^{i} *sabhak*, of these.	ओहि सभक *oh*^{i} *sabhak*. of those.
Loc.	एहि सभ मेँ *eh*^{i} *sabh mẽ*. in these.	ओहि सभ मेँ *oh*^{i} *sabh mẽ*, in those.

Instead of एहि *eh*[i], we may have, throughout, एह *eh* or ऐह *aih*, and similarly for ओहि *oh*[i], we may have ओह *oh* or औह *auh*. I have not noted any instrumental form of ओ *ō*, corresponding to the एँ *ẽ* of ई *ī*. The genitives singular एकर *ēkar* and ओकर *ōkar* are contractions of एहि कर *eh*[i] *kar* and ओहि कर *oh*[i] *kar* respectively. I have not met with forms like एहिक *ehik* or ओहिक *ohik*, as we might expect. The plural suffix may be सबहि *sabah*[i] instead of सभ *sabh*. लोकनि *lok*[a]*ni* cannot be used, as the pronouns refer only to inanimate objects.

As examples of these inanimate non-honorific pronouns, we may quote :—

ई एकर आठम बिआन थिकै *ī ēkar āṭham biān thikai*, this is the eighth calving of this one (referring to a cow).

ई ले जाह *ī le jāh*, take away this.

एहि नहिँ जनली अहाँ भद्री छी *eh*[i] *nah*[ĩ] *jan*[a]*lī ahā̃ bhadrī chī*, I did not know this, that your honour is Bhadri.

एहि सँ ई फल बहराइअछि *eh*[i] *sã ī phal bah*[a]*rāi-ach*[i], from this this fruit comes out, *i.e.*, the moral of this is the following :—

ओहि मेँ किछु लाभ नहिँ *oh*[i] *mẽ kicch*[u] *lābh nah*[ĩ], in that there is no profit.

कौआ ओकर गुद्दा खाए गेल *kauā ōkar guddā khāe gēl*, the crow ate up its kernel.

As an emphatic form of these pronouns we have इहे *ihe*, this indeed, and उहे *uhe* or वैह *waih*, that indeed, as in दीना भद्री जिबैत चल उहे गबैत रहै *dinā bhadrī jibait chal, uhe gabait rahai*, (when) Dinā and Bhadrī were alive, that is the very song they used to sing ; वैह चोराए कै लै गेल अछि *waih corāe kai lai gēl ach*[i], it is he who has stolen (the property) and carried it off.

146. (*b*) Non-Honorific Animate.

This is declined like the inanimate pronoun, except that एकरा *ek^{a}rā* is substituted for एहि *eh^{i}* and ओकरा *ok^{a}rā* for ओहि *oh^{i}*. Thus :—

Singular.

Nom.	इ *i* or ई *ī*, this	ओ *ō*, that.
Instr.	एकरें *ek^{a}rẽ*, एकरा सँ *ek^{a}rā sã*, by this.	ओकरा सँ *ok^{a}rā sã*, by that.
Dat.	एकरा *ek^{a}rā*, एकरा कें *ek^{a}rā kẽ*, to this.	ओकरा *ok^{a}rā*, ओकरा कें *ok^{a}rā kẽ*, to that.
Gen.	एकर *ēkar*, of this.	ओकर *ōkar*, of that.

Plural.

Nom.	इ सभ *i sabh*, ई सभ *ī sabh*, etc., these.	ओ सभ *ō sabh*, etc., those.
Dat.	एकरा सभ (कें) *ek^{a}rā sabh* (*kẽ*), to these.	ओकरा सभ (कें) *ok^{a}rā sabh* (*kẽ*), to those.

Similarly for the other cases. I have not noted any instrumental form of ओ *ō*, corresponding to the एकरें *ek^{a}rẽ* of ई *ī*. In the plural, instead of सभ *sabh*, we can, as usual, have सबहि *sabah^{i}* or लोकनि *lok^{a}ni*. As examples of these animate non-honorific pronouns, we may quote :—

ओ आइकाल्हि गाभिनि अछि *ō āikālh^{i} gābhin^{i} ach^{i}*, nowadays she is in calf (referring to a cow).

ओकरा एहि तरहें घबड़ाएल देखि कँ *ok^{a}rā eh^{i} tar^{a}hẽ ghab^{a}ṛāel dēkh^{i} kã*, having seen him distracted in this manner.

In the following ओकरा *ok^{a}rā* is irregularly used to refer to an inanimate object. तखन ओ सभ ओकरा झट पट तोड़ि देलक *takhan ō sabh ok^{a}rā jhaṭ-paṭ tōṛ^{i} dēlak*, then they at once broke it (*sc.* a stick).

एकर आठम बिआन *ēkar āṭham biān*, her eighth calving.

जेहि सौं ओकर परबरश होइक से अवश्य० कर्त्तव्य० थीक *jehi saũ ōkar parabaraś hōik sē abasya kartabya thīk*, we must certainly do what is necessary for its (the child's) support.

एकरा सभ कें किछु कै देखाबी *ekarā sabh kē̃ kichu kai dekhābī*, having done something, let me show it to all these (*viz.* to his sons).

एकरा सबहि कें हमरा लग पठाए देह *ekarā sabahi kē̃ hamarā lag paṭhāe daih*, send all these (*viz.*, dogs) to me.

हिं *hĩ* added to these oblique forms gives emphasis, while हुं *hũ* when suffixed, means 'also.' Thus एकरहिं कें *ekarahĩ kē̃*, it is to *this* one; ओकरहुं पठाए दिऔक *okarahũ paṭhāe diauk*, send him also. Observe that the final आ *ā* of एकरा *ekarā* and ओकरा *okarā* is shortened before these suffixes.

147. (*c*) Honorific.

The old honorific oblique forms of ई *ī* and ओ *ō* are हिनि *hini* and हुनि *huni* respectively. We meet them variously spelt. Sometimes we have हिन *hin* and हुन *hun*; sometimes हिन्हि *hinhi* and हुन्हि *hunhi*, and sometimes हिन्ह *hinh* and हुन्ह *hunh*. For the sake of convenience I shall only employ हिनि *hini* and हुनि *huni* in the paradigms, but it should be remembered that the other forms are often met with. Indeed, the most usual form of the genitive is हिनक *hinak* and हुनक *hunak*, and not हिनिक *hinik* and हुनिक *hunik*. These old oblique forms are only employed as adjectives, and, being honorific, rarely occur in the literary style, though one hears them in conversation. We have an example in हुनि स्वामिक कारन *huni swāmik kāran*, for the sake of that (respected) husband (the prospective wife is speaking), in the song of Salhēs.

148. The modern oblique form is the oblique genitive of the old oblique form. Thus, हिनका *hin*^{a}*kā* and हुनका *hun*^{a}*kā*, of which हिनिका *hinikā*, हिन्हका *hinh*^{a}*kā*, हिन्हिका *hinhikā*, and हुनिका *hunikā*, हुन्हका *hunh*^{a}*kā*, हुन्हिका *hunhikā*, are optional varieties.

149. The declension of the honorific pronoun is the same as that of the non-honorific, substituting हिनका *hin*^{a}*kā* and हुनका *hun*^{a}*kā*, or any of the optional spellings, for एकरा *ek*^{a}*rā* and ओकरा *ok*^{a}*rā*, respectively. Thus :—

Singular.

Nom.	इ *i* or ई *ī*, this.		ओ *ō*, that.	
Instr.	हिनका सँ *hin*^{a}*kā sã*, by this.		हुनका सँ *hun*^{a}*kā sã*, by that.	
Dat.	हिनका *hin*^{a}*kā*, हिनका कँ *hin*^{a}*kā kẽ*,	to this.	हुनका *hun*^{a}*kā*, हुनका क *hun*^{a}*kā kẽ*,	to that.
Gen.	हिनक *hinak*. हिनकर *hin*^{a}*kar*.	of this.	हुनक *hunak*, हुनकर *hun*^{a}*kar*.	of that.

Plural.

Nom. इ सभ *i sabh*, ई सभ *ī sabh*, etc., these. ओ सभ *ō sabh*, etc., those.

Dat. हिनका सभ (कँ) *hin*^{a}*kā sabh* (*kẽ*), to these. हुनका सभ (कँ) *hun*^{a}*kā sabh* (*kẽ*), to those.

Similarly for the other cases. As usual, in the plural we can use सबहि *sabah*^{i} or लोकनि *lok*^{a}*ni* instead of सभ *sabh*. Examples of the use of this form of the demonstrative pronoun are :—

हिनका फुरसति देब *hin*^{a}*kā phursat*^{i} *dēb*. I will give him leave to depart.

हुनका माए बाप गारी देलक *hun*^{a}*kā māe bāp gārī dēlak*, have the father and mother given abuse to her (*i.e.*, have they abused her).

हुनिका माता नहि *hunikā mātā nah*ⁱ, to him there is no mother, he has no mother.

हुनक कानब सुनि *hunak kānab sun*ⁱ, hearing her weeping.

150. The above genitives एकर *ēkar*, ओकर *ōkar*, हिनक *hinak*, or हिनकर *hin*ᵃ*kar* and हुनक *hunak* or हुनकर *hun*ᵃ*kar*, are usually all put into the oblique form when agreeing with a noun in an oblique case. Examples of this will be found in § 134 *ante*.

The Relative and Correlative Pronouns.

151. The Relative Pronoun is जे *jē*, who, which, and its Correlative is से *sē*, he, she, it, that.

152. As in the case of the Demonstrative Pronouns, each has two forms, a non-honorific and an honorific; and the non-honorific form, again, may be animate or inanimate. There is, however this difference, that in the Instrumental, Ablative, and Genitive singular, and throughout the plural, the form usually employed for inanimate nouns may also be employed for animate ones.

153. When used as adjectives, the oblique forms (जाहि *jāh*ⁱ and ताहि *tāh*ⁱ) of the non-honorific inanimate declension are used when in agreement with a noun in an oblique case. Examples of the adjectival use of these pronouns are as follows:—

जे चीज बस्तु सभ अहाँक नोकसान भेल अछि, से सभ पहुँचत *jē cīj bast*ᵘ *sabh ahā̃k nok*ᵃ*sān bhēl ach*ⁱ, *sē sabh pahũcat*, all your property which has been spoilt, will arrive (*i.e.*, be restored).

जे लोक आएल छल से लोक गेल *jē lōk āel chal*, *sē lōk gēl*, the man who came, went.

जाहि लोकक खेत ताहि लोकक धान *jāh*ⁱ *lōkak khēt*, *tāh*ⁱ *lōkak dhān*, the person who owns the field, owns the paddy.

जाहि बन सिकिओ ने डोलै ताहि बन हन्सा छै लड़ै *jāh^i ban siki-ō ne ḍōlai, tāh^i ban hansā chai laṛai*, (in) the forest where even the reeds are motionless, his soul is fighting.

154. When used as a substantive, the inanimate non-honorific form is declined as follows. The Instrumental, Ablative, and Genitive singular, and the whole of the plural can be also used to refer to animate nouns.

155. (*a*) Non-Honorific Inanimate.

Singular.

	जे *jē*, which, who.	से *sē*, he, she, it, that.
Nom.	जे *jē*, which.	से *sē*, that.
Acc.	जाहि (कँ) *jāh^i (kẽ)*, to which.	ताहि (कँ) *tāh^i (kẽ)*, to that.
Instr.	जँ *jẽ* / जाहि सँ *jāh^i sā̃*, by which, by whom.	तँ *tẽ* / ताहि सँ *tāh^i sā̃*, by that, by him.
Dat.	जाहि (कँ) *jāh^i (kẽ)*, to which.	ताहि (कँ) *tāh^i (kẽ)*, to that.
Abl.	जाहि सँ *jāh^i sā̃*, from which, from whom.	ताहि सँ *tāh^i sā̃*, from that, from him.
Gen.	जसु *jas^u*, of which, of whom.	तसु *tas^u*, of that, of him.
Loc.	जाहि मँ *jāh^i mẽ*, in which.	ताहि मँ *tāh^i mẽ*, in that.

Plural.

Nom.	जे सभ *jē sabh*, which, who.	से सभ *sē sabh*, those, they.
Acc.	जाहि सभ (कँ) *jāh^i sabh kẽ*, which, who.	ताहि सभ (कँ) *tāh^i sabh (kẽ)*, those, they.
Instr.	जाहि सभ सँ *jāh^i sabh sā̃*, by which, by whom.	ताहि सभ सँ *tāh^i sabh sā̃*, by those, by them.
Dat.	जाहि सभ (कँ) *jāh^i sabh (kẽ)*, to which, to whom.	ताहि सभ (कँ) *tāh^i sabh (kẽ)*, to those, to them.

Abl. जाहि सभ सँ *jāhi sabh sã*, from which, from whom. ताहि सभ सँ *tāhi sabh sã*, from those, from them.

Gen. जाहि सभक *jāhi sabhak*, of which, of whom. ताहि सभक *tāhi sabhak*, of those, of them.

Loc. जाहि सभ मेँ *jāhi sabh mẽ*, in which, in whom. ताहि सभ मेँ *tāhi sabh mẽ*, in those, in them.

Instead of जाहि *jāhi* and ताहि *tāhi*, we sometimes find in poetry जा *jā* and ता *tā*. We also sometimes have जेहि *jehi* and तेहि *tehi*, which are properly Bhojpuri. From this last we have an instrumental जेहिँ *jehĩ* and तेहिँ *tehĩ*, which are used adverbially, to mean 'as,' 'so.' The Genitives जसु *jasu*, and तसु *tasu*, are only used in proverbs and poetry. In one place Vidyāpati has तासि *tāsi* (xviii, 7). I have not met forms like जाहिक *jāhik* and ताहिक *tāhik*, which we might expect. The plural suffix may, as usual, be सबहि *sabahi* or लोकनि *lokani* instead of सभ *sabh*. As examples of this form of the honorific pronoun we may quote :—

जे आएल से गेल *jē āel sē gēl*, he who came, went.

जाहि सँ नाम चलैन्हि से हमर किरिया करैह *jāhi sã nām calainhi, sē hamar kiriyā karaiah*, in order that (*lit.* from which) our name may continue, so perform our funeral rites.

In the following the final ि i of जाहि *jāhi* has been lengthened for the sake of metre.

जाही सँ किछु पाबिअ सहिअ कडुइ बेन *jāhī sã kichu pābiă, sahiă karui bēn*, from whomsoever you would receive benefits, you must bear abusive words.

कैएक कथा सभ सिखाए दिअहु कि जाहि सँ तोहरा लाभ हैतहु *kaiek kathā sabh sikhāe diahu, ki jāhi sã tohrā lābh haitahu*, I will teach you several sayings from which there will be gain to you.

जकरा जा सँ रीती दुरहुक दुरि गेलें दोगुन पिरीती *jakarā jā sã rītī durahuka duri gēlē doguna pirītī*, to whom, with whom there is affection (*i.e.*, when there is mutual affection), the love is twice as strong the more distant they are from each other (Vidyāpati, xlvi. 1).

ता सम *tā sama*, like that (Vidyapati, xvi. 2).

जेहि सों ओकर परबरश होइक *jeh*^{i} *suũ ōkur par*^{a}*baraś hōik*, so that (*lit.* from which) its support may be, (we must take precautions for the child's support).

तेहि अबसर *teh*^{i} *abasara*, at that time (Vid. xxviii. 4).

जेहिँ ऐलाह तेहिँ गेला, *jeh*^{ĩ} *ailăh teh*^{ĩ} *gēlā*, as he came, so he went.

जसु मन परम तरासे *jasu mana parama tarāsē*, in whose heart there is exceeding fear (Vid. vii. 5).

तसु साहस नहिँ सीमा *tasu sāhasa nahī sīmā*, there is no limit to her courage (Vid. vii. 4).

तासि रिपु *tāsi ripu*, his foe (Vid. xviii. 7).

156. Several emphatic forms of these pronouns have been noted. Such are जैह *jaih*, who, सेह *seh*, सैह *saih*, सोए *sōe*, even he: सेओ *sēō*, सेहो *sēhō*, सेहओ *seh-o*, he also. Thus,—

सैह चतुर जन जैह बुझत अबधारी *saiha catura jana jaiha bujhata abadhārī*, they alone are wise who can understand it correctly (Vid. xvii. 7).

तनिका सेह पै नाह *tanikā seh pai nāh*, he alone (will be) a husband to her.

चानन लाग बिखम सर सोए *cānana lāga bikhama sara sōe*, the application of sandalwood,—even that is an intolerable arrow (Vid. xvii. 3).

सेहओ दुरि गेला *seha-o duri gēlā*, that also went far away (Vid. lxxiii. 4).

सेहो थिक ओहि ठामा *sēhō thika ohi ṭhāmā*, that also is in that place (Vid. xvii. 3).

157. It will have been noticed from the above that while से *sē* is generally employed as a correlative, it is sometimes used as an independent demonstrative pronoun. Its Instrumental singular appears under various forms, such as तैं *taĩ*, तौं *taũ*, तौ *tau*, तो *tō*, or with emphatic ई *ī*, तेंई *tẽī*, or with emphatic ओ *o*, तेंओ *tẽo*, तैओ *taio*, or तैअओ *taiao*, all of which are commonly used adverbially. Thus:—

तें नहिं करथि गरासे *tẽ nahĩ karathi garāsē*, *therefore* he does not devour it (Vid. xiv. 8).

तैं नहिं कमल सुखाई *taĩ nahĩ kamala sukhāī*, *therefore* the lotus does not wither (Vid. xiv. 6).

तौं पय जीबे अधर सुधा रस जौं पय पीबे *taũ paya jībē, adharu sudhā-rasu jaũ paya pībē*, *so long* will it live, as long as it sips the nectar of the lower lip (Vid. ii. 5).

तो पय जीबथि जीबे *tō paya jībathi jībē*, so long will he remain living (Vid. x. 10).

तेंई बहि गेल हावा *tẽī bah[i] gēl hāwā*, *exactly so* did the wind blow.

तेंओ धसल केस पासे *tẽo dhasalu kēśu pāsē*, *therefore also* my hair was disordered (Vid. xl. 7).

तैओ तुलित नहिं भेला *taio tulita nahĩ bhēlā*, *still* it did not equal (the beauty of thy face) (Vid. vi. 4).

तैअओ कुमुदिनि करय अनंदा *taiao kumudini karaya anandā*, *nevertheless* the water-lily rejoices (Vid. xlvi. 6).

158. (*b*) Non-Honorific Animate.

This is declined like the inanimate pronoun, except that जकरा *jak*^{a}*rā* is substituted for जाहि *jāh*^{i}. and तकरा *tak*^{a}*rā* for ताहि *tāh*^{i}. Thus:—

Singular.

Nom.	जे *jē*, who.	से *sē*, he, she, that.
Instr.	जकरेँ *jak*^{a}*rē̃*, / जकरा सँ *jak*^{a}*rā sã*, } by whom.	तकरेँ *tak*^{a}*rē̃*, / तकरा सँ *tak*^{a}*rā sã*, } by him, &c.
Dat.	जकरा (केँ) *jak*^{a}*rā* (*kē̃*), to whom.	तकरा (केँ) *tak*^{a}*rā* (*kē̃*), to him, &c.
Gen.	जकर *jakar*, whose.	तकर *takar*, his, her, its.

Plural.

Nom.	जे सभ *jē sabh*, who.	से सभ *sē sabh*, they.
Dat.	जकरा सभ (केँ) *jak*^{a}*rā sabh* (*kē̃*), to whom.	तकरा सभ (केँ) *tak*^{a}*rā sabh* (*kē̃*), to them.

Similarly for the other cases. In the plural, as usual, सबहि *subah*^{i} or लोकनि *lok*^{a}*ni* may be substituted for सभ *sabh*. Occasionally we come across जेकर *jēkar* instead of जकर *jakar*, जेकरा *jek*^{a}*rā* instead of जकरा *jak*^{a}*rā*, तेकर *tēkar* instead of तकर *takar*, and तेकरा *tek*^{a}*rā* instead of तकरा *tak*^{a}*rā*. These are properly Bhojpurī forms.

As examples of these non-honorific animate pronouns we may quote:—

जकर खेत तकर धान *jakar khēt. takar dhān*, whose is the field, his is the paddy-crop.

जकर लाठी तकर महीस *jakar lāṭhī takar mahīs*, he who owns the cudgel owns the buffalo.

जकरा सँ रस चूबि रहल अछि *jak*ᵃ*rā sa͂ ras cūb*ⁱ *rahal ach*ⁱ, (grapes) from which the juice is exuding (here the pronoun is, exceptionally, inanimate).

जेकर बनल अखड़वा तेकर बारहो मास *jĕkar banal akhaṛ*ᵃ*wā tĕkar băr*ᵃ*ho mās*, he whose (fields) are ready in *Āṣāḍh*, is ready also all the year round.

हिँ *h*ĩ (even), and हुँ *h*ũ (also), are added as in the case of demonstratives. Thus (Vid. l. 4).

> एहि अवसर पहु मिलन जेहन सुख ।
> जकरहिँ होए से जान ॥
>
> *ehi abasara pahu milana jehana sukha* ।
> *jakarahĩ hoe sē jāna* ॥

Only she that hath experienced them, knows the bliss of the tryst with the beloved at such a time.

159. (c) Honorific Animate.

The honorific oblique forms of जे *jĕ* and से *sĕ* are जनि *jan*ⁱ and तनि *tan*ⁱ, respectively. We thus get the following declension which is exactly parallel to that of ई *ī* and ओ *ō* :—

Singular.

Nom.	जे *jĕ*, who.	से *sĕ*, he, she, that.
Instr.	जनिका सँ *janikā sa͂*, by whom.	तनिका सँ *tanikā sa͂*, by him, her.
Dat.	जनिका (केँ) *janikā* (*kẽ*), to whom.	तनिका (केँ) *tanikā* (*kẽ*), to him, her.
Gen.	जनिक *janik*, जनिकर *janikar*, whose.	तनिक *tanik*, तनिकर *tanikar*, his, hers.

Plural.

Nom. जे सभ *jē sabh*, who. से सभ *sē sabh*, they.

Dat. जनिका सभ (कें) *janikā sabh* (*kē̃*), to whom. तनिका सभ (कें) *tanikā sabh* (*kē̃*), to them.

And so on for the other cases. As usual, in the plural we can use सबहि *subah*ⁱ, or लोकनि *lok*ᵃ*ni* instead of सभ *sabh*. Examples of these honorific forms are :—

जेहन जनिकर चाकरी तेहनें सन भरि देथि *jehan janikar cāk*ᵃ*rī, teh*ᵃ*nē-san bhar*ⁱ *dēth*ⁱ, as is each one's (*lit.* whose) service, exactly so he pays in full.

केओ जमानत दै कें बचलाह जनिका अमला नेही *keõ jamānat dai kē̃ bac*ᵃ*lāh, janikā am*ᵃ*lā nēhī*, some, to whom there was affection on the part of the court officials, got off by giving bail.

जनिक एहन धनि *janika ehana dhani*, (a man) whose wife is so (beautiful), (Vid. li. 2).

कि कहब तनिक गेआने *ki kahaba tanika geānē*, what shall I say (about) his wisdom? (Vid. xxii. 2).

160. I have not noted any occurrence of the employment of the oblique genitive of जे *je*, though, of course, it is commonly heard colloquially. For से *sē*, we have the following pair of examples :—

Direct Genitive—

लाख गारि देलें, तकर उतर हम नहिं किछु कहलोक *lākh gār*ⁱ *dēlē̃, takar utar ham nah*ⁱ *kich*ᵘ *kah*ᵃ*lunk*, a thousand abuses didst thou give me, but I said to thee no answer to (*lit.* of) it.

Oblique Genitive—

तकरा बल सें गुलामी जट चरबैत छथि *tak*ᵃ*rā bal sē̃ gulāmī jaṭ car*ᵃ*bait ach*ⁱ, through her might Gulāmi Jaṭ is grazing (cattle).

161. Interrogative Pronouns.

There are two interrogative pronouns, *viz.*, के *kē*, who? and की *kī*, what? The former only refers to animate objects, and the latter only to inanimate.

162. When employed as adjectives के *kē* and की *kī* become कोन *kōn* or कौन *kaun*, but when agreeing with a noun in the nominative singular की *kī* may remain unchanged. Examples of the adjectival use of these pronouns are :—

के *kē*,—ओ कोन लोक थीक *ō kōn lōk thīk*, what caste is he?

कोन लोकक घोड़ छैक *kōn lōkak ghōṛ chaik*, of what person is (this) the horse, *i.e.*, what person owns the horse?

कौन गरू परलौ *kaun garū parªlau*, what misfortune has befallen you?

पुछैत छैन्हि जे कौन लोगक हबेली छीक *puchait chainhⁱ jē kaun lōgak habēlī chīk*, you are asking, '(of a man) of what caste is this the house?'

कौन उपाय जाएब जोगिया नगर *kaun upāy jāeb jogiyā nagar*, by what device shall we go to Jogiyā town?

की *kī*,—ई कोन बिआन थिकैक *ī kōn biān thikaik*, what calving is this? (*i.e.*, how many times has she calved before?)

ओकरा मेँ कोन गुन छैक *ōkªrā mē̃ kōn gun chaik*, what virtue is there in it?

कोन लोटा मेँ पानि लाएल छह *kōn lōṭā mē̃ pāni lāel chah*, in what vessel have you brought the water?

कौन दिसा के अबैत होए कहहु बुझाय *kaun disā kē abait hōai kahahu bujhāy*, tell (me) in what direction he may be coming.

फेरि की झगड़ा अछि *phērⁱ kī jhagªṛā achⁱ*, then what (cause of) quarrel can there be?

की नाम छिक *kī nām chhik*, what name is it?

163. The declension of के *kē* (the animate pronoun) closely follows that of the animate forms of जे *jē*.

There are, as usual non-honorific and honorific declensions. They are as follows :—

Singular.

	Non-honorific.	*Honorific.*
Nom.	के *kē*, who? which?	के *kē*, who? which?
Instr.	ककरेँ *kakᵃrē̃*, ककरा सँ *kakᵃrā sã*, } by whom?	कनिका सँ *kanikā sã*, by whom?
Dat.	ककरा (केँ) *kakᵃrā* (*kē̃*), to whom?	कनिका (केँ) *kanikā* (*kē̃*), to whom?
Gen.	ककर *kakar*, whose?	कनिक *kanik*, कनिकर *kanikar*, whose?

Plural.

Nom.	के सभ *kē sabh*, who?	के सभ *kē sabh*, who?
Dat.	ककरा सभ (केँ) *kakᵃrā sabh* (*kē̃*), to whom?	कनिका सभ केँ *kanikā sabh kē̃*, to whom?

and so on for the other cases. In the plural, as usual, सबहि *sabahⁱ* or लोकनि *lakᵃni*, may be substituted for सभ *sabh*. Occasionally we come across केकर *kēkar* instead of ककर *kakar*, and केकरा *kekᵃrā* instead of ककरा *kakᵃrā*, but these are properly Bhojpuri forms. I have not come across काहि *kāhⁱ* corresponding to जाहि *jāhⁱ* in the modern language, but Vidyāpati employs it in passages such as काहि कहब दुख *kāhi kahabu dukha*, to whom shall I tell my distress? (lxi. 2.)

As examples of these animate interrogative pronouns, we may quote :—

ककर घोड़ छैक *kakar ghōṛ chaik*, whose horse is it?

केकर एहन जमाए *kēkara ehana jamāe*, who has such a son-in-law (Vid. lxxxi. 4)?

ककरा दे के जोगिया जाँजरि भेजब समाद *kakᵃrā dē ke jogiyā jā̃jarⁱ bhējab samād*, having given whom (*i.e.*, by means of whom) shall we send word to Jogiyā Jā̃jari.

लुबुधल नयन हटय के पार *lubudhala nayana haṭaya kē pāra*, who can turn aside a greedy eye? (Vid. iv. 3).

I have not come across any instances of the honorific forms in literature, but they are occasionally heard colloquially.

164. The inanimate interrogative pronoun is कि *ki* or की *kī*, what? It is often written किश्च *kia* or किए *kiē*, especially in poetry. Its declension is quite irregular, and is as follows :—

Singular.

Nom. कि *ki*, की *kī*, or किश्च *kia*, what?

Acc. कथी कें, *kathī kē̃*, or की *kī*, what?

Instr. कथीँ *kathī̃*, कथी सँ *kathī sã̄*, by what?

Dat. कथी लै *kathī lai*, किऐ *kiai*, किए *kiē*, or किए *kie*, to or for what? why?

Abl. कथी सँ *kathī sã̄*, from what?

Gen. कथीक *kathīk*, of what?

Loc. कथी मेँ *kathī mē̃*, in what?

Plural wanting. Note the form of the Dative. This case has many variations. I have noted कि ला *ki lā*, कि लै *ki lai*, की ला *kī lā*, की लै *kī lai*, कथी ला *kathī lā*, कथी लै *kathī lai*. लै *lai* is often written लय *lay* or लए *lae*, and instead of कथी *kathī*, we often have कथि *kathi*. Like the dative, the instrumental कथीँ *kathī̃* is used to mean 'why?'

Examples of this pronoun are :—

कि कहब तनिक गेआने *ki kahuba tanika geānē*, what shall I say (about) his wisdom ? (Vid. xxii. 2).

अपनेक बकरी की भेल *apᵃnek bakᵃrī kī bhēl*, what has happened to your goat ?

की छैक *kī chaik*, what is it ?

किअ भेल *kia bhēl*, what has happened ?

किअ कहौ हे मुसाहु *kia kahau, hē musāhᵘ*, O Musāhu, what have you to say ?

किए बिधाता लिखि मोहि देल *kiē bidhātā likhi mohi dēl*, why hath God written (it) for me (in my fate) ? (Vid. lvii. 1).

कथी में पानि लाएल छह *kathī mẽ pāni lāel chāh*, in what have you brought the water ?

कथी हमरा चोर बनबैछी *kathī homᵃrā cōr banᵃbaichī*, why do you make me out a thief ?

कथि लए कंश पटकलह मोहि *kathi lae kaṁśa paṭakalāha mōhi*, why, O Kaṁśa, didst thou dash me down (Manbōdh's *Harivaṁśa*. i. 37).

फोटरा गीदर कथि ला मरद औतार लेलें *phoṭᵃrā gīdar kathi lā marad autār lēlẽ*, O Phoṭᵃrā, the jackal, why has a man taken your form ?

क्यो कह नन्द महर किए मान *kyō kaha nanda mahara kie māna*, others (*lit.* some) said. 'Why does King Nanda agree ?' (Manbōdh. vii. 45).

Indefinite Pronouns.

165. These are केओ *keo*, anyone, someone ; किछु *kichᵘ*, anything, something ; and कैएक *kaiek*, several.

166. केओ *keo*, anyone, someone, appears under various forms. I have noted केओ *keō*, क्यो *kyō*, and केअओ *keao*. In old poetry we sometimes meet केदहु *kēduhu*.

167. When used as an adjective, it usually takes the form कोनो *kōno* or कौनो *kauno*, but we sometimes find केओ *keo* used instead.

The following are examples of its use as an adjective:—

कोनो नेना नहिं आएल *kōno nenā nahi̇ ãel*, no boy came.

कोनो गृहस्थक फुलवाड़ी में *kōno gṛhasthak phulᵃwāṛī mẽ*, in the garden of a certain householder.

कोनो बातक मन में अंदेशा मति राखी *kōno bātak man mẽ andēśā matⁱ rakhī*, do not have anxiety in your mind about anything.

कौनो मुसहर ने घर से होइत अछि बाहिर *kauno musahar nẽ ghar se hōit achⁱ bāhir*, no Musahar comes out of the house.

कौनो बात के हरकति नहिं *kauno bāt kē harᵃkatⁱ nahⁱ*, there is no inconvenience for (want of) anything.

केओ अपूर्व ढंगक लोक *keo apūrb ḍhaṅgak lōk*, a man of some extraordinary kind, or some man of an extraordinary kind.

It will be seen that when used as an adjective, it can refer to inanimate objects as well as animate ones.

168. When used as a substantive, it has an oblique form ककरहुँ *kakᵃrahũ*, often written ककरो *kakᵃrō*. Its genitive is ककर *kakᵃrō*. In poetry we sometimes find a form काहु *kāhu* instead of ककरहुँ *kakᵃrahũ*, with a genitive काहुक *kāhuka*. It is therefore thus declined:—

Singular.

Nom.	केओ *keo*, केओ *keō*, क्यो *kyō*, or केअओ *keaō*,	anyone, someone.
Acc.	ककरहुँ, *kak^{a}rah$^{\tilde{u}}$*, or ककरहुँ कें *kak^{a}rah$^{\tilde{u}}$ kẽ*	someone, or anyone.
Inst.	ककरहुँ सँ *kak^{a}rah$^{\tilde{u}}$ sẽ*, by anyone, etc.	
Dat.	ककरहुँ *kak^{a}rah$^{\tilde{u}}$*, or ककरहुँ कें *kak^{a}rah$^{\tilde{u}}$ kẽ*	to anyone, etc.
Abl.	ककरहुँ सँ *kak^{a}rah$^{\tilde{u}}$ sẽ*, from anyone, etc.	
Gen.	ककरो *kak^{a}rō*, of anyone, etc.	
Loc.	ककरहुँ मे *kak^{a}rah$^{\tilde{u}}$ mẽ*, in anyone, etc.	

The plural is the same as the singular. ककरो *kak^{a}rō* may be used for ककरहुँ *kak^{a}rah$^{\tilde{u}}$* throughout.

Examples of the use of this pronoun are:—

केओ नहिं आएल *keo nahĩ āel*, no one came.

क्यो घर अँगना केअओ दुआरि *kyō ghara ãganā keao duāri*, some (danced) in the courtyard of the house and some in the doorway (Manbōdh's *Harivaṁśā*, ii. 45).

निज भुज बल ककरहुँ नहिं गनए *nija bhuja bala kakarahũ nahi ganae*, (on account of) the strength of their own arms they esteem no one (Manbōdh, vi. 33).

किछु नहिं ततहुँ काहु सौं भेल *kichu nahĩ tatahũ kāhu sõ bhēla* from that quarter nothing (*i.e.*, no help) came from anyone (Manbōdh, i. 7).

क्यो नहिं मानए काहुक हटल *kyō nahĩ mānae kāhuka haṭalu*, no one heeds the remonstrances of anyone (Manbōdh, iv. 17).

169. The indefinite pronoun inanimate is किछु *kich^{u}* or किच्छु *kicch^{u}*. It means 'anything' and 'something.' When it means 'anything,' the oblique form is the same as the nominative, but

when it means 'something' its oblique form is कथू *kathū*. We therefore have the following declensions :—

170. किछु *kich*ᵘ, or किच्छु *kicch*ᵘ anything.

Nom. किछु *kich*ᵘ, anything.

Acc. किछु कें *kich*ᵘ *kẽ*, anything.

Inst. किछु सँ *kich*ᵘ *sã*, by anything.

Dat. किछु कें *kich*ᵘ *kẽ*, to anything.

Abl. किछु सँ *kich*ᵘ *sã*, from anything.

Gen. किछुक *kichuk*, of anything.

Loc. किछु में *kich*ᵘ *mẽ*, in anything.

171. किछु *kich*ᵘ, or किच्छु *kicch*ᵘ something.

Nom. किछु *kich*ᵘ, something.

Acc. कथू कें *kathū kẽ*, something.

Inst. कथू सँ *kathū sã*, by something.

Dat. कथू कें *kathū kẽ*, to something.

Abl. कथू सँ *kathū sã*, from something.

Gen. कथूक *kathūk*, of something.

Loc. कथू में *kathū mẽ*, in something.

Examples of the use of this pronoun are :—

ओहि ग्राम में ककरो किछु नहिं छैक *ohⁱ grām mẽ kakᵃrō kich*ᵘ *nahⁱ chaik*, in that village no one has anything.

किछु अमोट पठबिहँ *kich*ᵘ *amōṭ paṭhabihã*, send (me) some mango conserve.

ओ औखध कथू में धैल होतैक *ō aukhadh kathū mẽ dhail hotaik*, that medicine must be put into something.

172. The Indefinite pronoun कैएक *kaiek*, some, several, is an adjective, and is not declined. An example of its use is:—

> तोहरा कैएक कथा सभ सिखाए दिअऊ *toh*ᵃ*ra kaiek kathā sabh sikhāe diuh*ᵘ. I will teach you several matters.

Derivative Pronominal Forms.

173. The following table gives in a succinct shape the various derivative pronominal forms. It explains itself, and further comment is unnecessary:—

	Near Demonstrative.	Remote Demonstrative.	Interrogative.	Relative.	Correlative.
	ई *ī*, this.	ओ *ō*, that.	के *kē*, who?	जे *jē*, who, which.	से *sē*, that.
Time.	एखन *ekhan*, now.	तखन *takhan*, then.	कखन *kakhan*, when?	जखन *jakhan*, when.	तखन *takhan*, then.
Place.	एतय *etay*, here.	ओतय *otay*, there.	कतय *katay*, where?	जतय *jatay*, where.	ततय *tatay*, there.
	एम्हर *ēmhar*, hither.	ओम्हर *ōmhar*, thither.	केम्हर *kēmhar*, whither?	जेम्हर *jēmhar*, whither.	तेम्हर *tēmhar*, thither.
Manner.	एना *ēnā*, thus.	ओना *ōnā*, in that way.	केना *kēnā*, how?	जेना *jēnā*, as.	तेना *tēnā*, so.
Likeness.	एहन *ehan*, or ऐसन *aisan*, like this.	ओहन *ohan*, like that.	केहन *kehan*, like what?	जेहन *jehan*, like as.	तेहन *tehan*, like the same.
Quantity or Number.	एतेक *etek*, this much.	ओतेक *otek*, that much.	कतेक *katek*, how much?	जतेक *jatek*, as much.	ततेक *tatek*, so much.

PART III.

CONJUGATION.

CHAPTER I.

PRELIMINARY.

A. General Remarks.

174. The conjugation of the verb forms the most complicated part of Maithilī Grammar. Like the verbs of many partially cultivated languages, it has few parts for which there are not two or three optional forms. These are not local peculiarities, but may often be used by the same speaker as his fancy or as the rhythm of the sentence dictates. In many cases I cannot find that they represent different shades of meaning.

175. Maithilī verbs may conveniently be divided into the two classes of *Transitive* and *Intransitive*. These differ in the conjugation of the tenses formed from the past participle. In the paradigms of the regular verb, the verb देखब *dēkhab*, to see, will be used as the example of a transitive verb, and the verb सूतब *sūtab*, to sleep, as the example of an intransitive verb. It will be observed that in both these verbs the root-vowel is long, and it must be carefully remembered that in the conjugation of all such verbs, the root-vowel is liable to be shortened, under the rules given in § 32 and ff. *ante.* It is most important to bear this in mind, as the whole system of conjugation is full of it.

176. There is one exception to this rule of the shortened antepenultimate, and this is that when ऐ *ai*, or औ *au*, is *final*, it counts as only one syllable (even when written अइ *ai*, अए *ae*, or अउ *au*, अओ *ao*, respectively) and not as two (see §§ 13, 33 *ii*). Thus under the general rule, we should expect the *ē* in the form देखै *dēkhai*, to be shortened; but it is not. The reason for this apparent irregularity is that in verbal forms a final ऐ *ai* always represents an older अहि *ahⁱ*, and a final औ *au* always represents an older अहु *ahᵘ*, each of which. under the rule, counts only as one syllable. देखै *dēkhai* is for देखहि *dēkhahⁱ*, and देखौ *dekhau* is for देखहु *dekhahᵘ*, and in both of these older forms the long *ē* is quite regular. The apparent exception disappears when ऐ *ai* or औ ceases to be final. Thus in देखैक *dekhaik* (for देखहिक *dekhahik*) and देखौक *dekhauk* for देखहुक *dekhahuk*), the shortening of the *ē* to *e* is quite regular.

B. Root. Verbal Nouns and Participles.

177. It will be more convenient to deal with the finite tenses after we have described the root and the various verbal nouns and participles. The **Root** of every verb is the same as the shortest form of the second person non-honorific of the Old Present. Thus the 2nd pers. non-hon. Old Present of देखब *dēkhab*, to see, is देख *dēkh*, which is also the root.

178. The **Verbal nouns** are three in number.

(*a*) The first verbal noun is formed by adding इ ⁱ to the root. Thus देखि *dēkhⁱ* the act of seeing (see § 57). The final इ ⁱ is often omitted in writing and pronunciation, so that we have देख *dēkh* instead of देखि *dēkhⁱ*. Its oblique form is देखै *dēkhai* or देखँ *dēkha*, and the rules for its declension together with examples are given in § 80 *ante*. Some roots ending in vowels are irregular in the formation of the first verbal noun.

179. (*b*) The second verbal noun is usually formed by adding अब *ab* to the root (see § 67) and is generally employed as the infinitive; thus देखब *dēkhab*. the act of seeing, to see. Its oblique form is देखबा *dekhᵃbā*, and the rules for its declension together with examples are given in § 81 *ante*.

Verbs whose roots end in आ *ā* form their infinitives in एब *eb*. Thus from जा *jā*, we have जाएब *jāeb*, to go.

Those whose roots end in आब *āb*, also form their infinitives in एब *eb*, but with the elision of the ब *b* of the root. Thus from the root पाब *pāb*, obtain, we have the infinitive पाएब *pāeb*, to obtain. In poetry we often find ओब *ob* instead of एब *eb* in this case. Thus पाओब *pāob*.

Those verbs whose roots end in इ *i* or ई *ī*, form the infinitive in अब *ab* or उब *ub*. Thus, सि *si*, sew, makes सिअब *siab* or सिउब *siub*.

Those verbs whose roots end in ऊ *ū*, form the infinitive in अब *ab* or इब *ib*. Thus चू *cū*, drip, makes चूअब *cūab*, or चूइब *cūib*, to drip.

Those verbs whose roots end in ओ *ō*, form the infinitive in अब *ab* or एब *eb*. Thus the root धो *dhō*, wash, makes धोअब *dhōab* or धोएब *dhōeb*, to wash.

Irregular are :—

√ हो *hō*, become, Infinitive होएब *hōeb* or हैब *haib*.

√ दे *dē* give, Infinitive देब *dēb*.

√ ले *lē* take, Infinitive लेब *lēb*.

This verbal noun is derived from the Sanskrit future passive participle in तव्य *tavya*, and is hence employed in the formation of the future tense.

180. (*c*) The third verbal noun is formed by adding अल *al* to the root (see § 63). thus देखल *dekhal*, the act of seeing. The oblique form is देखला *dekhalā*, and the rules for its declension together with examples are given in § 81, *ante*. This verbal noun is generally the same as the past participle, but when the latter is irregular the verbal noun sometimes takes the regular form. Thus the √ जा *jā*, go, has its past participle (irregular) गेल *gēl*, but its third verbal noun is जाएल *jāel*. From this example it will be seen that (compare the second verbal noun), it ends sometimes in एल *el* instead of अल *al*. The rule is the same as in the case of अब *ab*.

The instrumental or locative of this verbal noun (or perhaps of the past participle) in अल *al*, is often used absolutely to indicate continued action. Thus :—एक गमारि गोआरिनि माथ पर मटकुरी धैलें चलि जाइछलि *ek gamāri goārini māth par maṭakurī dhailẽ cali jāichali*, a foolish milkmaid, *by placing a curd-pot on her head*, was going along. That is to say, she was going along with a curd-pot on her head.

Similarly we have from the √ ले *lē*, take, लेलें जाएब *lēlẽ jāeb*, to take away with one, लेलें आएब *lēlẽ āeb*, to bring with one. In such common phrases न *n* is often substituted for ल *l*, so that we have लेनें जाएब *lēnẽ jāeb* or even नेनें आएब *nēnẽ āeb*. These forms are different in meaning from forms such as लै जाएब *lai jāeb* (Hindi ले जाना *lē jānā*) to take away or लै आएब *lai āeb* (Hindī ले आना *lē ānā*) or लाएब *lāeb* (Hindī लाना *lānā*) to bring. They correspond rather to the Hindī लिये जाना *liyē jānā*, to take away *with one*.

Examples of such forms are :—

हमरा समाद नैहर लेनें जाह *hamarā samāda naihara lēnẽ jāhū*, take away with you a message for my father's house also (*Vid.* lxxix. 10).

अहिरा गोआर समाद नेनें अबैत छैक *ahirā goār samād nēnẽ abait chaik*, Ahirā Goār is bringing the news with him.

लै जाह सलहेस कें ... कचे बाँस के फठा सों पीठि ओदारि देब *lai jāh salahēs kẽ ... kacē bā̃s ke phaṭhā saũ pīṭhi odāri dēb*, take away Salhēs ... with a split piece of green bamboo flay his back. (बाँस के *bā̃s ke* is not a Maithilī form. It is borrowed, as often happens in folktales, from another dialect, *viz.*, Bhojpurī. The correct Maithilī would be बाँसक *bā̃sak* or बाँस केर *bā̃s kēr*.)

जकर बेदुली लाएल तकर तिरिआ केहन सुरखी *jakar beduli lāel takar tiriā kehan surakhī*, how fair must the woman who owns the spangle which you brought !

181. **The Noun of Agency,** corresponding to the Hindī noun in वाला *wālā*, is formed by adding बाह *bāh* or वाह *wāh* to the root. Thus देखबाह *dekh°bāh* or देखवाह *dekh°wāh*, a **seer,** one who sees. See § 72.

182. The **Present Participle** is formed by adding ऐत *ait*, often written अइत *ait* or अयित *ayit*, to the root (see § 64). Thus देखैत *dekhait*, देखइत *dekhait*, or देखयित *dekhayit*, seeing. The ऐ *ai* of this termination is very unstable. Thus with verbs whose roots end in a long vowel, the termination becomes इत *it*, as in जाइत *jāit*, going; होऐत *hōait*, or होइत *hōit*, becoming. The √ सि *si*, sew, has सिऐत *siait*, सिउत *siut*, and सिइत *siit*, but √ पी *pī*, drink, makes पिबैत *pibait*, just as √ पाब *pāb*, obtain, has पबैत *pabait*. The √ दे *dē*, give, and the √ ले *lē*, take, have, respectively, दैत *dait* and लैत *lait* for their present participles. In the Past Conditional tense, which is formed from this participle, the ऐत *ait* is, as a rule, similarly weakened. Thus देखितहुँ *dekhitah*[ũ], (if) I had seen.

183. By adding the oblique termination हिं *h*[i] to the weakened present participle we get a form called the "**Adverbial Participle.**" Thus देखितहिं *dekhitah*[i], on seeing, in the act of seeing, immediately on seeing, equivalent to the Hindī देखते-ही *dēkh*[a]*tē-hī*. The following are examples of the employment of these participles:—

कनैत खिजैत धामी आएल *kanait* (√ कान *kān*) *khijait* (√ खीज *khīj*) *dhāmī āel*, Dhāmī came weeping and feeling angry (note the shortening of the antepenultimate vowel).

हमरा सबहिक देखैत स्वामि-धन वृथा नष्ट होइछ *ham°rā sab°hik dekhait swāmi-dhan vṛthā naṣṭ hōich*, in our presence [*lit.* (in the) seeing of us] our master's property is being destroyed.

दीना राम के धरितहिं भद्रीक एहुनी केहुनी छुटि गेल *dīnā rām kē dharitah*[i] *bhadrīk ehunī kehunī chuṭ*[i] *gēl*, immediately on (Phoṭ°rā's) seizing Dīnā Rām, Bhadri's knees and elbows were freed.

184. The **Past Participle** is usually formed by adding अल *al* to the root (see § 68). When the root ends in a vowel, or in आब *āb*, the vowel of the suffix is liable to change, much as the termination अब *ab* of the second verbal noun is changed. Thus:—

Verbs whose roots end in आ *ā*, add एल *el*. Thus √ घबड़ा *ghabᵃrā*, to be agitated, past participle घबड़ाएल *ghabᵃṛāel*.

Verbs whose roots end in आब *āb*, add ओल *ol*. Thus, from √ पाब *pāb*, obtain, पाओल *pāol*.

Verbs whose roots end in इ *i* or ई *ī*, add अल *al* or उल *ul*. Thus from √ सि *si*, sew, सिअल *sial* or सिउल *siul*, from √ पी *pī*, drink, पीउल *pīul*.

Verbs whose roots end in ऊ *ū* take अल *al* or इल *il*. Thus, from √ चू *cū*, drip, चूअल *cūal* or चूइल *cūil*.

Verbs whose roots end in ओ *ō* take अल *al* or एल *el*. Thus, from √ धो *dhō*, wash, धोअल *dhōal* or धोएल *dhōel*.

Six verbs have irregular past participles as follows:—

√ कर *kar*, do	Past Participle	कैल *kail*.
√ धर *dhar*, seize, place	..	धैल *dhail*.
√ मर *mar*, die	..	मरल *maral* or मुइल *muil*.
√ दे *dē*, give	..	देल *dēl*.
√ ले *lē*, take	..	लेल *lēl*.
√ हो *hō*, become	..	भेल *bhēl*.

The past participle भेल *bhēl*, added to another past participle, imparts to it more of the character of an adjective, and, at the same time, adds completeness to the idea. Thus, सूतल भेल, *sūtal bhēl*, asleep; देखल भेल *dēkhal bhēl*, seen.

The instrumental of the past participle is employed in conjugation to form the perfect and pluperfect tenses.

I have not come across many good instances in literature of the use of the past participle as an adjective. It is, of course, extremely commonly employed in the formation of the tenses. The following may be taken as examples of the adjectival use :—

एक गरीब परोसिया जाड़क मारल घर सँ निकसि आएल, *ek garīb parosiyā jāṛak māral ghar sȧ̃ nikas^i āel*, a poor neighbour. struck of (*i.e.* by) cold. came forth from (his) house.

एक कंगाल कोनो पहुँचल अतीथि सँ पुछलक, *ek kaṅgāl kōno pahũcal atith^i sȧ̃ puchalak*, a beggar once asked from a certain arrived pilgrim (*i.e.* a pilgrim who had arrived).

185. **The Conjunctive Participle** corresponds to the Hindī देख कर *dēkh kar*, having seen, and is properly the same in form as the first verbal noun. Thus, देखि *dēkh^i* (or देख *dēkh*), having seen. This is the form we generally find in poetry or proverbs. but in the modern language it is usual to add the suffixes के *ke*. कैं *kaĩ*, कँ *kȧ̃*, or कैकँ *kaikȧ̃*. Thus देखि के *dēkh^i ke*. देखि कैं *dēkh^i kaĩ*, देखि कँ *dēkh^i kȧ̃*, or देखि कैकँ *dēkh^i kaikȧ̃*. having seen. A poetical form of कँ *kȧ̃* is कहुँ *kah^u*. thus डूबि कहुँ *dūb^i kah^u*, having dived. The following verbs have irregular conjunctive participles. Only the short form is given in each case. The suffixes can be added as usual :—

कर *kar*, do	Conj. Part.	करि *kar^i*, के *ke*, कै *kai*, or कय *kay*. कए *kae*, कँ *kȧ*.
धर *dhar*, seize. place.	..	धरि *dhar^i*, धै *dhai*, or धय *dhay*. धए *dhae*, धँ *dhȧ*.
आ *ā*, come	..	आबि *āb^i*, आइ *āi*, or आय *āy*.
दे *dē*, give	..	दे *dē*, दै *dai*, दय *day*, दए *dae*. देइ *dei*. दँ *dȧ*.
ले *lē*, take	..	ले *lē*, लै *lai*, लय *lay*, लए *lae*, लेइ *lei*. लँ *lȧ*.
हो *hō*, become	..	होइ *hoi*, भै *bhai*. भय *bhay*, भए *bhae*.

C. Finite Tenses.

186. **Gender.**—As in the case of nouns, the Maithilī verb has two genders, Masculine and Feminine. Feminine forms are,

as a rule, only used when the subject is a feminine animate being. The first person never shows any distinction of gender, nor do those forms (see § 188, below) in which respect is shown to the object. It follows that only those forms of the 2nd and the 3rd persons, whose objects are non-honorific (Groups I and II below), ever change for the feminine gender. Even in these persons there are many forms which are of common gender.

187. **Long and Redundant Forms.**—Verbs have short, long, and redundant forms just like nouns. I have not discovered any difference in their meaning. The long form is most often made by adding ऐ *ai* to the short form, and the redundant form by adding क *k* to the long form. Thus we have (short form) देखैछी *dekhaichī*, I see, of which the long form is देखैछिऐ *dekhaichiai*, and the redundant form is देखैछिऐक *dekhaichiaik*. Similarly, we have (short form) देखलक *dekhᵃlak*, he saw, long form देखलकै *dekhalᵃkai*, redundant form देखलकैक *dekhalᵃkaik*. In some forms of the second person the long form is made by adding अँह *åh* or अहु *ahᵘ* and the redundant form by adding अँहक *ᵃhåk* or अहुक *ᵃhuk* with variations of spelling, which will appear in the paradigms. Thus, देख *dēkh*, thou seest, long form देखँह *dēkhåh* or देखहु *dēkhahᵘ*, redundant form देखहँक *dekhᵃhåk* or देखहुक *dekhᵃhuk*.

These long and redundant forms are confined to those groups of inflexions in which the object is non-honorific (*vide* § 188). Even then, there is no long or redundant form for the third person when the subject is honorific. They are thus confined to the following cases.

First and second persons—Subject non-honorific, object non-honorific (Group I), or subject honorific, object non-honorific (Group II).

Third person—Subject non-honorific, object non-honorific (Group I).

These groups are described below in § 188.

Examples of the employment of these long and redundant forms are as follows :—

1st Person. Short Form :—मारब धनुखा देब खँसाब, *mārab*

dhanukhā, dēb khasāy. I will strike him (with an arrow) from the bow, I will fell him.

Long Form:—एहि बेरिया मारबै धरती देबै लोटाय, *eh^{i} beriyā mār^{a}bai, dhar^{a}tī dēbai loṭāy*, at this time I will strike him, I will cause him to roll upon the ground.

Redundant Form:—ताहि ठाम देबैक धुनी खसाय, *tāh^{i} ṭhām debaik dhunī khasāy*, at that place we shall set (*lit.* cause to fall) our fire (on the ground).

3rd Person. Short Form:—घड़ि एक चलबे पहर बिति गेल *ghaṛ^{i} ek cal^{a}bē pahar bit^{i} gēl*, after travelling a few (*lit.* one) half-hours, a watch (of the day) passed.

Long Form:—तखन गेलै गंगुआ हजमुआ, *takhan gēlai Gāguā haja-muā*, then Gangū the barber went.

Redundant Form.—सात नींदे सूतलि छलैक फेकुनी काँचे नींद में उठलैक चिहाय, *sāt nīdē sūtal^{i} chalaik phekunī, kācē nīd mē uṭh^{a}laik cihāy*, Phekuni was sleeping in seven sleeps (at once), and in drowsiness she started up.

188. **Number. Non-honorific and Honorific forms.**—Before going further it must be explained once for all that the Maithili verb does not change for number. There is no distinction between singular and plural. On the other hand, there is a distinction between the non-honorific and honorific forms (which, indeed, by derivation, are respectively singular and plural). In the finite tenses there are thus four groups of forms for each person, according as the subject or as the object is treated honorifically.

These four groups are :—

(I) Subject non-honorific ; object non-honorific. *E.g.*, he (a slave) or it sees him (a slave) or it.

(II) Subject honorific ; object non-honorific. *E.g.*, he (a king) sees him (a slave) or it.

(III) Subject non-honorific ; object honorific. *E.g.*, he (a slave) or it sees him (a king).

(IV) Subject honorific ; object honorific. *E.g.*, he (a king) sees him (a king).

Except in the case of the 3rd person of group IV, all the

forms of groups III and IV (in which the object is honorific) are made from the long forms of groups I and II (in which it is non-honorific) respectively, by lengthening the final vowels when necessary, and adding न्हि *nh*^{i}.

In the case of the 3rd person of group IV, there is no long form of the 3rd person of group II from which to make it. It is therefore made from the short form of the 3rd person of group II, in a manner similar to that of the formation of the other persons of group IV.

Examples of these third and fourth groups are:—

1st person: long form, groups I and II, देखैछिऐ *dekhaichiai*, I see; groups III and IV, देखैछिऐन्हि *dekhaichiainh*^{i}.

2nd person: long form, group I, देखैछहु *dekhaichah*^{u}, you see; group III, देखैछहून्हि *dekhaichahūnh*^{i}.

2nd person: long form, group II, देखैछिऐ *dekhaichiai*, you (honorific) see; group IV, देखैछिऐन्हि *dekhaichiainh*^{i}.

3rd person: long form, group I, देखैछै *dekhaichai*, he sees; group III, देखैछैन्हि *dekhaichainh*^{i}.

3rd person: short form, group II, देखैछथि *dekhaichath*^{i}, he (honorific) sees; group IV, देखैछथीन्हि *dekhaichathīnh*^{i}.

In the above explanations I have employed the words "slave" and "king" to illustrate the non-honorific and honorific forms respectively, but, in common use, the distinction is not nearly so marked as this. As a practical guide, we may say that human beings are generally referred to by honorific forms, unless they are distinctly inferior, such as low-caste people, slaves, etc. On the other hand, inanimate things and irrational animals are almost always referred to as non-honorific.

In regard to Groups III and IV, I have said that the *object* must be honorific. The object may be the direct object or may be the indirect object. Either has the same effect on the verbal form. Thus, in the second, fourth and sixth of the following examples, of the use of these forms, the honorific object is indirect:—

First person (Groups I and II) and second person (Group II) (long forms) (as will be seen from § 190, these three are always the same in form). एहि बेरिया मारबै धरती देबै लोटाय, *ehi beriyā mārabai, dharatī debai loṭāy*, this time I will strike him and cause him to roll over (on) the ground.

First person (Groups III and IV) and second person (Group IV). सभ मशाला लछमी दाइ कें अपने चुप्पे देबैन्हि, *sabh maśālā Lachamī Dāi kẽ apane cuppē debainhi*, your Honour will give all the spices privately to (the respected) Lakṣmī Dāi.

Second person (Group I) (long form). कोन दिसा के अबैत होइ कहहु बुझाय, *kōn disā kē abait hōai kahahu bujhāy*, explain and tell in what direction he is coming.

Second person (Group III). कालू सदा अम्मा निरसों के कहहुन्हि जोगिया जाई, *Kālū Sadā Ammā Nirasō kē kahahūnhi Jogiyā jāī*, say to (the respected) Kālū Sadā and mother Nirsō, 'go to Jogiyā.'

Third person (Group I) (long form). ओकरा एहि तरहें घबड़ाएल देखि कँ एक मनुष्य॰ कहलकै, *okarā ehi tarahẽ ghabaṛāel dekhi kã ek manuṣya kahalakai*, seeing him (the fool) thus agitated a certain man said to him—.

Third person (Group III). मोनशी कहलथीन्हि नहिं हौ, अर्जी लिखैछी। ओ कहलकैन्हि तँ हमरो सही कै दिअ, *monaśī kahalathīnhi* (Group IV), '*nahi hau, arjī likhaichī.*' *Ō kahalakainhi*, '*tã hamarō sahī kai dia*, the (respected) scribe I said (politely) to (the unknown and respected stranger), 'it is not (what you think it is, —*hau* not *hai*. see § 101), I am writing a petition.' He (*i.e.* the stranger who was an impudent fool) said (to the respected scribe), 'then please to put my signature also.'

Third person (Group II) (short form). देहि दुनू भाइ छोड़ि देलथि, *dehi dunū bhāi choṛi delathi*, the two (famous) brothers (the heroes of the story) left their bodies.

Third person (Group IV). कालू सदा दीना भद्री के बैसै देलथीन्हि, *Kālū Sadā Dīnā Bhadrī kē baisai delathīnhi*, (the respected) Kālū Sadā made (the two famous brothers) Dīnā and Bhadri sit down.

Another example occurs above under 'Third person (Group III).'

189. So far we have been dealing only with transitive verbs. Intransitive verbs have only an indirect object, and, in their case, the use of Groups III and IV is rather lax. They are, of course, employed when the indirect object is honorific, but they are also found when the verb has no object at all and when the *subject*, not the object is honorific. Thus: –

तखन गंगा-जी कहै लगलथीन्हि, *takhan Gaṅgā-jī kahai lagal^a-thīnh^i*, then they began to say to (the holy) Ganges.

बहुत दिन भेलैन्हि अहाँ लोकनि तकाजा नहिँ करैछिऐन्हि, *bahut din bhelainh^i ahā̃ lok^ani takājā nah^ĩ karaichiainh^i*, many days (have) passed (since) you (*honorific*) have pressed (the respected Bhōlā Sāhu) (for the money he owes).

In the former of these two examples it will be seen that the honorific object is indirect. In the second example the close connection with a sentence having an honorific subject and an honorific direct object as well, is responsible for the form of भेलैन्हि *bhelainh^i*.

Instances of intransitive verbs with an honorific subject are much more common, especially when the subject is plural. In fact we have here a survival of the old plural signification of these forms (see the first paragraph of § 188).

Thus:—

दीना भद्री मरि गेलैन्हि, *Dīnā Bhadrī mar^i gelainh^i* (Group III), Dīnā and Bhadrī are dead. Here, if the verb were transitive, the subject would be non-honorific, as the form belongs to Group III. In an intransitive verb it is honorific plural.

जाहि सँ नाम चलैन्हि से हमर किरिया करँह, *jāh^i sã nām calainh^i sē hamar kiriyā karȁh*, perform our funeral rites that our (famous) names may be current (*i.e.* endure).

कोनो धनिक कँ दुइ बेटा रहैन्हि । जखन हुनक बाप मरि गेलथीन्हि *kōno dhanik kẽ dui bēṭā rahainhi* (Group III). *Jakhan hunak bāp mari gelathīnhi*, to a certain (respected) rich man there were two (respected) sons. When the (respected) father of (the respected) them died ....

190. **Person.**—It is in denoting the persons that the complex character of the Maithili verb is most manifest. There are many forms for each person. The following is a brief sketch of personal terminations.

In the first case we must note that the first person is the same whether the subject is honorific or not; also that the second person honorific is always the same as the first person. Thus देखैछी *dekhaichī* means I or we (non-honorific), or I or we (honorific) see, or thou (honorific) seest, or you (honorific) see.

191. **The rule of attraction.**—In the case of some of the personal terminations, there is an important rule to be applied. It is called *the rule of attraction*, and is peculiar to Bihāri. We have seen that when the object of a verb is honorific certain special forms are used. Similarly, there are special forms when the object is in the second person. These forms only occur in the case of forms with a non-honorific object whose terminations contain the letter ऐ *ai*, and are made by changing ऐ *ai* to औ *au*. Thus देखलक *dekh^a^lak*, देखलकै *dekhal^a^kai*, or देखलकैक *dekhal^a^kaik*, he saw, but देखलक *dekh^a^lak*, देखलकौ *dekhal^a^kau*, or देखलकौक *dekhal^a^kauk*, he saw *you*. The relationship of the second person with the object need not be very direct, as will be seen from the fourth of the following examples :—

मुरता नेना कँ मारलकै, *Mur^a^tā nēnā kẽ māral^a^kai*, Murtā struck the boy.

मुरता तोहरा कँ मारलकौ, *Mur^a^tā toh^a^rā kẽ māral^a^kau*, Murtā struck you.

ओकरा गाड़ी में कोन माल छै, *ok^a^rā gāṛī mẽ kōn māl chai*, what goods are there in his cart ?

तोहरा गाड़ी में कोन माल छौ *tōh^a^rā gāṛī mẽ kōn māl chau*, what goods are there in your cart ?

Note further, as to spelling, that the ै *ai* is quite frequently written अइ *ai*, अए *ae* or even अय *ay*, so that instead of छै *chai* in the penultimate example we may have छइ *chai*, छए *chae* or छय *chay*. Similarly instead of ौ *au*, we may have अउ *au* or अओ *ao*. Thus instead of छौ *chau* we sometimes see written छउ *chau* or छओ *chao*. Historically, these ौ *au* terminations are contractions of अहु *ahu*, and we sometimes come across this spelling, especially in poetry. Thus for दिऔ *diau*, let me give you, I have met दिअहु *diahu*, which has the same meaning.

192. It will be remembered that the 2nd person honorific is always the same as the first person. With regard to this there is one reservation, viz., *that the rule of attraction does not apply to the second person.* Thus देखैछिऔ *dekhaichiau*, means only 'I, or we. see you'; it does not mean 'you (honorific) see you.' In the second person the termination ौ *au* is only used to refer to the subject. Thus in the *Git Dina-bhadri* (149). we have जेबौ जोगिया जहाँ गाम *jaibau Jogiyā jahā̃ gām*, you will go to where is the village of Jogiyā. In the first person जेबौ *jaibau* would mean 'I will go to your (house, or some such word).' Moreover 'you see you' would be an impossible idea in Maithili. We should have to say 'you see (your) self,' which is a different thing altogether and does not bring in the rule of attraction. It thus follows that the rule of attraction only applies to the first and third persons. Examples are :—

First person, देखलिऐ *dekhaliai*, देखलिऐक *dekhaliaik*, I or we saw; देखलिऔ *dekhaliau* or देखलिऔक *dekhaliauk*, I or we saw you.

Third person, non-honorific subject, non-honorific object देखलकै *dekhalakai* or देखलकैक *dekhalakaik*, he or they saw; देखलकौ *dekhalakau* or देखलकौक *dekhalakauk*, he or they saw you.

I have very rarely come across forms like देखलकौन्हि *dekhalakaunhi* (from देखलकैन्हि *dekhalakainhi*), he (non-honorific) saw you (honorific) (Group III), but I doubt if they were correct. I have never met such in conversation. At the same time it may be noted that in the present conjunctive there is a form in औन्हि *aunh*[i], which is peculiar to this tense, and which has no special reference to the 2nd person. It has nothing to do with the rule of attraction.

On the other hand, just as a redundant form is obtained by changing ऐ *ai* to ऐक *aik*, so a redundant form is quite commonly made by changing औ *au* to औक *auk*. Thus the redundant form of देखलिऔ *dekh*[a]*liau* is देखलिऔक *dekh*[a]*liauk*. as in the above examples.

193. **Other Personal Terminations.**—Before taking up the general aspect of this question, we may notice the frequently occurring terminations अथि *ath*[i] and अन्हि *anh*[i]. These are peculiar in the third person in the second group, in which the subject only is honorific. *In the tenses formed from the past participle,* अथि *ath*[i] is used only with transitive verbs, but अन्हि *anh*[i] is not subject to this restriction.

In the case of intransitive verbs, we have आह *ăh*, instead of अथि *ath*[i], in the tenses formed from the past participle. But आह *ăh* is not confined to the 3rd person. In the 3rd person it is honorific like अथि *ath*[i], but it can also be employed for the second person *non-honorific*. Thus सुतलाह *sut*[a]*lăh* means either 'he or they (honorific) slept.' or else 'thou or you (non-honorific) slept.'

आह *ăh*. is also used honorifically in the third person of the future of both transitive and intransitive verbs.

आह *ăh* has a feminine form ईह *īh* or ईहि *īh*[i]. Thus सुतलीह *sut*[a]*līh* or सुतलीहि *sut*[a]*līh*[i], she or they (fem.) (honorific) slept or thou or you (fem. non-hon.) slept. अथि *ath*[i] and अन्हि *anh*[i] have no special feminine forms. They are of common gender.

We may give the following examples of the use of these terminations :—

अन्हि *anh*[i].

Past Conditional (formed from present participle)—औतन्हि दुरागमन करैतन्हि जमैया जाँजरि, *antanh*[i] (intransitive), *durāgaman karaitanh*[i] (transitive) *jamaiyā Jā̃jar*[i] (if) (the two famous) sons-in-law had come, they would have performed (the ceremony of) *durāgaman* at Jānjari.

Past Indicative (formed from past participle)—बड़ फभैत दीना भद्री कैलन्हि दुनू भाइ, *bar phajhait Dinā Bhadri kailanh*[i] (transitive) *dunū bhāi*. great indignity did the two (famous) brothers, Dīnā and Bhadrī (to me).

Perfect (formed from past participle)—फेर ऐलन्हि अछि से देखलक लोग सभ, *pher ailanh*[i] *ach*[i] *sē dekh*[a]*lak lōg sabh*, the people saw (that) (the respected Dīnā and Bhadrī) have come back.

In old poetry, this termination is often written as a suffix, without the disappearance of the initial अ *a*. Thus, we have in Manbōdh's *Haribans* :—

कनक मुकुट झलकल-अन्हि द्वार, *kanaka mukuṭa jhalakala-anhi dwāra*, the golden diadem gleamed in the doorway.

जनि झपटल-अन्हि बाज बटेरि, *jani jhapaṭala-unhi bāja baṭēri*, as a falcon swooped upon a quail

In the old poetry we even find this termination suffixed to the termination आह *āh* as in the following passage from the same poem :—

कहु खन नाचथि गाबथि गीत ।
खैताह-अन्हि से परलए बीत ॥

Kahu khana nācathi gābathi gīta.
Khaitāha-anhi sē paralae bīta.

(The child Kṛṣṇa) sometimes danceth and sometimes singeth songs. (if) he will eat (transitive future), a whole age passeth away (*i.e.*, an age used to pass even in getting him away from his play to eat).

So we have it added to the termination अथि *ath*^{i}, in the following from the same :—

पूछथि-अन्हि तौं भद्वा कहब, *pūchathi-anhi taũ bhad*^{a}*bā kahaba*, if he (Kṛṣṇa) ask you, then you will say that it is an unlucky day.

अथि *ath*^{i}.

Old Present (formed from the root) :—

कनक धामी के कहिहौन्हि बुझाय। दुनू बेटीक कहिहौन्हि जे कोहबर करथि तैयार। दुनू जमाय मारल गेलैन्हि।

Kanak Dhāmī kē kahihaunh^{i} *bujhāy, dunū bēṭīk kahihaunh*^{i} *jē koh*^{a}*bar karath*^{i} (transitive) *taiyār, dunū jamāy māral gelainh*^{i},

Tell and explain to (the respected) Kanak Dhāmī. Tell him that the two (respected) sons-in-law for whom he (the respected one) is preparing the marriage bowers of his two daughters, have been slain.

कालू सदा बैठल रहथि दरबाजा, *Kālū Sadā baiṭhal rahath*^{i} (intransitive) *dar*^{a}*bājā* (the respected) Kālū Sadā was (*lit.* remains) seated at his doorway.

Past indicative (formed from past participle) :—

देहि दुनू भाइ छोड़ि देलथि, *dēh*^{i} *dunū bhāi chōṛ*^{i} *dēlath*^{i}, the two (famous) brothers left their bodies

आह *ăh*. *Third person honorific.*

Future Indicative (transitive or intransitive) :—राजा भीम सेन कहताह हाल हम नहिं जानी, *rājā Bhīm Sain kah*^{a}*tăh hāl, ham nah*^{ĩ} *jānī*, Rājā Bhīm Sēn will tell (transitive) the affair, we do not know.

जाहि तरह जाति में रहताह से उपाय के देबहीन्हि, *jāh*^{i} *tarah jāt*^{i} *mẽ rah*^{a}*tăh sē upāy ke deb*^{a}*hīnh*^{i}, you will arrange so that they may remain (intransitive) in caste.

Past Indicative (only intransitive) :—भद्रीक आगू सल्हेस भै गेलाह ठाढ़ि, *Bhadrik āgū Salhēs bhai gēlāh ṭhāṛh*^{i}, before Bhadri (the famous) Salhēs took his stand.

Feminine examples are :—डेगे डेगे चललीह जोजन भरि जाइ जुमलीह अपना फुलवाड़ी, *ḍēgē ḍēgē cal*^{a}*līh, jōjan bhar*^{i} *jāi jum*^{a}*līh ap*^{a}*nā phul*^{a}*wāṛī*, step by step she went, having gone a full league she arrived at her garden.

धामीक सबद सुनि उठलीहि दीना भद्रीक माइ चिहाय, *Dhāmīk subad sun*^{i} *uṭh*^{a}*līh*^{i} *Dīnā Bhadrīk māi cihāy*, hearing Dhāmī's voice, the mother of Dīnā and Bhadrī started up.

Second person non honorific : कोन गरू परल जे सुतलाह खटबाढ़ि, *kaun garū paral jē sut*^{a}*lăh khaṭ*^{a}*bāṛ*^{i}, what calamity has befallen (you) that you are sleeping on your bed ?

194. **Tenses.** The tenses of the Maithilī verb are the same as in Bengali, and are conjugated very similarly in their main principles.

We may divide them into—

(*a*)—Tenses formed from the root.
(*b*)—The Future.
(*c*)—Tenses formed from the Present Participle.
(*d*)—Tenses formed from the Past Participle.

The first three classes are conjugated in the same way whether a verb is transitive or intransitive ; but the tenses formed from the past participle are conjugated differently according to whether the verb is transitive or intransitive. In this respect, we may note that the verb substantive is treated as intransitive.

The following is a list of the more usual tenses :—

(*a*) (1) Old Present Indicative
(2) Present Conditional
(3) Imperative
formed from the root.

(*b*) (4) Future Indicative
of mixed formation.

(*c*) (5) Past Conditional
(6) Present Indicative
(7) Imperfect Indicative
formed from the present participle.

(*d*) (8) Past Indicative
(9) Perfect Indicative
(10) Pluperfect Indicative
formed from the past participle.

195. I now proceed to give the personal terminations of these tenses in the case of regular verbs whose roots end in consonants. When a root ends in a vowel, the addition of the termination causes some anomalies which will be discussed under the head of Vocalic Roots in Chapter IV. Similarly, there are a few irregular verbs which will be specially dealt with in Chapter V.

Some of the examples which I give of the various terminations, are instances of these anomalous formations. I had to do this when no other examples were available. In such cases I have invariably drawn attention to the fact, or have given a reference to the section where the anomaly is dealt with.

When there are two or more forms in use for one person of one group or section of a group, I put the one most commonly employed first. The order of forms in the following paradigms has nothing to do with derivation. In fact, the oldest forms, being seldom employed, usually come last. For instance, the termination *iah*ᵘ of the long form of the first person, Groups I and II with the object in the second person, of the Old Present, is certainly the original of the termination *iau*. But I put *iau* first because it is the one commonly met with. *Iah*ᵘ is seldom heard, and the third termination given in the paradigms, *iå*, only occurs in poetry. Unless feminine forms are specially given, all forms are of common gender.

196. The three tenses formed from the root,—the Old Present, the Present Conditional, and the Imperative,—are all really variants of one tense. Custom has, however, ordained slight variations in the conjugation according to the use to which the tense is put. It will be seen (§ 201) that this tense is also employed as a future.

(*a*) (1) The **Old Present** is not much used now-a-days, except in poetry and proverbs and in idiomatic phrases, such as की कही *kī kahī*, what am I to say? It is conjugated by adding the personal terminations to the root direct. These are as follows:—

PERSON.	SHORT FORM.		LONG FORM.		REDUNDANT FORM.			
	GROUP I. (Subject: non-honorific. Object: non-honorific.)	GROUP II. (Subject: honorific. Object: non-honorific).	GROUP I. (Subject: non-honorific. Object: non-honorific).	GROUP II. (Subject: honorific. Object: non-honorific).	GROUP I. (Subject: non-honorific. Object: non-honorific).	GROUP II. (Subject: honorific. Object: non-honorific).	GROUP III. (Subject: non-honorific. Object: honorific).	GROUP IV. (Subject: honorific. Object: honorific).
1	*ĩ*, (Groups I and II)		*iai* Or (with object in 2nd person). *iau*, *iaũ*^{u}, or **iā̃* (Groups I and II)		*iaik*. Or (with object in 2nd person). *iauk*. (Groups I and II)		*iainh*^{i} (Groups III and IV)	
2	(The bare root).	Same as 1st person.	*ā̃h*, *ah*^{u}, *au*; fem. *ah*^{i}, *ā̃h*^{i}.	Same as 1st person, but no forms for object in 2nd person.	*ahā̃k*, *ahuk*, *ahik*.	Same as 1st person, but no forms for object in 2nd person.	*ahũnh*^{i}.	Same as 1st person.
3	*ĕ*. **a*, **u* **ahĩ*.	*ath*^{i}.	*ai* (*ae*). Or (with object in 2nd person.) *au* (or *ah*^{u}.)	......	*aik*. Or (with object in 2nd person.) *auk*.	......	*ainh*^{i}.	*athĩnh*^{i}. *athũnh*^{i}.

In the above, forms which are chiefly employed in poetry are marked with an asterisk Besides these we may mention a non-honorific first person singular in *ŏ* occasionally used by the vulgar, and an old form of the second person in *asi*, found in Vidyāpati. Thus:—

पुरबहि बन्दौं सुरुज *purubahi̐ bandŏ suruj*, in the East I worship the sun.

मृगमद पंक करसि अँग राजा *mrga-mada paṅka karasi ãga rājā*, with paste of musk dost thou anoint (thy) limbs Vid. xii. 2)

As examples of the use of this tense, we may quote the following:—

First Person: मरी पिश्रास पिश्राबऊ पानि, *marī piāsa piābahu pāni*, I die of thirst, give me water to drink (Vid. xii, 2).

आज देखिऐ सखि बड़ि अनुमनि सनि, *ăja* (for *āja*) *dekhiai sakhi baṛi anumani sani*, to-day, O friend, I see her very melancholy (Vid. xxxiv, 1).

कहियो न जनिश्रौ पँचा उधार, *kahiyŏ na janiau* (√ *jān*) *pãca udhār*, never do we know (of) borrowing or taking (things) on credit from you.

देखिअ तुअ अपरुब सभ साज, *dekhiă tua aparuba sabha sāja*, I see thee arrayed in wondrous raiment (Vid. xii, 1).

दौरी गाम सुनिऐक, *Daurī gām suniaik*, I hear (the name of) the village Daurī.

Second Person:—(I have not come across any instance of the second person of this tense used in literature There are examples of this person in the Present Conditional, and in the Imperative.)

Third Person: नहिँ नहिँ करे नयन ढर लोरे, *nahĩ nahĩ karē nayana ḍhura lōrē*, she says 'no, no.' and tears flow from her eyes (Vid. xxviii 5).

साजनि ताक जिबन थिक सार। जे मन दइ कर पर उपकार *sājani tāka jibana thika sāra, jē mana dai karu para upkāra*, O friend, behold, his life is precious, who willingly rendereth assistance to others (Vid. iii, 3).

राऊ दूरि बसु निश्ररो न आबथि तैँ नहिँ करथि गरासे, *Rāhu dūri basu niaro na ābathi, tē nahĩ karathi garāsē*, Rāhu (the demon of eclipse) (*i.e.*, her hair) dwelleth afar off, and doth not approach (the sun and moon, *i.e.*, her eyes), and therefore he doth not eclipse them (Vid. xiv, 8).

कटला तरु जक खसु अड़राय, *kaṭalā taru jaka khasu aṛarāya*, she falls screaming like a severed tree (Man. ii, 52).

भनहिं बिद्यापति, *bhanahī Bidyāpati*, saith Vidyāpati (Vid. passim).

आगु आगु डोली चलै पाछू पाछू दुनू भाइ, *āgū āgū ḍōlī calai, pāchū pāchū dunū bhāi*, in front go the litters (and) behind the two brothers.

हाथ माँथ मीड़ै पीटै, *hāth mā̃th mīṛai pīṭai*, she wrings her hands and beats her head (in sorrow).

दौरी गाम सुनिऐक बसैक हिरिया तमोलिनि जिरिया लोहाइनि, *Daurī gām suniaik basaik Hiriyā Tamōlin[i] Jiriyā Lohāin[i]*, I hear (the name of) a village called Daurī, (where) dwell Hirā Tamōlini and Jirā Lohāini.

इतनी लिखैक मिनतिया, *it[a]nī likhaik minatiyā*, so much (in the way of) respectful salutations he writes.

दीना भद्रीक कनैन्हि जोगिया दोस्त महीम, *Dīnā Bhadrīk kanainh[i]* (√ *kān*) *Jogiyā dōst mahīm*, the friends and lovers of (the respected) Dīnā and Bhadrī all weep in Jogiyā.

198. (*a*) (2). The **Present Conditional** is only a variant of the Old Present, from which it is derived. It prefers to substitute औ *au* for ऐ *ai*, in the third person. In this case the औ *au* (also written अहु ah^{u} or ओ *ō*) does not indicate that the object is in the second person. The forms in ऐ *ai* of the Old Present are also occasionally met in this tense. The following are the terminations. Those marked with an asterisk are chiefly used in poetry:—

PERSON.	SHORT FORM.		LONG FORM.		REDUNDANT FORM.			
	GROUP I. (Subject: non-honorific. Object: non-honorific.)	GROUP II. (Subject: honorific. Object: non-honorific.)	GROUP I. (Subject: non-honorific. Object: non-honorific.)	GROUP II. (Subject: honorific. Object: non-honorific.)	GROUP I. (Subject: non-honorific. Object: non-honorific.)	GROUP II. (Subject: honorific. Object: non-honorific.)	GROUP III. (Subject: non-honorific. Object: honorific.)	GROUP IV. (Subject: honorific. Object: honorific.)
1	*ī*		*iai* Or (with object in 2nd person.) *iau*, iah^{u}, **iå*		*iaik* Or (with object in 2nd person). *iauk*		$iainh^{i}$	
2	(The bare root).	Same as 1st person.	*åh*, ah^{u}, *au*; fem. $ah^{\tilde{i}}$, $\mathring{a}h^{\tilde{i}}$.	Same as 1st person, but no forms for object in 2nd person.	*ahåk*, *ahuk*, *ahik*.	Same as 1st person, but no forms for object in 2nd person.	$ah\bar{u}nh^{i}$.	Same as 1st person.
3	*ē*, **a*, **u*.	ath^{i}, ath^{u}.	*au*, ah^{u}, *ō*, (sometimes *ai*).	...	*auk* (sometimes *aik*)	...	$ainh^{i}$ $aunh^{i}$.	$ath\bar{i}nh^{i}$, $ath\bar{u}nh^{i}$.

The following are examples of the use of this tense :—

First person :—आठम दीन चोर माल हाजिर करी नहिं हाजिर करी तौ नौम दीन तोहरा सौं बिबाह करी, *āṭham dīn cōr māl hājir karī* (future) ; *nahi hājir karī* (pres. conditional), *tau naum dīn tohᵃrā saũ bibāh karī* (future), on the eighth day I will produce the thief (and) the stolen), property ; (if) I do not produce (them), then on the ninth day I will marry you.

की कहिऔक *kī kahiauk*, what am I to say (on your behalf).

Second person :—जखन अपने चाही तखन तोड़वा लेल जाइ, *jakhan apᵒne cāhī, takhan toṛᵒwā lēl jāī*, when you, sir, may desire, then have (the fruit) plucked and take it away.

सत्य० पूछी *satya pūchī*, (if) your honour ask the truth.

Third person :—आगि लागल झोँपड़ी जे निकसै से लाभ, *āgi lāgal jhõpᵒṛī, jē nikᵒsē sē lābh*, when a cottage is on fire whatever may come out (may be rescued), that is (clear) profit.

कौन दिशा के अबैत होए कहहु बुझाय, *kaun disā kē abait hōai kahahu bujhāy*, tell clearly in what direction he is (*lit.* may be) coming.

नहिं पतियाहु तौ अबिहें, *nahi patiyāhu* (√ *patiyā + ahu*) *to ăbihẽ*, if she do not believe you, then come.

जाहि सौं नाम चलैन्हि से हमर किरिया करह, *jāhi sõ nām calainhi sē hamar kiriyā karăh*, perform our funeral rites that our name may endure.

199. (*a*) (3). The **Imperative** is again a variant of the Present Conditional. The first person usually ends in ऊ *ū*, instead of ई *ī*, although the latter is also used. There are a number of alternative forms of the second person. The following are the terminations. To these the termination गँ *gå*, also employed for the future, is often added without affecting the sense. Terminations marked with an asterisk are chiefly used in poetry.

PERSON.	SHORT FORM.		LONG FORM.		REDUNDANT FORM.			
	GROUP I. (Subject: non-honorific. Object: non-honorific.)	GROUP II. (Subject: honorific. Object: non-honorific.)	GROUP I. (Subject: non-honorific. Object: non-honorific.)	GROUP II. (Subject: honorific. Object: non-honorific.)	GROUP I. (Subject: non-honorific. Object: non-honorific.)	GROUP II. (Subject: honorific. Object: non-honorific.)	GROUP III. (Subject: non-honorific. Object: honorific.)	GROUP IV. (Subject: honorific. Object: honorific.)
1	*ū* (sometimes *i*)	*ū* (sometimes *i*)	*iai* Or (with object in 2nd person.) *iau*, *iah*^{u}, **iå*	*iai* Or (with object in 2nd person.) *iau*, *iah*^{u}, **iå*	*iaik* Or (with object in 2nd person.) *iauk*	*iaik* Or (with object in 2nd person.) *iauk*	*iainh*^{i}.	*iainh*^{i}.
2	(The bare root.) also *ĕ*.	Same as 1st person.	*åh*, *ah*^{u}. *au*, *aũ*; fem. *ah*^{ĩ}, *ãh*^{ĩ}	Same as 1st person, but no forms for object in 2nd person.	*ahåk* (*ahŏk*), *ahuk* *ahīk*, *auk*.	Same as 1st person, but no forms for object in 2nd person.	*ahūnh*^{i}.	Same as 1st person.
3	*ĕ*, **a*, **u*.	*ath*^{i}, *ath*^{u}.	*au*, *ah*^{u}, *ō*, (sometimes *ai*.)	...	*auk*, (sometimes *aik*.)	...	*aunh*^{i}.	*athīnh*^{i} *othūnh*^{i}.

The following are examples of the use of this tense:—

First Person:—चलू तीनू मामा भगिना कटैया सिकार, *calū tīnū māmā bhaginā Kaṭaiyā sikār*, let us three, uncle and nephews, go to hunt in the Kaṭaiyā forest.

बाप माइ के कहू-गँ ठेकान, *bāp māi kē kahū-gå ṭhekān*, let us tell our father (and) mother our whereabouts.

तीर खैँचि मुसाहु बनियाँ के मारी, *tīr khaĩci Musāhu Baniyā̃ kē mārī*, drawing an arrow let me kill Musāhu Baniyā.

किछु सीखि लेए तँ पठाय दिऐक, *kicchu sīkhi lēē, tå paṭhāy diaik*, let him learn something (first), and then let me send him.

Second Person:- जेहि मुँहेँ धैलेँ कटैया ओहि मुँहेँ धर अपना बाप के, *jehi* (for *jāhi*) *mũhẽ dhailẽ Kaṭaiyā, ohi mũhẽ dhar apanā bāp kē*, with the mouth with which you (non-honorific) seized (me) (in) Kaṭaiyā, with the same mouth seize your own father (an abusive phrase).

अपना अपना घर मेँ सुन्नर खाएक करे-गँ, *apanā apanā ghar mẽ sunnar khāek karẽ-gå*, each in your own house prepare beautiful food. (A mother-in-law is addressing her daughters-in-law. Hence non-honorific terms are used).

आबि कै अप्पन मुदै बान्हू, *ābi kai appan mudai bānhū*, having come, bind your foe. (A wife is addressing her husband respectfully).

चलू सामी भोजन करू, *calū sāmī bhōjan karū*, come, my husband, make your meal.

एहन बात मति कहँह बहुत तामस मति करँह, *ehan bāt mati kahåh, bahut tāmas mati karåh*, say not such words, make not much anger. (One brother addresses another familiarly).

ताकहु ममा हरिन सुगरक ठाठ, *tākahu, mamā, harin sugarak ṭhāṭh*, look, uncle, for herds of deer and boar.

एक बेरि हुकुम दिहु, *ek bēri hukum dihu*, give (me) the order but once (cf. the example of दिअँ *diå*, in § 200).

भनहिँ बिद्यापति सुनिऐ मनाइनि, *bhanahī Bidyāpati suniai Manāini*, saith Vidyāpati, 'hear, O Manāini.' (Vid. lxxxii., 8).

कहहँक जे जातिक योगी छी, *kahᵃhȧk jē jātik Jōgī chī*, say 'we are Jōgīs by caste.'

पुछहुक जे कोन लोग छी, *puchᵃhuk jē kōn lōg chī*, ask (them), 'what is your Honours' caste ?'

बहोरन ममा के लाबहोक बोलाय, *Bahōran mamā kē lăbᵃhōk bolāy*, call and bring Bahōran (our) uncle.

हमरा बालकक संग ओकरहुँ पठाय दिऔक, *hamᵃrā bālakak saṅg okarohᵘ paṭhāy diauk*, send him also with my boy.

कालू सदा अम्मा निरसो के कहहुन्हि जोगिया जाई, *Kālū Sadā ammā Nirᵃsō kē kahᵃhūnhⁱ Jogiyā jāī*, say to the respected Kālū Sadā and mother Nirsō 'go to Jogiyā.'

Third Person :—किच्छु सीखि लेए तँ पठाय दिऐक, *kicchᵘ sīkhⁱ lēē tȧ̃ paṭhāy diaik*, let him learn something, then let me send him.

जाहि मुँहेँ धैलक फोटरा गीदर जेठ भाइ के ताहि मुँहेँ धरौ हमरा के, *jāhⁱ mūhē̃ dhailak Phoṭᵃrā gīdar jēṭh bhāi kē, tāhⁱ mūhē̃ dharau hamᵃrā kē*, with the mouth with which Phoṭrā the jackal has seized my elder brother, with the same mouth let him seize me.

200. There are various forms of a respectful imperative in the second person, made by adding इहेँ *ihē̃*, इअ *iȧ* (or इय *iyȧ*), इअह *iȧh*, इहँ *ihȧ*, इऔक *iauk*, इहौक *ihauk*, इहौन्हि *ihaunhⁱ*, इहथि *ihathⁱ*, or बहीन्हि *bahīnhⁱ* to the root. These I call **Mild Imperatives.** There are also some periphrastic respectful forms made by combining the 2nd verbal noun in ल *l*, with the Imperative or Future of the √ जा *jā*, go, which I call the **Respectful Imperative** and the **Respectful Future** respectively. Examples of these are as follows :—

नहि पतियाऊ तो आबिहेँ, *nahⁱ patiyāhᵃ, to ăbihē̃*, if she do not believe you, then please to come.

दीश निगम दुइ आनि मिलाबिय ।
ताहि दिअ बिधि मुख आध ॥

Dīsa nigama dui āni milābiya (m.c. for *milābiyȧ*).
Tăhi dia (m.c. for *diȧ*) *Bidhi-mukha ȧdha* (Vid. xvii., 4).

Join the (ten) directions to the (four) vēdas, and to that add half the (four) faces of Brahmā.

एक बेरि हुकुम दिअ, *ek bēr*ⁱ *hukum diȧ*, please give (me) the order but once. (cf. the example of दिहु *dih*ᵘ, in § 199).

हम तोहरा एक कहिनी सुनबैछिअहु जकरा सभ दीन मन रखिअह, *ham toh*ᵃ*rā ek kahinī sun*ᵃ*baichiah*ᵘ *jak*ᵃ*rā sabh dīn man rakhiȧh*, I tell you a story, which please remember all your days.

तहाँ तों बैसिह हम जाइत छी दौरी गाम, *tahā̃ tō̃ baisihȧ*, *ham jāit chī Daurī gām*, please sit there, I am going to Daurī village.

चढ़िऔक ममा परसाक गाछ, *caṛhiauk mamā par*ᵃ*sāk gāch*, O uncle please climb up the *parsā* tree.

दादा हो अहिरा गोआर के कहिहौक जाइ बथान, *Dādā hō*, *Ahirā Gōār kē kahihauk jāī bathān*, O brother, say to Ahirā Goār, 'go to (your) cow-shed.'

दुनू बेटीक कहिहौन्हि जे कोहबर करथि तैयार दुनू जमाय मारल गेलैन्हि, *dunū bēṭīk kahihaunh*ⁱ *jē koh*ᵃ*bar karath*ⁱ *taiyār*, *dunū jamāy māral gelainh*ⁱ, please tell (him) that the two sons-in-law for whom he is preparing the marriage bowers of his two daughters have been killed.

से हो सारा मानिहथि हमर दिनमा, *sē hō sārā mānihath*ⁱ *hamar din*ᵃ*mā* (for *din*ᵃ*wā*), therefore, O brother-in-law, accept (or, 'let my brother-in-law accept') my day (*i.e.*, the date fixed by me).

एक सेर अन्न घटि नहिं देबहीन्हि, *ek sēr ann ghaṭ*ⁱ *nah*ⁱ̃ *deb*ᵃ*hīnh*ⁱ, please do not give one seer of grain less (than the right amount).

Respectful Imperative :—जखन अपने चाही तखन तोड़बा लेल जाय, *jakhan ap*ᵃ*ne cāhī*, *takhan toṛ*ᵃ*bā lēl jāy*, when you, sir, may desire, then be good enough to have the fruit plucked and take it.

Respectful Future :—देखल जाएत, *dēkhal jāet*, you will be pleased to see, *i.e.*, be good enough to look and see.

NOTE.—The Respectful Imperative and Respectful Future are really impersonal passives. लेल जाय *lēl jāy*, is, literally, 'let it be taken.' So देखल जाएत *dēkhal jāet*, is, 'it will be seen (by you).' This use of the impersonal passive as a form of respect, is carried to great lengths in the Naipālī language spoken immediately to the north of Mithilā.

201 (*b*). The **Future** tense in Maithilī is formed in three ways. In the first place it may be the same as the present conditional. We often find the forms of the present conditional or imperative employed in the sense of the future. It may be noted that, in the cognate Kāśmīrī language, the only form of the future is made in the same way.

In the second place, a number of the forms of the future are based on the second verbal noun, which ends in ब *b* (देखब *dēkhab*, to see).

In the third place, a number of the forms of the future are based on the present participle, ending in ऐत *ait* (देखैत *dekhait*, seeing). In this case the termination of the participle is lightened by changing ऐत *ait* to अत *at* (देखत *dēkhat*) or इत *it* (देखित *dēkhit*).

202. The idea of future time can be emphasized by adding गॅ *gå* (in old Maithili गै *gai* or गए *gae*) to any of these forms. The addition of this termination is quite optional, and is most common in conversation. Examples of the use of this termination taken from literature are as follows. Those of गै *gai* and गए *gae* are in poetry and are taken from Manbōdh's Haribans :—

एछि दही कें बेचब-गॅ आओर कंचा सबहि सँ आम कीनि लेब, *ch*ⁱ *dahī kē̃ bēcab-gå, āor kañcā sabah*ⁱ *sā̃ ām kīn*ⁱ *lēb*, I'll sell these curds, and with the pice (I get for them) I will buy mangoes. (This example shows how purely optional the use of गॅ *gå* is. It is employed with one future and not with the other).

बाप माइ के कहू-गॅ ठेकान, *bāp māi-kē kahū-gå ṭhekōn*, we shall (*i.e.*, let us) inform (our) parents as to (our) whereabouts.

अपना अपना घर में सुन्नर खाएक करें-गॅ, *ap*ᵒ*nā ap*ᵒ*nā ghar mē̃ sunnar khāek karē̃-gå*, you will prepare beautiful food each in her own room.

मारब-गै हम काल्हि बथान, *māraba-gai hama kālhi bathāna*, to-morrow will I destroy the cowsheds.

तखनुक हरख कहब-गए काहि, *takhanuka harakha kahaba-gae kāhi*, to whom shall I tell the joy of that moment?

The second and third of the above examples have also been given as examples of imperatives. Grammatically, the termination गँ *gå* shows that they are futures, used in the sense of polite imperatives. They are the first form of the future, which is identical with the present conditional and imperative.

It is hardly necessary to point out the correspondence of this termination with the Hindī गा *gā* in forms such as देखूँ-गा *dēkhū̃-gā*, I shall see.

It is unnecessary to give a table of the terminations of the first form of the future. They are identical with those of the present conditional and imperative. One example may be given in which the same word is used once as a future conditional, and once as a future indicative :—

नहिं हाजिर करी तौ नौम दीन तोहरा सौँ बिबाह करी, *nah*ⁱ *hājir karī, tau naum dīn toh*ᵃ*rā saũ bibāh karī*, If I shall not produce (the thief) then I will marry you on the ninth day.

Other examples are :—

एहि उपकारक बदला तोहरा कैएक कथा सिखाय दिअहु, *eh*ⁱ *up*ᵃ*kārak bad*ᵃ*lā toh*ᵃ*rā kaiek kathā sikhāy diah*ᵘ, in return for this favour I will teach you (object in second person) certain things.

किछु सीखि लेए तँ पठाय दिऐक, *kicch*ᵘ *sīkh*ⁱ *lēē, tå paṭhāy diaik*, let him learn something, and then I will send him (to school).

203. (*b*, 4). **Future Indicative**, second form, based on the second verbal noun in ब *b*. The terminations are added directly to the root. Vulgarly, we often hear म *m* instead of ब *b*. Thus देखमौक *dekh^{a}mauk* instead of देखबौक *dekh^{a}bauk*, I shall see you. This second form only occurs in the first and second persons. After roots ending in vowels, the junction vowel is often some other vowel instead of ^{a}, following in this the second verbal noun.

PERSON.	SHORT FORM.		LONG FORM.		REDUNDANT FORM.			
	GROUP I. (Subject: non-honorific. Object: non-honorific.)	GROUP II. (Subject: honorific. Object: non-honorific.)	GROUP I. (Subject: non-honorific. Object: non-honorific.)	GROUP II. (Subject: honorific. Object: non-honorific.)	GROUP I. (Subject: non-honorific. Object: non-honorific.)	GROUP II. (Subject: honorific. Object: non-honorific.)	GROUP III. (Subject: non-honorific. Object: honorific.)	GROUP IV. (Subject: honorific. Object: honorific.)
1	*ab*, *^{a}bahũ*, *^{a}bõ*,		*^{a}bai* Or (with object in 2nd person.) *^{a}bau*, *^{a}bahu*		*^{a}baik* Or (with object in 2nd person.) *^{a}bauk*		*^{a}bainhi*	
2	*^{a}bẽ*	Same as 1st person.	*^{a}bah*, *^{a}bau*, *^{a}bahŏ*; fem. *^{a}bãhi*.	Same as 1st person, but no forms for object in 2nd person.	*^{a}bahak*, *^{a}bahik*.	Same as 1st person, but no forms for object in 2nd person.	*^{a}bahũnhi*.	Same as 1st person.
3	Wanting.	Wanting.	Wanting.	Wanting.	Wanting.	Wanting.	Wanting.	Wanting.

The following are examples of this form of the future:—

First Person: नहिं पतियाहु तो आबिहें देबहु गोआही गुजराय, *nahi̐ patiyāhᵘ to ăbihē̃, dēbahᵘ (dē + ᵃbahᵘ) goăhī gujarăy,* if she do not believe you, please come, (and) I will bear testimony.

सभ के देबों हम चारि सेर बोनि, *sabh kē dēbō̃ (dē + ᵃbō̃) ham cārⁱ sēr bonⁱ*, to all will I give four seers (of grain) as daily wages.

मारब धनुखा देब खसाय, *mārab dhanukhā, dēb khasāy,* I will smite him with (an arrow from my) bow and fell him.

कजरा नदी कैसन उतरब पार, *Kajᵃrā nadī kaisan utᵃrab pār,* how shall we cross the river Kajᵃrā?

[*N.B.*—This form in अब *ab* is the one in general use].

नहिं हो मामा घुरबै चलह कटैया सिकार, *nahi̐, hō māmā, ghurᵃbai; calăh Kaṭaiyā sikār,* we will not return, O uncle; come to hunt in Kaṭaiyā.

दुरमति लागल रे छौंड़ा पूत तोरा एक थापड़ मारबौ, *durᵃmatⁱ lăgal rē chaũṛā pūt, tōrā ek thāpaṛ mārᵃbau,* are you mad, you son of a boy? I will give you a slap.

घर में चोरी भेल चोर माल पकड़ि कै हाजिर कै दह तखन तोहरा फुरसति देबहु बीच में नहिं देबहु, *ghar mē̃ cōrī bhēl; cōr māl pakaṛⁱ kai hājir kai dăh, takhan tohᵃrā phurᵃsatⁱ dēbahᵘ; bīc mē̃ nahi̐ dēbahᵘ*, a theft has taken place in (my) house; arrest the thief and his booty, then will I release you; till then I will not set you free.

उनटि के हम नहिँ किच्छु कहबैक, *unaṭⁱ ke ham nahi̐ kicchᵘ kahᵃbaik,* I will make no reply (to her).

Second Person: हमरा गाइक दूध पीबें, *hamᵃrā gāik dūdh pībē̃,* will you drink the milk of *my* cow? (a rude question.)

निरसो अम्मा के कहबौ बुझाय, *Nirᵃsō ammā kē kahᵃbau bujhāy,* you will explain to mother Nirsō.

धाबाक धारि तोरि माँझी हाँक हो मामा। माँझी बैठल

हमरा देह पर । कहब हबाल । परसाक गाछ पर से हेँठ होबहो, *dhābāk dhār*^{i} *tōr*^{i} *mā̃chī haūk, hō māmā. Mā̃chī baiṭhat* (3rd person) *ham*^{a}*rā dēh par. Kahab* (1st person) *habāl. Par*^{a}*sāk gāch par sē hē̃ṭh hob*^{a}*hō* (2nd person). tear off a branch of the *dhābā* tree, and drive off the flies. The flies will settle on our corpses. I will tell you a circumstance (that concerns us). Will you come down from the *parsā* tree ?

तखन जाय पुछबहून्हि सखी केँ, *takhan jāy puch*^{a}*bahūnh*^{i} *sakhī kē̃*, (one girl addresses another) then you will go and ask our (respected) friend.

आधा आधा सभ मशाला लछमी दाइ केँ अपने चुप्पे देबैन्हि, *ādhā ādhā sabh maśālā Lach*^{a}*mī Dāi kē̃ ap*^{a}*ne cuppē debainh*^{i}, your Honour will give half of each of the delicacies privately to the respected Lachmī Dāi.

The following is an example of the suffix अन्हि *anh*^{i} as used by Manbōdh (see § 193).

कहलन्हि कुबलय पिड़ लै आनि ।

द्वार धरब-अन्हि भिनसर जानि ॥

kah^{a}*lanhi kubalae piṛa lai āni,*
dwāra dharaba-anhi (for *dhar*^{a}*bainh*^{i}) *bhinasara jāni.*

He said, " having brought (the Elephant) Kuvalaya Piḍa at dawn, warily you will place him at the door."

204. (*b*) (4). **Future**, third form, based on the present participle ending in ऐत *ait*, of which the ऐ *ai* is usually weakened to अ *a*, but sometimes to इ *i*. The terminations are to be added to the root direct. This form is mainly used in the third person. In the first person it is only found in groups I and II, and in the 2nd person only in group II, and even here it is not common.

PERSON.	SHORT FORM.		LONG FORM.		REDUNDANT FORM.			
	GROUP I. (Subject: non-honorific. Object: non-honorific.)	GROUP II. (Subject: honorific. Object: non-honorific.)	GROUP I. (Subject: non-honorific. Object: non-honorific.)	GROUP II. (Subject: honorific. Object: non-honorific.)	GROUP I. (Subject: non-honorific. Object: non-honorific.)	GROUP II. (Subject: honorific. Object: non-honorific.)	GROUP III. (Subject: non-honorific Object: honorific.)	GROUP IV. (Subject: honorific. Object: honorific.)
1	*itah*^{e}.		*^{a}tiai* Or (with object in 2nd person.) *^{a}tiau*, *^{a}tiah^{u}*.		*^{a}tiaik* Or (with object in 2nd person.) *^{a}tiauk*.		Wanting.	
2	Wanting.	Same as 1st person.	Wanting.	Same as 1st person, but no forms for object in 2nd person.	Wanting.	Same as 1st person, but no forms for object in 2nd person.	Wanting.	Wanting.
3	*at*; fem. *at^{i}*.	*^{a}tath^{i}*, *^{a}tath^{u}*, *^{a}tăh*; fem. *^{a}tīh* or *^{a}tīh^{i}*	*^{a}tai* Or (with object in 2nd person). *^{a}tau*, *^{a}tah^{u}*.	......	*^{a}taik* Or (with object in 2nd person.) *^{a}tauk*.	......	*^{a}tainh^{i}*	*^{a}thĩnh^{i}* *^{a}thũnh^{i}*.

Examples of this form of the future as follows. Only one example has been noted in literature of the 1st person, and none of the 2nd person. The example of the first person will be found in the third sentence below:—

Third Person: जिब जाएत परान बचत तैओ ने परसा गाछ पर सँ हेँठ होबोँ, *jib jāet, parān bacat, taio nē par^{a}sā gāch par sē hēṭh hōbõ*, (whether) my life will go (*i.e.*, will be lost), (or whether) my life will be saved, still I will not descend from the Parsā tree.

मधुपुर रमनि जखन हरि देखति ।
हरखित जनम कृतारथ लेखति ॥

madhupura ramani jakhana hari dekhati,
harakhita janama kṛtāratha lekhati. (Manbōdh.)

When a damsel of Madhupur will see Hari,
She will rejoice and will consider her life's desire
fulfilled.

सामी सलहेस जौँ मिलतथि सामी सलहेस लै राज भोगितहुँ । नहिं मिलताह हिआ हारि घुरब । सोग सन्ताप सौँ पानि धसि खसब, *sāmī sal^{a}hēs jaũ mil^{a}tath^{i}, sāmī sal^{a}hēs lai rāj bhogitah^{u}* (1st person). *Nah^{i} mil^{a}tāh, hiā hār^{i} ghurab. Sōg santāp saũ pāni dhas^{i} khasab*, (if) my lord Salhēs will be met (by me), with my lord Salhēs will I enjoy the kingdom. If he will not be met (by me), losing my heart (heart-broken) will I return. In sorrow and affliction will I plunge into water (and drown myself).

[Note in this example two different forms of the first person and two different forms of the third person honorific. In each case the two forms of each pair are quite identical in meaning.]

निरसो देलन्हि बजर केवाड़ ठोकि जे बाबू सुतले रहताह नहिं जैताह *Nir^{a}sō dēlanh^{i} bajar kewāṛ ṭhōk^{i}, jē bābū sut^{a}lē rah^{a}tāh nah^{i} jaitāh*, Nirsō shut adamantine doors (*i.e.*, shut the door tightly) saying, 'my sons will remain asleep, and will not depart.'

मोरंग छैक पनियाँ कुपनियाँ बहिरे धरतै साहुक कलबुज, *Mōraṅg chaik paniyā̃ ku-paniyā̃, bahirē dhar^{a}tai sāhuk kal^{a}buj*, in the

Mōrang the water is bad water, and will seize from without the body of the Sāhu (and fill him with disease).

ताहिर मीयाँक बेटी छै बड़ जोगतान। एक थापड़ मारतौ पानि नहिं पीबैं, *tāhir mīyā̃k bēṭī chai baṛ jōgᵃtān. Ek thāpaṛ mārᵃtau pāni nahⁱ pībē̃*, Tāhir Miyā̃'s daughter is a great sorceress. She will give you one slap and you will never drink water (again) (*i.e.*, you will be killed).

पाँचो मिलि के करतहु सन्स्कार, *pā̃cō milⁱ ke karᵃtahᵘ sanskār*, the five will unite and perform your funeral ceremonies.

तोहरा सभक केसो टेढ़ नहिं हैतहु, *tohᵃrā sabhak kēs-ō ṭēṛh nahⁱ haitahᵘ* (indirect obj. in 2nd pers.), not even a hair of one of you will be bent.

बरख बारह लगतैक खेपवा, *barakh bārah lagᵃtaik khepᵃwā*, the expedition will last twelve years.

As an example of Manbōdh's suffix अन्हि *anhⁱ*, we have खैताह-अन्हि, *khaităh-anhi*, already quoted in § 193.

205. (*c*) (5). The **Past Conditional** is formed from the present participle, to which the personal terminations are added directly. In the short form of group I, no termination is added in the third person, the bare present participle being here employed alone.

The present participle ends in ऐत *ait*, as in देखैत *dekhait*, seeing. When personal terminations are added, this termination is usually lightened to इत *it*, thus देखित *dēkhit*. This lightening is not however obligatory, and we sometimes hear the ऐ *ai* retained. This is not a peculiarity of any particular form, but depends entirely on the personal equation of the writer or the speaker. Sometimes the ऐत *ait* is lightened to अत *at* (देखत *dēkhat*), instead of इत *it*. This also is a case of personal equation.

The following are the terminations of this tense. I have included the lightened participial termination in each instance, so that the terminations as given, are to be added to the root direct. In every instance *ai* or ᵃ may (as has been explained) be substituted for the initial *i* of the termination. The terminations commencing with *i* are, however, much the most usual.

206. (*c*) (5) **Past Conditional.** The terminations are added to the root direct.

PERSON.	SHORT FORM.		LONG FORM.		REDUNDANT FORM.			
	GROUP I. (Subject: non-honorific. Object: non-honorific.)	GROUP II. (Subject: honorific. Object: non-honorific.)	GROUP I. (Subject: non-honorific. Object: non-honorific.)	GROUP II. (Subject: honorific. Object: non-honorific.)	GROUP I. (Subject: non-honorific. Object: non-honorific.)	GROUP II. (Subject: honorific. Object: non-honorific.)	GROUP III. (Subject: non-honorific. Object: honorific.)	GROUP IV. (Subject: honorific. Object: honorific.)
1	*itah*$^{\tilde{u}}$*, *ıtī* (seldom used).		*itiai* Or (with object in 2nd person.) *itiau*, *itiah*^{u}.		*itiaik* Or (with object in 2nd person). *itiauk*.		*itiainh*^{i}.	
2	*itẽ*.	Same as 1st person.	*itàh*; fem. *itah*$^{\tilde{i}}$ or *itāh*$^{\tilde{i}}$.	Same as 1st person, but no forms for object in 2nd person.	*it*^{a}*hàk*, *it*^{a}*hik*.	Same as 1st person, but no forms for object in 2nd person.	*it*^{a}*hūnh*^{i}	Same as 1st person.
3	*ait*; fem. *ait*^{i}.	*itath*^{i}, *itanh*^{i}.	*itai* Or (with object in 2nd person.) *itau*, *itah*^{u}.	......	*itaik* Or (with object in 2nd person.) *itauk*.	......	*itainh*^{i}.	*it*^{a}*thīnh*^{i} *it*^{a}*thūnh*^{i}.

* or *aitah*$^{\tilde{u}}$ or ^{a}*tah*$^{\tilde{u}}$ and so throughout except in the short form of the 3rd person of group I.

The following are examples of the use of this tense :—

First Person :—जौँ हमहुँ तोहरा जकाँ बनीज-ब्यापार करितहुँ आओर अन्न तौलितहुँ तखन आइ पाओ भरि अन्न एम्हर ओम्हर सँ माँगि नहिँ खैतहुँ, *jaŭ hamah*^{ū} *toh*^{a}*rā jakā̃ banīj-byāpār karitah*^{ū}, *āor ann taulitah*^{ū}, *takhan āi pāo bhar*^{i} *ann ēmhar ōmhar sā̃ mā̃g*^{i} *nah*^{ī} *khaitah*^{ū} (for *khā* + *itah*^{ū}), if I also, like you, had done trading and had weighed out food, I should not have eaten to-day a quarter of a seer of food begged from here and there.

जनितहुँ तो बगहा मेँ बरदी तमाकू लदबैतिऐ, *janitah*^{ū} *to bag*^{a}*hā mē̃ bar*^{a}*dī tamākū lad*^{a}*baitiai*, if I had known, I would have loaded a bullock in Baghā with tobacco.

Second Person (also *Third Person*) :—जौँ तोँ हमरा नहिँ छाड़ितह आओर मारि दितह तखन ओ मोती तोहरा हाथ लगैत, *jō̃ tō̃ ham*^{a}*rā nah*^{ī} *chăṛităh āor mār*^{i} *dităh, takhan ō mōtī toh*^{a}*rā hāth lagait*, if you had not let me go and had killed me, then that pearl would have come into your hand.

Third Person :—जिबैत रहैत तो जोगिया अबैत पलटि, *jibail rahait to jogiyā abait palaṭ*^{i}, if they had been alive they would have come back to Jogiyā.

आन केओ रहितथि मारितहुँ मुक्का दितहुँ खँसाय, *ān keo rahitath*^{i} *mări-tah*^{ū} *mukkā ditah*^{ū} *khā̃sāy*, if it had been any other person (than you, our respected mother), we should have struck him with a blow of the fist, and knocked him down.

औतन्हि दुरागमन करैतन्हि जमैया जाँजरि, *autanh*^{i} *durāgaman karai-tanh*^{i} *jamaiyā jā̃jar*^{i}, if they had come to Jā̃jari his sons-in-law would have performed the ceremony of *durāgaman*.

Sometimes the imperfect tense indicative is employed in the sense of the past conditional. An example is जो जिबैत चलाह दीना भद्री जोगिया नगर कौनो मुसहरनी नहिँ कैलक सिँगार, *jo jibait chalăh dīnā bhadrī jogiyā nagar, kauno musahar*^{a}*nī nah*^{ī} *kailak sī̃gār*, if Dīnā and Bhadrī had been alive in Jogiyā town, no Musahar's wife would have dared to adorn herself. In this example the past tense indicative is also employed in the apodosis in the sense of the past conditional.

19

207. (*c*) (6) **Present Indicative.**
(*c*) (7) **Imperfect Indicative.**

These two tenses are formed by combining the present participle with Auxiliary Verbs. They will be dealt with under the head of periphrastic tenses (Chapter III).

208. (*d*) (8) **Past Indicative.**—This tense is formed from the past participle in अल *al* (देखल *dēkhal*), which in the case of transitive verbs is a passive. Thus देखल, *dēkhal*, means 'seen,' and when we want to say 'I saw' we must say 'seen by me.' We have observed that nouns and pronouns have nothing corresponding to the agent case in Hindi. The 'by me,' 'by you,' or 'by him,' etc., which forms the subject of the verb, is therefore indicated by the terminations suffixed in conjugating the tense. देखलहुँ, *dekh*ᵃ*lah*ⁿ, means 'seen by me,' 'I saw'; देखलैंह, *dekh*ᵃ*låh*, means 'seen by you', 'you saw'; देखलक *dekh*ᵃ*lak*, means 'seen by him,' 'he saw'; and so on.

On the other hand the past participle of an intransitive verb is not necessarily passive. सूतल, *sūtal* means 'slept,' and in conjugation 'I slept' may be represented by either 'it was slept by me' or by 'slept I.' In Maithilī both principles are followed in conjugating intransitive verbs. This is most manifest in the periphrastic tenses formed from the past participle, the perfect and the pluperfect, but we also see clear traces of it in the conjugation of the past indicative. Here there is a mixture of forms. For 'I slept' we usually say 'it was slept by me'; but for 'you slept' we do not say 'it was slept by you' (सुतलैंह *sut*ᵃ*låh*) but we say सुतलोह *sut*ᵃ*lăh*, i.e., slept you. It thus follows that the conjugation of the past tense of an intransitive verb sometimes agrees with that of the past tense of a transitive verb, and sometimes differs.

At the present day all sense of the *reason* for this difference has disappeared from the language. No native of Mithilā, when employing the past tense of a transitive verb, is aware that he is using a passive idiom. To him the pasts of both kinds of verbs are conjugated in as straightforward a manner as the English, I loved, thou lovedst, he loved. All that he is conscious of is that in the tenses formed from the past participle, the conjugation of transitive verbs differs from that of intransitive ones, and, for practical purposes this is all that need be known. It is unnecessary to consider देखलहुँ *dekh*^{a}*lah*^{ũ} as meaning 'it was seen-by-me,' and it is quite sufficient to consider it as meaning 'I saw,' just as सुतलहुँ *sut*^{a}*lah*^{ũ} means 'I slept'; but it is useful to know the origin of the difference, and for that reason the above explanation has been given.

We commence with giving the terminations of the past tense of the **transitive** verb.

209. (*d*) (8) **Past Indicative** of a **Transitive** verb. The terminations to be added to the root direct.

PERSON.	SHORT FORM.		LONG FORM.		REDUNDANT FORM.			
	GROUP I. (Subject : non-honorific. Object : non-honorific.)	GROUP II. (Subject : honorific. Object : non-honorific.)	GROUP I. (Subject : non-honorific. Object : non-honorific.)	GROUP II. (Subject : honorific. Object : non-honorific.)	GROUP I. (Subject : non-honorific. Object : non-honorific.)	GROUP II. (Subject : honorific. Object : non-honorific.)	GROUP III. (Subject : non-honorific. Object : honorific.)	GROUP IV. (Subject ; honorific. Object : honorific.)
1	^{a}lahũ, al, ^{a}lĩ ; fem. al^{i}.	^{a}lahũ, al, ^{a}lĩ ; fem. al^{i}.	^{a}lai, ^{a}liai Or (with object in 2nd person.) ^{a}lau, ^{a}lah^{u}, ^{a}liau, ^{a}liah^{u}	^{a}lai, ^{a}liai Or (with object in 2nd person.) ^{a}lau, ^{a}lah^{u}, ^{a}liau, ^{a}liah^{u}	^{a}laik, ^{a}liaik Or (with object in 2nd person.) ^{a}lauk, ^{a}liauk.	^{a}laik, ^{a}liaik Or (with object in 2nd person.) ^{a}lauk, ^{a}liauk.	^{a}lainh^{i}, ^{a}liainh^{i}.	^{a}lainh^{i}, ^{a}liainh^{i}.
2	al$^{\tilde{e}}$, ^{a}laĩ	Same as 1st person.	^{a}lăh ; fem. ^{a}līh^{i} ^{a}lĭh^{i}.	Same as 1st person, but no forms for object in 2nd person.	^{a}lahăk, ^{a}lahīk	Same as 1st person, but no forms for object in 2nd person.	^{a}lahũnh^{i}.	Same as 1st person.
3	^{a}lak (al ; fem. al^{i}.)	^{a}lanh^{i} (^{a}lath^{i}.)	al^{a}kai Or (with object in 2nd person) al^{a}kau.	...	al^{a}kaik Or (with object in 2nd person.) al^{a}kauk.	...	al^{a}kainh^{i}.	al^{a}thīnh^{i}. al^{a}thũnh^{i}.

In the above paradigm the termination *al* (fem. *al*^{i}) properly belongs to the first person in the short form of Group I. In the case of intransitive verbs, it is not used in the first person, but is used in the third person of the same group. In old (*e.g.*, in Manbōdh's *Haribans*) poetry, and in the speech of the illiterate (*e.g.*, in the song of Salhēs), this termination is, however, also used in the third person of the transitive verbs. I have, therefore, inserted it also under the third person, placing it within marks of parenthesis to show that its use in this person is not regular.

In the third person of Group II, the termination ^{a}*lanh*^{i} is the one in common use. I have only noted one occurrence in literature of the form ^{a}*lath*^{i}.

The following are examples of the use of this tense :—

First Person :—भन मनबोध पछाँ किछु रहल ।
कथा प्रसंग आगु हम कहल ॥

Bhana Manabōdha pachā̃ kichu rahala.[1]
Kathā prasaṅga āgu hama kahala.[1]

Saith Manbōdh, 'this occurred (intransitive, 3rd person) somewhat subsequently. In the order of (my) tale I said (transitive, 1st person) it too soon.'

कहियो न देखल गेहुमनक फेँच पर खंजन फहराइत *kahiyō na dēkhal gehumanak phẽc par khañjan phah*^{a}*rāit*, never (before) did I see a khañjan-bird hovering over the hood of a cobra.

गोड़ लगैत छी पैयाँ परैत छी एहि नहिं जनली अहाँ भद्री छी *gōṛ lagait chī, paĩyā̃ parait chī, eh*^{i} *nah*^{ĩ} *jan*^{a}*lī ahā̃ bhadrī chī*, I clasp (your) legs, I fall at (your) feet, I did not know this, that Your Honour was Bhadrī.

जनम सँ पुजलहुँ मोकामा गढ़ मेँ, *janam sā̃ puj*^{a}*lah*^{ũ} *mokāmā gaṛh mẽ*, from (my) birth, did I worshipped (thee) in Mokāmā fort.

बालपन अधरा बान्हलि पर पुरुख मुँह नहिं देखलि जनम पाए सिन्दुर नहिं माँग पहिरलि । ऊनका कारन काँचे बाँसक कोहबर बान्हलि लाल पलंग सभ रंग सेज ओछाओलि सिकिया चीरि कै बेनिया बनाओलि,

---

[1] *i.e., rahal, kahal.* Being in verse, the final *a* is pronounced. See § 9.

bāl^{a}pan ac^{a}rā bānhal^{i}, par purukh mūh nah^{ĩ} dēkhal^{i}, janam pāe sindur nah^{ĩ} mā̃g pahiral^{i} ; hun^{a}kā kāran kā̃cē bā̃sak koh^{a}bar bānhal^{i}, lāl palaṅg sabh rang sēj ochāol^{i} (for *ochāb + al^{i}*), *sikiyā cir^{i} kai beniyā banāol^{i}* (*banāb + al^{i}*), (a woman speaks) I tied up my girlhood with my body-cloth, the face of another man I did not see, from my birth I did not wear vermilion on the parting of my hair. For him did I build a bridal arbour of fresh bamboos, on a crimson bed did I overspread a mattress of varied colours, and with a split reed did I apply silver spots to my brow.

लाख अपराध कैलौक। लाख गारि देलें। तकर उतर हम नहिं किछु कहलौक, *lākh ap^{a}rādh kailauk, lākh gār^{i} dēlẽ, takar ūtar ham nah^{ĩ} kich^{u} kah^{a}lauk*, I committed a hundred thousand faults against you; a hundred thousand abusive words did you give me; (and yet) no answer of that (abuse) did I say to you.

Second Person: जाहि मरद लै जोबन सेबलें से मरद बैसल छौक देबहा नदीक धार, *jāh^{i} marad lai jōban seb^{a}lẽ, sē marad baisal chauk deb^{a}hā nadīk dhār*, the man for whom you have kept your virginity, is seated for you by the stream of the river Debhā.

कौन गरू परलौ बड़ भोरे छेंकल दुआर, *kaun garū par^{a}lau baṛ bhōrē chẽkal duār*, what misfortune has befallen you that your Honour has obstructed my door very early in the morning?

बिनु अपराधें गरदनियाँ देलह, *bin^{u} ap^{a}rādhẽ gar^{a}daniyā̃ dēlah*, without fault (*i.e.*, for no fault) you gave them neck-thrusting (*i.e.*, you thrust them away by the neck).

Third Person: केओ नहिं चिन्हलक जोगियाक लोग, *keo nah^{ĩ} cinh^{a}lak, jogiyāk lōg*, none of the people of Jogiyā recognised them.

देखलक सल्हेस जे बड़ अजगुत भेल, *dekh^{a}lak salhēs jē baṛ aj^{a}gut bhēl*, Salhēs saw that (something) very extraordinary (had) happened.

चटि दे धैलक पटि दे मारलक बान्हलक पछुआड़ि धै कें, *caṭ^{i} dē dhailak, paṭ^{i} dē mār^{a}lak, bā̃nh^{a}lak pachuāṛ^{i} dhai ke*, giving abruptness (*i.e.*, suddenly) he seized (him), giving instantaneousness (*i.e.*, instantly) he struck (him), seizing him from behind he bound him.

This termination *^{a}lak* is very common.

The following are examples of the irregular omission of the final *ak*.

हँसि हँसि कुसल पुछल ब्रजनाथ, *hāsi hāsi kusala puchala braja-nātha*, smilingly Vrajanāth asked his welfare. (Manbōdh, vii, 28)

कै देब सबइ सबहुँ एह कहल ।
निज अनुचर सभ कहल हकार ।

'kai deba sabai' sabahũ eha kahala,......
nija anucara sabha kahala hakāra. (Manbōdh, ii, 34, 35).

All of them said this 'we will do everything'...........His attendants all uttered a howl.

बाजै लागल भद्री दीना सौं साजल जबाब, *bājai lāgal* (intransitive) *bhadrī, dīnā saũ sājal* (for *sāj*^{a}*lak*) *jabāb*, Bhadrī began to speak, to Dīnā he arranged his answer.

तखन दौना मालिनि दछिनक चीर पहिरि लेलि पाटी सम्हारि लेलि नैना काजर पेन्हि लेलि ... ... असलै कसबीनि भेलि, *takhan daunā mālin*^{i} *dachinak cīr pahir*^{i} *lēl*^{i} (transitive), *pāṭī samhār*^{i} *lēl*^{i}, *nainā kājar pēnh*^{i} *lēl*^{i}........... *ās*^{a}*lē kas*^{a}*bīn*^{i} *bhēl*^{i} (intransitive), then Daunā Mālin apparelled herself in garments of the south, arranged her flat temple-locks, (and) applied collyrium to her eyes............(in appearance) she became a real harlot.

[It will be seen that in the last two examples, taken from modern prose, the irregular form of the transitive verbs seems to be suggested by the neighbourhood of an intransitive verb with the same subject.]

फेर मारलन्हि दीना राम फोटरा के देलन्हि खसाय, *pher mār*^{a}*lanh*^{i} *dīnā rām phoṭ*^{a}*rā kē dēlanh*^{i} *khasāy*, again (the respected) Dīnā Rām smote Phoṭrā and dashed him down (*dēlanh*^{i} for *dē* + ^{a}*lanh*^{i}).

अपन बहु बेटी रखलन्हि घर सुताय । हमर बेटी पुतहु देखलन्हि नाँगट उघारि, *apan bah*^{u} *bēṭī rakh*^{a}*lanh*^{i} *ghar sutāy, hamar bēṭī putuh*^{u} *dekh*^{a}*lanh*^{i} *nãgaṭ ughār*^{i}, he (the respected one) put his own daughter-in-law and daughter to sleep in his house, and (came here and) having uncovered them saw my daughter and daughter-in-law naked.

[As an example of Manbōdh's method of employing the suffix अन्हि *anh*^{i} (§ 193), we may quote:—

सबहु देखल-अन्हि जे छल जागल, *sabahu dekhala-anhi jē chala jāgala*, every one who was awake saw (what happened).]

[The solitary example of the form in ^{a}*lath*^{i} which I have noted occurs in the song of Dīnā Bhadrī. It is as follows:—

देहि दुनू भाइ छोड़ि देलथि, *dēh*^{i} *dunū bhāi chōṛ*^{i} *dēlath*^{i} (for *dē* + ^{a}*lath*^{i}), the two brothers left their bodies (and disappeared).]

कथा सभ सौँ बहुत बुझौलकै परंतु केओ किछु नहिँ मानलकै, *kathā sabh saũ bahut bujhaul*^{a}*kai* (for *bujhāb* + *al*^{a}*kai*), *parant*^{u} *keo kicch*^{u} *nah*^{ĩ} *mănal*^{a}*kai*, he remonstrated much with them by words, but no one heeded (him) at all.

ददा हो नहिँ बुझलकौ, दुनू पुतहु के फजिहति कैलक, *dadā hō, nah*^{ĩ} *bujhal*^{a}*kau; dunū putuh*^{u} *kē phajihat*^{i} *kailak*, brother, she did not understand you; she has done indignity to her daughters-in-law.

तखन ओकरा सभक बाप कहलकैक, *takhan ok*^{a}*rā sabhak bāp kaha-l*^{a}*kaik*, then their father said to them.

ओ कहलकैन्हि हमरो नमस्कार लिखि दिऔन्हि । मोनसी कहलथीन्हि नहिँ हौ *ō kahal*^{a}*kainh*^{i} '*ham*^{a}*rō namaskār likh*^{i} *diaunh*^{i}'; *mon*^{a}*sī kahal*^{a}*thīnh*^{i} '*nah*^{ĩ} *hau*,' he (the ignorant fool, not respected) said (politely to the respected scribe) 'please write my compliments also.' The (respected) scribe said (politely, to the fool, whom he treated with respect) 'it is not (what you think).'

210. (*d*) (8) **Past Indicative** of an **Intransitive** verb. The terminations to be added to the root direct.

PERSON.	SHORT FORM.		LONG FORM.		REDUNDANT FORM.			
	GROUP I. (Subject : non-honorific. Object : non-honorific.)	GROUP II. (Subject : honorific. Object : non-honorific.)	GROUP I. (Subject : non-honorific. Object : non-honorific.)	GROUP II. (Subject : honorific. Object : non-honorific.)	GROUP I. (Subject : non-honorific. Object : non-honorific.)	GROUP II. (Subject : honorific. Object : non-honorific.)	GROUP III. (Subject : non-honorific Object (indirect : honorific.)	GROUP IV. (Subject : honorific. Object (indirect : honorific.)
1	^{a}*lah*$^{\tilde{a}}$ ^{a}*lī.*		^{a}*liai* Or (with indirect object in 2nd person.) ^{a}*liau*, ^{a}*lia̍h*^{u}.		^{a}*liaik* Or (with indirect object in 2nd person.) ^{a}*liauk.*		^{a}*liainh*^{i}	
2	^{a}*lẽ*, ^{a}*laĩ.*	Same as 1st person.	^{a}*lăh* ; fem. ^{a}*līh*, ^{a}*līh*^{i}.	Same as 1st person, but no forms for object in 2nd person.	^{a}*lahẵk*, ^{a}*lahīk.*	Same as 1st person, but no forms for object in 2nd person.	^{a}*lahūnh*^{i}.	Same as 1st person.
3	*al* ; fem. *al*^{i}.	^{a}*lăh* (fem. ^{a}*līh*, ^{a}*līh*^{i}) ; ^{a}*lanh*^{i}.	^{a}*lai* Or (with indirect object in 2nd person.) ^{a}*lau*, ^{a}*lah*^{u}.	...	^{a}*laik* Or (with indirect object in 2nd person.) ^{a}*lauk.*	...	^{a}*lainh*^{i}.	*al*^{a}*thīnh*^{i} *al*^{a}*thūnh*^{i}.

Regarding the employment of those forms of Groups I and II which refer to the object in the second person, and the forms (Group III and IV) in which the object is honorific, reference should be made to §§ 191, 192 and § 189.

The following are examples of the use of this tense :—

First Person:—आन दिन भरि छवा उतरलहुँ पार, *ān din bhar*ⁱ *chawā utaralah*ᵘ *pār*, on other days I crossed (the river) (with the water only) up to the calves of my legs.

बारह बरख जोगिया जाँजरि बसलहुँ, *bārah barakh jogiyā jā̃jar*ⁱ *bas*ᵒ*lah*ᵘ, for twelve years lived we in Jogiyā Jānjari.

बारह बरिस नैहर सासुर बसली, *bārah baris naihar sāsur bas*ᵒ*lī*, for twelve years did we live in our fathers' houses and in those of our fathers-in-law.

Second Person :—रे गमार तों हमर तीनू कथा एखनहिं बिसरि गेलें, *rē gamār, tõ hamar tīnū kathā ekhanah*ĩ *bisar*ⁱ *gēlē̃* (for *gē*+ᵒ*lē̃*) O fool, you already forgot my three statements.

कौन गरू परल जे सुतलाह खटबारि, *kaun garū paral jē sut*ᵒ*lāh khaṭ*ᵒ*bār*ⁱ, what calamity befell (you) that you (the respected one) slept (*i.e.*, art lying prone) upon (your) bed.

Third Person :—अम्माक सबद सुनि दीना भद्री उठल चिहाय, *ammāk subad sun*ⁱ *dīnā bhadrī uṭhal cihāy*, when they heard their mother's words, Dīnā and Bhadrī started up.

गोसाँउनीक घर पैसलि दीना भद्रीक सिरमा बैसलि, *gosā̃unīk ghar paisal*ⁱ ; *dīnā bhadrīk sir*ᵒ*mā baisal*ⁱ, she entered the shrine of the family Goddess ; she sat by the head of Dīnā and Bhadrī's bed.

चललाह भद्री गुलामी के उद्देस, छौँड़ाक रूप धैलक। भद्री चलल बरा डीह बथान, *cal*ᵒ*lāh bhadrī gulāmī kē udēs : chaũṛāk rūp dhailak bhadrī calal barā ḍīh bathān*, (the respected) Bhadrī went to search for Gulāmī : he took the shape of a little boy : (now no longer respected, being but a village lad) Bhadrī went to the cowshed in Barā Ḍih.

डिया डारि के चललीह मालिनि। कनैत चललीह मालिनि स्वामीक उद्देस। डेगे डेगे चललीह। जोजन भरि जाय जुमलीह अपना फुलबाड़ी। फूल देखि धरती खसलीह मुरझाय। तखन लोटि लोटि कानै लगलीहि फुलबाड़ी में। ऊनक कानब सुनि संग समाज सखी बहीन भोर होइत आएलि,

hiyā hōr^{i} *kui cal*^{a}*līh mālin*^{i} *: kanait*^{i} *cal*^{a}*līh mālin*^{i} *swāmīk udēs : ḍēgē ḍēgē cal*^{a}*līh : jōjan bhar*^{i} *jāy jum*^{a}*līh up*^{a}*nā phul*^{a}*bāṛī : phūl dēkh*^{i} *dhar*^{a}*tī khus*^{a}*līh mur*^{a}*chāy : takhan lōṭ*^{i} *lōṭ*^{i} *kānai lag*^{a}*līh phul*^{a}*bāṛī mẽ : hunak kānab sun*^{i} *saṅg samāj sakhī bahin bhōr hōit āel*^{i}, broken-hearted went (the respected) Mālin: weeping went Mālin to search for her husband: step by step she went: she travelled for a whole league and arrived at her garden: seeing the flowers she fell fainting: then, rolling on the ground, she began to weep: hearing the sound of her weeping her (not respected) companions, female friends, (and) sisters came at dawn.

As a specimen of Manbōdh's use of the suffix *anh*^{i} (§ 193), we may quote:—

पैर परल-अन्हि प्रेम जनाए । *paira parala-anhi prēma janāe* (The respected) Akrūra expressing (his) affection fell at (Kṛṣṇa's) feet (Man. vii, 27).

Similarly झपटल-अन्हि *jhapaṭala-anhi*, he swooped (Man. x, 17), and झलकल-अन्हि *jhalakala-anhi*, he glittered (Man. ix, 11).

कानै लगलै बरुआ चारू गुनबें, *kānai lag*^{a}*lai barua* (long form of *bār*, a boy) *cārū gun*^{a}*bẽ*, the boy began to weep in a pretty way.

कौन गरू परलौ, *kaun garū par*^{a}*lau*, what misfortune has befallen you?

किछु बाकी रहलैक काल्हि सोम दिन के ले जैहें, *kich*^{u} *bākī rah*^{a}*laik, kālh*^{i} *sōm din kē lē jaihẽ*, something remained wanting (to complete the full weight), let her take that away on Monday.

फोटरा के देखि अजगुत भेलौक, *phoṭ*^{a}*rā kē dēkh*^{i} *aj*^{a}*gut bhelauk*, having seen Phoṭrā, it was wonderful to you.

दीना भद्री मरि गेलैन्हि, *dīnā bhadrī mar*^{i} *gelainh*^{i}, (the respected) Dinā and Bhadrī (have) died.

तखन गंगा-जी कहै लगलथीन्हि जे नाओ गेल भसिया, *takhan gaṅgā-jī kahai lagal*^{a} *thīnh*^{i} *jē 'nāo gēl bhasiyā,'* then the holy Ganges began to say that 'the boats were washed away.'

211. In order to make the Transitive and Intransitive conjugations of this tense quite clear, the student may be reminded that some terminations are common to transitive and intransitive verbs, while others are peculiar to transitive, and others again to transitive verbs. This is made plain in the two following tables:—

(*d*) (8). **Past Indicative.** Terminations common to Transitive and to Intransitive verbs.

PERSON.	SHORT FORM.		LONG FORM.		REDUNDANT FORM.			
	GROUP I. (Subject: non-honorific. Object: non-honorific.)	GROUP II. (Subject: honorific. Object: non-honorific.)	GROUP I. (Subject: non-honorific. Object: non-honorific.)	GROUP II. (Subject: honorific. Object: non-honorific.)	GROUP I. (Subject: non-honorific. Object: non-honorific.)	GROUP II. (Subject: honorific. Object: non-honorific.)	GROUP III. (Subject: non-honorific. Object: honorific.)	GROUP IV. (Subject: honorific. Object: honorific.)
1	*^{a}lī, ^{a}lah^{ũ}.*		*^{a}liai* Or (with object in 2nd person.) *^{a}liau, ^{a}liah^{u}.*		*^{a}liaik.* Or (with object in 2nd person.) *^{a}liauk.*		*^{a}liainh^{i}.*	
2	*^{a}lẽ, ^{a}laĩ.*	Same as 1st person.	...	Same as 1st person, but no forms for object in 2nd person.	*^{a}lahãk* *^{a}lahīk.*	Same as 1st person, but no forms for object in 2nd person.	*^{a}lahūnh^{i}.*	Same as 1st person.
3	...	*^{a}lanh^{i}.*	...	...	...	...	...	*al^{a}thīnh^{i}, al^{a}thūnh^{i}.*

(*d*) (8). **Past Indicative.** Terminations used only by Transitive or by Intransitive verbs, respectively.

PERSON.	SHORT FORM.		LONG FORM.		REDUNDANT FORM.			
	GROUP I. (Subject: non-honorific. Object: non-honorific.)	GROUP II. (Subject: honorific. Object: non-honorific.)	GROUP I. (Subject: non-honorific. Object: non-honorific.)	GROUP II. (Subject: honorific. Object: non-honorific.)	GROUP I. (Subject: non-honorific. Object: non-honorific.)	GROUP II. (Subject: honorific. Object: non-honorific.)	GROUP III. (Subject: non-honorific. Object: honorific.)	GROUP IV. (Subject: honorific. Object: honorific.)
1	Transitive: *al*: fem. al^{i}		Transitive: ^{a}lai Or (with object in 2nd person.) Transitive: ^{a}lau, $^{a}lah^{u}$.		Transitive: $^{a}laik$ Or (with object in 2nd person.) Transitive: $^{a}lauk$.		Transitive: $^{a}lainh^{i}$.	
2	...	Same as 1st person.	Transitive: $^{a}l\breve{a}h$; fem. $^{a}l\bar{i}h^{i}$, $^{a}l\bar{i}h^{i}$. Intransitive: $^{a}l\breve{a}h$; fem. $^{a}l\bar{i}h$, $^{a}l\bar{i}h^{i}$.	Same as 1st person, but no forms for object in 2nd person.	...	Same as 1st person, but no forms for object in 2nd person.	...	Same as 1st person.
3	Transitive: ^{a}lak Intransitive: *al*; fem. al^{i}.	$^{a}lath^{i}$. $^{a}l\breve{a}h$; fem. $^{a}l\bar{i}h$, $^{a}l\bar{i}h^{i}$.	Trans. $al^{a}kai$. Intrans.: ^{a}lai Or (with object in 2nd person.) Trans.: $al^{a}kau$. Intrans.: ^{a}lau.	...	Trans.: $al^{a}kaik$ Intrans.: $^{a}laik$. Or (with object in 2nd person.) Trans.: $al^{a}kauk$. Intrans.: $^{a}lauk$.	...	Transitive: $al^{a}kainh^{i}$. Intransitive: $^{a}lainh^{i}$.	

212. (*d*) (9). **Perfect Indicative.**
(*d*)(10). **Pluperfect Indicative.**

These two tenses are formed by combining the past participle with auxiliary verbs. They will be dealt with under the head of periphrastic tenses (Chapter III).

CHAPTER II.

Verbs Substantive and Auxiliary Verbs.

213. The Verb Substantive is freely employed in the formation of periphrastic tenses;—*viz.* of the Present Indicative, the Imperfect Indicative, the Perfect Indicative, and the Pluperfect Indicative. There are several forms of the verb substantive, all of which are in common use.

214. The verb substantive most frequently met with is that formed from the root अछ *ach*, be. It is defective in its conjugation, the only parts used being the present and past tenses and the present participle. Moreover, in the modern language, except in one form of the 3rd person of the present, and in the present participle, the initial अ *a* is always dropped, so that the word for 'I am' is छी *chī*, not अछी *achī*. In the older language, however, of poetry and occasionally in folktales, the initial अ *a* is commonly preserved. In poetry, moreover, the final ऐ *ai* of the long form of the first person (including the 2nd person honorific), is often weakened to अ *a*, so that we have छिअ *chia* for छिऐ *chiai* for 'I am,' 'you are.' In the following paradigm such poetical forms are given within marks of parenthesis.

The conjugation of the present tense of this verb is based on the conjugation of the old Present (see § 197) of the regular verb, but presents a few abnormal forms. The conjugation of the past tense follows that of the past tense of the regular intransitive verb. This verb is conjugated as follows :—

√ अछ *ach*, be.

Present Participle :—अछैत *achait* ; fem. अछैति *achaiti*, being.

215. Present. I am, &c.

PERSON.	SHORT FORM.		LONG FORM.		REDUNDANT FORM.			
	GROUP I. (Subject: non-honorific. Object: non-honorific.)	GROUP II. (Subject: honorific. Object: non-honorific.)	GROUP I. (Subject: non-honorific. Object: non-honorific.)	GROUP II. (Subject: honorific. Object: non-honorific.)	GROUP I. (Subject: non-honorific. Object: non-honorific.)	GROUP II. (Subject: honorific. Object: non-honorific.)	GROUP III. (Subject: non-honorific. Object: honorific.)	GROUP IV. (Subject: honorific. Object: honorific.)
1	छी *chi*, (अछी *achī*.)		छिऐ *chiai*, (छिअ *chia*) Or (with object in 2nd person.) छिऔ *chiau*, छिअहु *chiah*^{u}.		छिऐक *chiaik* Or (with object in 2nd person.) छिऔक *chiauk*.		छिऐन्हि *chiainh*^{i}.	
2	छें *chẽ*, छैं *chaĩ*.	Same as 1st person.	छह *chah*; fem. छहिं *chahĩ*.	Same as 1st person, but no forms for object in 2nd person.	छहँक *chahãk*, छहीक *chahīk*.	Same as 1st person, but no forms for object in 2nd person.	छहुन्हि *chahũnh*^{i}.	Same as 1st person.
3	अछि *ach*^{i}; or छिक *chik*, छीक *chīk*; fem. छीकि *chīk*^{i}.	छथि *chath*^{i}	छै *chai*, छिकै *chikai* (अछै *achai*) Or (with object in 2nd person.) छौ *chau*, छहु *chah*^{u} छिकौ *chikau*, छिकहु *chikah*^{u}	...	छैक *chaik*, छिकैक *chikaik*. Or (with object in 2nd person.) छौक *chauk*, छिकौक *chikauk*.	...	छैन्हि *chainh*^{i}.	छथीन्हि *chathīnh*^{i}. छथून्हि *chathūnh*^{i}.

216. **Past.** I was, &c.

PERSON.	SHORT FORM.		LONG FORM.		REDUNDANT FORM.			
	GROUP I. (Subject : non-honorific. Object : non-honorific.)	GROUP II. (Subject : honorific. Object : non-honorific.)	GROUP I. (Subject : non-honorific. Object : non-honorific.)	GROUP II. (Subject : honorific. Object : non-honorific.)	GROUP I. (Subject : non-honorific. Object : non-honorific.)	GROUP II. (Subject : honorific. Object : non-honorific.)	GROUP III. (Subject : non-honorific. Object : honorific.)	GROUP IV. (Subject : honorific. Object : honorific.)
1	चलहुँ *chalah*$^{\tilde{u}}$, चली *chalī.*		चलिऐ *chaliai* Or (with object in 2nd person.) चलिऔ *chaliau*, चलिअहु *chaliah*^{u}.		चलिऐक *chaliaik* Or (with object in 2nd person.) चलिऔक *chaliauk.*		चलिऐन्हि *chaliainh*^{i}	
2	चलें *chalẽ*, चलैं *chalaĩ.*	Same as 1st person.	चलाह *chalāh*; fem. चलीह *chalih* चलीहि *chalih*^{i}.	Same as 1st person, but no forms for object in 2nd person.	चलहँक *chal*^{a}*hā̃k*, चलहीक *chal*^{a}*hīk.*	Same as 1st person, but no forms for object in 2nd person.	चलहुँन्हि *chal*^{a}*hũnh*^{i}.	Same as 1st person.
3	चल *chal* ; fem. चलि *chal*^{i}.	चलाह *chalāh* ; (अचलाह *ach*^{a}*lāh*) fem. चलीह *chalih* चलीहि *chalih*^{i}.	चलै *chalai* Or (with object in 2nd person.) चलौ *chalau*, चलहु *chalah*^{u}	...	चलैक *chalaik* Or (with object in 2nd person.) चलौक *chalauk*	...	चलैन्हि *chalainh*^{i}	चलथीन्हि *chal*^{a}*thīnh*^{i}, चलथून्हि *chal*^{a}*thūnh*^{i}.

The following are examples of the use of this verb, as a verb substantive. Many other examples will be found under the head of the periphrastic tenses.

217. **Present.** *First Person* :—जातिक जोगी छी, *jātik jōgī chī*, by (lit. of) caste we are Jōgis.

हम धरमक बेटा छी, *ham dharamak bēṭā chī*, I am the son of Virtue (*i.e.*, I am telling the truth).

हम हलधर अनुचर छिअ जकर ।
चउदह भुवन हुकुम चल तकर ॥

hama haladhara anucara chia jakara ।
caudaha bhuban hukuma cala takara ॥ (Man. ix, 66.)

The fourteen worlds move at His commands, whose servants I and Haladhara are.

Second Person :—कोन लोग छी, *kōn lōg chī*, what caste are Your Honours ?

एहि नहि जनली अहाँ भद्री छी, *ehi nahi janalī ahā̃ bhadrī chī*, this I did not know (that) Your Honour is Bhadri.

Third Person :—कखन जाएत दिन कत अछि बेरि, *kakhana jāeta* (m.c. for *jāet*) *dina kata achi bēri*, when will the day go how much time is (left) ? (Vid. xii, 3).

एहि अछि काली फनि दुरबार, *ehi achi kālī phani durabāra*, (in) this (place) is the invincible snake Kālī (Man. iv, 19).

चारिम एक कथा आओर अछि, *cārim ek kathā āor achi*, there is one more, a fourth, statement (which I am going to tell you).

हमरा बेटा जेहन छथि से खूब जनै छी, *hamarā bēṭā jehan chathi sē khūb jonai-chī*, you know well what sort (of temper) there is to my (respected) son.

कमल भमर जग अछए अनेक, *kamala-bhramara jaga achae* (for *achai*) *anēka*, lotus(-loving) bees there are many in (this) world (Vid. xlv, 1).

सन्तति ओकर आज धरि अछए, *santati ōkara ăja* (m. c. for *āja*) *dhari achae* (for *achai*), his descendants exist to this day (Man. xiii, 18).

ताहिर मीयाँक बेटी छै बड़ जोगतान, *tāhir mīyā̃k bēṭī chai baṛ jōgatān*, Tāhir Miyā̃'s daughter is a great sorceress.

जे काल धैलक अहि तोहरा से छौ लगे में, *jē kāl dhailak ahi tohrā sē chau lagē mẽ*, the death (*i.e.*, the murderer) which has seized you is still close to you.

तोहरा घर में एक चन्द्रहार छहु, *tohrā ghar mẽ ek candrahār chahu*, in your house there is to you a necklace.

बकस में छौ-टा रुपैया छैक ओ मसाला सभ छैक, *bakas mẽ chau-ṭā rupaiā chaik ō masālā sabh chaik*, in the box are six rupees, and there are dainties.

की नाम छिक। कालू सदा नाम छीक, *kī nām chik? kālū sadā nām chīk*, what is (your) name? (my) name is Kālū Sadā.

श्री लछमी देवि कें नेना छोट छैन्हि, *śrī lachmī dēbi kẽ nēnā chōṭ chainhi*, to the respected Lakṣmī Dēvī there is a little baby (not respected), *i.e.*, she has had a baby.

सामीक अरजल छथीन्हि कुटुम भल, *sāmīk arjal chathīnhi kuṭum bhal*, the welfare of (a respected wife's) relations is the gain of (the respected) husband.

218. **Past.** *First Person* :—नान्हि-टा छली हम बाप माइक नाम नहिँ जनली, *nānhi-ṭā chalī ham bāp māik nām nahĩ janlī*, (a man is speaking) I was a baby, and did not know the name of my father and mother.

हम तोहर बैरी छलिअहु, *ham tōhar bairī chaliahu*, I was to you your enemy.

Second Person :—I have not come across any example of this person in literature.

Third Person :—हमरा पेट में मुर्गीक अंडहु सँ पैघ एक मोती छल, *hamrā pēṭ mẽ murgīk aṇḍa-hu sã paigh ek mōtī chal*, in my belly there was a pearl bigger than even a hen's egg.

गोबिंद गमन सुनल ब्रज-नारि।
जे छलि जतए बैसलि हिय हारि॥

gōbĩda gamana sunala braj-nāri ।
jē chali jatae baisali hia hāri ॥

When the women of Braj heard of the departure of Kṛṣṇa, they all sat down broken-hearted (Man. vii, 33).

अछलाह मोट छोट जे भेल ।
कोट गेलाह नहिं लाजक लेल ॥

achalăha mōṭa chōṭa jē bhēla ।
kōṭa gelăha nahī̃ lājaka lēla ॥

Those who had been (lit. were) (so) stout (and valiant, and) had (now) become (so) small, out of shame did not return to the fortress (Man. x, 50).

एक चिलहोरिक लोल में एक घोंघा छलै, *ek cil^a hōrik lōl mẽ ek ghõghā chalai*, there was a shell-fish in the beak of a kite.

भाइ जेठ छलहु से मारल गेल कटैया, *bhāi jēṭh chalah^u sē māral gēl kaṭaiyā*, he who was to-you your eldest brother has been killed in Kaṭaiyā.

Present Participle. तोहरा अछैत घर में चोरी भेल, *toh^a rā achait* (a sort of 'ablative absolute') *ghar mẽ cōrī bhēl*, while you were present (*i.e.*, while you were in charge) a theft took place in the house.

निज धनि अछैति नइ उपभोगब ।
केबल परहिक आसे ॥

nija dhani achaiti nai upabhōgaba ।
kēbala parahi-ka āsē ॥

You, while having your own wife, will not be content with her but your hope is only for another's wife (Vid. li, 6).

अछइत बस्तु न करिअ निरासे *achaita bastu na karia* (m. c. for *kariă*) *nirāsē*, do not disappoint him as long as any thing remaineth (to thee) (Vid. iii, 4).

This verb is very frequently used with a genitive or dative of possession to mean 'to have.' Thus from Manbōdh (vi, 34, 35).

चानुर मुष्टि हमर अछि माल ।......
करि बर अछि मोहि कुबलए पीड़ ।

cānura muṣṭi hamara achi māla ।......
kari bara achi mohi kubalae pīṛa ।

Of me are (*i.e.*, I have) (two) wrestlers, Cānura and Muṣṭi... to me is (*i.e.*, I have) an excellent elephant (named) Kuvalaya Piḍa. Similarly Vidyâpati (lxxix, 7).

नहिं मोरा टका अछि नहिं धेनु गाइ *nahĩ mōrā ṭakā achi nahĩ dhēnu gāī*, I have no money and no milch cow.

√ अह *ah*, be.

219. Another form of the verb substantive which we frequently hear in conversation is connected with the Hindī है *hai*, is, and may be said to be based on the root अह *ah*, be. It is still more defective than the root अछ *ach*; indeed, I have only met two forms of it, *viz.*:

अहि *ahⁱ*, he is.

हौ *hau*, he is (object in 2nd person).

The latter form would postulate the existence of है *hai*, but I have not come across it. Examples of the use of these two forms are :—

थोरेक आम हमरा संग अहि *thōrek ām hamᵃrā saṅg ahⁱ*, a few mangoes are in my possession.

देस देस आओर गाम गाम घुमला सँ की लाभ अहि *dēs dēs āor gām gām ghumᵃlā sã kī lābh ahⁱ*, what profit is there from wandering about from country to country and from village to village ?

मोनसी कहलथीन्हि नहिं हौ *monᵃsī kahalᵃthīnhⁱ 'nahĩ hau,'* the (respected) scribe said (politely) 'it is not (what you think).'

The use of this root is regular in the Magᵃhī and Bhojᵃpurī dialects of Bihārī. In them the verb is much more fully conjugated.

√ थिक *thik*, be.

220. Instead of the verb √ अछ *ach*, the verb √ थिक *thik* may be substituted, but only in the present tense.

221. The √ थिक *thik* is by origin the strong form of the √ *थि *thi*, which is derived from the Sanskrit स्थित *sthita*, stood. स्थित *sthita* is the past participle of the Sanskrit intransitive √ स्था *sthā*, stand. It should therefore be remembered that √ थिक *thik is by origin a past participle of an intransitive verb.*

Although, therefore, it is now only used in the sense of the present tense, it takes the terminations of the past tense of an intransitive verb, the letter ल *l* being omitted. It will be remembered that this ल *l* is the sign of the past tense, and in this case it is not required, as the √ थिक *thik* is already in the past.

The following is therefore the conjugation of the √ थिक *thik* in the present tense. It is not used in any other tense.

222. **Present.** I am, &c.

PERSON.	SHORT FORM.		LONG FORM.		REDUNDANT FORM.			
	GROUP I. (Subject: non-honorific. Object: non-honorific.)	GROUP II. (Subject: honorific. Object: non-honorific.)	GROUP I. (Subject: non-honorific. Object: non-honorific.)	GROUP II. (Subject: honorific. Object: non-honorific.)	GROUP I. (Subject: non-honorific. Object: non-honorific).	GROUP II. (Subject: honorific. Object: non-honorific).	GROUP III. (Subj.: non-honorific. Object: honorific).	GROUP IV. (Subject honorific. Object: honorific).
1	थिकहुँ *thikah$^{\tilde{u}}$*		थिकिऐ *thikiai* Or (with object in 2nd person.) थिकिऔ *thikiau*, थिकिअहु *thikiah^{u}*		थिकिऐक *thikiaik* Or (with object in 2nd person.) थिकिऔक *thikiauk*.		थिकिऐन्हि *thikiainh^{i}*.	
2	थिकेँ *thikẽ*, थिकैँ *thikaĩ*.	Same as 1st person.	थिकाह *thikāh*; fem. थिकीह *thikīh*, थिकीहि *thikīh^{i}*.	Same as 1st person, but no forms for object in 2nd person.	थिकहँक *thik^{a}hãk* थिकहीक *thik^{a}hīk*.	Same as 1st person, but no forms for object in 2nd person.	थिकहुन्हि *thik^{a}hũnh^{i}*,	Same as 1st person.
3	थिक *thik*, थीक *thīk*; fem. थीकि *thīk^{i}*.	थिकाह *thikāh*; fem. थिकीह *thikīh*, थिकीहि *thikīh^{i}*.	थिकै *thikai* Or (with object in 2nd person.) थिकौ *thikau*, थिकहु *thikah^{u}*	...	थिकैक *thikaik*. Or (with object in 2nd person.) थिकौक *thikauk*	...	थिकैन्हि *thikainh^{i}*.	थिकथीन्हि *thik^{a}thīnh^{i}*, थिकथून्हि *thik^{a}thūnh^{i}*.

The following are examples of the use of this form of the present of the Verb Substantive.

First Person :—पहिल खंड हम लेब किऐक-तँ हम जंगलक राजा थिकहुँ *pahil khaṇḍ ham lēb, kiaik-tã ham jaṅgalak rājā thikahũ*, the first portion I shall take because I am king of the forest.

जाति के हम नटिन थिकहुँ *jāti ke ham naṭin thikahũ*, by caste I (fem.) am a *naṭin.*

Second Person :—के तों थिकाह ककर कुल जानि ।
बिनु परिचय नहिं देब पिढ़ि पानि ॥
थिकहुँ पथुकजन राज कुमार ।
धनिक बिओग भरमि संसार ॥

kē tõ thikāha kakara kula jāni ।
binu paricaya nahī deba piṛhi pāni ॥
thikahũ pathukajana rāja-kumāra ।
dhani-ka biōga bharami (m.c. for *bharamī*) *sansāra* ॥

'Who are you (respected) and of what family? Without previous acquaintance I give no man a seat or water.'

'I am a traveller and a Rājpūt; and, separated from my love, I roam over the world' (Vid. lxxx, 2, 3).

Third Person :—दीना भद्रीक गीत सपनोती थिक *dīnā bhadrīk gīt sapanautī thik*, the song of Dinā (and) Bhadrī is (like) a dream (to us).

बिद्यापति एह गाओल सजनी गे
ई थिक नब रस रीती ।
बयस जुगल सम चित थिक सजनी गे
दुहु मन परम हुलासे ॥

bidyāpati eha gāola, sajanī gē,
ī thika naba rasa rītī ।
bayasa jugala, sama cita thika, sajanī gē,
duhu mana parama hulāsē ॥

(Saith) Vidyāpati, 'this I sang, O friend. This is the way of new delights. Their ages are equal, their souls are in unison.

O friend. In the hearts of both is supremest rapture.' (Vid. xxiii, 11, 12).

तखन सलहेस कहैत छथीन्हि जे कोन चोर थीक *takhan sal°hēs kahait chathīnh' jē 'kōn cōr thīk,'?* then Salhēs says, 'who is the thief'?

धैलक तरह जेहन गोट थीक *dhailaka taraha jehana goṭa thīka,* he took every form which was (possible for him to take). (Man. vii, 3).

तो-हुँ थीकि मोर माए *tō-hũ thīk' mōr māi,* my mother is you also (*i.e.*, you also are my mother).

हमर सक नहिं थीकि *hamar sak nahĩ thīk'*, my power is not (*i.e.*, I am not able). Here, quite exceptionally, an inanimate word is treated as a feminine, and has a feminine verb after it.

ई कोन बिआन थिकैक। ई एकर आठम बिआन थिकै *ī kōn biān thikaik? ī ēkar āṭham biān thikai,* what calving (of the cow) is this? It is her eighth calving.

चानन सौं अनुरागल थिकइन्हि
भसम चढ़ाबथि अंग।
भनहिं बिद्यापति सुनिऐ मनाइनि
थिकाह दिगंबर भंग॥

cānana sõ anurāgala thikainhi,
bhasama caṛhābathi aṅga ।
bhanahĩ bidyāpati suniai manāini
thikāha digumbara bhaṅga ॥

He is painted with sandal-wood,
He smears ashes on his body.
Saith Vidyāpati, 'hear, O Mēnā,
It is the god Digambar Bhang.'

(Vid. lxxxii, 6, 8).

√ रह *rah*, remain.

223. Instead of the verb √ अछ *ach*, the verb √ रह *rah* may be substituted, but only in the past tense. That is to say, instead of छली *chalī*, I was, we may say रही *rahī*.

The verb √ रह *rah* means literally 'remain,' and when used as a verb substantive this meaning is retained. The verb is taken to signify 'I was such and such, and I remain so.' Hence 'I remain' is considered as equivalent to 'I was.' When used in the sense of 'I was' although the signification is one of past time, the verb is therefore conjugated in the old present and not in the form of the past tense.

The following is therefore the conjugation of the verb √ रह *rah* in the sense of the past tense of the verb substantive. It is not used for any other tense of the verb substantive. In the sense of 'remain' this verb is conjugated throughout, and is quite regular.

224. Old Present for Past. 'I was,' &c.

PERSON.	SHORT FORM. GROUP I. (Subject : non-honorific. Object : non-honorific.)	SHORT FORM. GROUP II. (Subject : honorific. Object : non-honorific.)	LONG FORM. GROUP I. (Subject : non-honorific. Object : non-honorific.)	LONG FORM. GROUP II. (Subject : honorific. Object : non-honorific.)	REDUNDANT FORM. GROUP I. (Subject : non-honorific. Object : non-honorific.)	REDUNDANT FORM. GROUP II. (Subject : honorific. Object : non-honorific.)	GROUP III. (Subj. : non-honorific. Object : honorific.)	GROUP IV. (Subject : honorific. Object : honorific.)
1	रही *rahī.*		रहिऐ *rahiai* Or (with object in 2nd person.) रहिऔ *rahiau*, रहिअहु *rahiah^u*		रहिऐक *rahiaik* Or (with object in 2nd person.) रहिऔक *rahiauk.*		रहिऐन्हि *rahiainh^i.*	
2	रह *rah.*	Same as 1st person.	रहँह *rahăh* ; fem. रहुहिँ *rahahĩ*, रहँहिँ *rahãhĩ.*	Same as 1st person, but no forms for object in 2nd person.	रहँक *rah^{a}hăk* रहहीक *rah^{a}hīk*	Same as 1st person, but no forms for object in 2nd person.	रहहुन्हि *rah^{a}hūnh^i.*	Same as 1st person.
3	रहे *rahē,* *रह *raha.*	रहथि *rahath^i*	रहै *rahai* Or (with object in 2nd person.) रहौ *rahau*, रहहु *rahah^u.*	...	रहैक *rahaik* Or (with object in 2nd person.) रहौक *rahauk.*	...	रहैन्हि *rahainh^i.*	रहथीन्हि *rah^{a}thīnh^i*, रहथून्हि *rah^{a}thūnh^i.*

The following are examples of the use of the √ रह *rah* as a Verb Substantive.

First Person :—I have not noted any instances of the use of this person as a verb substantive. It occurs as an auxiliary verb.

Second Person :—The same remarks apply.

Third Person : प्रलए काल तहँ रह नहिँ घाटि, *pralae kāla tahã raha nahĩ ghāṭi*, (the crash) was not less than (that at) the time of the general destruction of the universe (Man. v, 39).

रहथि मिथिला मेँ बीरेश्वर नामक मन्त्री, *rahath*[i] *mithilā mẽ bīrēśwar nāmak mantrī*, in Mithilā there was a prime-minister named Virēśwara.

गुड़कल गुड़कल भिड़ुकल जाए ।
जतए रहए दुइ ब्रिच्छ अकाए ॥

guṛakala guṛakala bhiṛukala jāe ।
jatae rahae (for *rahai*) *dui briccha akāe* ॥

Rolling, rolling, bouncing, it goes to where were two huge trees (Man. iii, 10).

जखन धै लेलेँ चलेँ तखन छाड़ब की रहौ, *jakhan dhai lēlẽ chalẽ takhan chāṛab kī rahau*, (lit.) when you had seized me, then what letting go was there (to you) (*i e.* why did you let me go)?

हाड़ जे मुँह मेँ रहैक से-हो गमौलक, *hāṛ jē mũh mẽ rahaik, sē-hō gamaulak*, the bone which was in his mouth, he lost that also.

कोनो धनिक कैँ दुइ बेटा रहैन्हि, *kōnō dhanik kẽ dui bēṭā rahainh*[i], to a certain rich man there were two (respected) sons.

225. It is thus seen that there are several forms of the verb substantive. All these can also be used as auxiliary verbs in the formation of periphrastic tenses. The √ अछ *ach* is the one generally employed, but we frequently meet the others used instead of it. This should be borne in mind, as, in the paradigms, I shall in the main confine myself to the forms with √ अछ *ach*.

The following summary of the short forms of the 3rd person will serve as a reminder.

अछि *ach*^{i}, or अहि *ah*^{i}, or थिक *thik* } he is

छल *chal*, or रहै *rahē* } he was.

---

226. The √ हो *hō*, become, as a Verb Substantive, and as an Auxiliary Verb.

It will have been observed that the Verbs Substantive just described are all defective, possessing amongst them all only two finite tenses,—the present indicative, and the past indicative. The remaining tenses, when required, are furnished by the corresponding forms of the √ हो *hō*, become. This verb is also employed in the formation of some of the rarer periphrastic tenses (see § 241).

The verb √ हो *hō* is anomalous in several of its forms, and will be fully described under the head of irregular verbs (§ 322).

For our present purposes it is sufficient to note here the following tenses, which are employed as auxiliaries :—

(2) *Present Conditional* :—होइ *hōi*, (if) I become, (if) I be.

(4) *Future Indicative* :—हैब *haib* or होएब *hoeb*, I shall become, I shall be.

(5) *Past Conditional* :—होइतहुँ *hōitah*^{u}, (if) I had become, (if) I had been.

The past is भेलहुँ *bhēlah*^{u}, I became. It is not employed either as a Verb Substantive or as an Auxiliary Verb.

CHAPTER III.

PERIPHRASTIC TENSES.

227. In the list of tenses given in § 194, the following are periphrastic :—

(c) (6) Present Indicative
(7) Imperfect Indicative
Formed from the Present Participle.
(d) (9) Perfect Indicative
(10) Pluperfect Indicative
Formed from the Past Participle.

Besides these there are six rare tenses, which can theoretically be made with the aid of the √ हो *hō*, become, as an auxiliary verb. They run parallel to the corresponding tenses in Hindi, but I have met only one instance of them in my reading. They are dealt with in § 241.

228. (c) (6) The **Present Indicative** is formed by conjugating the present tense of the auxiliary verb with the present participle. Thus देखैत *dekhait*. seeing; छी *chī*, I am; देखैत छी *dekhait chī*, I see. Or we may have देखैत अछि *dekhait ach*, he sees (there is no first person for this form of the auxiliary); or देखैत थिकहुँ *dekhait thikah*, I see. Of course, instead of छी *chī*, we can have छिऐ *chiai*, छिओ *chiau*, छिऐक *chiaik*, and so on. In all cases that goes without saying.

In this tense (and also in the imperfect) it is very common to drop the final त *t* of the present participle, and to write it as one word with the auxiliary. Thus देखैछी *dekhai-chī*, I see. and so throughout. Here, although *written* in the Nāgarī character as one word, the two do not form a real compound This is seen in cases in which the present participle does not end in ऐत *ait*, but, as is the case with some vocalic roots, in इत *it* preceded by a long vowel (see Chapter IV). In such cases the suffixed auxiliary does not bring in the rule of the short antepenultimate, as it would if it was really compounded with the participle. Thus, the present participle of the √ खा *khā*, eat, is खाइत *khāit*, and the present indicative is खाइछी *khāi-chī*, not खइछी *khaichī*, I am eating. In transliteration, I, therefore, insert a hyphen between the participle and the auxiliary as shown above.

In the short form of Group I in the 3rd person there is a further slight optional irregularity. For "he sees," the usual (but not, by any means, the only) form is देखइछि *dekhaïch*[i] or even देखइछ *dekhaïch*, as well as देखैत अछि *dekhait achh*[i] or देखैछि *dekhai-achh*[i]. It should be noted carefully that this is always pronounced *dekha-ichh*[i] or *dekha-ichh*, and that the *a* and the *i* never coalesce into ऐ *ai* as is usually the case (see § 13). Here the two letters always form two distinct syllables.

In the feminine, the feminine of the present participle (देखैति *dekhait*[i]) should be used. The final ति *t*[i] is elided exactly like the masculine त *t*.

It will be remembered that there are various ways of spelling the present participle. We may have देखैत *dekhait*, or देखइत *dekhaït* or देखएत *dekhaet*, or देखयित *dekhayit*. As explained in § 13, this is only a matter of spelling, not of pronunciation.

The following are therefore the terminations of this tense :—

229 (c) (6). **Present Indicative.** Uncontracted form. The terminations to be added to the root direct.

PERSON.	SHORT FORM. GROUP I. (Subject: non-honorific. Object: non-honorific.)	SHORT FORM. GROUP II. (Subject: honorific. Object: non-honorific.)	LONG FORM. GROUP I. (Subject: non-honorific. Object: non-honorific.)	LONG FORM. GROUP II. (Subject: honorific. Object: non-honorific.)	REDUNDANT FORM. GROUP I. (Subject: non-honorific. Object: non-honorific.)	REDUNDANT FORM. GROUP II. (Subject: honorific. Object: non-honorific.)	GROUP III. (Subject: non-honorific. Object: honorific.)	GROUP IV. (Subject: honorific. Object: honorific.)
1	*ait chi*; fem. *ait^{i} chi.*		*ait chiai*; fem. *ait^{i} chiai* Or (with object in 2nd person.) *ait chiau*; fem. *ait^{i} chiau.*		*ait chiaik*; fem. *ait^{i} chiaik* Or (with object in 2nd person.) *ait chiauk*; fem. *ait^{i} chiauk.*		*ait chiainh^{i}*; fem. *ait^{i} chiainh^{i}.*	
2	*ait chẽ*; fem. *ait^{i} chẽ.*	Same as 1st person.	*ait chah̃*; fem. *ait^{i} chahĩ.*	Same as 1st person, but no forms for object in 2nd person.	*ait chahâk*; fem. *ait^{i} chahâk*	Same as 1st person, but no forms for object in 2nd person.	*ait chahũnh^{i}*; fem. *ait^{i} chahũnh^{i}.*	Same as 1st person.
3	*ait ach^{i}*; fem. *ait^{i} ach^{i}.*	*ait chath^{i}*; fem. *ait^{i} chath^{i}.*	*ait chai*; fem. *ait^{i} chai* Or (with object in 2nd person.) *ait chau*; fem. *ait^{i} chau*	......	*ait chaik*; fem *ait^{i} chaik* Or (with object in 2nd person.) *ait chauk*; fem *ait^{i} chauk*	......	*ait chainh^{i}*; fem. *ait^{i} chainh^{i}.*	*ait chathĩnh^{i}*; fem. *ait^{i} chathinh^{i}.*

230. (*c*) (6) **Present Indicative.** Contracted forms. The terminations to be added to the root direct. All forms are common gender, unless special feminine forms are given.

PERSON.	SHORT FORM.		LONG FORM.		REDUNDANT FORM.			
	GROUP I. (Subject: non-honorific. Object: non-honorific.)	GROUP II. (Subject: honorific. Object: non-honorific.)	GROUP I. (Subject: non-honorific. Object: non-honorific.)	GROUP II. (Subject: honorific. Object: non-honorific.)	GROUP I. (Subject: non-honorific. Object: non-honorific.)	GROUP II. (Subject: honorific. Object: non-honorific.)	GROUP III. (Subject: non-honorific. Object: honorific.)	GROUP IV. (Subject: honorific. Object: honorific.)
1	*ai-chī.*		*ai-chiai* Or (with object in 2nd person.) *ai-chiau.*		*ai-chiaik* Or (with object in 2nd person.) *ai-chiauk.*		*ai-chiainh*^{i}.	
2	*ai-chē̃.*	Same as 1st person.	*ai-chăh*; fem. *ai-chah*^{i}.	Same as 1st person, but no forms for object in 2nd person.	*ai-ch*^{a}*hăk.*	Same as 1st person, but no forms for object in 2nd person.	*ai-ch*^{a}*hŭnh*^{i}.	Same as 1st person.
3	*ai-ach*^{i} or (more usually) *aĭch*^{i} or *aĭch.*	*ai-chath*^{i}.	*ai-chai* Or (with object in 2nd person.) *ai-chau.*	...	*ai-chaik* Or (with object in 2nd person.) *ai-chauk.*	...	*ai-chainh*^{i}.	*ai-ch*^{a}*thīnh*^{i}.

In the above paradigms I have omitted duplicate forms of the Verb Substantive. They can easily be supplied.

It is unnecessary to do more than remind the student that any other form of the verb substantive (अछि *ah*^{i}, छौ *hau*, थिकहुँ *thikah*^{u}, &c.), can be used instead of those given above.

The following are examples of the use of this tense :—

First Person :—गोड़ लगैत छी पैयाँ परैत छी एहि नहिं जनली अहाँ भद्री छी, *gōr lagait chī, paĩyā̃ parait chī, eh*^{i} *nah*^{i} *jan*^{a}*lī ahā̃ bhadrī chī*, I clasp (your) legs, I fall at (your) feet, this I did not know that your Honour is Bhadrī.

भाइ चिट्ठी लिखैछी, *bhāi ciṭṭhī likhai-chī*, brother, I am writing a letter.

देखैत अछी सूखल डारि पर बादिल कागा बोलैत अछि मरन मरन, *dekhait achī* (old form of *chī*) *sūkhal ḍār*^{i} *par bādil kāgā bolait ach*^{i} *maran maran*, I see on a branch the fearful crow is saying 'Death, Death.'

भेद बताए दैति छी, *bhēd batāe dait*^{i} *chī*, I (fem.) tell an artifice.

एहि कथा पर हम तोहरा एक कहिनी सुनबैछिअहु, *eh*^{i} *kathā par ham toh*^{a}*rā ek kahinī sun*^{a}*bai-chiah*^{u}, on this account I (fem.) cause you to hear (*i.e.*, tell you) a story.

हम रे अहिरा पुछैत छिऔक बड़ साधु भाब, *ham, rē ahirā, puchait chiauk baṛ sādh*^{u} *bhāb*, I am asking you, O cowherd, in a very gentle manner.

आन दिन देखिऔक कटैया बड़ सोहाबन आजू कटैया देखैछिऔक बड़ भयाबन, *ān din dekhiauk* (old present) *kaṭaiyā baṛ sohāban, ājū kaṭaiyā dekhai-chiauk baṛ bhayāban*, on other days I see (*i.e.*, used to see) the Kataiyā (forest) (about which you speak) very pleasant. To-day I see it very terrible.

Second Person :—कहलन्हि जे अहिरा कहाँ जाइछैं, *kah*^{a}*lanh*^{i} *jē 'ahirā, kahā̃ jāi-chaĩ'* (the present participle of √जा *jā* is *jāit*, not *jāait*, see §§ 282, 310), (the respected Bhadrī) said, 'O cow herd, where are you (not respectful) going.'

जाहि मरद लाय एतेक मगरूमी देखबैति छैं ताहि मरद के हम बरा डीहे देखब, *jāh*^{i} *marad lāy etek mag*^{a}*rūmī dekh*^{a}*bait*^{i} *chaĩ, tāh*^{i} *marad kē ham barā ḍihē dēkhab*, the man on whose account you (fem.) show so much pride, I will see at Barā Ḍih.

हे बाबू हबेलीक की पुछैत छी? मुसहरक हबेली छीक, *hē bābū, habēlīk kī puchait chī? Musah*^{a}*rak habēlī chīk*, O gentlemen, Are you asking (the caste) of the house? It is the house of a Musahar.

हमरा बेटा जेहन छथि से खूब जनैछी, *ham*^{a}*rā bēṭā jehan chath*^{i}*, sē khūb janai-chī*, you (fem.) know well what sort of (temper) there is to my son (*i.e.*, what a temper he has).

केना के मारैत छँह हो भगिना फोटरा फेर भेल तैयार, *kenā ke mărait chăh, hō bhaginā, phoṭ*^{a}*rā pher bhēl taiyār*, how are you hitting (him), O Nephews? Phoṭarā is again ready (to attack you).

एक ठाम रहि कँ स्वामी में लय किऐ नहिं लगबैछँह आओर कोनो मठ में बैसि कँ दाताक गुन किऐ नहिं गबैछँह, *ek ṭhām rah*^{i} *kă swāmī mē lay kiai nah*^{ĩ} *lag*^{a}*bai-chăh? Āor kōnō maṭh mē bais*^{i} *kă dātāk gun kiai nah*^{ĩ} *gabai-chăh*, why do you not remain in one place and devote yourself to the contemplation of the Master? Why do you not sit in some temple and sing the goodness of the Giver?

किएक सबहु होइछिअ मति मूढ़, *kieka sabahu hoi-chia* (the present participle of √हो *hō* often takes the form होइत *hoit*, see § 322) *mati mūṛha*, why are you all of foolish mind (Manbōdh, v. 22)?

अहाँ लोकनि तकाजा नहिं करैछिऐन्हि, *ahā̃ lok*^{a}*ni takājā nah*^{i} *karai-chiainh*^{i}, you (respected people) are not pressing (the respected person) (to pay his debts).

Third person:—ओकर नाम केओ ने बाट बटोही धरैत अछि, *ōkar nām keo nē bāṭ baṭōhī dharait ach*^{i}, no traveller on the road takes (*i.e.*, utters) his name.

फोटरा बरा डीहा में गाइ भड़कबैत अछि, *phoṭ*^{a}*rā barā ḍīhā mē gāi bhaṛ*^{a}*kabait ach*^{i}, Phoṭarā is scaring the cattle in Barā Ḍih.

सदा भूकि भूकि कैं हमरा सभ कें भड़कबैअछि, *sadā bhūk*^{i} *bhūk*^{i} *kaĩ ham*^{a}*rā sabh kē̃ bhaṛ*^{a}*kabai-ach*^{i}, always on the bark (the dogs) are scaring us (*or* causing us to quarrel).

भद्री के पाँच से फजिहति करैति अछि, *bhadrī kē pā̃c sai phajihatⁱ* *karaitⁱ achⁱ*, to Bhadrī she makes use of five hundred infamies (*i.e.*, abuses him).

तिरिया पुछैअछि जातिक ठेकान, *tiriyā puchai-achⁱ jātik ṭhekān*, a woman is asking (fem.) information as to (our) name.

बिद्यापति भन इहो न निक थिक ।
जग भरि करइछि निंदा ॥

Bidyāpati bhana 'ihō na nika thika ।
jaga bhari karaïchi nindā' ॥

Saith Vidyāpati, 'this also is not right, the whole world blames it' (Vid. xxxv, 6).

जनि जल-हीन मीन जक फिरइछि ।
अहोनिसि रहइछि जागी ॥

jani jala-hīna mīna jaka phiraïchi ।
ahonisi rahaïchi jāgī ॥

Like a fish without water, she twists and turns, and day and night she remains awake (Vid. lxxvi, 8).

अपनेक ओतय कतेक मोट चलैअछि, *ap^anek otay katek mōṭ calai-ahⁱ*, how many well-buckets are working in your (farm)?

स्वामि-धन वृथा नष्ट होइछ, *swāmi-dhan bṛthā naṣṭ hoïch* (the present participle of √हो *hō* is होइत *hoit*, see § 322), my master's property is being needlessly wasted.

केवल आलसी कैं स्वामी वस्तु देअबयित छथि कपट सैं निरालसी लोक भी खायित छथि, *kēbal āl^asī kā̃ swāmī bast^u deabayit chathⁱ; kapaṭ sō̃ nirālasī lōk bhī khāyit chathⁱ*, (my) master is causing goods (*i.e.*, food) to be given only to lazy people; (but) by means of deceit people who are not lazy are also eating. (This and the preceding are from Candā Jhā's version of the *Puruṣa Parīkṣā*, p. 51. Note the spelling of the present participle).

दीना राम कहैत छथि, *dinā rām kahait chathⁱ*, Dinā Rām says (so and so).

ओ लोकनि गमार थिकाह जे बैरी कें सत्यबादी बुझैछथि, *ō lokᵃni gamār thikăh, jē baīrī kē̃ satyabādī bujhai-chathⁱ*, those people are fools who consider enemies as speakers of the truth.

मालिनि कर जोरि मिनती करैछथि, *mālinⁱ kar jōrⁱ minᵃtī karai-chathⁱ*, (the respected) Mālini (name of a woman) is making supplication with hands joined together.

अबैति छौ गोआही गुजराब, *abaitⁱ chau goāhī gujᵃrāb*, she is coming to make you bear testimony.

अम्मा निरसो कालू सदा ओ अहिरा गोआर समाद नेनें अबैत छैक, *ammā nirᵃsō, kālū sadā, o ahirā goār samād nēnē̃ abait chaik*, Mother Nirsō, Kālū Sadā, and Ahirā the cowherd, are coming with the news.

एक जानबर दच्छिन सौँ अबैत छौक, *ek jānᵃbar dacchin saũ abait chauk*, an animal is coming towards you from the south.

दीना भद्री ठाढ़ भेलाह पुछैत छैन्हि जे कोन लोगक हबेली छीक, *dīnā bhadrī thāṛh bhēlăh, puchait chainhⁱ jē 'kōn, lōyak habēlī chīk,'* Dīnā Bhadri stood, they are asking (politely) 'of what caste is (this) the house ?'

कालू सदा के कहैत छथीन्हि जे हमहुँ मुसहर छी, *kālū sadā kē kahait chathīnhⁱ jē hamahᵘ musahar chī*, they (the respected ones) say (politely) to Kālū Sadā that, 'we also are Musahars.'

तखन पुछैछथीन्हि चंपा *takhan puchai-chathīnhⁱ campā*, then (the respected) Campā (name of a woman) asks (politely).

No example of the use of the √थिक *thik* as an auxiliary occurs in the above examples. I have failed to find such in literature, where it seems to be only used as a verb substantive. We, however, occasionally hear it employed as an auxiliary in conversation.

231. (c) (7). The **Imperfect Indicative** is formed by conjugating the past tense of the Auxiliary Verb with the present participle. Thus देखैत *dekhait*, seeing; छलहुँ *chalahᵘ*, I was; देखैत छलहुँ *dekhait chalahᵘ*, I was seeing. Or we may say देखैत रही *dekhait rahī*.

As in the present tense it is very common to drop the final त *t* of the present participle, and to write it as one word with the auxiliary. Thus देखैछलहुँ *dekhai-chalah*ŭ, and so throughout.

In the feminine, the feminine of the present participle (देखैति *dekhait*ⁱ) should be used. The final ति *t*ⁱ is elided exactly like the masculine त *t*.

As in the Present Indicative (see § 228) there are the usual variations of spelling of the present participle.

The following are therefore the terminations of this tense:—

232. (*c*) (7). **Imperfect Indicative.** Uncontracted form. The terminations to be added to the root direct.

PERSON.	SHORT FORM.		LONG FORM.		REDUNDANT FORM.			
	GROUP I. (Subject: non-honorific. Object: non-honorific.)	GROUP II. (Subject honorific. Object: non-honorific.)	GROUP I. (Subject: non-honorific. Object: non-honorific.)	GROUP II. (Subject: honorific. Object: non-honorific.)	GROUP I. (Subject: non-honorific. Object: non-honorific.)	GROUP II. (Subject: honorific. Object: non-honorific.)	GROUP III. (Subject: non-honorific. Object: honorific)	GROUP IV. (Subject: honorific. Object: honorific.)
1	*ait chalah*$^{\tilde{u}}$; fem. *ait*^{i} *chalah*$^{\tilde{u}}$.		*ait chaliai*; fem. *ait*^{i} *chaliai* Or (with object in 2nd person.) *ait chaliau*; fem. *ait*^{i} *chaliau*.		*ait chaliaik*; fem. *ait*^{i} *chaliaik* Or (with object in 2nd person) *ait chaliauk*; fem. *ait*^{i} *chaliauk*.		*ait chaliainhi*; fem. *ait*^{i} *chaliainh*^{i}.	
2	*ait chal*$^{\bar{e}}$; fem. *ait*^{i} *chalē*.	Same as 1st person.	*ait chalăh*; fem. *ait*^{i} *chalīh*.	Same as 1st person, but no forms for object in 2nd person.	*ait chal*^{a}*hăk*; fem. *ait*^{i} *chal*^{a}*hăk*	Same as 1st person, but no forms for object in 2nd person.	*ait chal*^{a}*hūn-h*^{i}; fem *ait*^{i} *chal*^{a}*hūnh*^{i}.	Same as 1st person.
3	*ait chal*; fem *ait*^{i} *chal*^{i}.	*ait chalăh*; fem. *ait*^{i} *chalīh*.	*ait chalai*; fem. *ait*^{i} *chalai* Or (with object in 2nd person.) *ait chalau*; fem. *ait*^{i} *chalau*.	......	*ait chalaik*; fem. *ait*^{i} *chalaik* Or with object in 2nd person.) *ait chalauk*; fem. *ait*^{i} *chalauk*.	......	*ait chalainh*^{i}; fem *ait*^{i} *chalainh*^{i}.	*ait chal*^{a}*thīn-h*^{i}; fem. *ait*^{i} *chal*^{a}*thīnh*^{i}.

233. (*c*) (7). **Imperfect Indicative.** Contracted form. Terminations to be added to the root direct. All forms are common gender, unless feminine forms are given.

PERSON.	SHORT FORM.		LONG FORM.		REDUNDANT FORM.			
	GROUP I. (Subject: non-honorific. Object: non-honorific.)	GROUP II. (Subject: honorific. Object: non-honorific.)	GROUP I. (Subject: non-honorific. Object: non-honorific.)	GROUP II (Subject: honorific. Object: non-honorific.)	GROUP I. (Subject: non-honorific. Object: non-honorific.)	GROUP II. (Subject: honorific. Object: non-honorific.)	GROUP III. (Subject: non-honorific. Object: honorific.)	GROUP IV. (Subject: honorific. Object: honorific.)
1	*ai-ch^{a}lahū*.		*ai ch^{a}liai* Or (with object in 2nd person.) *ai ch^{a}liau*.		*ai-ch^{a}liaik* Or (with object in 2nd person.) *ai-ch^{a}liauk*.		*ai-ch^{a}liainh^{i}*.	
2	*aich^{a}lĕ*.	Same as 1st person.	*ai-ch^{a}lăh*; fem. *ai-ch^{a}lih*.	Same as 1st person but no forms for object in 2nd person.	*ai-ch^{a}lahăk*.	Same as 1st person but no forms for object in 2nd person.	*ai-ch^{a}lahŭnh^{i}*.	Same as 1st person.
3	*ai-chal*; fem. *ai-chal^{i}*.	*ai-ch^{a}lăh*; fem. *ai-ch^{a}lih*.	*ai ch^{a}lai* Or (with object in 2nd person.) *ai-ch^{a}lau*.	......	*ai-ch^{a}laik* Or (with object in 2nd person.) *ai-ch^{a}lauk*.	.. ...	*ai-ch^{a}lainh^{i}*	*ai-chal^{a}-thinh^{i}*.

In the course of my reading, I have only noted this tense in the third person. All three persons are heard in conversation. The following are examples of the third person :—

ओ बाहर ठाढ़ भेल हाथ मिड़ैत छल, *ō bāhar ṭhāṛh bhēl hāth miṛait chal*, he stood outside (and) was wringing his hands.

दीना भद्री जिबैत छल उहे गबैत रहै, *dīnā bhadrī jibait chal uhe gabait rahai*, (when) Dīnā (and) Bhadrī were living, they were singing (*i.e.*, used to sing) that very song.

एक मोनसी बजार में बैसल चिट्ठी लिखैछल, *ek mon°sī, bajār mē baisal, ciṭṭhī likhai-chal*, a scribe, seated in the market, was writing a letter.

एक गमारि गोआरिनि माथ पर मटकुरी धैलें चलि जाइछलि, *ek gamāri goārini māth par maṭ°kurī dhailē cali jāi-chali* (the present participle of the √जा *jā* is जाइत *jāit*, see §§ 282, 310), a foolish milkmaid was going along with a pot of curds on her head.

234. (*d*) (9). **Perfect Indicative.**—This tense is conjugated in two ways. The first form is the one most commonly met with, and is made on the same principle both for transitive and intransitive verbs. All that is necessary is to take the corresponding form of the past indicative and to suffix to it the third person of the present of the auxiliary verb,—usually in the form अछि *achi* or अहि *ahi*. Note that in whatever person the verb may be, the auxiliary is always in the third person. Thus :—

Past, देखलहुँ *dekh°lahũ*, I saw.

Perfect, देखलहुँ अछि *dekh°lahũ achi* or देखलहुँ अहि *dekh°lahũ ahi*, I have seen.

Past, देखल *dēkhal*, I saw.

Perfect, देखल अछि *dēkhal achi* or देखल अहि *dēkhal ahi*, I have seen.

Past, देखलेंह *dekh°lẽh*, you saw.

Perfect, देखलेंह अछि *dekh°lẽh achi* or देखलेंह अहि *dekh°lẽh ahi* you have seen.

Past, देखलक *dekh*ᵃ*lak*, he saw.

Perfect, देखलक अछि (or अहि) *dekh*ᵃ*lak ach*ⁱ (or *ah*ⁱ), he has seen.

Past, सुतलहुँ *sut*ᵃ*lah*ᵘ, I slept.

Perfect, सुतलहुँ अछि (or अहि) *sut*ᵃ*lah*ᵘ *ach*ⁱ (or *ah*ⁱ) I have slept.

Past, सुतलाह *sut*ᵃ*lăh*, you slept.

Perfect, सुतलाह अछि (or अहि) *sut*ᵃ*lăh ach*ⁱ (or *ah*ⁱ) you have slept.

Past, सुतलै *sut*ᵃ*lai*, he slept.

Perfect, सुतलै अछि (or अहि) *sut*ᵃ*lai ach*ⁱ (or *ah*ⁱ) he has slept.

It will be remembered that the short form of the third person of the past tense of transitive verbs ends in ᵃ*lak* (thus देखलक *dekh*ᵃ*lak*, he saw), while in the case of intransitive verbs it ends in *al* (सूतल *sūtal*, he slept). We never say सुतलक *sut*ᵃ*lak*. In the perfect tense, however, the form सुतलक *sut*ᵃ*lak* is regularly employed, and is, indeed, the customary form. Thus सुतलक अछि (or अहि) *sut*ᵃ*lak ach*ⁱ (or *ah*ⁱ), he has slept.

The origin of this mode of forming the perfect is well illustrated by this last form. It will be remembered that all the terminations of the past of transitive verbs and most of those of the past of intransitive verbs are really pronouns in the case of the agent. अहुँ *ah*ᵘ, means 'by me,' अक *ak*, means 'by him,' and so on. Thus देखल+अहुँ *dekh*ᵃ*l + ah*ᵘ, means 'seen-by-me,' *i.e.*, I saw, and देखल+अक *dekh*ᵃ*l + ak* means 'seen by him,' he saw. Adding अछि *ach*ⁱ (or अहि *ah*ⁱ) we get देखल+अहुँ अछि *dekh*ᵃ*l + ah*ᵘ *ach*ⁱ, (it) is seen by me, a sort of impersonal verb with the resultant meaning 'I have seen.' Similarly देखल+अक अछि *dekh*ᵃ*l + ak ach*ⁱ is, 'it is seen by him,' *i.e.*, he has seen. In the case of intransitive verbs, सूतल *sūtal*, meaning simply 'asleep,' is a past participle, employed like the Hindi past participle सोया *sōyā*, to mean 'he slept.' But if we want to say 'he has slept,' we must make an impersonal verb सुतल+अक अछि *sut^{a}l+ak ach^i*, it is slept by him, *i.e.*, 'he has slept.' सूतल अछि *sūtal ach^i* (see below) would mean rather 'he is asleep.'

This one case of the use of सुतलक *sut^{a}lak* instead of सूतल *sūtal* is the only instance in which the conjugation of this form of the perfect differs from that of the past (omitting, of course, consideration of the added अछि *ach^i* or अहि *ah^i*), and it is quite unnecessary to give a table of the terminations.

235. The following are examples of this form of the perfect:—

First Person:—एक बकस पठाओल अछि से अहाँक हेतु, *ek bakas paṭhāol* (see § 273) *ach^i*, *sē ahā̃k hēt^u*, I have sent a box, it is for you.

सूपत बेँचि के देली अहि, *sūpat bē̃c^i ke dēlī* (see § 314) *ah^i*, I have given in barter (*lit.* having sold) the full weight.

रोपलहुँ अछि, *rop^{a}lah^u ach^i*, I have planted (see below).

अहाँ कें खोलाओलि अछि, *ahā̃ kē̃ kholāol^i* (see § 273) *ach^i*, I (fem.) have caused you to be freed.

Second Person:—कोन जिआन भेल अछि जे हमरा बाँधि देल अछि से हाल कह, *kōn jiān bhēl ach^i jē ham^{a}rā bā̃lh^i dēl* (see § 314) *ach^i*, *sē hāl kah*, explain what fault has occurred that you have bound me.

एहि बेरि कुसिआर रोपलहुँ अछि बा नहिं। कुसिआर तँ रोपलहुँ अछि, *eh^i bēr^i kusiār rop^{a}lah^u ach^i* (2nd person) *bā nah^ĩ? Kusiār tā̃ rop^{a}lah^u ach^i* (1st person), this time have you planted any sugarcane or no? I have indeed planted sugarcane (but it has not turned out well).

Third Person:—केबार अम्मा निरसो ठोकलक अहि, *kebār ammā nir^{a}sō ṭhok^{a}lak ah^i*, Mother Nirsō has shut the door.

दीना भद्री मरि गेलैन्हि तखन फेर ऐलन्हि अछि, *dīnā bhadrī mar^i gelainh^i, takhan pher ailanh^i ach^i*, Dīnā and Bhadrī died (*past*), then (*i.e.*, now) they have come (*perfect*) back again.

सौदा देऊ पुराय औरो बकिए रहलोक अछि, *saudā dēhᵘ purāy, auro bakiē rahᵃluuk achⁱ*, give the goods in full weight, more also has remained in arrear (with you) (*i.e.*, you have still to give more to make full weight).

236. The second form of the perfect is not so common as the first form. It is made in exactly the reverse way to the method of making the first form. Here it is the present tense of the auxiliary verb which is conjugated with the past participle. In the case of transitive verbs the participle is put in the instrumental case,—thus देखलेँ छी *dekhᵃlẽ chī*, I have seen—or in the locative,—thus देखले छी *dekhᵃlē chī*. In both of these forms न *n* is often substituted for ल *l*, especially by the vulgar,—thus देखनेँ छी *dekhᵃnẽ chī* or देखने छी *dekhᵃnē chī*. The past participle, whether in the instrumental or in the locative, does not change for gender.

In the case of intransitive verbs, the past participle is in the nominative form, and is liable to inflection for gender. Thus सूतल छी *sūtal chī*, fem. सूतलि छी *sutalⁱ chī*, I have slept. This form of intransitive verbs has very often (in fact generally) very little of the *meaning* of the perfect tense about it. सूतल छी *sūtal chī*, for instance, generally means 'I am asleep' rather than 'I have slept.' Sometimes, however, the sense of the perfect is quite plain. Examples of both uses will be found below.

It is unnecessary to give tables of the termination of this form of the perfect. In transitive verbs the past participle (in the instrumental or locative) is unchangeable (either for person or for gender). In intransitive verbs it is only changeable for gender. The only thing that changes for person is the auxiliary verb, and of this any appropriate form may be used.

237. The following are examples of this form of the perfect of transitive verbs:—

First Person:—अपनेक ओतय कतेक मोट चलै अछि । तीनि मोट तँ लधलेँ छी, *apᵃnek otay katek mōṭ calai-ahⁱ? Tīnⁱ mōṭ tā̃ ludhᵃlẽ chī*, how many well-buckets (worked by cattle) are in use in your (farm)? Well, I have yoked three well-buckets.

हम एकरा मारबा में बहुत दौड़-धूप कैलें छी, *ham ekᵃrā mārᵃbā mẽ bahut daur-dhūp kailẽ* (see § 306) *chī*, I have made great exertions in killing it.

Second Person :—ई कहिनी नहिं सुनलें छह, *ī kahinī nahi sunᵃlẽ chah*, have you not heard this saying ?

I have not noted in literature any instance of the occurrence of the third person of this form of the perfect of a transitive verb.

The following are examples of the use of this tense in an intransitive verb :—

First Person :—सबेरेक चलल छी, *sabērēk calal chī*, I have started (*i.e.*, I started) at dawn.

सुनंह गंगा चोरि कै आएल छी, *sunah gangā, cōrⁱ kai āel* (see § 312) *chī*, hear, O Ganges, having committed theft, I have come (*or* am come).

I have not come across any example of the second person.

Third Person :—पानि बरिसला बिना बड़ हानि भेल अछि, *pāni barisᵃlā binā baṛ hānⁱ bhēl* (see § 322) *achⁱ*, owing to the rain not falling there has been great loss.

अंगूर सभक एहन गुच्छ सभ पाकल टट्टी में लटकि रहल अछि कि जकरा सँ रस चूबि रहल अछि, *ãgūr sabhak ehan gucch sabh pākal taṭṭī mẽ laṭakⁱ rahal achⁱ, ki jakᵃrā sã ras cūbⁱ rahal achⁱ*, such ripe bunches of grapes having hung from the trellis have remained (*i.e.*, are there), that the juice has remained dripping (cf. § 342) (*i.e.*, keeps dripping).

से जनमल अछि (*v.l.* छथि) मारत तोहि, *sē janamala achi* (or *chathi*) *mārata tōhi*, he has taken birth (who) will kill thee (Man. i. 377).

जाहि मरद लै जोबन सेबलें से मरद बैसल छौक देबहा नदीक धार, *jāhⁱ marad lai jōban sebᵃlẽ, sē marad baisal chauk debᵃhā nadīk dhār*, the man for whom you kept your virginity, that man is seated (for you) by the stream of the river Debhā.

238. The **Pluperfect Indicative** is formed on the same principles as the second form of the perfect, substituting the past tense of the verb substantive for the present of the verb substan-

tive. Thus देखलें *dekh°lē̃*, (देखले *dekh°lē*, देखनें *dekh°nē̃*, देखने *dekh°nē*) छलहुँ *chalahũ*, I had seen; सूतल छलहुँ *sūtal chalahũ*, I had slept. Instead of छलहुँ *chalahũ*, etc., we may as usual have रही *rahī*, etc. There is nothing corresponding to the first form of the perfect; we never meet forms like देखलहुँ छल *dekh°lahũ chal.*

This tense not only has the sense of a pluperfect, but is also used to signify that the action happened a long time ago. Thus, देखलें छलहुँ *dekh°lē̃ chalahũ* means either 'I had seen,' or 'I saw a long time ago.'

I have given सूतल छलहुँ *sūtal chalahũ* (fem. सूतलि छलहुँ *sūtal[i] chhalahũ*) as the form of the pluperfect of an intransitive verb. It is necessary to add that natives of Mithilā tell me that (in this tense only) intransitive verbs may also be treated as if they were transitive so that we can also have सुतलें छलहुँ *sut°lē̃ chalahũ*. I have, however, never met such a form in literature.

It is unnecessary to give a table of the terminations of this tense. The following are examples of its use in literature:—

239. (*a*) Transitive verbs—

First Person:—हम तोहरा पहिले हस्सी में उड़ौने रहिअहु, *ham toh°rā pahilē hassī mē̃ uṛaunē* (see § 273 ff.) *rahiahu*, formerly (long ago) I ridiculed you in sport.

Second Person:—जखन धै लेलें (or लेनें or लेने) छलें तखन छाड़ब की रहौ, *jakhan dhai* (see § 314) *lēlē̃* (or *lēnē̃* or *lēnē*) *chalē̃ takhan chāṛab kī rahau*, when you had caught me, then what letting go was there to you (*i.e.*, why did you let me go)?

Third Person:—जतवा जनि कर लेनें छलि सुन्दरि ।
से सभ सोपलक ताही ॥

jatawā jani kara lenē̃ chali sundari ।
sē sabha sopalaka tāhī ॥

The fair one made over everything to those from whom she had taken them (Vid. x. 2). Here लेनें *lēnē̃* is shortened to लेनें *lenē̃* for the sake of metre.

240. (*b*) Intransitive verbs—

First Person :—राति हम सूतल छलहुँ अप्पन (for अपना) सिरकी मेँ, *rāt*[i] *ham sūtal chalah*[ū] *oppan* (for *ap*[a]*nā*) *sir*[a]*kī mē̃*, at night I was asleep in my own tent.

गेल छलहुँ *gēl chalah*[ū], I had gone. See next example.

Second Person :—कथी लै ओतय गेल छलहुँ। ओतय हमर खेत अछि। ओकरा देखै गेल छलहुँ, *kathī lai otay gēl chalah*[ū]*? otay hamar khēt ach*[i]. *Ok*[a]*rā dēkhai gēl chalah*[ū], why had you gone there? My field is there. I had gone to see it.

Third Person :—अपन सभ धन उड़ाय भिखारि भै गेल छल, *apan sabh dhan urāy bhikhāri bhai gēl chal*, having squandered all his property, he had become a beggar.

राम राम कहि के उठल छलाह, *rām, rām, kah*[i] *ke uṭhal chalăh*, crying 'Rām, Rām' he was arisen (*i.e.*, arose).

अहिरा गोआर गेल कटैया भद्री बैसल रहै, *ahirā goār gēl kaṭaiyā, bhadrī baisal rahai*, Ahirā Goār went to Kaṭaiyā; Bhadrī was seated (there).

सात नीँदे सूतलि छलि फेकुनी, *sāt nī̃dē sūtal*[i] *chal*[i] *phekunī*, Phekunī (name of a woman) was asleep in seven sleeps.

It will be noted that, as in the case of the perfect, many of the examples of the intransitive verb are not true pluperfects (so far as sense goes) at all.

The √हो *hō as an Auxiliary.*

241. In Hindī there is a set of periphrastic tenses formed with the √हो *hō*, become, as the auxiliary. Most of them are very rare. As given in the grammars, under various fancy names, they are :—

चलता होऊँ, *cal*[a]*tā hōū̃*, I may be going.
चलता होऊँगा, *cal*[a]*tā hōū̃gā*, I shall be going.
चलता होता, *cal*[a]*tā hōtā*, had I been going.
चला होऊँ, *calā hōū̃*, I may have gone.
चला होऊँगा, *calā hōū̃gā*, I shall have gone.
चला होता, *calā hōtā*, had I gone.

It would be, no doubt, possible to concoct parallel tenses in Maithilī, but I have never met any example of any of them except one of the first, which, also, I may add, is the one which is most common in Hindī.

The one example which I have noted is :—

कोन दिसा के अबैत होइ कहहु बुझाय, *kōn disā kē abait hōai kahahu bujhāy*, having explained tell (*i.e.*, tell clearly) in what direction he may be (*i.e.*, is probably) coming.

It will be sufficient to dismiss this and the other connected tenses with these remarks. I shall not refer to them again. If met with they will be easily recognized.

In the following chapter I give a complete paradigm of the conjugation of the regular transitive and of the regular intransitive verb, with roots ending in consonants. The roots chosen as examples are √देख *dēkh*, see, and √सूत *sūt*, sleep.

CHAPTER IV.

CONJUGATION OF THE REGULAR VERB.

242. In the following paradigms attention must be again called to the regular shortening of the antepenultimate vowel as explained in §§ 32 and ff and § 176. When the vowel of the root is आ *ā*, the practice is to shorten it to अ *a*, not to आ॑ *ă*, unless this would cause ambiguity. Thus one form of the third person past indicative of the √लाग *lāg*, begin, is लगलै *lag^a lai*, not लागलै *lăg^a lai*, because in Maithilī there is no √लग *lag*, begin, with which it can be confused. But the long form of the first person of the same tense of the √मार *mār*, strike, is मारलौ *măr^a lai*, not मरलौ *mar^a lai*, because the latter might be confused with the मरलै *mar^a lai*, he died, the long form of the third person of the √ *mar*, die.

A. TRANSITIVE VERB.

√देख *dēkh*, see.

243. (*a*) (1) Old Present, 'I see,' &c.

PERSON.	SHORT FORM. GROUP I. (Subject: non-honorific. Object: non-honorific.)	SHORT FORM. GROUP II. (Subject: honorific. Object: non-honorific.)	LONG FORM. GROUP I. (Subject: non-honorific. Object: non-honorific.)	LONG FORM. GROUP II. (Subject: honorific. Object: non-honorific.)	REDUNDANT FORM. GROUP I. (Subject: non-honorific. Object: non-honorific.)	REDUNDANT FORM. GROUP II. (Subject: honorific. Object: non-honorific.)	GROUP III. (Subject: non-honorific. Object: honorific.)	GROUP IV. (Subject: honorific. Object: honorific.)
1	देखी *dēkhī*, *देखौं *dēkhõ*.		देखिऐ *dekhiai* Or (with object in 2nd person.) देखिऔ *dekhiau*, देखिअड़ *dekhiahu* *देखिअ *dekhiä*.		देखिऐक *dekhiaik* Or (with object in 2nd person.) देखिऔक *dekhiauk*.		देखिऐन्हि *dekhiainhi*.	
2	देख *dēkh*, *देखसि *dēkhasi*	Same as 1st person.	देखह *dēkhah*, देखहु *dēkhahu*, देखौ *dēkhau*; f. देखहिं *dēkhahĩ* देखहिँ *dēkhãhĩ*.	Same as 1st person, but no forms for object in 2nd person.	देखहक *dekhahak* देखहुक *dekhahuk*, देखहीक *dekhahik*	Same as 1st person, but no form for object in 2nd person.	देखहुन्हि *dekhahũnhi*.	Same as 1st person
3	देखे *dēkhē*, *देख *dēkha*, *देखु *dēkhu*, *देखहिँ *dēkhahĩ*.	देखथि *dēkhathi*.	GROUP I. देखै *dēkhai* Or (with object in 2nd person.) देखौ *dēkhau*, देखहु *dēkhahu*.		GROUP I. देखैक *dekhaik* Or (with object in 2nd person.) देखौक *dekhauk*		देखैन्हि *dekhainhi*	देखथीन्हि *dekhathīnhi*, देखथून्हि *dekhathũnhi*.

* Chiefly used in poetry, or in the old language. Regarding the long *ē* in देखै *dēkhai*, देखौ *dēkhau*, see § 176.

244. (*a*) (2) **Present Conditional,** '(if) I see, I may see,' &c.

PERSON.	SHORT FORM.		LONG FORM.		REDUNDANT FORM.			
	GROUP I. (Subject: non-honorific. Object: non-honorific.)	GROUP II. (Subject: honorific. Object: non-honorific.)	GROUP I. (Subject: non-honorific. Object: non-honorific.)	GROUP II. (Subject: honorific. Object: non-honorific.)	GROUP I. (Subject: non-honorific. Object: non-honorific.)	GROUP II. (Subject: honorific. Object: non-honorific.)	GROUP III. (Subject: non-honorific. Object: honorific.)	GROUP IV. (Subject: honorific. Object: honorific.)
1	देखी *dēkhī.*		दॆखिऐ *dekhiai* Or (with object in 2nd person.) दॆखिऔ *dekhiau,* दॆखिअहु *dekhiah*^{u} *दॆखिअँ *dekhiȧ.*		दॆखिऐक *dekhiaik* Or (with object in 2nd person.) दॆखिऔक *dekhiauk.*		दॆखिऐन्हि *dekhiainh*^{i}	
2	देख *dēkh.*	Same as 1st person.	देखह *dēkhȧh,* देखहु *dēkhah*^{u}, देखौ *dēkhau ;* f. देखहि *dēkhah*^{i} देखहिँ *dēkhãh*^{i}.	Same as 1st person, but no forms for object in 2nd person.	दॆखहक *dekh*^{a}*hȧk* दॆखहुक *dekh*^{a}*huk* दॆखहीक *dekh*^{a}*hik*	Same as 1st person, but no form for object in 2nd person.	दॆखहुन्हि *dekh*^{a}*hũnh*^{i}.	Same as 1st person.
3	देखे *dēkhē,* *देख *dēkha,* *देखु *dēkhu.*	देखथि *dēkhath*^{i} देखथु *dēkhath*^{u}.	GROUP I. देखौ *dēkhau,* देखहु *dēkhah*^{u}, देखो *dēkhō,* (sometimes) देखै *dēkhai*		GROUP I. दॆखौक *dekhauk,* (sometimes) दॆखैक *dekhaik.*		दॆखैन्हि *dekhainh*^{i}, दॆखौन्हि *dekhaunh*^{i}.	दॆखथीन्हि *dekh*^{a}*thīnh*^{i}, दॆखथुन्हि *dekh*^{a}*thũnh*^{i}.

* Chiefly used in poetry or in the old language.

245. (*a*) (3) **Imperative,** 'let me see, see thou,' &c.

PERSON.	SHORT FORM.		LONG FORM.		REDUNDANT FORM.			
	GROUP I. (Subject: non-honorific. Object: non-honorific.)	GROUP II. (Subject: honorific. Object: non-honorific.)	GROUP I. (Subject: non-honorific. Object: non-honorific.)	GROUP II. (Subject: honorific. Object: non-honorific.)	GROUP I. (Subject: non-honorific. Object: non-honorific.)	GROUP II. (Subject: honorific. Object: non-honorific.)	GROUP III. (Subject: non-honorific. Object: honorific.)	GROUP IV. (Subject: honorific. Object: honorific.)
1	देखू *dēkhū*, (sometimes) देखी *dēkhī*.		दॆखिऐ *dekhiai* Or (with object in 2nd person.) दॆखिऔ *dekhiau*, दॆखिअऽ *dekhiah*^{u} *दॆखिअँ *dekhiã*.		दॆखिऐक *dekhiaik* Or (with object in 2nd person.) दॆखिऔक *dekhiauk*.		दॆखिऐन्हि *dekhiainh*^{i}.	
2	देख *dēkh*, देखँ *dēkhẽ*.	Same as 1st person.	देखह *dēkhăh*, देखऽ *dēkhah*^{u}, देखौ *dēkhau*, देखौं *dēkhaũ*; f. देखहिं *dēkhahĩ*, देखँहिं *dēkhãhĩ*.	Same as 1st person, but no forms for object in 2nd person.	दॆखहक *dekh*^{a}*hăk*, दॆखहोक *dekh*^{a}*hōk*, दॆखहुक *dekh*^{a}*huk*, दॆखहीक *dekh*^{a}*hīk*, दॆखौक *dekhauk*.	Same as 1st person, but no form for object in 2nd person.	दॆखहुन्हि *dekh*^{a}*hũnh*^{i}.	Same as 1st person.
3	देखे *dēkhē*, *देख *dēkha*, *देखु *dēkhu*.	देखथि *dēkhath*^{i}. देखथु *dēkhath*^{u}.	GROUP I. देखौ *dēkhau*, देखऽ *dēkhah*^{u}, देखो *dēkhō*, (sometimes) देखै *dēkhai*		GROUP I. दॆखौक *dekhauk*, (sometimes) दॆखैक *dekhaik*.		दॆखौन्हि *dekhaunh*^{i}	दॆखथीन्हि *dekh*^{a}*thīnh*^{i} दॆखथून्हि *dekh*^{a}*thūnh*^{i}.

* Chiefly used in poetry, or in the old language.

246. Mild Imperative.

Second person.—देखिहेँ *dekhihẽ*, देखिअ॑ *dekhiȧ*, देखिय॑ *dekhiyȧ*, देखिअह *dekhiȧh*, देखिह॑ *dekhihȧ*, देखिऔक *dekhiauk*, देखिहौक *dekhihauk*, देखिहौन्हि *dekhihaunhi*, देखिहथि *dekhihathi*, देखबहीन्हि *dekhabahīnhi*, please to see.

247. Respectful Imperative.

Second person.—देखल जाई *dēkhal jāī*, देखल जाओ *dēkhal jāo*, be pleased to see.

248. Respectful Future.

Second person.—देखल जाएत *dēkhal jāet*, देखल जाएत-ग॑ *dēkhal jāet-gȧ*, you will be pleased to see, be good enough to see.

249. Future Indicative.

First Form.—This is the same as the present conditional (*a*) (2), to which the termination ग॑ *gȧ* (poetically गै *gai* or गए *gae*) may optionally be added. Thus देखी *dēkhī* or देखी-ग॑ *dēkhī-gȧ*, I shall see.

250. (*b*) (4) **Future Indicative.** Second form. 'I shall see,' &c. The termination गँ *gå* (गै *gai* or गए *gae*) may be added throughout.

PERSON.	SHORT FORM.		LONG FORM.		REDUNDANT FORM.			
	GROUP I. (Subject: non-honorific. Object: non-honorific.)	GROUP II. (Subject: honorific. Object: non-honorific.)	GROUP I. (Subject: non-honorific. Object: non-honorific.)	GROUP II. (Subject: honorific. Object: non-honorific.)	GROUP I. (Subject: non-honorific. Object: non-honorific.)	GROUP II. (Subject: honorific. Object: non-honorific.)	GROUP III. (Subject: non-honorific. Object: honorific.)	GROUP IV. (Subject: honorific. Object: honorific.)
1	देखब *dĕkhab*, देखबहुँ *dekh^{a}bah$^{\tilde{u}}$*, देखबौं *dekh^{a}bŏ̃.*		देखबै *dekh^{a}bai* Or (with object in 2nd person.) देखबौ *dekh^{a}bau*, देखबहु *dekh^{a}bah^{u}.*		देखबैक *dekh^{a}baik* Or (with object in 2nd person.) देखबौक *dekh^{a}bauk.*		देखबैन्हि *dekh^{a}bainh^{i}.*	
2	देखबें *dekh^{a}bẽ.*	Same as 1st person.	देखबह *dekh^{a}băh,* देखबौ *dekh^{a}bau,* देखबहो *dekh^{a}bahŏ;* fem. देखबहिं *dekh^{a}bãh^{i}.*	Same as 1st person, but no forms for object in 2nd person.	देखबहक *dekh^{a}bahăk,* देखबहीक *dekh^{a}bahīk.*	Same as 1st person, but no form for object in 2nd person.	देखबहुन्हि *dekh^{a}bahũnh^{i}.*	Same as 1st person.
3	Wanting.	Wanting.	Wanting.	Wanting.	Wanting.	Wanting.	Wanting.	Wanting.

251. (*b*) (4) **Future Indicative.** Third Form. 'I shall see,' &c. The termination गँ *gã* (गै *gai* or गए *gae*) may be added throughout.

PERSON.	SHORT FORM.		LONG FORM.		REDUNDANT FORM.			
	GROUP I. (Subject: non-honorific. Object: non-honorific.)	GROUP II. (Subject: honorific. Object: non-honorific.)	GROUP I. (Subject: non-honorific. Object: non-honorific.)	GROUP II. (Subject: honorific. Object: non-honorific.)	GROUP I. (Subject: non-honorific. Object: non-honorific.)	GROUP II. (Subject: honorific. Object: non-honorific.)	GROUP III. (Subject: non-honorific. Object: honorific.)	GROUP IV. (Subject: honorific. Object: honorific.)
1	देखितहुँ *dekhitah*^{u}.		देखतिऐ *dekh*^{a}*tiai* Or (with object in 2nd person.) देखतिओ *dekh*^{a}*tiau*, देखतिअहु *dekh*^{a}*tiah*^{u}.		देखतिऐक *dekh*^{a}*tiaik*, Or (with object in 2nd person.) देखतिओक *dekh*^{a}*tiauk*.		Wanting.	
2	Wanting.	Same as 1st person.	Wanting.	Same as 1st person, but no forms for object in 2nd person.	Wanting.	Same as 1st person, but no form for object in 2nd person.	Wanting.	Wanting.
3	देखत *dēkhat*; fem. देखति *dēkhat*^{i}.	देखतथि *dekh*^{a}*tath*^{i}, देखतथु *dekh*^{a}*tath*^{u}, देखताह *dekh*^{a}*tāh*; f. देखतीह *dekh*^{a}*tīh*, देखतीहि *dekh*^{a}*tīh*^{i}.	GROUP I. देखतै *dekh*^{a}*tai* Or (with object in 2nd person.) देखतौ *dekh*^{a}*tau*, देखतहु *dekh*^{a}*tah*^{u}		GROUP I. देखतैक *dekh*^{a}*taik* Or (with object in 2nd person.) देखतौक *dekh*^{a}*tauk*.		देखतैन्हि *dekh*^{a}*tainh*^{i}.	देखथीन्हि *dekh*^{a}*thīnh*^{i}, देखथून्हि *dekh*^{a}*thūnh*^{i}.

252. (*c*) (5) **Past Conditional,** '(if) I had seen,' &c.; 'I should have seen,' &c.

PERSON.	SHORT FORM.		LONG FORM.		REDUNDANT FORM.			
	GROUP I. (Subject: non-honorific. Object: non-honorific.)	GROUP II. (Subject: honorific. Object: non-honorific.)	GROUP I. (Subject: non-honorific. Object: non-honorific.)	GROUP II. (Subject: honorific. Object: non-honorific.)	GROUP I. (Subject: non-honorific. Object: non-honorific.)	GROUP II. (Subject: honorific. Object: non-honorific.)	GROUP III. (Subject: non-honorific. Object: honorific.)	GROUP IV. (Subject: honorific. Object: honorific.)
1	देखितहुँ *dekhitah^{ŭ}** देखिती *dekhitī* (rare).		देखितिऐ *dekhitiai* Or (with object in 2nd person.) देखितिऔ *dekhitiau*, देखितिअहु *dekhitiah^{u}*		देखितिऐक *dekhitiaik* Or (with object in 2nd person.) देखितिऔक *dekhitiauk.*		देखितिऐन्हि *dekhitiainh^{i}.*	
2	देखितेँ *dekhitĕ.*	Same as 1st person.	देखितह् *dekhitah*; fem. देखितहिँ *dekhitahĭ*, देखिताँहिँ *dekhitā̃h^{ĭ}.*	Same as 1st person, but no forms for object in 2nd person.	देखितहक *dekhit^{a}hak*, देखितहीक *dekhitahīk.*	Same as 1st person, but no form for object in 2nd person.	देखितहुन्हि *dekhit^{a}hŭnh^{i}.*	Same as 1st person.
3	देखैत *dekhait*; fem. देखैति *dekhait^{i}.*	देखितथि *dekhitath^{i}*, देखितन्हि *dekhitanh^{i}.*	GROUP I. देखितै *dekhitai* Or (with object in 2nd person.) देखितौ *dekhitau*, देखितहु *dekhitah^{u}.*		GROUP I. देखितैक *dekhitaik* Or (with object in 2nd person) देखितौक *dekhitauk.*		देखितैन्हि *dekhitainh^{i}.*	देखितथीन्हि *dekhit^{a}thīnh^{i}*, देखितथून्हि *dekhit^{a}thūnh^{i}.*

* Or देखैतहुँ *dekhaitah^{ŭ}* or देखतहुँ *dekh^{a}tah^{ŭ}*, and so throughout, except in the short form of the 3rd person of Group I.

253. (*c*) (6) **Present Indicative.** Uncontracted form. 'I see,' &c.; 'I am seeing,' &c.
(The Auxiliary verb does not change for gender, except in the second person of the long form of Group I.)

PERSON.	SHORT FORM.		LONG FORM.		REDUNDANT FORM.			
	GROUP I. (Subject: non-honorific. Object: non-honorific.)	GROUP II. (Subject: honorific. Object: non-honorific.)	GROUP I. (Subject: non-honorific Object: non-honorific.)	GROUP II. (Subject: honorific. Object: non-honorific.)	GROUP I. (Subject: non-honorific. Object: non-honorific.)	GROUP II. (Subject: honorific. Object: non-honorific)	GROUP III. (Subject: non-honorific. Object: honorific.)	GROUP IV. (Subject: honorific. Object: honorific)
1	देखैत छी *dekhait chī*; fem. देखैति छी *dekhait^i chī*.		देखैत छिऐ *dekhait chiai*; fem. देखैति छिऐ *dekhait^i chiai*. Or (with object in 2nd person.) देखैत छिऔ *dekhait chiau*; fem. देखैति छिऔ *dekhait^i chiau*.		देखैत छिऐक *dekhait chiaik*; fem. देखैति छिऐक *dekhait^i chiaik*. Or (with object in 2nd person.) देखैत छिऔक *dekhait chiauk*; fem. देखैति छिऔक *dekhait^i chiauk*.		देखैत छिऐन्हि *dekhait chiainh^i*; fem. देखैति छिऐन्हि *dekhait^i chiainh^i*.	
2	देखैत छेँ *dekhait chẽ*; fem. देखैति छेँ *dekhait^i chẽ*.	Same as 1st person.	देखैत छह *dekhait chah*; fem. देखैति छहिँ *dekhait^i chahĩ*.	Same as 1st person, but no forms for object in 2nd person.	देखैत छहक *dekhait chahak*; fem. देखैति छहक *dekhait^i chahak*.	Same as 1st person, but no forms for object in 2nd person.	देखैत छहुन्हि *dekhait chahũnh^i*; fem. देखैति छहुन्हि *dekhait^i chahũnh^i*	Same as 1st person.
3	देखैत अछि *dekhait ach^i*; fem. देखैति अछि *dekhait^i ach^i*.	देखैत छथि *dekhait chath^i*; fem. देखैति छथि *dekhait^i chath^i*.	GROUP I. देखैत छै *dekhait chai*; fem. देखैति छै *dekhait^i chai*. Or (with object in 2nd person.) देखैत छौ *dekhait chau*; fem. देखैति छौ *dekhait^i chau*.		GROUP I. देखैत छैक *dekhait chaik*; fem. देखैति छैक *dekhait^i chaik*. Or (with object in 2nd person.) देखैत छौक *dekhait chauk*; fem. देखैति छौक *dekhait^i chauk*.		देखैत छैन्हि *dekhait chainh^i*; fem. देखैति छैन्हि *dekhait^i chainh^i*.	देखैत छथीन्हि *dekhait chathīnh^i*; fem. देखैति छथीन्हि *dekhait^i chathīnh^i*.

254. (*c*) (6) **Present Indicative.** Contracted form. 'I see,' &c.; 'I am seeing,' &c. (The feminine is the same as the masculine, except in the second person of the long form of Group I.)

PERSON.	SHORT FORM.		LONG FORM.		REDUNDANT FORM.			
	GROUP I. (Subject: non-honorific. Object: non-honorific.)	GROUP II. (Subject: honorific. Object: non-honorific.)	GROUP I. (Subject: non-honorific. Object: non-honorific.)	GROUP II. (Subject: honorific. Object: non-honorific.)	GROUP I. (Subject: non-honorific. Object: non-honorific.)	GROUP II. (Subject: honorific. Object: non-honorific.)	GROUP III. (Subject: non-honorific. Object: honorific.)	GROUP IV. (Subject: honorific. Object: honorific.)
1	देखैछी *dekhai-chī.*		देखैछिऐ *dekhai-chiai* Or (with object in 2nd person) देखैछियौ *dekhai-chiau.*		देखैछिऐक *dekhai-chiaik* Or (with object in 2nd person.) देखैछियौक *dekhai-chiauk.*		देखैछिऐन्हि *dekhai-chiainh^{i}.*	
2	देखैछेँ *dekhai-chĕ*	Same as 1st person.	देखैछह *dekhai-chah*; fem. देखैछहि *dekhai-chah^{i}.*	Same as 1st person, but no forms for object in 2nd person.	देखैछहक *dekhai-ch^{a}hăk.*	Same as 1st person, but no forms for object in 2nd person.	देखैछहुन्हि *dekhai-ch^{a}hŭnh^{i}.*	Same as 1st person.
3	देखैअछि *dekhai-ach^{i}*; more usually, देखइछि *dekhaïch^{i}*, देखइछ *dekhaïch.*	देखैछथि *dekhai-chath^{i}.*	GROUP I. देखैछै *dekhai-chai* Or (with object in 2nd person.) देखैछौ *dekhai-chau.*		GROUP I. देखैछैक *dekhai-chaik* Or (with object in 2nd person.) देखैछौक *dekhai-chauk.*		देखैछैन्हि *dekhai-chainh^{i}.*	देखैछथीन्हि *dekhai-ch^{a}thīnh^{i}.*

In both the above forms of the Present Indicative, any optional form of the present tense of the auxiliary verb may be employed, as explained in § 230.

255. (*c*) (7) **Imperfect Indicative.** Uncontracted form. 'I was seeing,' &c. (The auxiliary verb does not change for gender, except in the third person of the short form of Group I and of Group II, and in the long form of the second person of Group I).

PERSON.	SHORT FORM.		LONG FORM.		REDUNDANT FORM.			
	GROUP I. (Subject: non-honorific. Object: non-honorific.)	GROUP II. (Subject: honorific. Object: non-honorific.)	GROUP I. (Subject: non-honorific. Object: non-honorific.)	GROUP II. (Subject: honorific. Object: non-honorific.)	GROUP I. (Subject: non-honorific. Object: non-honorific.)	GROUP II. (Subject: honorific. Object: non-honorific.)	GROUP III. (Subject: non-honorific. Object: honorific.)	GROUP IV. (Subject: honorific. Object: honorific.)
1	देखैत चलहुँ *dekhait chalah^{u}*; f. देखैति चलहुँ *dekhait^{i} chalah^{u}*.		देखैत चलिऐ *dekhait chaliai*; fem. देखैति चलिऐ *dekhait^{i} chaliai* Or (with object in 2nd person.) देखैत चलिऔ *dekhait chaliau*; f. देखैति चलिऔ *dekhait^{i} chaliau*.		देखैत चलिऐक *dekhait chaliaik*; f. देखैति चलिऐक *dekhait^{i} chaliaik* Or (with object in 2nd person.) देखैत चलिऔक *dekhait chaliauk*; f. देखैति चलिऔक *dekhait^{i} chaliauk*.		देखैत चलिऐन्हि *dekhait chaliainh^{i}*; fem. देखैति चलिऐन्हि *dekhait^{i} chaliainh^{i}*.	
2	देखैत चलैं *dekhait chalaĩ*; fem. देखैति चलैं *dekhait^{i} chalaĩ*.	Same as 1st person.	देखैत चलाह *dekhait chalāh*; f. देखैति चलीह *dekhait^{i} chalīh*.	Same as 1st person, but no forms for object in 2nd person.	देखैत चलहँक *dekhait chal^{a}hãk*; f. देखैति चलहँक *dekhait^{i} chal^{a}hãk*.	Same as 1st person, but no forms for object in 2nd person.	देखैत चलहुन्हि *dekhait chal^{a}hũnh^{i}*; f. देखैति चलहुन्हि *dekhait^{i} chal^{a}hũnh^{i}*	Same as 1st person.
3	देखैत चल *dekhait chal*; fem. देखैति चलि *dekhait^{i} chal^{i}*.	देखैत चलाह *dekhait chalāh*; f. देखैति चलीह *dekhait^{i} chalīh*.	GROUP I. देखैत चलै *dekhait chalai*; fem. देखैति चलै *dekhait^{i} chalai* Or (with object in 2nd person.) देखैत चलौ *dekhait chalau*; fem. देखैति चलौ *dekhait^{i} chalau*.		GROUP I. देखैत चलैक *dekhait chalaik*; f. देखैति चलैक *dekhait^{i} chalaik* Or (with object in 2nd person.) देखैत चलौक *dekhait chalauk*; fem. देखैति चलौक *dekhait^{i} chalau*.		देखैत चलैन्हि *dekhait chalainh^{i}*; fem. देखैति चलैन्हि *dekhait^{i} chalainh^{i}*.	देखैत चलथीन्हि *dekhait chal^{a}thinh^{i}*; f. देखैति चलथीन्हि *dekhait^{i} chal^{a}thinh^{i}*.

256. (*c*) (7) **Imperfect Indicative.** Contracted Form. 'I was seeing,' &c. (The feminine is the same as the masculine, except in the third person of the short form of Group I and of Group II, and in the long form of the second person of Group I.)

PERSON.	SHORT FORM.		LONG FORM.		REDUNDANT FORM.			
	GROUP I. (Subject: non-honorific. Object: non-honorific.)	GROUP II. (Subject: honorific. Object: non-honorific.)	GROUP I. (Subject: non-honorific. Object: non-honorific.)	GROUP II. (Subject: honorific. Object: non-honorific.)	GROUP I. (Subject: non-honorific. Object: non-honorific.)	GROUP II. (Subject: honorific. Object: non-honorific.)	GROUP III. (Subject: non-honorific. Object: honorific.)	GROUP IV. (Subject: honorific. Object: honorific.)
1	देखैछलहुँ *dekhai-chalahũ.*		देखैछलिऐ *dekhai-chaliai* Or (with object in 2nd person) देखैछलिऔ *dekhai-chaliau.*		देखैछलिऐक *dekhai-chaliaik* Or (with object in 2nd person.) देखैछलिऔक *dekhai-chaliauk.*		देखैछलिऐन्हि *dekhai-chali-ainhi.*	
2	देखैछलैं *dekhai-chalẽ.*	Same as 1st person.	देखैछलाह *dekhai-chalăh,* देखैछलीह *dekhai-chalih.*	Same as 1st person, but no forms for object in 2nd person.	देखैछलहक *dekhai-chalahăk.*	Same as 1st person, but no forms for object in 2nd person.	देखैछलहुन्हि *dekhai-chala-hũnhi.*	Same as 1st person.
3	देखैछल *dekhai-chal*; fem. देखैछलि *dekhai-chali.*	देखैछलाह *dekhai-chalăh*; fem. देखैछलीह *dekhai-chalih.*	GROUP I. देखैछलै *dekhai-chalai* Or (with object in 2nd person.) देखैछलौ *dekhai-chalau.*		GROUP I. देखैछलैक *dekhai-chalaik* Or (with object in 2nd person.) देखैछलौक *dekhai-chalauk.*		देखैछलैन्हि *dekhai-chal-ainhi.*	देखैछलथीन्हि *dekhai-chala-thīnhi.*

In both the above forms of the Imperfect Indicative any optional form of the past tense of the auxiliary verb may be employed, as explained in § 231.

257. (*d*) (8) **Past Indicative.** 'I saw,' &c.

PERSON.	SHORT FORM. GROUP I. (Subject: non-honorific. Object: non-honorific.)	SHORT FORM. GROUP II. (Subject: honorific. Object: non-honorific.)	LONG FORM. GROUP I. (Subject: non-honorific. Object: non-honorific).	LONG FORM. GROUP II. (Subject: honorific. Object: non-honorific.)	REDUNDANT FORM. GROUP I. (Subject: non-honorific. Object: non-honorific.)	REDUNDANT FORM. GROUP II. (Subject: honorific. Object: non-honorific.)	GROUP III. (Subject: non-honorific. Object: honorific)	GROUP IV. (Subject: honorific. Object: honorific)
1	दॆखलहुँ *dekh^{a}lahũ*, देखल *dēkhal*, दॆखली *dekh^{a}lī*; f. देखलि *dēkhal^{i}* instead of देखल *dēkhal*.		दॆखलै *dekh^{a}lai*, दॆखलिऐ *dekh^{a}liai* Or (with object in 2nd person.) दॆखलौ *dekh^{a}lau*, दॆखलहु *dekh^{a}lah^{u}*, दॆखलिऔ *dekh^{a}liau*, दॆखलिअहु *dekh^{a}liah^{u}*.		दॆखलैक *dekh^{a}laik*, दॆखलिऐक *dekh^{a}liaik* Or (with object in 2nd person.) दॆखलौक *dekh^{a}lauk*, दॆखलिऔक *dekh^{a}liauk*.		दॆखलैन्हि *dekh^{a}lainh^{i}*, दॆखलिऐन्हि *dekh^{a}liainh^{i}*.	
2	दॆखलें *dekh^{a}lẽ*, दॆखलैं *dekh^{a}laĩ*.	Same as 1st person.	दॆखलह *dekh^{a}lăh*; fem. दॆखलिहि *dekh^{a}lih^{i}* दॆखलीहि *dekh^{a}līh^{i}*.	Same as 1st person, but no forms for object in 2nd person.	दॆखलहक *dekh^{a}lahăk*, दॆखलहीक *dekh^{a}lahik*.	Same as 1st person, but no forms for object in 2nd person.	दॆखलहुन्हि *dekh^{a}lahũnh^{i}*.	Same as 1st person.
3	दॆखलक *dekh^{a}lak*, *देखल *dēkhal*; f *देखलि *dēkhal^{i}*.	दॆखलन्हि *dekh^{a}lanh^{i}*, *दॆखलथि *dekh^{a}lath^{i}*	GROUP I. दॆखलकै *dekhal^{a}kai* Or (with object in 2nd person.) दॆखलकौ *dekhal^{a}kau*.		GROUP I. दॆखलकैक *dekhal^{a}kaik* Or (with object in 2nd person.) दॆखलकौक *dekhal^{a}kauk*.		दॆखलकैन्हि *dekhal^{a}kainh^{i}*	दॆखलथीन्हि *dekhal^{a}thĩnh^{i}*, दॆखलथून्हि *dekhal^{a}thũnh^{i}*.

* These forms are peculiar to poetry. In the modern language they are only used by the vulgar.

258. (*d*) (9) **Perfect Indicative.** First Form. 'I have seen,' &c.

PERSON.	SHORT FORM.		LONG FORM.		REDUNDANT FORM.			
	GROUP I. (Subject: non-honorific. Object: non-honorific.)	GROUP II. (Subject: honorific. Object: non-honorific.)	GROUP I. (Subject: non-honorific. Object: non-honorific.)	GROUP II. (Subject: honorific. Object: non-honorific.)	GROUP I. (Subject: non-honorific. Object: non-honorific.)	GROUP II. (Subject: honorific. Object: non-honorific.)	GROUP III. (Subject: non-honorific. Object: honorific.)	GROUP IV. (Subject: honorific. Object: honorific.)
1	देखलहुँ अछि *dekh^{a}lah$^{\tilde{u}}$ ach^{i}.*		देखलै अछि *dekh^{a}lai ach^{i}* Or (with object in 2nd person.) देखलौ अछि *dekh^{a}lau ach^{i}.*		देखलैक अछि *dekh^{a}laik ach^{i}* Or (with object in 2nd person.) देखलौक अछि *dekh^{a}lauk achi.*		देखलैन्हि अछि *dekh^{a}lainh^{i} ach^{i}*	
2	देखलें अछि *dekh^{a}lẽ ach^{i}.*	Same as 1st person.	देखलह अछि *dekh^{a}lah ach^{i}*; f. देखलिहि अछि *dekh^{a}līh^{i} ach^{i}.*	Same as 1st person, but no forms for object in 2nd person.	देखलहक अछि *dekh^{a}lahak ach^{i}.*	Same as 1st person, but no forms for object in 2nd person.	देखलहन्हि अछि *dekh^{a}lahãnh^{i} ach^{i}.*	Same as 1st person
3	देखलक अछि *dekh^{a}lak ach^{i}.*	देखलन्हि अछि *dekh^{a}lanh^{i} ach^{i}.*	GROUP I. देखलकै अछि *dekhal^{a}kai ach^{i}* Or (with object in 2nd person.) देखलकौ अछि *dekhal^{a}kau ach^{i}.*		GROUP I. देखलकैक अछि *dekhal^{a}kaik ach^{i}* Or (with object in 2nd person.) देखलकौक अछि *dekhal^{a}kauk ach^{i}.*		देखलकैन्हि अछि *dekhal^{a}kainh^{i} ach^{i}.*	देखलथीन्हि अछि *dekhal^{a}thīnh^{i} ach^{i}.*

Any other optional form of the preterite indicative may be substituted for those given above. Thus देखल अछि *dēkhal ach^{i}*, देखलिऐ अछि *dekh^{a}liai ach^{i}*, etc. Also, instead of अछि *ach^{i}* we may substitute any other optional form of the third person of the present of the auxiliary verb; but the ones in ordinary use are अछि *ach^{i}* and अहि *ah^{i}*.

259. (*d*) (9) **Perfect Indicative.** Second Form. 'I have seen,' &c.

PERSON.	SHORT FORM.		LONG FORM.		REDUNDANT FORM.			
	GROUP I. (Subject: non-honorific. Object: non-honorific.)	GROUP II. (Subject: honorific. Object: non-honorific.)	GROUP I. (Subject: non-honorific. Object: non-honorific.)	GROUP II. (Subject: honorific. Object: non-honorific.)	GROUP I. (Subject: non-honorific. Object: non-honorific.)	GROUP II. (Subject: honorific. Object: non-honorific.)	GROUP III. (Subject: non-honorific. Object: honorific.)	GROUP IV. (Subject: honorific. Object: honorific.)
1	देखलें छी *dekh^{a}lē chi.*		देखलें छिऐ *dekh^{a}lē chiai* Or (with object in 2nd person) देखलें छिऔ *dekh^{a}lē chiau.*		देखलें छिऐक *dekh^{a}lē chiaik* Or (with object in 2nd person.) देखलें छिऔक *dekh^{a}lē chiauk.*		देखलें छिऐन्हि *dekh^{a}lē chiainh^{i}.*	
2	देखलें छें *dekh^{a}lē chē.*	Same as 1st person.	देखलें छह *dekh^{a}lē chah*; cf. देखलें छहिं *dekh^{a}lē chahī.*	Same as 1st person, but no forms for object in 2nd person.	देखलें छहक *dekh^{a}lē chahak.*	Same as 1st person, but no forms for object in 2nd person.	देखलें छहुन्हि *dekh^{a}lē chahũnh^{i}.*	Same as 1st person.
3	देखलें अछि *dekh^{a}lē ach^{i}.*	देखलें छथि *dekh^{a}lē chath^{i}.*	GROUP I. देखलें छै *dekh^{a}lē chai* Or (with object in 2nd person.) देखलें छौ *dekh^{a}lē chau.*		GROUP I. देखलें छैक *dekh^{a}lē chaik* Or (with object in 2nd person.) देखलें छौक *dekh^{a}lē chauk.*		देखलें छैन्हि *dekh^{a}lē chainh^{i}.*	देखलें छथीन्हि *dekh^{a}lē chathīnh^{i}.*

Instead of देखलें *dekh^{a}lē*, we often hear देखले *dekh^{a}lē*. The vulgar often substitute देखनें *dekh^{a}nē* or देखने *dekh^{a}nē*, and these forms are also occasionally used by the educated.

Any optional form of the present tense of the auxiliary verb may be employed, as explained in § 236.

260. (*d*) (10) **Pluperfect Indicative.** 'I had seen,' &c.; 'I saw a long time ago,' &c.

PERSON.	SHORT FORM.		LONG FORM.		REDUNDANT FORM.			
	GROUP I. (Subject: non-honorific. Object: non-honorific.)	GROUP II. (Subject: honorific. Object: non-honorific.)	GROUP I. (Subject: non-honorific. Object: non-honorific.)	GROUP II. (Subject: honorific. Object: non-honorific.)	GROUP I. (Subject: non-honorific. Object: non-honorific.)	GROUP II. (Subject: honorific. Object: non-honorific.)	GROUP III. (Subject non-honorific. Object: honorific.)	GROUP IV. (Subject: honorific. Object: honorific.)
1	देखलें चलहुँ *dekh^{a}lẽ chalahũ*.		देखलें चलिऐ *dekh^{a}lẽ chaliai* Or (with object in 2nd person.) देखल चलिऔ *dekh^{a}lẽ chaliau*		देखलें चलिऐक *dekh^{a}lẽ chaliaik* Or (with object in 2nd person.) देखलें चलिऔक *dekh^{a}lẽ chaliauk*		देखलें चलिऐन्हि *dekh^{a}lẽ chaliainh^{i}*.	
2	देखलें चलें *dekh^{a}lẽ chalẽ*.	Same as 1st person.	देखलें चलाह *dekh^{a}lẽ chalāh*; f. देखलें चलीह *dekh^{a}lẽ chalīh*.	Same as 1st person, but no forms for object in 2nd person.	देखलें चलहुँक *dekh^{a}lẽ chal^{a}hŭk*.	Same as 1st person, but no forms for object in 2nd person.	देखलें चल-हुन्हि *dekh^{a}lẽ chal^{a}hũnh^{i}*.	Same as 1st person.
3	देखलें चल *dekh^{a}lẽ chal*; f. देखलें चलि *dekh^{a}lẽ chal^{i}*.	देखलें चलाह *dekh^{a}lẽ chalāh*; f. देखलें चलीह *dekh^{a}lẽ chalīh*.	GROUP I. देखलें चलै *dekh^{a}lẽ chalai* Or (with object in 2nd person.) देखलें चलौ *dekh^{a}lẽ chalau*.		GROUP I. देखलें चलैक *dekh^{a}lẽ chalaik* Or (with object in 2nd person.) देखलें चलौक *deh^{a}lẽ chalauk*.		देखलें चलैन्हि *dekh^{a}lẽ cha-lainh^{i}*.	देखलें चलथीन्हि *dekh^{a}lẽ chal^{a}-thīnh^{i}*.

As in the perfect देखले *dekh^{a}lē*, देखनें *dekh^{a}nẽ* or देखने *dekh^{a}ne* are found instead of देखलें *dekh^{a}lẽ*.

Any optional form of the past tense of the auxiliary verb may be employed, as explained in § 238.

261. Verbal Nouns and Infinitives.

(1) देखि *dēkh*ⁱ (or देख *dēkh*) (oblique form, देखै *dēkhai* or देखँ *dēkhā̃*), the act of seeing.

(2) देखब *dēkhab* (obl. form, देखबा *dekh*ᵃ*bā*), the act of seeing, to see.

(3) देखल *dēkhal* (obl. form, देखला *dekh*ᵃ*lā*), the act of seeing.

262. Noun of Agency.

देखबाह *dekh*ᵃ*bāh* or देखवाह *dekh*ᵃ*wāh*, one who sees.

263. Participles.

Present:—देखैत *dekhait* (fem. देखैति *dekhait*ⁱ), seeing.

Past:—देखल *dēkhal* (fem. देखलि *dēkhal*ⁱ), seen.

Conjunctive:—देखि *dēkh*ⁱ (देख *dēkh*), देखि कैं *dēkh*ⁱ *kaĩ*, देखि कँ *dēkh*ⁱ *kā̃*, or देखि कैकँ *dēkh*ⁱ *kaikā̃*, having seen.

Adverbial:—देखितहिं *dekhitah*ⁱ̃, on seeing, in the act of seeing, immediately on seeing.

B. INTRANSITIVE VERB.

√सूत *sūt*, sleep.

264. It is only necessary to give paradigms of those tenses of the intransitive verb which are formed from the past participle. In the other tenses it is conjugated exactly like the transitive verb.

As the intransitive verb has no direct object, those forms of the verb which have special reference to the object, *viz.*, Groups III and IV, and the long forms in औ *au* of Groups I and II can only refer to the indirect object. The mode of their employment is explained in § 189.

265. (*d*) (8) **Past Indicative.** 'I slept,' &c.

PERSON.	SHORT FORM.		LONG FORM.		REDUNDANT FORM.		GROUP III. (Subject: non-honorific. Object (indirect): honorific.)	GROUP IV. (Subject: honorific. Object (indirect): honorific.)
	GROUP I. (Subject: non-honorific. Object: non-honorific.)	GROUP II. (Subject: honorific. Object: non-honorific.)	GROUP I. (Subject: non-honorific. Object: non-honorific.)	GROUP II. (Subject: honorific. Object: non-honorific.)	GROUP I. (Subject: non-honorific. Object: non-honorific.)	GROUP II. (Subject: honorific. Object: non-honorific.)		
1	सुतलहुँ *sut^{a}lah^{ũ}*, सुतली *sut^{a}lī*.		सुतलिऐ *sut^{a}liai* Or (with indirect object in 2nd person.) सुतलिऔ *sut^{a}liau*, सुतलिअऽ *sut^{a}liah^{u}*.		सुतलिऐक *sut^{a}liaik* Or (with indirect object in 2nd person.) सुतलिऔक *sut^{a}liauk*.		सुतलिऐन्हि *sut^{a}liainh^{i}*.	
2	सुतलेँ *sut^{a}lẽ*, सुतलैँ *sut^{a}laĩ*.	Same as 1st person.	सुतलाह *sut^{a}lāh*; fem. सुतलीह *sut^{a}līh*, सुतलीहि *sut^{a}līh^{i}*.	Same as 1st person, but no forms for object in 2nd person.	सुतलहँक *sut^{a}lahãk*, सुतलहीक *sut^{a}lahīk*.	Same as 1st person, but no forms for object in 2nd person.	सुतलहुन्हि *sut^{a}lahũnh^{i}*.	Same as 1st person.
3	सूतल *sūtal'*; fem. सूतलि *sūtal^{i}*.	सुतलाह *sut^{a}lāh* (fem. सुतलीह *sut^{a}līh*, सुतलीहि *sut^{a}līh^{i}*); सुतलन्हि *sut^{a}lanh^{i}*.	GROUP I. सुतलै *sut^{a}lai* Or (with indirect object in 2nd person.) सुतलौ *sut^{a}lau*, सुतलऽ *sut^{a}lah^{u}*.		GROUP I. सुतलैक *sut^{a}laik* Or (with indirect object in 2nd person.) सुतलौक *sut^{a}lauk*.		सुतलैन्हि *sut^{a}lainh^{i}*.	सुतलथीन्हि *sutal^{a}thīnh^{i}*, सुतलथून्हि *sutal^{a}thūnh^{i}*.

266. (*d*) (9) **Perfect Indicative.** First form. 'I have slept,' &c.

PERSON.	SHORT FORM.		LONG FORM.		REDUNDANT FORM.			
	GROUP I. (Subject: non-honorific. Object: non-honorific.)	GROUP II. (Subject: honorific. Object: non-honorific.)	GROUP I. (Subject: non-honorific. Object: non-honorific.)	GROUP II. (Subject: honorific. Object: non-honorific.)	GROUP I. (Subject: non-honorific. Object: non-honorific.)	GROUP II. (Subject: honorific. Object: non-honorific.)	GROUP III. (Subject: non-honorific. Object (indirect): honorific.)	GROUP IV. (Subject: honorific. Object (indirect): honorific.)
1	सुतलहुँ अछि *sut^{a}lah$^{\bar{u}}$ ach^{i}.*		सुतलिऐ अछि *sut^{a}liai ach^{i}* Or (with ind. obj. in 2nd person.) सुतलिऔ अछि *sut^{a}lian ach^{i}.*		सुतलिऐक अछि *sut^{a}liaik ach^{i}* Or (with ind. obj. in 2nd person.) सुतलिऔक अछि *sut^{a}liauk ach^{i}.*		सुतलिऐन्हि अछि *sut^{a}liainh^{i} ach^{i}.*	
2	सुतलें अछि *sut^{a}lẽ ach^{i}.*	Same as 1st person.	सुतलाह अछि *sut^{a}lāh ach^{i}*; f. सुतलीह अछि *sut^{a}līh ach^{i}.*	Same as 1st person, but no forms for object in 2nd person.	सुतलहक अछि *sut^{a}lahak ach^{i}.*	Same as 1st person, but no forms for object in 2nd person.	सुतलहुन्हि अछि *sut^{a}lahũnh^{i} ach^{i}.*	Same as 1st person.
3	सुतलक अछि *sut^{a}lak ach^{i}.*	सुतलाह अछि *sut^{a}lāh ach^{i}*; fem. सुतलीह अछि *sut^{a}līh ach^{i}.*	GROUP I. सुतलै अछि *sut^{a}lai ach^{i}* Or (with ind. obj. in 2nd person.) सुतलौ अछि *sut^{a}lau ach^{i}.*		GROUP I. सुतलैक अछि *sut^{a}laik ach^{i}* Or (with ind. obj. in 2nd person.) सुतलौक अछि *sut^{a}lauk ach^{i}.*		सुतलैन्हि अछि *sut^{a}lainh^{i} ach^{i}.*	सुतलथीन्हि अछि *sutal^{a}thīnh^{i} ach^{i}.*

Any optional form of the Past Indicative may be substituted for those given above. Thus सुतली अछि *sut^{a}li ach^{i}*, I have slept, instead of सुतलहुँ अछि *sut^{a}lah$^{\bar{u}}$ ach^{i}.*

Also, instead of अछि *ach^{i}* we may substitute any of the optional forms of the third person of the present of the auxiliary verb; but the ones in ordinary use are अछि *ach^{i}* and अहि *ah^{i}.*

267. (*d*) (9) **Perfect Indicative.** Second Form. 'I have slept,' &c.; 'I am asleep,' &c.

PERSON.	SHORT FORM.		LONG FORM.		REDUNDANT FORM.		GROUP III. (Subject: non-honorific. Object (indirect): honorific.)	GROUP IV. (Subject: honorific. Object (indirect): honorific.)
	GROUP I. (Subject: non-honorific. Object: non-honorific.)	GROUP II. (Subject: honorific. Object: non-honorific.)	GROUP I. (Subject: non-honorific. Object: non-honorific.)	GROUP II. (Subject: honorific. Object: non-honorific.)	GROUP I. (Subject: non-honorific. Object: non-honorific.)	GROUP II. (Subject: honorific. Object: non-honorific.)		
1	सूतल छी *sūtal chī*; fem. सूतलि छी *sūtal^{i} chī*.		सूतल छिऐ *sūtal chiai*; fem. सूतलि छिऐ *sūtal^{i} chiai* Or (with indirect object in 2nd per.) सूतल छियौ *sūtal chiau*; fem. सूतलि छियौ *sūtal^{i} chiau*.		सूतल छिऐक *sūtal chiaik*; fem. सूतलि छिऐक *sūtal^{i} chiaik* Or (with indirect object in 2nd per.) सूतल छियौक *sūtal chiauk*; fem. सूतलि छियौक *sūtal^{i} chiauk*.		सूतल छिऐन्हि *sūtal chiainh^{i}*; fem. सूतलि छिऐन्हि *sūtal^{i} chiainh^{i}*.	
2	सूतल छेँ *sūtal chẽ*; fem. सूतलि छेँ *sūtal^{i} chẽ*.	Same as 1st person.	सूतल छह *sūtal chăh*; fem. सूतलि छहिँ *sūtal^{i} chahĩ*.	Same as 1st person, but no forms for object in 2nd person.	सूतल छहक *sūtal chahăk*; f. सूतलि छहक *sūtal^{i} chahăk*.	Same as 1st person, but no forms for object in 2nd person.	सूतल छहुन्हि *sūtal chahũnh^{i}*; f. सूतलि छहुन्हि *sūtal^{i} chahũnh^{i}*.	Same as 1st person.
3	सूतल अछि *sūtal ach^{i}*; fem. सूतलि अछि *sūtal^{i} ach^{i}*.	सूतल छथि *sūtal chath^{i}*; f. सूतलि छथि *sūtal^{i} chath^{i}*.	GROUP I. सूतल छै *sūtal chai*; f. सूतलि छै *sūtal^{i} chai* Or (with ind. obj. in 2nd person.) सूतल छौ *sūtal chau*; f. सूतलि छौ *sūtal^{i} chau*.		GROUP I. सूतल छैक *sūtal chaik*; f. सूतलि छैक *sūtal^{i} chaik* Or (with ind. obj. in 2nd person.) सूतल छौक *sūtal chauk*; f. सूतलि छौक *sūtal^{i} chauk*.		सूतल छैन्हि *sūtal chainh^{i}*; fem. सूतलि छैन्हि *sūtal^{i} chainh^{i}*.	सूतल छथीन्हि *sūtal chathīnh^{i}*; fem. सूतलि छथीन्हि *sūtal^{i} chathīnh^{i}*.

Any optional form of the present tense of the auxiliary verb may be employed, as explained in § 236.

268. (*d*) (10) **Pluperfect Indicative.** 'I had slept,' &c.; 'I slept a long time ago,' &c.; 'I was asleep,' &c.

PERSON.	SHORT FORM.		LONG FORM.		REDUNDANT FORM.			
	GROUP I. (Subject: non-honorific. Object: non-honorific.)	GROUP II. (Subject: honorific. Object: non-honorific.)	GROUP I. (Subject: non-honorific. Object: non-honorific.)	GROUP II. (Subject: honorific. Object: non-honorific.)	GROUP I. (Subject: non-honorific Object: non-honorific.)	GROUP II. (Subject: honorific. Object: non-honorific.)	GROUP III. (Subject: non-honorific. Object (indirect): honorific.)	GROUP IV. (Subject: honorific. Object indirect): honorific.)
1	सूतल* चलहुँ *sūtal chalahũ*; f. सूतलि* चलहुँ *sūtal^{i} chalahũ*.		सूतल चलिऐ *sūtal chaliai*; fem. सूतलि चलिऐ *sūtal^{i} chaliai* Or (with ind. obj. in 2nd person) सूतल चलिऔ *sūtal chaliau*; fem. सूतलि चलिऔ *sūtal^{i} chaliau*.		सूतल चलिऐक *sūtal chaliaik*; fem. सूतलि चलिऐक *sūtal^{i} chaliaik* Or (with ind. obj. in 2nd person.) सूतल चलिऔक *sūtal chaliauk*; f. सूतलि चलिऔक *sūtal^{i} chaliauk*.		सूतल चलिऐन्हि *sūtal chaliainh^{i}*; fem. सूतलि चलिऐन्हि *sūtal^{i} chaliainh^{i}*.	
2	सूतल चलैं *sūtal chalẽ*; fem. सूतलि चलैं *sūtal^{i} chalẽ*.	Same as 1st person.	सूतल चलाह *sūtal chalāh*; f. सूतलि चलीह *sūtal^{i} chalīh*.	Same as 1st person, but no forms for object in 2nd person.	सूतल चलहक *sūtal chal^{a}hāk*; f. सूतलि चलहक *sūtal^{i} chal^{a}hāk*.	Same as 1st person, but no forms for object in 2nd person.	सूतल चलहुन्हि *sūtal chal^{a}hũnh^{i}*; f. सूतलि चलहुन्हि *sūtal^{i} chal^{a}hũnh^{i}*.	Same as 1st person.
3	सूतल चल *sūtal chal*; fem. सूतलि चलि *sūtal^{i} chal^{i}*.	सूतल चलाह *sūtal chalāh*, fem. सूतलि चलीह *sūtal^{i} chalīh*.	GROUP I. सूतल चलै *sūtal chalai*; fem सूतलि चलै *sūtal^{i} chalai* Or (with ind. obj. in 2nd person.) सूतल चलौ *sūtal chalau*; fem. सूतलि चलौ *sūtal^{i} chalau*.		GROUP I. सूतल चलैक *sūtal chalaik*; fem. सूतलि चलैक *sūtal^{i} chalaik* Or (with ind. obj. in 2nd person.) सूतल चलौक *sūtal chalauk*; fem. सूतलि चलौक *sūtal^{i} chalauk*.		सूतल चलैन्हि *sūtal chalainh^{i}*; f. सूतलि चलैन्हि *sūtal^{i} chalainh^{i}*.	सूतल चलथीन्हि *sūtal chal^{a}thīnh^{i}*; fem. सूतलि चलथीन्हि *sūtal^{i} chal^{a}thīnh^{i}*

* Or (both masc. and fem.) सुतलैं *sut^{a}lẽ*, or (less commonly, and mostly by the uneducated) सुतले *sut^{a}lē*, सुतनैं *sut^{a}nẽ*, or सुतने *sut^{a}nē*.

Any optional form of the past tense of the auxiliary verb may be employed, as explained in § 238.

CHAPTER V.

Vocalic Roots.

269. The roots of the verbs conjugated in the preceding chapter end in a consonant. If a root ends in a vowel, the same terminations are added, but when these commence with a vowel, changes, which require explanation, occur in the method of suffixing them to the root.

The same is the case with verbs whose roots end in आब *āb*, in which the ब *b* represents an older semi-vowel व *v*, which is, as a general rule, ultimately derived from a Sanskrit प *p*. The conjugation of these verbs runs parallel with that of verbs in आ *ā*, but at the same time differs from them in certain particulars. Owing to the nature of these roots in आब *āb*, I class them as vocalic roots for convenience of treatment.

Vocalic roots may end in आ *ā*, आब *āb*, इ *i*, ई *ī*, ए *ē*, ऊ *ū* or ओ *ō*. They will be dealt with in that order.

Roots in आ *ā* and आब *āb*.

270. Of all vocalic roots these are by far most common. Verbs whose roots end in आ *ā* include all potential passives (see § 333), a large number of intransitive verbs, and the transitive verb √ खा *khā*, eat.

Verbs whose roots end in आब *āb* include nearly all causals and double causals (see §§ 334 and ff), a certain number of transitive verbs, and the intransitive verbs √गाब *gāb*, sing., √पछताब *pach*ᵃ*tāb*, repent, and √आब *āb*, come. √आब *āb* is irregular in some of its forms and will be dealt with in § 312, although in this chapter I have freely used regular forms in the examples. √गाब *gāb* follows the other roots in आब *āb*, except that as they are transitive and it is usually intransitive, it in such cases takes the intransitive forms of the past tenses. When used as a transitive verb it is conjugated as such. Thus,—गाओल *gāol*, he sang (intransitive); but (Vid. xxiii, 11) एह गाओल *eh gāol*, I sang this (transitive).

271. As a great many verbs have both potential passive and causal forms, we frequently notice pairs of each conjugation running side by side. Thus from the √देख *dēkh*, see, we have the potential passive √देखा *dēkhā*, be visible, and the causal √देखाब *dēkhāb*, cause to see, show. The past participle of the former would be देखाएल *dekhāel* and of the latter देखाओल *dekhāol*. देखैलहुँ *dekhailahū̃* would mean 'I was visible.' देखौलहुँ *dekhaulahū̃* would mean 'I caused to see.'

The following are examples of these roots, with the past participle in each case :—

A. Verbs in आ *ā*.

Root.	Past Participle.
देखा *dēkhā*, be visible,	देखाएल *dekhāel*.
अघा *aghā*, be satiated.	अघाएल *aghāel*.
घबड़ा *ghabᵃṛā*, be confused,	घबड़ाएल *ghabᵃṛāel*.
हड़बड़ा *haṛᵃbaṛā*, be flurried,	हड़बड़ाएल *haṛᵃbaṛāel*.
खा *khā*, eat,	खाएल *khāel*.

B. Verbs in आब *āb*.

Root.	Past Participle.
देखाब *dēkhāb*, show,	देखाओल *dekhāol*.
पाब *pāb*, obtain,	पाओल *pāol*.
गाब *gāb*, sing,	गाओल *gāol*.
पछताब *pachᵃtāb*, repent.	पछताओल *pachᵃtāol*.

272. As usual (*vide* §§ 32 ff) the termination आ *ā* or आब *āb* is liable to be shortened in the antepenultimate. It is usually, however, retained long before a final ऐ *ai* or औ *au*. Thus पाबै *pābai*. पाबौ *pābau*, as explained in § 176. Before ऐत *ait* of the

present participle आब *āb* is as usual shortened, as in पबैत *pabait*. Verbs in आ *ā*, on the other hand, make the present participle as in खाइत *khāit* or खायित *khāyit*.

When the final vowel of a root in आ *ā* comes before a termination beginning with अ *a*, the two together become आए *āe*. Thus खा *khā* + अल *a* becomes खाएल *khāel* (really for खायल *khāyal*, with euphonic य् *y* inserted), eaten or I ate; खा *khā* + अब *ab* becomes खाएब *khāeb*, to eat or I shall eat. Before ऐ *ai*, it usually remains unchanged, as in देखाऐ *dekhāai*, he sees, but in the present participle, the termination ऐत *ait* becomes इत *it*, and before the इ *i* the आ *ā* either remains unchanged or inserts a य् *y*; thus, as above, खाइत *khāit* or खायित *khāyit*, eating. As usual (see §§ 11, 14) इ *i* is often employed for ए *e*, and *vice versa*, so that we may meet forms such as खाइल *khāil*, खाइब *khāib* or खाएत *khāet*. In all these cases, when the आ *ā* is shortened under the antepenultimate rule, the two vowels together become ऐ *ai* (often written, as usual अइ *ai* or अए *ae*, see § 13). Thus खैलहुँ *khailahũ*, I ate, खैबै *khaibai*, I shall eat, खैतहुँ *khaitahũ* (if) I had eaten.

273. With roots ending in आब *āb*, the procedure is somewhat different. As a general rule, before अ *a*, the आब *āb* plus अ *a* becomes आओ *āo*. Thus देखाब *dēkhāb* + अब *ab* becomes देखाओब *dekhāob* (poetical form; for the usual form see below), I shall show; देखाब *dēkhāb* + अल *al* becomes देखाओल *dekhāol*, I showed. In the form देखाबथि *dekhābathi* (3rd person, Short Form, Group II, Old Present), the ब *b* is preserved unchanged.

Before terminations commencing with ऐ *ai* or औ *au* the ब *b* is usually retained. Thus देखाबै *dekhābai*, देखाबौ *dekhābau* (3rd person, Long Form, Group I, Old Present); Present Participle देखबैत *dekhᵃbait*, with shortening of the antepenultimate. Before इ *i* or ई *ī*, आब *āb* remains unchanged, as in देखाबी *dekhābī*, I show.

274. In the modern language there is a tendency to assimilate the conjugation of roots in आब *āb* to that of those in आ *ā*. A glance at the paradigm will show that many optional forms are borrowed from the latter conjugation. In the 2nd verbal noun and in the future the conjugation in आ *ā* has almost ousted the original one. We have just seen that the old poetical form of the first person future was देखाओब *dekhāob*, I shall show. In the modern language it is, however, always देखाएब *dekhāeb*. A reference to the paradigm will show how completely the original *o*-conjugation has disappeared in the future. It has only survived in the third form of the tense.

On the other hand, the past tense, the one most frequently employed, strongly preserves the *o*-conjugation. The conjugation of roots in आ *ā*, has here entirely failed to gain a footing. In this tense, and elsewhere in similar circumstances, when आओ *ā-o* becomes अओ *a-o*. under the antepenultimate rule, the two adjacent vowels coalesce, and are usually written औ *au*. Thus, देखाओल *dekhāol* or देखौलहुँ *dekhaulahŭ*, I showed.

275. In the following paradigms, I take as the model of a root in आ *ā* the √देखा *dēkhā*, be visible, and as the model of a root in आब *āb*, √देखाब *dēkhāb*, show. I only give the short and long forms of Groups I and II. The redundant forms of these two groups, and the forms of Groups III and IV can be made from these without any difficulty. In cases where any difficulty is likely to arise, I solve it in additional notes. It is only necessary to give the four simple tenses, the verbal nouns, and the participles. The periphrastic tenses can easily be made from these materials. Even for the four simple tenses, I only give the most common forms.

One other remark should be made. I have throughout spoken of roots ending in आब *āb*. This termination is very often written आव *āw* or *āv*, and is even so pronounced in South Mithilā. Thus, instead of देखाबी *dekhābī*, we hear देखावी *dekhāwī* or *dekhāvī*, and so throughout. There is no doubt that in the best standard Maithili the correct forms are those with ब *b*, though व *w* forms will often be found in literature (generally due to careless writing).

276. (*a*) (1) **Old Present.**

'I am visible,' &c. — 'I show,' &c.

PERSON.	'I am visible': SHORT FORM. GROUP I. (Subject: non-honorific. Object: non-honorific.)	SHORT FORM. GROUP II. (Subject: honorific: Object: non-honorific.)	LONG FORM. GROUP I. (Subject: non-honorific. Object: non-honorific.)	LONG FORM. GROUP I. (Subject: honorific. Object: non-honorific.)	'I show': SHORT FORM. GROUP I. (Subject: non-honorific. Object: non-honorific.)	SHORT FORM. GROUP II. (Subject: honorific. Object: non-honorific.)	LONG FORM. GROUP I. (Subject: non-honorific. Object: non-honorific.)	LONG FORM. GROUP II. (Subject: honorific. Object: non-honorific.)
1	देखाइँ *dekhāĩ*, देखाऊँ *dekhāũ*.		देखैऐ *dekhaiai* Or (with object in 2nd person.) देखैऔ *dekhaiau*.		देखाबी *dekhābi* (देखाइँ *dekhāĩ*), देखाबूँ *dekhābũ* (देखाऊँ *dekhāũ*).		देखाबिऐ *dekhābiai* (देखैऐ *dekhaiai*) Or (with obj. in 2nd pers.) देखाबिऔ *dekhābiau* (देखैऔ *dekhaiau*).	
2	देखा *dēkhā*.	Same as 1st person.	देखाह *dekhāh*.	Same as 1st person, but no forms for object in 2nd person.	देखाब *dēkhāb*.	Same as 1st person.	देखाबह *dekhābah*, Red. form देखाबहक *dekhābahak*.	Same as 1st person, but no forms for object in 2nd person.
3	देखाए *dekhāe*, (often spelt देखाय *dekhāy*), देखाओ *dekhāo* (देखाव *dekhāw*).	देखाथि *dekhāthi*.	GROUP I. देखाऐ *dekhāai* Or (with object in 2nd person.) देखाऔ *dekhāau*, देखाहु *dekhāhu*.		देखाबे *dekhābē* (देखाए *dekhāe*.)	देखाबथि *dekhābathi*.	GROUP I. देखाबै *dekhābai* Or (with object in 2nd person.) देखाबौ *dekhābau*.	

For *ā*-verbs, in Groups III and IV, we have (1) देखैन्हि *dekhaiainhi*; (2) देखाहुन्हि *dekhāhūnhi*; (3) देखाऐन्हि *dekhāainhi*; देखाथीन्हि *dekhāthīnhi*.

277. (*b*) (4) **Future Indicative.** Second Form.

'I shall be visible,' &c. — 'I shall show,' &c.

PERSON.	'I shall be visible,' &c. SHORT FORM.		LONG FORM.		'I shall show,' &c. SHORT FORM.		LONG FORM.	
	GROUP I. (Subject: non-honorific. Object: non-honorific.)	GROUP II. (Subject: honorific. Object: non-honorific.)	GROUP I. (Subject: non-honorific. Object: non-honorific.)	GROUP II. (Subject: honorific. Object: non-honorific.)	GROUP I. (Subject: non-honorific. Object: non-honorific.)	GROUP II. (Subject: honorific. Object: non-honorific.)	GROUP I. (Subject: non-honorific. Object: non-honorific.)	GROUP II. (Subject: honorific. Object: non-honorific.)
1	देखाएब *dekhāeb.*		देखैबै *dekhaibai* Or (with object in 2nd person.) देखैबौ *dekhaibau.*		देखाएब *dekhāeb* (poetical) देखाओब *dekhāob.*		देखैबै *dekhaibai* Or (with object in 2nd person.) देखैबौ *dekhaibau.*	
2	देखैबैं *dekhaibẽ.*	Same as 1st person.	देखैबह *dekhaibăh.*	Same as 1st person, but no forms for object in 2nd person.	देखैबैं *dekhaibẽ.*	Same as 1st person.	देखैबह *dekhaibăh.*	Same as 1st person, but no forms for object in 2nd person.
3	Wanting.	Wanting.	GROUP I. Wanting.		Wanting.	Wanting.	GROUP I. Wanting.	

278. (*b*) (4) **Future Indicative.** Third Form.

'I shall be visible,' &c. — 'I shall show,' &c.

PERSON.	SHORT FORM.		LONG FORM.		SHORT FORM.		LONG FORM.	
	GROUP I. (Subject: non-honorific. Object: non-honorific.)	GROUP II. (Subject: honorific. Object: non-honorific.)	GROUP I. (Subject: non-honorific. Object: non-honorific.)	GROUP II. (Subject: honorific. Object: non-honorific.)	GROUP I. (Subject: non-honorific. Object: non-honorific.)	GROUP II. (Subject: honorific. Object: non-honorific.)	GROUP I. (Subject: non-honorific. Object: non-honorific.)	GROUP II. (Subject: honorific. Object: non-honorific.)
1	देखैतहुँ *dekhaitahũ*.		देखैतिऐ *dekhaitiai* Or (with object in 2nd person). देखैतिऔ *dekhaitiau*.		देखौतहुँ *dekhautahũ*.		देखौतिऐ *dekhautiai* Or (with obj. in 2nd person.) देखौतिऔ *dekhautiau*.	
2	Wanting.	Same as 1st person.	Wanting.	Same as 1st person, but no forms for object in 2nd person.	Wanting.	Same as 1st person.	Wanting.	Same as 1st person, but no forms for object in 2nd person.
3	देखाइत *dekhāit*.	देखैताह *dekhaitāh*.	GROUP I. देखैतै *dekhaitai* Or (with object in 2nd person.) देखैतौ *dekhaitau*.		देखाओत *dekhāot*.	देखौताह *dekhautāh*.	GROUP I. देखौतै *dekhautai* Or (with obj. in 2nd person.) देखौतौ *dekhautau*.	

279. (*c*) (5) **Past Conditional.**

'If I had been visible,' &c.; 'I should have been visible,' &c. 'If I had shown,' &c.; 'I should have shown,' &c.

PERSON.	SHORT FORM. GROUP I. (Subject: non-honorific. Object: non-honorific.)	SHORT FORM. GROUP II. (Subject: honorific. Object: non-honorific.)	LONG FORM. GROUP I. (Subject: non-honorific. Object: non-honorific.)	LONG FORM. GROUP II. (Subject: honorific. Object: non-honorific.)	SHORT FORM. GROUP I. (Subject: non-honorific. Object: non-honorific.)	SHORT FORM. GROUP II. (Subject: honorific. Object: non-honorific.)	LONG FORM. GROUP I. (Subject: non-honorific. Object: non-honorific.)	LONG FORM. GROUP II. (Subject: honorific. Object: non-honorific.)
1	देखैतहुँ *dekhaitahũ*		देखैतिऐ *dekhaitiai* Or (with object in 2nd person.) देखैतिऔ *dekhaitiau.*		देखबैतहुँ *dekh^{a}baitahũ*, देखबितहुँ *dekh^{a}bitahũ*, देखौतहुँ *dekhautahũ.*		देखबैतिऐ *dekh^{a}baitiai*, &c. Or (with obj. in 2nd pers.) देखबैतिऔ *dekh^{a}baitiau*, &c.	
2	देखैतेँ *dekhaitẽ.*	Same as 1st person.	देखैतह *dekhaitàh.*	Same as 1st person, but no forms for object in 2nd person.	देखबैतेँ *dekh^{a}baitẽ*, &c.	Same as 1st person.	देखबैतह *dekh^{a}baitàh*, &c.	Same as 1st person, but no forms for object in 2nd person.
3	देखाइत *dekhāit.*	देखैतथि *dekhaitathi.*	GROUP I. देखैतै *dekhaitai* Or (with object in 2nd person.) देखैतौ *dekhaitau.*		देखबैत *dekh^{a}bait.*	देखबैतथि *dekh^{a}baitathi*, &c.	GROUP I. देखबैतै *dekh^{a}baitai*, &c. Or (with obj. in 2nd. pers.) देखबैतौ *dekh^{a}baitau*, &c.	

Optional forms for *āb*-verbs throughout as in the first person, except in the short form of the 3rd person of Group I.

280. (*d*) (8) Past Indicative.

PERSON.	‘I became visible,’ &c. SHORT FORM. GROUP I. (Subject: non-honorific. Object: non-honorific.)	GROUP II. (Subject: honorific. Object: non-honorific.)	LONG FORM. GROUP I. (Subject: non-honorific. Object: non-honorific.)	GROUP II. (Subject: honorific. Object: non-honorific.)	‘I showed,’ &c. SHORT FORM. GROUP I. (Subject: non-honorific. Object: non-honorific.)	GROUP II. (Subject: honorific. Object: non-honorific.)	LONG FORM. GROUP I. (Subj. non-honorific. Object: non-honorific.)	GROUP II. (Subject: honorific. Object: non-honorific.)
1	दॆखैलहुँ *dekhailah*[*], दॆखैली *dekhaile.*		दॆखैलिऐ *dekhailiai* Or (with object in 2nd person.) दॆखैलिऔ *dekhailiau.*		दॆखौलहुँ *dekhaulah*[*], दॆखाओल *dekhāol*, दॆखौली *dekhaule.*		दॆखौलै *dekhaulai*, दॆखौलिऐ *dekhauliai* Or (with obj. in 2nd person.) दॆखौलौ *dekhaulau*, दॆखौलिऔ *dekhauliau.*	
2	दॆखैलेँ *dekhailē.*	Same as 1st person.	दॆखैलाह *dekhailāh.*	Same as 1st person, but no forms for object in 2nd person.	दॆखौलेँ *dekhaulē.*	Same as 1st person.	दॆखौलाह *dekhaulāh.*	Same as 1st pers., but no forms for obj. in 2nd pers.
3	दॆखाएल *dekhāel.*	दॆखैलाह *dekhailāh.*	GROUP I. दॆखैलै *dekhailai* Or (with object in 2nd person.) दॆखैलौ *dekhailau.*		दॆखौलक *dekhaulak.*	दॆखौलन्हि *dekhaulanhi.*	GROUP I. दॆखौलकै *dekhaulakai* Or (with obj. in 2nd person.) दॆखौलकौ *dekhaulakau.*	

* Here and elsewhere the diphthong is often written as in दॆखओलहुँ or दॆखउलहुँ (see § 13).

281. Verbal Nouns and Infinitives.

(1)

देखाय *dekhāy* (an optional and usual spelling of देखाइ *dekhāi* or देखाए *dekhāe*), the condition of being visible; obl. देखाए *dekhāe* or देखाय *dekhāy*.

देखाबि *dekhāb*^{i} or देखाय *dekhāy* (often spelt देखाइ *dekhāi* or देखाए *dekhāe*), the act of showing. The oblique form of देखाबि *dekhab*^{i} is देखाबै *dekhābai* (with the usual variations of spelling), or देखाबँ *dekhābã*. That of देखाय *dekhāy* is देखाए *dekhāe* or देखाय *dekhāy*.

(2)

देखाएब *dekhāeb*; obl. देखैबा *dekhaibā*; the condition of being visible, to be visible.

देखाएब *dekhāeb*; obl. देखैबा *dekhaibā*: the act of showing, to show.

(3)

देखाएल *dekhāel*; obl. देखैला *dekhailā*; the condition of being visible.

देखाओल *dekhāol*; obl. देखौला *dekhaulā*; the act of showing.

282. Participles.

Present.

देखाइत *dekhāit*, seeing. | देखबैत *dekh*^{a}*bait*, showing.

Past.

देखाएल *dekhāel*, seen. | देखाओल *dekhāol*, shown.

283. The following are examples of the use of verbs whose roots end in आ *ā*.

(*a*) (1) **Old Present** :—

फोटरा के तीर चढ़ाय कँ भट्ठी मारै। मरि जाय, *phoṭ*^{a}*rā kē tīr caṛhāy ke bhadrī mārai ; mar^i jāy*, Bhadri having aimed an arrow strikes Phoṭrā. He dies.

अम्मत अँगूर के खाओ, *ammat āgūr kē khāo*, who eats sour grapes ?

से कोन ठाम जतै नहिं जाथि। कै बेरि अँगनहुँ सौं बहराथि॥
कै बेरि साँप धरए लै जाथि। कै बेरि चून दही बदि खाथि॥

sē kona ṭhāma jatai nahī jāthi । *kai beri āganahū sō baharāthi* ॥
kai beri sāpa dharae lai jāthi । *kai beri cūna dahī badi khāthi* ॥

What place is there where he does not go ! How often does he go outside the court-yard ! How often does he catch hold of a snake and carry it away (thinking it a piece of rope) ! How often does he eat lime thinking it is curds. (Man. iii, 2. 4).

(*a*) (2) **Present Conditional** :—

नहिं पतियाऊ तो आबिहें, *nah^i patiyāh^u to ābihē*, (if) she do not have faith in you, then come.

(*a*) (3) **Imperative** :—

यार राखू मोर बात जाऊ जोगिया घर ... ... **अहाँ घुरि जाऊ** *yār rākhū mōr bāt, jāh^u jogiyā ghar ... ahā̃ ghuri jāū*, friend, heed my word, go home to Jogiyā ... let Your Honour return (home).

कहलकैन्हि हे अम्मा जाह जाह घर, *kahal^akainh^i*, '*hē ammā, jāh jāh ghar*,' he said respectfully, 'O mother, go, go home.'

खाह पिबँह चैन करँह, *khāh, pibah, cain karah*, eat, drink, be happy.

Precative Form :—**काल्हिक दिन लै जैहें** *kālhik din lē jaihē*, please take (it) away tomorrow.

(*b*) (4) **Future Indicative** :—

तीनु मम भगिना जाएब कटैया सिकार, *tīnū mamā bhaginā jāeb kaṭaiyā sikār*, we three, uncle and nephews, will go to Kaṭaiyā to hunt.

हमरो समधिया लै के जैबौ जोगिया, *ham^arō samadhiyā lē ke jaibau jogiyā*, having taken our message also, you will go to Jogiyā.

हमरा पेटक आगि एहि सँ नहिं मिझाएत (for **मिझाइत**, § 271) *ham^arā pēṭak āg^i eh^i sã nah^i mijhāet* (for *mijhāit*), the fire of my belly cannot be extinguished (potential passive) by this.

बाबू सुतले रहताह नहिँ जैताह, *bābū sut^{a}lē rah^{a}tăh ; nah^{i} jaităh.* (my) sons will remain asleep; they will not go.

खैताह-अन्हि से परलए बीत, *kaităha-anhi sē paralae bīta,* (if) he will eat, a whole age passeth away (see § 193).

(*c*) (5) **Past Conditional** :—

जौँ हमहुँ तोहरा जकाँ अन्न तौलितहुँ तखन आइ पाओ भरि एम्हर ओम्हर सँ माँगि नहिँ खैतहुँ, *jaũ hamah^{u} toh^{a}rā jakā̃ ann taulitah^{u} takhan āi pāo bhur^{i} ēmhar ōmhar sā̃ mā̃g^{i} nah^{i} khaitah^{u}*, if, like you, I had (traded and) weighed out food, I should not to-day have eaten after begging a quarter of a seer (of food) from here and there.

(*c*) (6) **Present Indicative** :—

कहलन्हि जे अहिरा कहाँ जाइछैँ। कहलक जे जाइछी गाइक बथान, *kah^{a}lanh^{i} jē 'ahirā kahā̃ jāichaī ?' kah^{a}lak jē jāi-chī gāik bathān,* he (honorific) said, 'O Ahīrā, where are you (non-honorific) going?' he (non-honorific) said, 'I am going to (my) cowshed.'

ठेहनी धैनेँ जाइत अछि उरसीक डीह, *ṭheh^{a}nī dhainē̃ jāit ach^{i} ur^{a}sīk ḍīh,* taking his crutch along with him, he is going to Ursī village.

(*d*) (8) **Past Indicative** :—

चित्ता आओर हुँड़ार नाँगड़ि सुटकाए कँ पड़ाएल, *cittā āor hūṛār nā̃gaṛ^{i} suṭ^{a}kāe kā̃ paṛāel,* the leopard and the wolf, hiding their tails, ran away.

तखन सबहु मिलि खाएल तार, *takhana sabahu mili khāela tāra,* then all, having united, ate (poetic for खैलक *khailak*) the *tāl* fruits. (Man. v, 11).

अग्नि प्रज्वलित देखि धूर्त सभ पड़यलाह (for पड़ैलाह) *agn^{i} prajwalit dēkh^{i} dhūrt sabh paṛay^{a}lăh* (for *paṛailăh*), seeing the fire blazing, the knaves ran away.

(*Note.*—Here we have an honorific form used in its original signification of a non-honorific plural. This sometimes occurs in literature).

जत पौलन्हि खैलन्हि सभ बस्तु, *jata paulanhi* (√पाब *pāb*) *khailanhi* (√खा *khā*) *sabha bastu,* all the things that he could get he ate. (Man. v, 30).

Verbal Nouns.

एतबाँ बचन सुनि दीना भद्री गेल खिसियाय, *et^{a}bā̃ bacan sun^i dīnā bhadrī gēl khisiyāy*, so much words having heard, Dīnā and Bhadrī became angry. (See § 342).

The genitive of खाय *khāy*, the act of eating, *viz.*, खाएक *khāek*, is used to mean "food." Thus अपना अपना घर मेँ सुन्नर खाएक करैँ-गँ *ap^{a}nā ap^{a}nā ghar mē̃ sunnar khāek karē̃-gá*. you will, each in your own house, prepare beautiful food.

ओना लेनेँ जैबे तो लोग कहतौ जे उढ़रा उढ़री छी, *onā lēnē̃ jaibē to lōg kah^{a}tau jē uṛk^{a}rā uṛh^{a}rī chī*, in taking them away with us (*i.e.*, if we take them away with us) in that way people will say to you that we are each a pair in concubinage.

नेरु हेरैनेँ जेहन धेनु गाइ, *nēru herainē̃* (for *herailē̃*) *jehana dhenu gāi*, like a cow on losing her calf. (Man. iii, 17).

Present Participle :—See *Present Indicative.*

Cf. also निरालसी लोक भोज्य खायित छथि, *nirāl^{a}sī lōk bhōjya khāyit* (for *khāit*) *chath^i*, people who are not lazy are eating food. (*Purush Parīkṣā*, p. 51).

Past Participle : See Past Indicative

Conjunctive Participle :

धामीक सबद सुनि उठलीहि दीना भद्रीक माइ चिहाय, *dhāmik sabad sun^i uṭh^{a}līh^i dīnā bhadrik māi cihāy*, having heard the voice of Dhāmī, the mother of Dīnā and Bhadrī, being startled, rose up.

284. The following are examples of the use of verbs whose roots end in आब *āb*.

(1) (*a*) (*b*) **Old Present, and Present Conditional**:—

जँ एकरा सभ केँ किछु कै देखाबी तँ चाही जे बुझि जाय, *já ek^{a}rā sabh kē̃ kicch^u kai dekhābī tá cāhī jē bujh^i jāy*, if, having done something I show it to them, then they ought to understand.

अबैति छौ गोआही गुजराब, *abait^i chau goāhī guj^{a}rāb*, she is coming to you (that) she may cause you to bear testimony.

बीछि बान कै फल सभ पाए, *bīchi bāna kai phula sabha pāe.* they all obtain as the fruit arrows (sharp as) scorpions. (Man. x, 52).

स्तुति उठि नित दिन सुरुज के हाँथ उठाबै, *sūti uṭhi nit din suruj kē hā̃th uṭhābai*, daily, when they go to rest, and when they rise, they raise their hands to the sun (and pray).

(1) (c) **Imperative :—**

रे धिया पुता ताहिर मियाँक हबेली देखाब, *rē dhiyā putā, tāhir miyā̃k habēlī dekhāb*, hulloa, girls and boys, show (me) Tāhir Miyā̃'s house.

चलह हो दादा धूनी उठाबह, *calah, hō dādā, dhūnī uṭhābah*, come. O brother, lift up the brazier (of fire).

बहोरन ममा के लाबहोक बोलाय, *bahōran mamā kē lābahōk bolāy*, having called uncle Bahōran, bring him (here).

(b) (4) **Future :—**

(*Old forms*) :—

आठम भए हम अपनहिं आओब ।
जेहन बनत पुनु तेहन बनाओब ॥

āṭhama bhae hama apanahĩ āob ।
jehana banata punu tehana banāoba ॥

I myself will come, having become (incarnate as) the eighth (child). as it will become (necessary), so will I bring it to pass. (Man. i, 32).

गाए महिसि सरकार लगाओब ।
लुटब सकल ब्रज जत धन पाओब ॥

gāe mahisi sarakāra lagāoba ।
luṭabu sakula braju jata dhanu pāoba ॥

I will confiscate to government his cows and she-buffaloes, and plunder all Vraja of all the wealth I can find (in it). (Man. vi, 28).

नन्दी सँ रस रीति बचाओब, *nandī sa̐ rasa rīti bacāoba*, thou wilt (*i.e.*, shouldest) conceal the way of love from (thy) sister-in-law. (Vid. xl, 12).

(*Modern forms*) :—

खूब अकड़ि अपन गहना कपड़ाक सुनरताई आओर मुँहक चमक-चिमक देखाएब, *khūb akaṛ*[i] *upan gah*[a]*nā kap*[a]*ṛāk sunar*[a]*tāī āor mũhak camak-cimak dekhāeb*, with much swagger I shall display the beauty of (my) ornaments and clothes. and the glory of my countenance.

हम अपनेक भल मानब आओर सदा गुन गाएब, *ham ap*[a]*nek bhal mānab āor sadā gun gāeb.* I shall revere you. and ever sing your praises.

जलदी रुपैआ असूल करू। नहिं तँ पीछू पछताएब, *jal*[a]*dī rupaiā asūl karū : nah*[i] *tã pīchū pach*[a]*tāeb.* realize (honorific) the money quickly ; otherwise you (honorific) will afterwards repent.

एकर उचित फल पैबह कालि, *ekara ucita phala paibaha* (for *paibáh*) *kāli*, on the morrow shalt thou obtain the fitting fruit of this. (Man. i. 38).

कहलक सोझ हमर जों आओत।
जिबइत जाए एकौ नहिं पाओत।

kahalaka sõjha hamara jõ āota ।
jībaita jāe ekau nahī pāota ।

said they. 'if they shall come before us, not one will obtain (permission) (*i.e.*, be able) to go away alive.' (Man. viii. 43).

चारू दीस बाट तकथि जे कोन दीस सौं सलहेस औताह, *cāru dīs bāṭ tākath*[i] *jē kōn dīs saũ sal*[a]*hēs autāh*, they watch the roads in the four directions, (to see) from what direction Salhēs will come.

(*c*) (5) **Past Conditional** :—

जनितहुँ तो बगहा में बरदी तमाकू लदबैतिऐ, *janitah*[ũ] *to bag*[a]*hā mẽ bar*[a]*dī tamākū lad*[a]*baitiai.* if I had known, I should have loaded a bullock with tobacco in Baghā.

जौहरी एकरा पबैत तो अत्यन्त खुसी होइत, *jauh*[a]*rī ek*[a]*rā pabait. to atyant khusī hoit*, (if) a jeweller had found this, he would have been very happy.

औतन्हि दुरागमन करैतन्हि जमैया जाँजरि, *autanh*[i], *durāgaman karaitainh*[i] *jamaiyā jãjar*[i]. (if) they had come to Jãjari, his sons-in-law would have celebrated the *durāgaman* ceremony.

(c) (6) **Present Indicative** :—

माइ बापक नाम छिपबैत छी, *māi bāpak nām chip*^{a}*bait chī*, we are concealing the names of our father and mother.

हम तोहरा एक कहिनी सुनबैछिअहु, *ham toh*^{a}*rā ek kahinī sun*^{a}*bai-chiah*^{u}, I am causing you to hear (telling you) a story.

कनौली में सात से पट्ठा अखाढ़ा में खेलबैत अछि, *kanaulī mẽ sāt sai paṭṭhā akhāṛhā mẽ khel*^{a}*bait ach*^{i}, in Kanauli he causes seven hundred athletes to play (*i.e.*, do gymnastics) on his arena.

But :—

एक से एकैस डण्ड खेलाइत अछि अखाढ़ा पर, *ek sai ekais daṇḍ khelāit ach*^{i} *akhāṛhā par*, he *performs* one hundred and twenty exercises (*cognate accusation of an intransitive verb*) on the arena.

सदा भूँकि भूँकि कैँ हमरा सभ कैँ भड़कबैअछि, *sadā bhū̃k*^{i} *bhū̃k*^{i} *kaĩ ham*^{a}*rā sabh kẽ bhaṛ*^{a}*kabai-ach*^{i}, they make us quarrel by their continual barking.

तीनु गोटे अबैत छथि *tīnū gōṭē abait chath*^{i}, the three (respected people) are coming.

अबैति छौ *abait*^{i} *chau*, she is coming to you. (See under Old Present).

पानि बिनु अबैत छौक तेजैत अबैत छौक परान, *pāni bin*^{u} *abait chauk, tejait abait chauk parān*, without water (*i.e.*, athirst) he is coming to you, he is coming to you giving up his life (*i.e.*, at the point of death).

(d) (8) **Past Indicative** :—

विद्यापति एह गाओल सजनी गे ।
ई थिक नब रस रीती ॥

bidyāpati eha gāola, sajanī gē ।
ī thika naba rasa rītī ॥

(Saith) Vidyāpati, 'I sang this, O friend,
This is the way of young love.' (Vid. xxiii, 11).

चौदह कोस पकड़िआ चौकीदारी लिखाओल चोरक बनार नहिं पाओल, *caudah kōs pakaṛiā caukīdārī likhāol, cōrak banār nah*^{i}

pāol. I caused (letters) to be written to the police of fourteen *kōs* (round) Pakaṛiā, and I found no trace of the thief.

की कहि कै हमरा बन्ध खोलौलिंहि, *kī kah*[i] *kai ham*[a]*rā bandh kholaulīh*[i], saying what (on what pretext) did you (fem.) get me released (from my) bonds ?

एक दिन ओ अपना बेटा सभ कें बजौलक, *ek din ō up*[a]*nā bēṭā sabh kē bajaulak,* one day he summoned his sons.

जत पौलन्हि खैलन्हि सभ बस्तु, *juta paulanhi khailanhi sabha bastu,* he (Kṛṣṇa) ate all the articles (of food) which he found. (Man. v. 30).

कथा सभ सँ बहुत बुझौलकै, *kathā subh sā̃ bahut bujhaul*[a]*kai,* he remonstrated much (with them) with many words.

(*a*) (9) **Perfect Indicative** :—

एक बकस पठाओल अछि से अहाँक हेतु, *ek bakas paṭhāol ach*[i], *sē ahā̃k hēt*[u], I have sent a box, it is for you.

तखन अहाँ कें खोलाओलि अछि, *takhan ahā̃ kē kholāol*[i] *ach*[i], then I (fem.) have released you.

(*d*) (10) **Pluperfect Indicative** :—

हम तोहरा पहिले हस्सी में उड़ौने रहिअहु, *ham toh*[a]*rā pahilē hassī mē uṛaunē* (for *uṛaulē*) *rahiah*[u], formerly I ridiculed you in sport.

Verbal Nouns :—

(1) (Obl.) आबए नहिं पाबए से करब, *ābae nahī̃ pābae sē karab* you will do that (by which) he will not get (power) to come (*i.e.* be able to come, *ābae* for *ābai*, obl. of *āb*[i]). (Man. viii, 46).

(3) पछतौला सँ की भै सकैअछि, *pach*[a]*taulā sā̃ kī bhai sakai-ach*[i], what can happen from regretting ?

Participles :—

Present :—See Present Indicative.

Past :—सगरो बनल बनाओल घर बिगड़ि गेल, *sag*[a]*rō banal banāol ghar bigaṛ*[i] *gēl,* all (her) ready-made house (*i.e.*, castle in the air) went to pieces.

Conjunctive :—

भद्री आबि के कहैत छथि, *bhadrī ābi ke kahait chathi*. Bhadrī, having come, is saying.

सभ मिलाए कँ तीनि से सँ किच्छु बढ़ि जाएत, *sabh milāe kā̃ tīni sai sā̃ kicch^a^ baṛhi jāet*, adding all together there will be something over three hundred.

हाथ धै के लेलक उठाय, *hāth dhai ke lēlak uṭhāy*, seizing by the hand, raising (them) up, he took (them) (*i.e.*, he lifted them up).

Roots in इ *i* and ई *ī*.

285. Roots in इ *i* and ई *ī* are conjugated exactly similarly, the only difference being that, according to the usual rule, the long ई *ī* is shortened to इ *i* when it falls in the antepenultimate. Indeed the two most important roots of this class, पि *pi* or पी *pī*, drink, and जि *ji* or जी *jī*, live, may have the *i* either long or short.

As the model verb, I take the √सि *si*, sew. It will be observed that in the case of the √सि *si* there are a number of optional forms, in which the letter ब *b* is inserted between two concurrent vowels. In the case of the two verbs √पि *pi* or पी *pī*, drink, and √जि *ji* or जी *jī*, live, it is important to note that they almost invariably employ the forms with ब *b*. Indeed, I may say, that I have never seen or heard the forms without the ब *b* in the case of these two verbs, though natives tell me they can be used. The fact is that in these two verbs the ब is not inserted, but really belongs to the root, as will be seen when we compare the Sanskrit forms पिबति *pibati*, he drinks, and जीवति *jīvati*, he lives. It should also be noted that these verbs have their present participles पिबैत *pibait* and जिबैत *jibait* respectively, and insert ब *b* in other places, where they are not found in the case of √सि *si*. In order to illustrate the peculiarities of these two verbs, I give the conjugation of √पि *pi* or पी *pī* alongside of that of √सि *si*, to facilitate comparison. In the case of √पि *pi* or पी *pī*, when there are two forms, one with long ई *ī* and the other with short इ *i*, I only give the one with long ई *ī*, and it must be remembered that a form with short इ *i* can also be used. √जि *ji* or जी *jī*, live. is conjugated exactly like √पि *pi* or पी *pī*.

286. (1) (*a*) Old Present.

'I sew,' &c. — 'I drink,' &c.

PERSON.	'I sew' SHORT FORM.		'I sew' LONG FORM.		'I drink' SHORT FORM.		'I drink' LONG FORM.	
	GROUP I. (Subject: non-honorific. Object: non-honorific.)	GROUP II. (Subject: honorific. Object: non-honorific.)	GROUP I. (Subject: non-honorific. Object: non-honorific.)	GROUP II. (Subject: honorific. Object: non-honorific.)	GROUP I. (Subject: non-honorific. Object: non-honorific.)	GROUP II. (Subject: honorific. Object: non-honorific.)	GROUP I. (Subj.: non-honorific. Object: non-honorific.)	GROUP II. (Subject: honorific. Object: non-honorific)
1	सिइ *sii.*		सिबिऐ *sibiai* Or (with object in 2nd person.) सिबिऔ *sibiau*		पीबी *pībī.*		पिबिऐ *pibiai* Or (with obj. in 2nd person.) पिबिऔ *pibiau.*	
2	सि *si.*	Same as 1st person.	सिअह *siăh,* सिबह *sibăh.*	Same as 1st person, but no forms for object in 2nd person.	पी *pī.*	Same as 1st person.	पीबह *pībăh.*	Same as 1st pers., but no forms for object in 2nd person.
3	सिए *siĕ.*	सिअथि *siathi,* सिबथि *sibathi.*	GROUP I. सिऐ *siai,* सिबै *sibai* Or (with object in 2nd person.) सिऔ *siau,* सिबौ *sibau.*		पीबे *pībĕ.*	पीबथि *pībathi.*	GROUP I. पीबै *pibai* Or (with obj. in 2nd person.) पीबौ *pībau.*	

287. (*b*) (4) **Future Indicative.** Second Form.

'I shall sew,' &c. — 'I shall drink,' &c.

PERSON.	SHORT FORM.		LONG FORM.		SHORT FORM.		LONG FORM.	
	GROUP I. (Subject: non-honorific. Object: non-honorific.)	GROUP II. (Subject: honorific. Object: non-honorific.)	GROUP I. (Subject: non-honorific. Object: non-honorific).	GROUP II. (Subject: honorific. Object: non-honorific.)	GROUP I. (Subject: non-honorific. Object: non-honorific.)	GROUP II. (Subject: honorific. Object: non-honorific.)	GROUP I. (Subject: non-honorific. Object: non-honorific.)	GROUP II. (Subject: honorific. Object: non-honorific.)
1	सिअव *siab.*		सिअवै *siabai*, सिवै *sibai* Or (with object in 2nd person.) सिअवौ *siabau*, सिवौ *sibau.*		पीउव *pīub.*		पीउवै *pīubai*, पीवै *pībai* Or (with obj. in 2nd person.) पीउवौ *pīubau*, पीवौ *pībau.*	
2	सिअवेँ *siabẽ*, सिवेँ *sibẽ.*	Same as 1st person.	सिअवऽह *siabăh*, सिवऽह *sibăh.*	Same as 1st person, but no forms for object in 2nd person.	पीउवेँ *pīubẽ*, पीवेँ *pībẽ.*	Same as 1st person.	पीउवऽह *pīubăh* पीवऽह *pībăh.*	Same as 1st person, but no forms for object in 2nd person.
3	Wanting.	Wanting.	Wanting.		Wanting.	Wanting.	Wanting.	

288. (*b*) (4) **Future Indicative.** Third Form.

'I shall sew,' &c. — 'I shall drink,' &c.

PERSON.	SHORT FORM. GROUP I. (Subject: non-honorific. Object: non-honorific.)	SHORT FORM. GROUP II. (Subject: honorific. Object: non-honorific.)	LONG FORM. GROUP I. (Subject: non-honorific. Object: non-honorific.)	LONG FORM. GROUP II. (Subject: honorific. Object: non-honorific.)	SHORT FORM. GROUP I. (Subject: non-honorific. Object: non-honorific.)	SHORT FORM. GROUP II. (Subject: honorific. Object: non-honorific.)	LONG FORM GROUP I. (Subject: non-honorific. Object: non-honorific.)	LONG FORM GROUP II. (Subject: honorific. Object: non-honorific.)
1	सिइतहुँ *siitahū̃*, सितहुँ *sitahū̃*.		सिअतिऐ *siatiai*, सितिऐ *sitiai* Or (with object in 2nd person.) सिअतिऔ *siatiau*, सितिऔ *sitiau*.		पिबितहुँ *pibitahū̃*, पिउतहुँ *piutahū̃*		पिउतिऐ *piutiai* Or (with obj. in 2nd person.) पिउतिऔ *piutiau*.	
2	Wanting.	Same as 1st person.	Wanting.	Same as 1st person, but no forms for object in 2nd person.	Wanting.	Same as 1st person.	Wanting.	Same as 1st person, but no forms for object in 2nd person.
3	सिअत *siat*, सिउत *siut*.	सिअतथि *siatathi*, सितथि *sitathi*.	GROUP I. सिअतै *siatai*, सितै *sitai* Or (with object in 2nd person.) सिअतौ *siatau*, सितौ *sitau*.		पीउत *piut*.	पिउतथि *piutathi*.	GROUP I. पिउतै *piutai* Or (with obj. in 2nd person.) पिउतौ *piutau*.	

289. (c) (5) Past Conditional.

PERSON.	'Had I sewn,' &c.; 'I should have sewn,' &c. — SHORT FORM. GROUP I. (Subject: non-honorific. Object: non-honorific.)	SHORT FORM. GROUP II. (Subject: honorific. Object: non-honorific.)	LONG FORM. GROUP I. (Subject: non-honorific. Object: non-honorific.)	LONG FORM. GROUP II. (Subject: honorific. Object: non-honorific.)	'Had I drunk,' &c.; 'I should have drunk,' &c. — SHORT FORM. GROUP I. (Subject: non-honorific. Object: non-honorific.)	SHORT FORM. GROUP II. (Subject: honorific. Object: non-honorific.)	LONG FORM. GROUP I. (Subj.: non-honorific. Object: non-honorific.)	LONG FORM. GROUP II. (Subject: honorific. Object: non-honorific.)
1	सिइतहुँ *siitahū̃*, सितहुँ *sitahū̃*.		सिइतिऐ *siitiai*, सितिऐ *sitiai* Or (with object in 2nd person.) सिइतिऔ *siitiau*, सितिऔ *sitiau*.		पिबितहुँ *pibitahū̃*		पिबितिऐ *pibitiai* Or (with obj. in 2nd person.) पिबितिऔ *pibitiau*.	
2	सिइतैँ *siitē̃*, सितैँ *sitē̃*.	Same as 1st person.	सिइतँह *siitāh*, सितँह *sitāh*.	Same as 1st person, but no forms for object in 2nd person.	पिबितैँ *pibitē̃*.	Same as 1st person.	पिबितँह *pibitāh*.	Same as 1st person, but no forms for object in 2nd person.
3	सिऐत *siait*.	सिइतथि *siitathi*, सितथि *sitathi*.	GROUP I. सिइतै *siitai*, सितै *sitai* Or (with object in 2nd person.) सिइतौ *siitau*, सितौ *sitau*.		पिबैत *pibait*.	पिबितथि *pibitathi*.	GROUP I. पिबितै *pibitai* Or (with obj. in 2nd person.) पिबितौ *pibitau*.	

290. (8) **Past Indicative.**

'I sewed,' &c. (Intransitive). 'I drank,' &c. (Transitive).

PERSON.	SHORT FORM. (Intransitive)		LONG FORM. (Intransitive)		SHORT FORM. (Transitive)		LONG FORM. (Transitive)	
	GROUP I. (Subject: non-honorific. Object: non-honorific.)	GROUP II. (Subject: honorific. Object: non-honorific.)	GROUP I. (Subject: non-honorific. Object: non-honorific.)	GROUP II. (Subject: honorific. Object: non-honorific.)	GROUP I. (Subject: non-honorific. Object: non-honorific.)	GROUP II. (Subject: honorific. Object: non-honorific.)	GROUP I. (Subj.: non-honorific. Obj.: non-honorific.)	GROUP II. (Subject: honorific. Obj.: non-honorific.)
1	सिअलहुँ *sialah*$^{\tilde{u}}$, सिउलहुँ *siulah*$^{\tilde{u}}$.		सिअलिऐ *sialiai*, सिउलिऐ *siuliai* Or (with object in 2nd person.) सिअलिऔ *sialiau*, सिउलिऔ *siuliau*.		पीउलहुँ *pĩulah*$^{\tilde{u}}$.		पीउलै *pĩulai* Or (with obj. in 2nd person.) पीउलौ *pĩulau*.	
2	सिअलेँ *sialẽ*, सिउलेँ *siulẽ*.	Same as 1st person.	सिअलाह *sialăh*, सिउलाह *siulăh*.	Same as 1st person, but no forms for object in 2nd person.	पीउलेँ *pĩulẽ*.	Same as 1st person.	पीउलह *pĩulăh*.	Same as 1st person, but no forms for object in 2nd person.
3	सिअल *sial*, सिउल *siul*.	सिअलाह *sialăh*, सिउलाह *siulăh*.	GROUP I. सिअलै *sialai*, सिउलै *siulai* Or (with object in 2nd person.) सिअलौ *sialau*, सिउलौ *siulau*.		पीउलक *pĩuluk*.	पीउलन्हि *pĩulanh*^{i}.	GROUP I. पिउलकै *piul*^{a}*kai* Or (with obj. in 2nd person.) पिउलकौ *piul*^{a}*kau*.	

291. Verbal Nouns.

(1) सि *si*; obl. सिऐ *siai* or सिबै *sibai*; the act of sewing.

(2) सिअब *siab*; obl. सिअबा *siabā*, सिबा *sibā*; the act of sewing, to sew.

(3) सिअल *sial*; obl. सिअला *sialā*, सिला *silā*; the act of sewing.

(1) पीबि *pībi*; obl. पीबै *pībai*; the act of drinking.

(2) पीउब *piub*; obl. पीउबा *pīubā*; the act of drinking, to drink.

(3) पीउल *pīul*; obl. पीउला *pīulā*; the act of drinking.

292. Participles.

Present.

सिउत *siut*, सिइत *siit*, सिऐत *siait*, sewing.

पिबैत *pibait*, drinking.

Past.

सिअल *sial*, सिउल *siul*, sewn.

पिउल *piul*, drunk.

---

293. It must be added that the root सि *si* also sometimes takes the forms of √ पि *pi* or पी *pī* (compare Sanskrit सीव्यति *sīvyati*, he sews), but those given above are the usual ones. These three roots (सि *si*, पि *pi*, जि *ji*) are the only roots in इ *i* which I have come across.

294. I have met no examples of √ सि *si* in literature, but the following are examples of the two others :—

(*a*) (1) **Old Present** :—

भनहिं बिद्यापति तौं पय जीबे ।
अधर सुधा-रस जौं पय पीबे ॥

bhanahī bidyāpati taū paya jībē ।
udhara sudhā-rasa jaū paya pībē ॥

Saith Vidyāpati, 'it (the bee) will live, so long as it drinketh the nectar of (your) lower lip.' (Vid. ii, 5).

लोभित मधुकर कौसल अनुसर ।
नव रस पिबु अबगाही ॥

lōbhita madhukara kausala anusaru ।
naba rasa pibu abagāhī ॥

The bee, tempted (by its sweetness), cleverly searcheth for it, and, diving (into the lotus) sips the fresh honey. (Vid. xxix, 2).

जाइ पिआबिऐ अधर सुधा रस ।
तौँ पय जीबथि जीबे ॥

jāi piābiai adhara sudhā rasa ।
taũ paya jībathi jībē ॥

Having gone (to her), cause her to drink (*causal verb*) the nectar of thy lower lip; then may she indeed live (present conditional) (*lit.*, live with life). (Vid. x. 10).

जमुना ह्रद बिखबत कै जानि ।
पसू पच्छि क्यों पिबै न पानि ॥

jamunā hrada bikhabata kai jāni ।
pasū pacchi kyō pibai na pāni ॥

Knowing the pool (in) the Jamunā (to be) like poison, no beast (or) bird drinks (its) water. (Man. iv, 20).

ता पर भमर पिबय रस सजनी गे ।
बैसल पंख पसारि ॥

tā para bhamara pibaya (for *pibai*) *rasa, sajanī gē* ।
baisala paṅkha pasāri ॥

On it, O friend, a bee drinks nectar, seated with outspread wings. (Vid. xv, 6).

(*a*) (3) **Imperative** :—

खाऽह पिबऽह चैन करऽह, *khāh, pibah, cain karah*, eat, drink, be happy.

जुग जुग जिबथु बसथु लख कोस ;
हमर अभाग हुनक कोन दोस ॥

juga juga jībathu, basathu lakha kōsa ।
hamara abhāga hunaka kona dōsa ॥

May he live for ages (even though) he dwell a hundred thousand *kōs* (away from me). It is my misfortune. What fault is it of his? (Vid. lviii, 2).

(*b*) (4) **Future** :—

तोँ हमरा गाइक दूध पीबैँ । मुंह भेलौक पिबैक । नहिं रे अहिरा दूध पीबै देबैँ तो एक जुम तमाकू दे, '*tō̃ hamarā gāik dūdh pībē̃! mūh bhelauk pibaik!*' '*nahi*, *rē ahirā, dūdh pībai dēbē̃, to ek jum tamākū dē*,' 'you will drink the milk of my cow! you have made (*lit.*, to you there is become) a mouth for (*lit.* of) drinking!' 'If you will not, O cowherd, give me milk to drink, then give me one mouthful of tobacco.' (Also example of 1st Verbal noun).

माधव आब न जीउति राही, *mādhaba āba, na jīuti rāhī*, O Mādhava, come. The fair one (*fem.*) will live no (longer) (Vid. x, 1).

(*c*) (6) **Present Indicative** :—

सीना गाइक दूध लै पिबैत अछि गुलामी जट, *sīnā gāik dūdh lai pibait achi gulāmī jaṭ*, Gulāmī Jaṭ takes and drinks the milk of the cow Sīnā.

(*c*) (7) **Imperfect Indicative** :—

दीना भद्री जिबैत चल उहे गबैत रहै, *dīnā bhadrī jibait chal uhē gabait rahai*, when Dīnā and Bhadrī were living, they used to sing that (song).

जो जिबैत चलाह दीना भद्री जोगिया नगर कोनो मुसहरनी नहिं कैलक सिंगार, *jō jibait chalāh dīnā bhadrī jogiyā nagar, kauno musaharni nahi kailak sĩgār*, if Dīnā and Bhadrī were living in Jogiyā town, not one Musahar's wife would (have dared to) adorn herself. (Here the Past Indicative is employed in the sense of the Past Conditional).

(*d*) (8) **Past Indicative** :—

एहन अएम तेजि पङ परदेस गेल ।
कुसुम पिउल मकरंदा ॥

ehana baesa teji pahu paradesa gela ।
kusuma piula (for *piulak*) *makarandā* ॥

At such (a tender) age my lord left me and went to a far country. (There) drank he the nectar of the flower. (Vid. lxvi, 8).

हरि भरि पेट पिउल दुध हरखि, *hari bhari pēṭa piula* (for *piulak*) *dudha harakhi*, Hari joyfully drank his bellyful of milk. (Man. ii, 51).

Verbal Nouns :—

(1) For **पीबै** *pībai* (obl.) and **पिबैक** *pibaik* (genitive), see example of future. So also **किछु दूध दैति अछि । नेना सभ कैं पिबैक भरि भै जाइत छैक**, *kicch*^{u} *dūdh dait*^{i} *ach*^{i} *? nēnā sabh kē̃ pibaik bhar*^{i} *bhai jāit chaik*, does she give any milk? There becomes the fill of drinking for the children (*i.e.*, she gives all that is wanted for the children).

जिबए दिअओ बरु बालक लेब, *jibae* (for *jībai*) *diao baru bālaka lēb*, allow (her) to live, but, rather take the child. (Man. ii, 8).

आबह बैसह पिबि लह पानि, *ābaha* (for *ābah*) *baisaha* (for *baisah*) *pibi laha* (for *lah*) *pāni*, come, sit down, take a drink of water (*pib*^{i} *lah* is an intensive compound, see § 342). (Vid. lxxx, 4).

Present Participle :—

जिबइत जाए एकौ नहिं पाओत, *jibaita jāe ekau nahī̃ pāota*, not one will be able to go away living. (Man. viii, 43).

जिबैत रहैत तो जोगिया अबैत पलटि, *jibait rahait to jogiyā abait palaṭ*^{i}, (if) they had remained living, then they would have returned back to Jogiyā.

देखलि सलहेस कैं कलालक भट्ठी पर दारू पिबैत, *dēkhal*^{i} *sal*^{o}*hēs kē̃ kalālak bhaṭṭhī par dārū pibait*, I (fem.) saw Salhēs drinking spirits at a grog-maker's still.

Conjunctive Participle :—

बौरम नदी मेँ पानि पीबि कै ऊपर होऐ, *bauram nadī mē̃ pāni pīb*^{i} *ke ūpar hōai*, he is (coming) up, having drunk water in the river Bauram.

Roots in ए *ē*.

295. Only two roots end in ए *ē*, *viz*. √दे *dē*, give, and ले *lē*, take. They are irregular throughout, and their conjugation will be given in chapter VI (§§ 314 ff).

Roots in ऊ *ū* and ओ *ō*.

296. These are conjugated as follows. It will be seen that, as in the case of verbs in इ *i*, *a* ब *b* is often optionally inserted. Sometimes we find य *y* instead of ब *b*. This is practically the only irregularity.

The model verbs are √चू *cū*, drip (intransitive) and √धो *dhō*, wash (transitive).

The most important of the roots in ओ *ō* is the √ हो *hō*, become. This is very irregular, and will be conjugated in chapter VI (§§ 322 ff).

297. (1) (*a*) **Old Present.**

'I drip,' &c. — 'I wash,' &c.

PERSON.	'I drip' SHORT FORM. GROUP I. (Subject: non-honorific. Object: non-honorific.)	'I drip' SHORT FORM. GROUP II. (Subject: honorific. Object: non-honorific.)	'I drip' LONG FORM. GROUP I. (Subject: non-honorific. Object: non-honorific.)	'I drip' LONG FORM. GROUP II. (Subject: honorific. Object: non-honorific.)	'I wash' SHORT FORM. GROUP I. (Subject: non-honorific. Object: non-honorific.)	'I wash' SHORT FORM. GROUP II. (Subject: honorific. Object: non-honorific.)	'I wash' LONG FORM. GROUP I. (Subj.: non-honorific. Obj.: non-honorific.)	'I wash' LONG FORM. GROUP II. (Subject: honorific. Obj.: non-honorific.)
1	चूइँ *cũĩ*, चूबी *cũbī*.		चुइऐ *cuiai*, चुबिऐ *cubiai*.		धोइँ *dhōĩ*, धोबी *dhōbī*.		धोइऐ *dhoiai*, धोबिऐ *dhobiai*.	
2	चू *cũ*.	Same as 1st person.	चूअँह *cũăh*, चूबँह *cũbăh*.	Same as 1st person, but no forms for object in 2nd person.	धो *dhō*.	Same as 1st person.	धोअँह *dhōăh*, धोबँह *dhōbăh*.	Same as 1st person, but no forms for object in 2nd person.
3	चूए *cũẽ*, चूबे *cũbē*.	चूअथि *cũathi*, चूबथि *cũbathi*.	GROUP I. चूऐ *cũai*, चूबै *cũbai*.		धोए *dhōē*, धोबे *dhōbē*, धोये *dhōyē*, धोय *dhōy*.	धोअथि *dhōathi*, धोबथि *dhōbathi*.	GROUP I. धोऐ *dhōai*, धोबै *dhōbai*.	

298. (*b*) (4) **Future Indicative.** Second form.

PERSON.	'I shall drip,' &c. SHORT FORM. GROUP I. (Subject: non-honorific. Object: non-honorific.)	SHORT FORM. GROUP II. (Subject: honorific. Object: non-honorific.)	LONG FORM. GROUP I. (Subject: non-honorific. Object: non-honorific.)	LONG FORM. GROUP II. (Subject: honorific. Object: non-honorific.)	'I shall wash,' &c. SHORT FORM. GROUP I. (Subject: non-honorific. Object: non-honorific.)	SHORT FORM. GROUP II. (Subject: honorific. Object: non-honorific.)	LONG FORM. GROUP I. (Subj.: non-honorific. Object: non-honorific.)	LONG FORM. GROUP II. (Subject: honorific. Object: non-honorific.)
1	चूअब *cūab*, चूइब *cūib*.		चुअबै *cuabai*, चुइबै *cuibai*, चूबै *cūbai*.		धोअब *dhōab*, धोएब *dhōeb*.		धोअबै *dhoabai*, धोएबै *dhoebai*, धोबै *dhōbai*.	
2	चूअबँ *cūabẽ*, चूइबँ *cūibẽ*, चूबँ *cūbẽ*.	Same as 1st person.	चूअबह *cūabåh*, चूइबह *cūibåh*, चूबह *cūbåh*.	Same as 1st person, but no forms for object in 2nd person.	धोअबँ *dhōabẽ*, धोएबँ *dhōebẽ*, धोबँ *dhōbẽ*.	Same as 1st person.	धोअबह *dhōabåh*, धोएबह *dhōebåh*, धोबह *dhōbåh*.	Same as 1st person, but no forms for object in 2nd person.
3	Wanting.	Wanting.	Wanting.		Wanting.	Wanting.	Wanting.	

299. (*b*) (4) **Future Indicative.** Third Form.

'I shall drip,' &c. — 'I shall wash,' &c.

PERSON.	'I shall drip' SHORT FORM. GROUP I. (Subject: non-honorific. Object: non-honorific.)	'I shall drip' SHORT FORM. GROUP II. (Subject: honorific. Object: non-honorific.)	'I shall drip' LONG FORM. GROUP I. (Subject: non-honorific. Object: non-honorific.)	'I shall drip' LONG FORM. GROUP II. (Subject: honorific. Object: non-honorific.)	'I shall wash' SHORT FORM. GROUP I. (Subject: non-honorific. Object: non-honorific.)	'I shall wash' SHORT FORM. GROUP II. (Subject: honorific. Object: non-honorific.)	'I shall wash' LONG FORM. GROUP I. (Subj.: non-honorific. Object: non-honorific.)	'I shall wash' LONG FORM. GROUP II. (Subject: honorific. Object: non-honorific.)
1	चूअतहुँ *cūatahŭ*, चूइतहुँ *cūitahŭ*,* चूतहुँ *cūtahŭ*.		चुअतिऐ *cuatiai*, चुइतिऐ *cuitiai*, चुतिऐ *cutiai*.		धोअतहुँ *dhōatahŭ*, धोएतहुँ *dhōetahŭ*, धोतहुँ *dhōtahŭ*.		धोअतिऐ *dhoatiai*, &c.	
2	Wanting.	Same as 1st person.	Wanting.	Same as 1st person, but no forms for object in 2nd person.	Wanting.	Same as 1st person.	Wanting.	Same as 1st person, but no forms for object in 2nd person.
3	चूअत *cūat*, चूइत *cūit*.	चूअतथि *cūatathi*, चूइतथि *cūitathi*, चूतथि *cūtathi*.	GROUP I. चुअतै *cuatai*, चुइतै *cuitai*, चूतै *cūtai*.		धोअत *dhōat*, धोएत *dhōet*.	धोअतथि *dhōatathi*, धोइतथि *dhōitathi*, धोतथि *dhōtathi*.	GROUP I. धोअतै *dhoatai*, धोइतै *dhoitai*, धोतै *dhōtai*.	

* Or चुबितहुँ *cubitahŭ*, and so throughout.

300. (e) (5) **Past Conditional.**

'(If) I had dripped,' &c.; 'I should have dripped,' &c. '(If) I had washed,' &c.; 'I should have washed,' &c.

PERSON.	SHORT FORM.		LONG FORM.		SHORT FORM.		LONG FORM.	
	GROUP I. (Subject: non-honorific. Object: non-honorific.)	GROUP II. (Subject: honorific. Object: non-honorific.)	GROUP I. (Subject: non-honorific. Object: non-honorific.)	GROUP II. (Subject: honorific. Object: non-honorific.)	GROUP I. (Subject: non-honorific. Object: non-honorific.)	GROUP II. (Subject: honorific. Object: non-honorific.)	GROUP I. (Subj.: non-honorific. Object: non-honorific.)	GROUP II. (Subject: honorific. Object: non-honorific.)
1	चूइतहुँ *cūitahŭ*,* चूतहुँ *cūtahŭ*.		चुइतिऐ *cuïtiai*, चुतिऐ *cutiai*.		धोएतहुँ *dhōetahŭ*, धोतहुँ *dhōtahŭ*.		धोएतिऐ *dhoetiai*, धोतिऐ *dhotiai*.	
2	चूइतें *cūitĕ*, चूतें *cūtĕ*.	Same as 1st person.	चूइतह् *cūităh*, चूतह् *cūtăh*.	Same as 1st person, but no forms for object in 2nd person.	धोएतें *dhōetĕ*, धोतें *dhōtĕ*.	Same as 1st person.	धोएतह् *dhōetăh*, धोतह् *dhōtăh*.	Same as 1st person, but no forms for object in 2nd person.
3	चूअत *cūat*, चूइत *cūit*, चूऐत *cūait*.	चूइतथि *cūitathi*, चूतथि *cūtathi*.	GROUP I. चुइतै *cuitai*, चूतै *cūtai*		धोअत *dhōat*, धोएत *dhōet*, धोऐत *dhōait*.	धोएतथि *dhoetathi*, धोतथि *dhōtathi*.	GROUP I. धोएतै *dhoetai*, धोतै *dhōtai*.	

* Or चुबितहुँ *cubitahŭ*, and so throughout.

301. (*d*) (8) **Past Indicative.**

'I dripped,' &c. (Intransitive). — 'I washed,' &c. (Transitive.)

PERSON.	SHORT FORM.		LONG FORM.		SHORT FORM.		LONG FORM.	
	GROUP I. (Subject: non-honorific. Object: non-honorific.)	GROUP II. (Subject: honorific. Object: non-honorific.)	GROUP I. (Subject: non-honorific. Object: non-honorific.)	GROUP II. (Subject: honorific. Object: non-honorific.)	GROUP I. (Subject: non-honorific. Object: non-honorific.)	GROUP II. (Subject: honorific. Object: non-honorific.)	GROUP I. (Subj.: non-honorific. Object: non-honorific.)	GROUP II. (Subject: honorific. Object: non-honorific.)
1	चूअलहुँ *cũalahũ*, चूइलहुँ *cũilahũ*.		चुअलिऐ *cualiai*, चुइलिऐ *cuiliai*.		धोअलहुँ *dhõalahũ*, धोएलहुँ *dhõelahũ*.		धोअलिऐ *dhoaliai*, धोएलिऐ *dhoeliai*.	
2	चूअलें *cũalẽ*, चूइलें *cũilẽ*.	Same as 1st person	चूअलाह *cũalāh*, चूइलाह *cũilāh*.	Same as 1st person, but no forms for object in 2nd person.	धोअलें *dhõalẽ*, धोएलें *dhõelẽ*.	Same as 1st person.	धोअलाह *dhõalāh*, धोएलाह *dhõelāh*.	Same as 1st person, but no forms for object in 2nd person.
3	चूअल *cũal*, चूइल *cũil*.	चूअलाह *cũalāh*, चूइलाह *cũilāh*.	GROUP I. चुअलै *cualai*, चुइलै *cuilai*.		धोअलक *dhõalak*, धोएलक *dhõelak*.	धोअलन्हि *dhõalanhi*, धोएलन्हि *dhõelanhi*.	GROUP I. धोअलकै *dhoalakai*, धोएलकै *dhoelakai*.	

302. Verbal Noun.

(1) चूबि *cūbⁱ*; obl. चूबै *cūbai*, चूऐ *cūai*; the act of dripping.

(1) धो *dhō*, धोइ *dhōi*, धोबि *dhōbⁱ*; obl. धोऐ *dhōai*, धोबै *dhōbai*; the act of washing.

303. Participles.

Present.

चूअत *cūat*, चूइत *cūit*, चूऐत *cūait* dripping.	धोअत *dhōat*, धोएत *dhōet*, धोऐत *dhōait*, washing.

Past.

चूअल *cūal*, चूइल *cūil*, dripped.	धोअल *dhōal*, धोएल *dhōel*, washed.

Probably ब *b* can be inserted in many more forms than are given above, but I have not met them. In conversation, a good deal depends on the personal equation of the speaker.

304. The only example of the use of a root in ऊ *ū* which I have noted in literature is the following:—

देखलक जे अंगूर एहन गुच्छ सभ पाकल टट्टी मे̃ लटकि रहल अछि कि जकरा सँ रस चूबि रहल अछि, *dekhᵃlak jē āgūr ehan gucch sabh pākal ṭaṭṭī mẽ laṭakⁱ rahal achⁱ, ki jakᵃrā sã ras cūbⁱ rahal achⁱ*, he saw that such bunches of grapes were hanging ripe from the trellis, that from them (*lit.* from which) the juice kept dripping (Intensive compound, see § 342).

Examples of roots in ओ *ō* are more common. Such are:—

(*a*) (1) **Old Present**:—

एक रोये अमाँ दोसर रोबे चन्ना हाए हाय ।
तेसर रोबै दूध छाड़ि बलकवा रे हाए हाय ॥

ek rōyē amā̃; dōsar rōbē cannā, hāe hāy;
tēsar rōbai dūdh chāṛⁱ balakᵃwā, rē, hāe hāy.

One (person), the mother, weeps; a second, Cannā weeps, alas, alas! A third, a child leaving (its mother's) milk, weeps, ah! alas, alas!

(*a*) (3) **Imperative** :—

बाबू गोड़ हाँथ धोऊ, *bābū gōṛ hā̃th dhōū*, gentlemen, wash your feet and hands.

जौड़ि जनु फोर्वह आओर काठी सबहि कें तोड़ि देह, *jauṛi janu phōăh, āor kāṭhī sabahi kẽ tōṛi daih*, do not open the string, and break the sticks.

(*d*) (8) **Past Indicative** :—

मारि लोभ सँ मुँह फोएलक, *māri lōbh sã mũh phōelak*, by reason of greed he opened his mouth.

1. **Verbal Noun** (oblique) :—

लगलाह कानै रोऐ, *lagolăh kānai rōai*, they began to wail (and) weep.

Past Participle :—

धोएल धाएल भेँड़ी पाँका लागै चाहै अछि, *dhōal dhāel bhẽṛī pā̃kā lāgai cāhai-achi*, the well-washed sheep is about to fall into the slough. (Proverb = there's many a slip, etc.)

Conjunctive Participle :—

रोय रोय कजलि दहाय गेल ना, *rōya* (for *rōi*) *rōya kajali dahāya gela* (m.c. for *gēla*) *nā*, lo, weeping, weeping the collyrium was washed away (from her eyes). (Vid. xxvi, 4).

बान्ह फोए हरि हिदए लगाओलि, *bānha phōe* (for *phōi*) *hari hridae lagāoli*, unloosing (his) bonds, she took Hari to her heart.

फेरि गृहस्थ फो कँ एक एक काठी देलकै, *phēri gṛhasth phō kã ek ek kāṭhī delokai*, then the farmer, having opened (the bundle), gave (them) the sticks one by one.

CHAPTER VI.

Irregular Verbs.

305. The following verbs are irregular :—

√कर *kar*, do, make.

√धर *dhar*, seize, place.

√मर *mar*, die.

√जा *jā*, go.

√आब *āb*, come.

√दे *dē*, give.

√ले *lē*, take.

√हो *hō*, become.

306. The roots कर *kar* and धर *dhar* are irregular in the formation of the past participle and of the tenses derived from it and also in the formation of the first and third verbal nouns. The two are conjugated on exactly parallel lines.

The past participle of the √कर *kar*, do, make, is कैल *kail*, often written कयल *kayal*, कएल (*i.e.*, कऍल) *kael*, or कइल *kail*. From this the past tense is formed as follows. As before, only the most commonly used forms of Groups I and II are given:—

(*d*) (8) **Past Indicative.** 'I did,' 'I made,' &c.

PERSON.	SHORT FORM.		LONG FORM.	
	GROUP I. (Subject: non-honorific. Object: non-honorific.)	GROUP II. (Subject: honorific. Object: non-honorific.)	GROUP I. (Subject: non-honorific. Object: non-honorific.)	GROUP II. (Subject: honorific. Object: non-honorific.)
1	कैलहुँ *kailah^{u}*, कैल *kail*.		कैलिऐ *kailiai*.	
2	कैलें *kailẽ*.	Same as 1st person.	कैलह *kailăh*.	Same as 1st person, but no forms for object in 2nd person.
3	कैलक *kailak*.	कैलन्हि *kailanh^{i}*.	GROUP I. कैलकै *kail^{a}kai*.	

Similarly the Perfect is कैलहुँ अछि *kailah^{u} ach^{i}* or कैलें छी *kailẽ chī*, and the Pluperfect is कैलें छलहुँ *kailẽ chalah^{u}*.

The first **verbal noun** is regularly करि *kar*ⁱ, but usually takes the form कै *kai*, कय *kay*, or कँ *kã*.

The third verbal noun, like the past participle is कैल *kail*, not करल *karal*, oblique कैला *kailā*.

The √धर *dhar*, seize, place, is conjugated exactly like the √कर *kar*, the ध् *dh* being substituted for the क् *k*.

307. The following are examples of the use of the irregular forms of these verbs.

जखनहिं लेल हरि कंचु अछोरि ।
कत परजुगुति कयल अंग मोरि ॥

jakhanahĩ lela hari kañcu achōri ।
kata parajuguti kayala ãga mōri ॥

when Hari snatched away my bodice, how many devices did I make, as I twisted my limbs. (Vid. xxxi, 1).

हम अपराध कैल, *ham apᵃrādh kail*, I committed a fault.

कहिओ जनम भरि चोरी नहिं कैली, *kahiō janam bhar*ⁱ *cōrī nah*ⁱ *kailī*, never in my whole life did I commit a theft.

लाख अपराध कैलौक, *lākh apᵃrādh kailauk*, a hundred thousand faults I committed against you.

मारि कोना कैलेँ फोटरा के, *mār*ⁱ *kenā kailẽ phōṭᵃrā kē*, how did you kill Photrā ?

जेहि मुँहेँ धैलेँ कटैया ओहि मुँहेँ धर अपना बाप के, *jeh*ⁱ *mũhẽ dhailẽ kaṭaiyā, oh*ⁱ *mũhẽ dhar apᵃnā bāp kē*, with the mouth with which you seized (me) in Kaṭaiyā, with the same mouth seize your own father.

तोँ हो ददा कैल गुलामीक साथ बैर, *tõ, hō dadā, kail gulāmīk sāth bair*, you, O brother, made enmity with Gulāmī.

तोँ एहि कथा पर भरोसा कैलह, *tõ eh*ⁱ *kathā par bharōsā kailah*. you made belief on (*i.e.*, you believed) this statement.

जेह कहलकै से कैलक, *jaih kahal^akai. sē kailak*, as he said, so he did.

अंगूरक टाट पर जाल लगाय कँ ओकरा धैलक, *āgūrak ṭāṭ par jāl lagāy kã ok^arā dhailak*, having put a net on a vine trellis, he caught it (the bird).

ओकरा मेँ कोन गुण छैक जे दाता ओकरा नेहाल कैलन्हि आओर हमरा कँगाल कैलन्हि, *ok^arā mē kōn guṇ chaik, jē dātā ok^arā nehāl kailanhⁱ āor ham^arā kāgāl kailanhⁱ*, what are his virtues that the Giver made blessings for him, and made me a beggar?

तीनू मामा भगिना धैलन्हि कटैया पन्थक बाट, *tinū māmā bhaginā dhailanhⁱ kaṭaiyā panthak bāṭ*, the three, uncle and nephews, took the path of the road (to) Kaṭaiyā.

केवल राहड़ि बाओग कैल अछि, *kēbal rāhaṛⁱ bāog kail achⁱ*, I have sown (*lit.* done sowing) only rāhaṛ.

हम एकरा मारबा मेँ बहुत दौड़-धूप कैलेँ छी। आओर तेसर खंड ई धैल अछि, *ham ek^arā mār^abā mē bahut dauṛ-dhūp kailẽ chī, āor tēsar khaṇḍ ī dhail achⁱ*. in killing this (deer) I have done much exertion. And this third portion I have placed (here).

क्यो करुना करि अभरन तेज, *kyō karunā kari abharana tēja*, some full of woe (*lit.* doing woe) cast aside their ornaments (Man. vii, 40).

हरि हरि कय पुनि उठति धरणि धरि।
रैनि गमाबय जागी॥

hari hari kaya (for *kai*) *puni uṭhati dharaṇi dhari* ।
raini gamābaya (for *gamābai*) *jāgī* ॥

crying (*lit.* doing) 'Hari, Hari,' again she (is) rising, having lain upon (*lit.* having seized) the ground; so waking passeth she the night (Vid. x, 7).

एकरा सभ कँ किछु कै देखाबी, *ek^arā sabh kē kicch^u kai dekhābī*. having done something, let me show it to all these (boys).

धैरज धै रहु मिलत मुरारि, *dhairaja dhai rahu, milata murāri*, having seized patience (*i.e.*, being patient), remain. Murāri will meet you (Vid. lxii, 6).

दौड़-धूप कैला सँ किच्छु नहिँ हैत, *daur-dhūp kailā sȧ̃ kicch[u] nah[ĩ] hait*, nothing will occur (*i.e.*, you will get no benefit) from running about.

In one instance Vidyāpati (lxvi, 1) has a kind of long form of the conjunctive participle, *viz.*, करिए *karie* for करि *kari* (poetical for करि *kar[i]*).

The verse runs:—

अवधि करिए पहु गेलाह, *abadhi karie pahu gēlăh*, my husband went, having fixed a date for his return. Compare टुटिए *ṭuṭiē* in § 344.

308. The conjugation of the √मर *mar*, die, closely resembles that of √कर *kar* and √धर *dhar*, allowance being made for the fact that it is an intransitive verb. It is only irregular in the fact that its present participle is मरैत *marait* or मुऐत *muait*, and that its past participle is मरल *maral* or मुइल *muil*. Its past conditional is therefore मरितहुँ *maritah[ũ]* or मुइतहुँ *muitah[ũ]*, and its past indicative is मरलहुँ *maralah[ũ]* or मुइलहुँ *muilah[ũ]*. The 3rd verbal noun is the same as the past participle. The oblique form of the first verbal noun is vulgarly मुऐ *muai* for मरै *marai*. See § 350.

309. I have not come across any forms of the irregular present participle in literature. The following are examples of tenses derived from the past participle:—

घन घन जे ऐलाह से मरल, *ghana ghana jē ailăha sē marala*, every troop that came (with him) died. (Man. x, 55).

ठामहि घूमि मुइल कै गोट, *ṭhāmahi ghūmi muila kai gōṭa*, several turned round and died on the spot. (Man. v, 41).

मुइल अरिष्ट भेल उपकार, *muila ariṣṭa bhēla upakāra*, the dead bull became a blessing. (Man. vi, 14).

मुइला पूतक बहुत नाओँ, *muilā* (oblique) *pūtak bahut nāō̃*, a dead son has many names (*i.e.*, is always spoken of affectionately). (Proverb).

हमरा मुइनेँ एक जरसी उद्धार, *ham[a]rā muinē̃* (for *muilē̃*, instr. of

3rd verb. noun) *ek* *ur*^{a}*sī udgār*, from our death joy has arisen only in (the village of) Ursī.

310. The √जा *jā*, go, is conjugated like an intransitive verb in आ *ā* (see §§ 270 ff.), but is irregular in its past participle, and in the tenses derived from it. The past participle is गेल *gel*, fem. गेलि *gēli*. On the other hand, the third verbal noun (that in ल *l*) is regular, and does not follow the past participle. It is जाएल *jāel*, obl. जैला *jailā*, not गेल *gēl*.

The following are the more usual forms of the tenses derived from the past participle :—

(*d*) (8). **Past Indicative.** 'I went,' &c.

<table>
<tr><th rowspan="2">PERSON.</th><th colspan="2">SHORT FORM.</th><th colspan="2">LONG FORM.</th></tr>
<tr><th>GROUP I.
(Subject : non-honorific. Object : non-honorific.)</th><th>GROUP II.
(Subject : honorific. Object : non-honorific.)</th><th>GROUP I.
(Subject : non-honorific. Object : non-honorific.)</th><th>GROUP II.
(Subject : honorific. Object : non-honorific.)</th></tr>
<tr><td>1</td><td colspan="2">गेलहुँ gēlah^{ū}.</td><td colspan="2">गेलिऐ geliai.</td></tr>
<tr><td>2</td><td>गेलें gēlē.</td><td>Same as 1st person.</td><td>गेलाह gēlāh.</td><td>Same as 1st person, but no forms for object in 2nd person.</td></tr>
<tr><td>3</td><td>गेल gēl.</td><td>गेलाह gēlāh.</td><td colspan="2">GROUP I.
गेलै gēlai.</td></tr>
</table>

The Perfect is गेलहुँ अछि *gēlah*^{ū} *ach*^{i} or गेल छी *gēl chī*, I have gone, I am gone. The Pluperfect is गेल छलहुँ *gēl chalah*^{ū} or गेलें छलहुँ *gēlē chalah*^{ū}, I had gone, I went a long time ago.

311. The following are examples of the use of the irregular forms of this verb :—

हम तोहरा हाथ सँ निकसि गेलहुँ *ham toh^{a}rā hāth sã̃ nikas^{i} gēlah^{u}*, having emerged from your hand, I went, *i.e.*, I escaped from your clutches.

नान्हिटा छली गे तिरिया हम रमिता भै गेली *nānhiṭā chalī, ge tiriyā ham ramitā bhai gēlī*, I was very young, O ladies, (when) I having become a wanderer went, *i.e.*, when I became a wanderer (see § 342 regarding the intensive compound **भै गेली** *bhai gēlī*).

तोँ हमर तीनू कथा एखनहि बिसरि गेलेँ, *tõ hamar tīnū kathā ekhanah^{i} bisar^{i} gēlẽ*, you went having forgotten (*i.e.*, you have entirely forgotten) already the three words of mine (§ 342).

एतबहिँ मेँ गेलाह खिसियाय, *etabah^{i} mẽ gēlăh khisiyāy*, at only this much did you go into a rage (§ 342).

कहाँ गेल किअ भेल थारू दोनबार, *kahā̃ gēl kia bhēl thārū don^{a}bār*, where has Tharū Donbār gone, what has become of him ?

एक कोस गेलाह हो बहोरन दुइ कोस गेलाह, *ek kōs gēlăh, hō bahōran, dui kōs gelăh*. O Bahōran, they went one *kōs*, they went two *kōs*.

माछी बैसलि दूध पर पाँखि गेलै लपटाय, *māchī baisal^{i} dūdh par, pā̃kh^{i} gelai* (m.c. for *gēlai*) *lap^{a}ṭāy*, a fly sat on milk, (and) his wings went entangled (in it) (§ 342).

मटकुरी माथ सँ खसि टुकरी टुकरी भै गेलैक, *maṭ^{a}kurī māth sã̃ khas^{i} ṭuk^{a}rī ṭuk^{a}rī bhai gelaik*, the pitcher having fallen from her head became (*i.e.*, was broken to) fragments (§ 342).

एक पैघ लोकक घर मेँ रातिक समय आगि लागि गेलैन्हि, *ek paigh lōkak ghar mẽ rātik samay āg^{i} lāg^{i} gelainh^{i}*, fire seized at night time the house of a rich man (§ 342).

हुनक बाप मरि गेलथीन्हि, *hunak bāp mar^{i} gel^{a}thīnh^{i}*, their (respected) father died (§ 342).

दुनू भाइ मारल गेलथून्हि कटैया खाप, *dunū bhāi māral gel^{a}thūnh^{i} kaṭaiya khāp*, the two (respected) brothers were killed in Kaṭaiyā Khāp (Passive § 331).

कथी लय ओतय गेल छलहुँ । ओतय हमर खेत अछि ओकरा देखै गेल छलहुँ, *kathī lay otay gēl chalahũ ? otay hamar khēt achi, okarā dēkhai gēl chalahũ*, why had you gone there ? My field is there, I had gone to see it.

It will be observed that this root is frequently used with the conjunctive participles of other verbs, to form what are called 'Intensive Compounds.' These will be fully explained in § 342. It is also used to form the passive voice as will be explained in § 331.

312. The √आब *āb*, come, is in most of its tenses conjugated like an intransitive verb in आब *āb*, see §§ 270 ff. Its past participle is, however, formed as if the root ended in आ *ā*, so that it is आएल *āel* (आयल *āyal* or आइल *āil*), not आओल *āol*. The following is therefore the conjugation of the past tense. Examples of the present, future, etc., will be found under the head of roots in आब *āb*.

(*d*) (8) **Past Indicative** 'I came,' &c.

PERSON.	SHORT FORM. GROUP I. (Subject: non-honorific. Object: non-honorific.)	SHORT FORM. GROUP II. (Subject: honorific. Object: non-honorific.)	LONG FORM. GROUP I. (Subject: non-honorific. Object: non-honorific.)	LONG FORM. GROUP II. (Subject: honorific. Object: non-honorific.)
1	ऐलहुँ *ailahũ*.		ऐलिऐ *ailiai*.	
2	ऐलें *ailẽ*.	Same as 1st person.	ऐलाह *ailàh*.	Same as 1st person, but no forms for object in 2nd person.
3	आएल *āel*.	ऐलाह *ailāh*.	GROUP I. ऐलै *ailai*.	

Similarly for the Perfect and Pluperfect.

The Present Participle is (regularly) अबैत *abait* (अबयित *abayit*). The 3rd singular Old Present is आबै *ābai* or आए *āē*, honorific आबथि *ābath*ⁱ, etc. The 1st singular future is आएब *āeb* (poetical also आओब *āob*). The Conjunctive Participle is आबि *āb*ⁱ, and also आइ *āi* (आय *āy*, etc.).

313. The following are examples of the use of this verb:—

खन परितज खन आबइ पास, *khana paritaja khana ābai pāsa*, sometimes she retreats and sometimes comes near him (Vid. viii, 3).

राहु दूरि बसु निअरो न आबथि, *rāhu dūri basu niaro na ābathi*, Rāhu dwelleth afar, (and) doth not approach her (Vid. xiv, 8).

फेरि पलटि मोरंग नहिँ आएब, *phēr*ⁱ *palaṭ*ⁱ *mōraṅg nah*ĩ *āeb*, again I will not come back to Mōrang.

गौरी आओत ना, *gaurī, āot nā*, O Gaurī, will he not come?

जिबैत रहैत तो जोगिया अबैत पलटि, *jībait rahait, to jogiyā abait palaṭ*ⁱ, if they had been living, then they would have come back to Jogiyā.

औतन्हि दुरागमन करैतैन्हि, *autanh*ⁱ *durāgaman karaitainh*ⁱ, if they had come they would have performed the *durāgaman*-ceremony.

दुइ चारि पैसा खातिर हम ऐलहुँ दरबाजा पर, *dui car*ⁱ *paisā khātir ham ailah*ũ *dar*ᵃ*bājā par*, for the sake of two or four pice I came to your doorway.

तीनू मिलि गेलाह हे बहोरन अकसर ऐलाह, *tīnū mil*ⁱ *gēlāh, hē bahōran, ak*ᵃ*sar ailāh*, the three went together, O Bahōran, (but) you came (back) alone.

कथी ला ऐलीह दरबाजा पर, *kathī lā ailīh dar*ᵃ*bājā par*, for what did you (fem.) come to the doorway?

एक बिदेशी आएल, *ek bidēsī āel*, a foreigner came.

सखि सभ देलि भवन कै सजनी गे।
घुरि आएलि सभ नारी॥

sakhi sabha dēli bhaban kai, sajanī gē
ghuri āeli sabha nārī ‖

O friend, the bridesmaids brought me to the chamber, and then all the women (left me and) went back home (Vid. xxiii, 7).

निअ पहु परिहरि आइलि कमल मुखि। *nia pahu parihari āili kamala-mukhi*, the lotus-faced girl came, having left her own husband (Vid. vii, 7).

अब ऐलांह दीनाक पास भद्री, *ab ailăh dīnāk pās bhadrī*, now Bhadrī came near to Dīnā.

ई देखि ओकरा मुंह में पानि भरि ऐलै, *ī dēkhⁱ okᵃrā mũh mẽ pāni bharⁱ ailai*, seeing this, water came into and filled his mouth (*i.e.*, his mouth watered).

कालू सदा कनैत कनैत ऐलैक जोगियाक गाम, *kālū sadā kanait kanait ailaik jogiyāk gām*, Kālū Sadā, weeping weeping, came to the village of Jogiyā.

An example of the present participle will be found under the head of roots in आब *āb* (§ 284).

314. The roots दे *dē*, give, and ले *lē*, take, are conjugated exactly alike. It is sufficient to give the conjugation of the √दे *dē*. That of √ले *lē* can be ascertained by simply substituting ल *l* for द *d* throughout.

These two verbs present many irregularities. These are partly due to the combination of the final vowel of the root with the terminations, but are also due to the fact that there are really two pairs of roots, *viz.*, √दे *dē* and √दि *di*, and √ले *lē* and √लि *li*. Sometimes one of the pair is used, and sometimes the other. Moreover, owing to दि *di* and लि *li* having short vowels, the long *ē* of दे *dē* and ले *lē* is often shortened by analogy, so that, although I have, as a rule, only written a long *ē* in the paradigms, a short *e* can always be substituted. This is shown from the use of these forms in poetry, where pairs like देब *dēb* and दॆब *deb*, लेब *lēb* and लॆब *leb*, देल *dēl* and दॆल *del*, लेल *lēl* and लॆल *lel* are of frequent occurrence. Numerous instances will be found in the examples given below.

Note that, as in the conjugation of the Old Present of the regular verb (see § 176), when a dissyllabic form ends in ऐ *ai* derived from अहि *ahⁱ* the long ए *ē* is not shortened on that account (though of course it may be shortened as above explained). Thus the long *ē* of देब *dēb* is not shortened in the form देबै *dēbai* (for *देबहि *dēbah*^{i}). In the redundant form दबैक *debaik* (for *देबहिक *deb^{a}hik*) it is, of course, shortened under the usual ante-penultimate rule.

I give the conjugation of the √ दे *dē* in Groups I and II pretty fully, as there are numerous irregular forms. The forms for Groups III and IV can easily be derived from these, and instances of them will be found among the examples.

315. (*a*) (1) **Old Present.** 'I give,' &c. **Future (First Form).** 'I shall give,' &c.

<table>
<tr><th rowspan="2">PERSON.</th><th colspan="2">SHORT FORM.</th><th colspan="2">LONG FORM.</th></tr>
<tr><th>GROUP I.
(Subject: non-honorific. Object: non-honorific.)</th><th>GROUP II.
(Subject: honorific. Object: non-honorific.)</th><th>GROUP I.
(Subject: non-honorific. Object: non-honorific.)</th><th>GROUP II.
(Subject: honorific. Object: non-honorific.)</th></tr>
<tr><td>I</td><td colspan="2">दी dī.</td><td colspan="2">दिऐ diai (poetical, दिअ dia).
Or (with object in 2nd person).
दिऔ diau, दिअहु diah^{u}.</td></tr>
<tr><td>2</td><td>दे dē, देसि dēsi (poetical).</td><td>Same as 1st person.</td><td>दिअ॑ह diăh, द॑ह dăh, दिअहु diah^{u} दिहु dih^{u}, देहु deh^{u}, दैह daih, दएह daeh.</td><td>Same as 1st person, but no forms for object in 2nd person.</td></tr>
<tr><td>3</td><td>दे dē, दिअ dia, देअ dea, देओ deo, देए dēē.</td><td>देथि dēth^{i}.</td><td colspan="2">GROUP I.
देऐ dēai,
Or (with object in 2nd person).
देऔ dēau.</td></tr>
</table>

Similarly, *mutatis mutandis*, the Present Conditional and the Imperative. See the examples of these tenses below.

316. (*b*) (4) Future. 'I shall give.'

PERSON.	Second Form. SHORT FORM. GROUP I. (Subject: non-honorific. Object: non-honorific.)	Second Form. SHORT FORM. GROUP II. (Subject: honorific. Object: non-honorific.)	Second Form. LONG FORM. GROUP I. (Subject: non-honorific. Object: non-honorific.)	Second Form. LONG FORM. GROUP II. (Subject: honorific. Object: non-honorific.)	Third Form. SHORT FORM. GROUP I. (Subject: non-honorific. Object: non-honorific.)	Third Form. SHORT FORM. GROUP II. (Subject: honorific. Object: non-honorific.)	Third Form. LONG FORM. GROUP I. (Subject: non-honorific. Object: non-honorific.)	Third Form. LONG FORM. GROUP II. (Subject: honorific. Object: non-honorific.)
1	देब *dēb*, देबों *dēbõ*, देबहुँ *dēbahũ*.		देबै *dēbai*. Or (with object in 2nd person.) देबौ *dēbau*, देबहु *dēbahu* (देमौ *dēmau*, vulgar.)		देतहुँ *dētahũ*.		देतिऐ *dētiai*, Or (with obj. in 2nd pers.). देतिऔ *dētiau*.	
2	देबें *dēbẽ*.	Same as 1st person.	देबह *dēbah*.	Same as 1st person, but no forms for object in 2nd person.	Wanting.	Same as 1st person.	Wanting.	Same as 1st person, but no forms for object in 2nd person.
3	Wanting.	Wanting.	Wanting.		देत *dēt*, दैत *dait*.	देतथि *dētathi*.	GROUP I. देतै *dētai*, Or (with obj. in 2nd pers.). देतौ *dētau*.	

317. (*c*) (5) **Past Conditional**: '(If) I had given,' &c.

PERSON.	SHORT FORM.		LONG FORM.	
	GROUP I. (Subject: non-honorific. Object: non-honorific).	GROUP II. (Subject: honorific. Object: non-honorific.)	GROUP I. (Subject: non-honorific. Object: non-honorific)	GROUP II. (Subject: honorific. Object: non-honorific.)
1	दितहुँ *ditah^{ũ}*.		दितिऐ *ditiai*, Or (with object in 2nd person). दितिऔ *ditiau*.	
2	दितें *ditẽ*.	Same as 1st person.	दितह *dităh*.	Same as 1st person, but no forms for object in 2nd person.
3	दैत *dait*, देइत *dẽit*.	दितथि *ditath^{i}*.	GROUP I. दितै *ditai*, Or (with object in 2nd person). दितौ *ditau*.	

318. (*d*) (8) **Past Indicative**: 'I gave,' &c.

PERSON.	SHORT FORM.		LONG FORM.	
	GROUP I. (Subject: non-honorific. Object: non-honorific)	GROUP II. (Subject: honorific. Object: non-honorific).	GROUP I. (Subj.: non-honorific. Object; non-honorific.)	GROUP II. (Subject: honorific. Object: non-honorific).
1	देलहुँ *dēlah^{ũ}*, देली *dēli*, देल *dēl* (fem. देलि *dēl^{i}*).		देलै *dēlai*, Or (with obj. in 2nd person.) देलौ *dēlau*.	
2	देलें *dēlẽ*.	Same as 1st person.	देलह *dēlăh*.	Same as 1st person, but no forms for object in 2nd person.
3	देलक *dēlak*.	देलन्हि *dēlanh^{i}*, देलथि *dēlath^{i}*.	GROUP I. देलकै *del^{a}kai*, Or (with obj. in 2nd person.) देलकौ *del^{a}kau*.	

319. Verbal Nouns.

1. दे *dē*, देइ *dēi*, दँ *dả*, दै *dai*, दय *day*, दए *dae*, दंए *dee*: the act of giving: obl. देमै *dēmai* or दीअँ *dīả*.
2. देब *dēb*, the act of giving, to give; obl. देबा *dēbā*.
3. देल *dēl*, the act of giving; obl. देला *dēlā*. Its instrumental is देलेँ *dēlẽ*, or देनेँ *dēnẽ*. Similarly, for √ले *lē*, we have लेलेँ *lēlẽ*, लेनेँ *lēnẽ*, or (a common corruption) नेनेँ *nēnẽ*.

320. Participles.

Present.

देत *dēt*, देइत *dēit*, or दैत *dait*, fem. देति *dētⁱ*, दैति *daitⁱ*, giving.

Past.

देल *dēl*, fem. देलि *dēlⁱ*, given.

321. The following are examples of the use of these two verbs. In several of the instances given these verbs form intensive compounds with the first verbal nouns of other verbs. In such cases the root meaning of 'giving' or 'taking' has almost disappeared. See § 342.

Old Present and First Form of Future:— कहिअ तँ सभ अभरन दिअ काढ़ि, *kahia tā sabha abharana dia kāṛhi*, if you say (the word) I will tear off the ornaments from my body (intensive compound, § 342) (Man. vii, 43).

तोहरा कैएक कथा सभ सिखाय दिअऊ, *tohᵃrā kaiek kathā sabh sikhāy diahᵘ*, I will teach you (§ 342, and so elsewhere below) several matters.

किच्छु सीखि लेए तँ पठाय दिएेक। बेस हमरा बालकक संग पठाय दिअौक, *kicchᵘ sīkhⁱ lēē, tả paṭhāy diaik. Bēs, hamᵃrā bālakak saṅg paṭhāy diauk*, let him learn a little, then I will send him. Good, send him with my son.

मदन बेदन दे मानस अन्त, *madana bedana dē mānasa anta*, Love gives pangs in the inmost recesses of my soul (Vid. lxi, 2).

तेल सिन्दुर सभ देलन्हि आओरि ।
चरि चरि चुर देअ (v. l. देओ) मथा गोआरि ।

tela sindura sabha dēlanhi āori ।
cari cari cura dea (or *deo*) *mathā goāri* ॥

Other herd-maidens all gave oil and vermilion, and going here and there put (*lit.* give) handfuls (of the same on each others') heads (Man. ii, 43).

ओ धरि दाओ कृष्ण देथि आड़, *ō dhari dāo kṛṣṇa dethi* (for *dēthi*) *āṛa*, adopting that trick Kṛṣṇa wards him off (*lit.* gives warding off) (Man. ix, 36).

राम भरोखा बैसि कँ सबहिक मोजरा लेथि ।
जेहन जनिकर चाकरी तेहनें सन भरि देथि ॥

Rāma jharōkhā baisi kā̃ sabahika mojarā lēthi ।
Jēhana janikara cākarī tehanē̃ sana bhari dēthi ॥

Rām sitteth at an upper window and taketh cognizance of all.
As each one's service is, so in full He payeth him.

उपर मँ सुगा देऐ चक भाउर, *upar mē̃ sugā dēai cak-bhāur*, above (them) the parrot flies in (*lit.* gives) circles.

Imperative : फेरि अपना मेँ बाँटि ली, *phēri apanā mē̃ bā̃ṭi lī*, afterwards, let us divide (it) amongst ourselves.

एक चुरुक दे पियाय, *ek curuk dē piyāy*, give one sip (of water) to drink.

ले गे गिरथाइनि हरवा ले, *lē, ge girathāini. harawā lē*, take, O mistress, take (my) strings of beads.

धोबिनि कहए मुख उक दे लगाए, *dhobini kahae mukha uka de lagāe*, he says to the Dhōbin 'thrust a torch in (their) faces' (Man. viii, 10).

तोरित केसि कँ देसि बजाए, *torita kēsi kē̃ dēsi bajāe*, quickly summon Kēsi (Man. vi, 22).

से इनाम देह हमरा तब तोहरा मन पुराएब, *sē inām dāh hamarā, tab toharā man purāeb*, give me that reward, (and) I will fulfil for you (your) heart's (desire).

एक बेरि ददा हुकुम दिहु, *ek bēr*ⁱ, *dadā, hukum dih*ᵘ, give, O brother, the order but once.

सूपत बेँचा देलौक सौदा देहु पुराय, *sūpat bẽcā delauk, saudā deh*ᵘ *purāy*, I have given you barter-price of full weight, give me (therefore) the full weight in commodities.

दुनू सेर बेँचा जोखि लेहु, *dunū sēr bẽcā jōkh*ⁱ *leh*ᵘ, take and weigh these two seers of grain as barter-price.

भनहिँ विद्यापति देह सुमति मति, *bhanahĩ bidyāpati daiha, sumati, mati*, saith Vidyāpati, O Wise One, give heed (Vid. xxvii, 5).

ब्राह्मण कें दएह, *brāhmaṇ kẽ daeh*, give to the Brāhmaṇ (from a private letter written to the author).

दुनू चार दुनू हाँथ दै बैठाय दहँक, *dunū cār dunū hãth dai baiṭhāy dahãk*, set down the two thatches with (*see below*) (your) two hands.

ओतहि रहथु दृढ़ फेरि हे सखि। दरसन देथु एक बेरि॥

otahi rahathu dṛṛh phēri, hē sakhi । *darasana dethu eka bēri* ॥

Let him dwell there permanently, but, O friend, let him give us a sight (of him) but once (in a way) (Vid. lxviii, 4).

Honorific Imperatives :—

एक बेरि हुकुम दिअँ, *ek bēr*ⁱ *hukum diā̃*, be pleased to give thy order but once.

नहिँ खलीफा एक बेरि ठाढ़ भै के कुस्ती लिअँ, *nah*ⁱ *khalīphā ek bēr*ⁱ *ṭhāṛh bhai ke kustī liā̃*, nay, Your Highness, once more stand up and wrestle a fall (*lit.* take a wrestle) (with me).

माधव जनि दीअहु मोर दोस, *mādhaba jani dīahu mora dōsa*, O Mādhava, do not give my blame (*i.e.*, blame me) (Vid. lxvii, 4).

सरन दिअओ सरनागत जानि, *sarana diao saranāgata jāni*, (addressed to Viṣṇu) grant (me) protection, considering (me) as one who has taken refuge (with thee) (Man. i, 18).

आजुक दिन दिऔक कमाय, *ājuk din diauk kamāy*, be pleased to work for this day (only).

हमरो नमस्कार लिखि दिऔन्हि, *hamarō namaskār likh*ⁱ *diaunh*ⁱ, please write down (*lit.* having written give) my compliments also.

एक सेर अन घटि नहिँ देबहीन्हि, *ek sēr an ghaṭ^i nah^ĩ deb^ahīnh^i*, please do not give (even) one seer too little.

Future :—

प्रातहिँ आध देश देब बाँटि, *prātahĩ ādha dēsa deba bā̃ṭi*, at dawn, having divided the country I will give (you) half (Man. vi, 31).

सिसु दुहु मारि नन्द लेब डाँड़ि, *sisu duhu māri nanda leba ḍā̃ṛi*, having killed the two children, I will take a fine from Nand (Man. vi, 27).

मारब धनुखा देब खसाय, *mārab dhanukhā, dēb khasāy*, I will kill him (with an arrow) from my bow, and will fell him.

तन्हिका भवन जनम हम लेब, *tanhikā bhabana janama hama lēba*, in his house I will take birth (Man. i, 21).

सभ के देबौँ हम चारि सेर बोनि, *sabh kē dēbõ ham cār^i sēr bon^i*, to all (others) I will give four seers (of grain) as wages.

देबहुँ गोआही गुजराय, *dēbah^ũ goāhī guj^aray*, I will bear testimony.

धरती देबै लोटाय, *dhar^ati dēbai loṭāy*, I will throw (him) on the ground.

तोरा देबौ मोती चूरक लड्डू, *tōrā dēbau mōtī-cūrak laḍḍū*, I will give you sweetmeats of fried pulse-grains.

तखन तोहरा फुरसति देबऊ बीच मे नहिँ देबऊ, *takhan toh^arā phur^asat^i dēbah^u*, *bīc mē nah^ĩ dēbah^u*, then I will give you leave to depart: in the meantime I will not give you (leave).

हम तोहरा बचा लेबऊ, *ham toh^arā bacā lēbah^u*, I will take care of you.

ताहि ठाम देबैक धूनी खँसाय, *tāh^i ṭhām debaik dhūnī khãsāy*, there will we set down our fire.

जौ लागि हाजिर करबै नहिं तौ लागि फुरसति नहिँ देबौक, *jau lāg^i hājir kar^abai nah^ĩ, tau lāg^i phur^asat^i nah^ĩ debauk*, as long as you do not produce (the thief), so long will I not give (Salhēs) leave to depart for you (*i.e.*, as you request).

नहिँ रे अहिरा दूध पीबै देबेँ, *nah^ĩ, rē ahirā, dūdh pībai dēbẽ*, (if) you will not, O cowherd, give (me) milk to drink.

बेरि बेरि देवकि गर्भ देब सब्य, *beri beri debaki garbha deba sabya*, turn and turn about shalt thou place all of them in Dēvakī's womb (Man. i, 29).

सातम संकरखित कै लेब । देवकि सौँ रोहिनि कैँ देब ॥

sātama saṅkarakhitu kai lēb । *dēbaki sō̃ rōhini kē̃ dēb* ॥

The seventh (child) thou shalt take, having withdrawn it from Dēvakī's (womb), and shalt give it to Rōhinī (Man. i, 30).

परलु अनाइत तेँ छथि अंतय । बालमु दोस न देबा ।

paralu anāita tē̃ chathi antaya । *bālamu dōsa na dēbā* (m.c. for *dēb*),

He is elsewhere unwillingly, thou shalt not (*i.e.*, do not) give blame to thy beloved (Vid. lxiv, 12).

जखन तोँ हमरा छाड़ि देबँह तखन कहबहु, *jakhan tō̃ hamarā chāṛi dēbah, takhan kahabahu*, when you will let me go, I will tell you.

से बकस खोलि दुइ-टा रुपैआ ओ आधा आधा सभ मशाला लछमी दाइ कँ अपने चुप्पे देबैन्हि, *sē bakas khōli dui-ṭā rupaiā ō ādhā ādhā sabh maśālā lachmī dāi kē̃ apne cuppē debainhi*, having opened the box you will please give to the respected Lakṣmī Dēvī two rupees and half of each of the dainties.

नारद देत-गए उकठी लारि, *nārada deta-gae ukaṭhī lārī*. Nārada will stir up some evil deed (Man. ii, 19).

हमरो काज भंग कै देत, *hamarō kāja bhaṅga kai dēta*, will he interrupt even my business (Man. v. 33)?

हमहूँ हेँठ होएब तो हमरो धै लेत, *hamahū hēṭh hōeb, to hamarō dhai lēt*, if I also shall descend, then he will seize me also.

देतौ लाख गारि बे अपराध, *dētau lākh gāri bē aparādh*, for no fault she will give you a hundred thousand abuses.

घर घर जोगियाक देतैक पुराय, *ghar ghar jogiyāk detaik purāy*, from house to house the (people) of Jogiyā will fulfil (our order).

Past Conditional:—एहि नहिं जनली अहाँ भद्री छी । हम सीना गाइक दूध दितहुँ पियाय, *ehi nahi janalī ahā̃ bhadrī chī : ham sīnā gāik dūdh ditahu piyāy*, I did not know that you are Bhadrī (or) I should have given you the milk of the cow Sīnā to drink.

जौं तौं हमरा नहिं छाड़ितँह आओर मारि दितँह तखन ओ मोती तोहरा हाथ लगैत, *jõ tõ hamᵃrā nahⁱ chāritáh, āor mārⁱ ditáh, takhan ō mōtī tohᵃrā hāth lagait,* if you had not let me go, and had killed me. then that pearl would have come into your possession.

Present Indicative:—सलहेसक पहरा सौं से तोरा इनाम दैत छी, *salᵃhēsak pahᵃrā saũ sē tōrā inām dait chī.* (what I stole) from Salhēs's guard, that give I thee as a reward.

मारैत अछि हाँक गाइ देइत अछि भड़काय, *mărait achⁱ hā̃k, gāi dēit achⁱ bhaṛᵃkāy,* they utter a howl, and throw the cows into disorder.

आलस्य एहने कीरा अहि जे धन कैं धूरा कै दैत अछि, *ālasya ehᵃnē kīrā ahⁱ, jē dhan kē̃ dhūrā kai dait achⁱ,* idleness is in such a manner a worm that it turns wealth to dust.

धिया पुता भद्री के लेइत छैन्हि डाँटि, *dhiyā putā bhadrī kē lēit chainhⁱ ḍā̃ṭⁱ,* the girls and boys scold Bhadrī.

किच्छु दूध दैति अछि, *kicchᵘ dūdh daitⁱ achⁱ,* is she (a cow) giving any milk?

Past Indicative:—

पथ अपराध पिशुन परचारल ।
तथिहुँ उतर हम देला ॥

patha aparādha piśuna paracārala ।
tathihũ utara hama dēlā (m.c. for *dēl*) ।

On the way the slanderers cast reproaches at me, and I answered them on the spot (Vid. xl, 9).

सूपत बैंचा देलौक, *sūpat bē̃cā delauk,* I gave you barter-price in full.

लाख अपराध कैलौक लाख गारि देलें, *lākh apᵃrādh kailauk, lākh gārⁱ dēlē̃,* a hundred thousand faults I committed against you. a hundred thousand abuses you gave me.

फोटरा गीदर कथी ला मरद औतार लेलें, *phoṭᵃrā gīdar kathī lā marad autār lēlē̃,* O Phoṭrā jackal, why did you take human form?

मेलि न मिलय देलहुँ हिम कोटि, *meli na milaya delahũ hima kōṭi,* even after bringing them together they do not unite. (though) thou didst give ten millions of gold (Vid. xxx, 3).

सेहो देल कोन काजे, *sēhō dela kona kājē*, even (if) you gave that, what good is it (Vid. lxiii, 2)?

पहिल बचन उतरो नहिं देलि ।
नैन कटाक्ष सँ जिव हरि लेलि ॥

pahila bacana utar-ō nahī̃ dēli
naina kaṭācha sū̃ (m.c. for *sā̃*) *jiba hari lēli* ||

Thou (*fem.*) gavest not even a reply to my first words, but with a glance of your eye you took away my life (Vid. xlix, 2).

बिह मोर परसन भेल । रघुपति दरसन देल ।

biha mora parasana bhēla |
raghupati darsana dēla (poet. for *dēlanhi*) ||

The Creator was pleased with me. Raghupati gave (me) a vision (of himself) (Vid. xi. 1).

रानी कें उठाय कै भीमसेनक खटिया पर देल, ओ सोनाक पलंग मथा पर राखि लेल, *rūnī kē̃ uṭhāy kai bhīm-sainak khaṭiyā par dēl* (vulgar for *dēlak*), *ō sōnāk palang mathā par rākhi lēl* (vulgar for *lēlak*), he lifted the queen and put her upon Bhīm Sēn's cot, while he took the golden bed and placed it upon (his own) head.

तोहर बदन सन चाँद होअथि नहिं ।
जैओ जतन बिह देला ॥

tohara badana sana cā̃da hoathi nahī̃ |
jaio jatana bihu dēlā (m.c. for *dēl*, poetical for *dēlanhi*).

The moon doth not equal thy face, however great efforts the Creator made (*lit.* gave) (Vid. vi, 3).

गमार भेंड़ा सभ एहि कपटी हुँड़ार सभक कथा मानि लेलक । आओर कुकुर सभ कें हुँड़ारक ओतय पठाय देलक, *gamār bhē̃ṛā sabh ehi kapaṭī hũṛār sabhak kathā māni lēlak, āor kukur sabh kē̃ hũṛārak otay paṭhāy dēlak*, the silly sheep believed the words of these deceitful wolves, and sent the dogs to where the wolves (were staying).

उमड़ि चलल कै लेलक सलाम, *umaṛi calala kai lelaka salāma*, he took leave to go and departed swaggering (Man. v, 36).

तिरिया देलन्हि सपना जोगिया गाम, *tiriyā dēlanh^i sap^anā jogiyā gām*, he gave (*i.e.*, showed) his wife a dream in Jogiyā village.

सबुज कमान लेलन्हि दीना भद्री हाँथ के, *sabuj kamān lēlanh^i dīnā bhadrī hāth-kē*, Dīnā and Bhadrī took up into their hands their green bows.

देहि दुनू भाइ छोड़ि देलथि, *dēh^i dunū bhāi chōṛ^i dēlath^i*, the two brothers abandoned their bodies.

कतहुँ सँ दुइ सै रुपैआक चाँनी ओहि रसायनी कें आनि देलकै, *katah^ũ sã dui sai rupaiāk cãnī oh^i rasāy^anī kē ān^i del^akai*, having brought from somewhere two rupees' worth of silver he gave it to that alchemist.

सुनू इन्द्रासन छपन कोटि देवता जे इन्द्र जनम देलैन्हि, *sunū indrāsan chapan kōṭ^i dēb^atā jē indra janam delainh^i* (vulgar for *del^akainh^i*) hear, ye fifty-six times ten million gods of heaven, (and) the Indra who gave me birth.

ई सुनि कँ अतीथि उत्तर देलथीन्हि, *ī sun^i kã atīth^i uttar del^athīnh^i*, having heard this the respected ascetic gave answer politely.

Perfect Indicative :—

सूपत बेँचि कँ देली अछि, *sūpat bēch^i ke dēlī ach^i*, having sold I have given the full weight.

जोराबर सिंघ राजपूत डोला के देलक अछि घेरि, *jorābar singh rāj^apūt ḍōlā kē dēlak ach^i ghēr^i*. Jorāwar Singh, the Rajput, has stopped the (brides') litters.

Pluperfect Indicative :—

जखन धै लेलें (or लेनें or लेने or नेनें) छलें तखन छाड़ब की रहौ, *jakhan dhai lēlē̃ (or lēnē̃ or lēnē, or nēnē̃) chalē̃, takhan chāṛab kī rahau*, when you had caught me, why did you let me go? (Literally, 'what letting go was there to you'?)

जतवा जनिकर लेनँ छलि सुन्दरि ।
से सभ सोपलक ताही ॥

jatawā janikara lenē chali sundari ।
sē sabha sopalaka tāhī ॥

The fair one made over everything to everyone from whom she had taken them (Vid. x, 2).

Verbal Nouns:—

(1) See Conjunctive Participle: (Obl.) हमरा एक बकरी लेमैक अछि, *hamᵃrā ek bakᵃri lemaik achⁱ*, there is to me (necessity) of taking a goat, *i.e.*, I want to get a goat.

देखाय देमै जाइत छी, *dekhāy dēmai jāit chī*, I am going for (*i.e.*, in order to) showing you.

(2) कँगालक पूछब आओर अतीथिक उत्तर देब, *kãgālak pūchab āor atīthik uttar dēb*, the question of the beggar, and the answer-giving of the holy man. (This is the title of a story).

(3) हाँथ लेलेँ बाढ़नि चलि भेलि, *hā̃th lēlē̃ bāṛhanⁱ calⁱ bhēlⁱ*, taking (*lit.* by taking) in her hand a broom she went away.

हमर समाद लेनेँ जाऊ जाँजरि, *hamar samād lēnē̃ jāū jā̃jarⁱ*, having taken my message go to Jānjari.

अहिरा गोआर समाद नेनेँ अबैत छैक, *ahirā goār samād nēnē̃ abait chaik*, Ahirā, the cowherd, is coming with (*lit.* on taking) the message.

Participles:—

Present:—See Present Indicative.

Past:—Compare Past Indicative.

The Past Participle, or possibly the 3rd verbal noun, of लेब *lēb*, is often used as a postposition meaning 'on account of,' 'for the sake of,' as in Man. ii, 38:—

लाजक लेल मुख हेरिओ न होअ, *lājaka lela mukha herio na hōa*, on account of shame, even looking you in the face does not take place.

Conjunctive:—चटि दे धैलक पटि दे मारलक, *caṭⁱ dē dhailak, paṭⁱ dē mārᵃlak*, giving abruptness (*i.e.*, suddenly) he seized (him), giving instantaneous (*i.e.*, instantly) he struck (him).

मोर समाद जोगिया ले जाह, *mōr samād jogiyā lē jāh*, having taken my message, go to Jogiyā.

बाज सभ ले के भेल तैयार, *bāj sabh lē ke bhēl taiyār*, taking his horses he became ready.

आस देइ फेरि करु न निरासे, *āsa dēi pheri karu na nirāsē*, having given hope, do not again make hopelessness (Vid. xlix, 4, corrected reading).

ककर सक अछि जे हमरा सोझा सँ उठा लँ जाएत, *kakar sak achi jē hamarā sōjhā sa͂ uṭhā la͂ jāet*. who has (sufficient) strength that he will lift (it) up from before me and take it away?

कतेक भूमि पर दै दै पटकलक, *katek bhūmi par dai dai paṭakalak*, how often placing it again and again on the ground she dashed it (*i.e.*, how often she dashed it on the ground. but without result).

डोँका कें लै कँ उड़लि, *ḍõkā kē̃ lai ka͂ uṛali*, taking the shell she flew (up in the air).

सीना बेना लै के चरबैत अछि बरा डीहक बथान, *sīnā bēnā lai ke carabait achi barā ḍīhak bathān*, he is herding (the cows) Sinā and Bēnā at the cowshed of Barā Ḍīh.

अपनहुँ मन दय बुझु अबगाहे, *apanahũ mana daya bujhu abagāhē*, having applied (*lit.* given) your mind consider deeply (Vid. ii, 4).

जानि असक्य बक्क दए छाड़, *jāni asakya bakka dae chāṛa*, knowing him to be invincible he suddenly (*lit.* giving suddenness) let him go (Man. ix, 36).

हरि अनुमति लए ई मति भेल, *hari anumati lae ī mati bhēla*, having taken Hari's permission, this was (their) determination (Man. i, 26).

पहिरि माल बर देए हरि राम । कैल प्रबेस नरेसक गाम ॥

pahiri māla. bara dee, hari rāma । kaila prabēsa narēsaka gāma ॥

Having put on the garlands, having given the boon. Hari and Balarāma entered the king's village (Man. viii, 19).

The Conjunctive Participles are often used as postpositions. दे *dē*, etc., in the meaning of 'through,' 'by means of.' and ले *lē*, etc., meaning 'for.'

बड़ेरिक उपर दे निकसि चलह, *baṛērik upar dē nikasi calåh*, come out by means of (going) over the ridge-pole (of the thatch).

दुनू चार दुनू हाँथ दै बैठाय दहक, *dunū cār dunū hā̃th dai baiṭhāy dahåk*. set down the two thatches with (*or* by means of) (your) two hands.

तकरा दे के भेजब समाद, *takᵃrā dē ke bhējab samād*, by means of him we will send the message.

जाहि मरद लै जोबन सेबलें, *jāhⁱ marad lai jōban sebᵃlē̃*, the man for whose sake you have kept your virginity.

322. The √हो *hō*. become, is also used to supply the missing tenses of the verb substantive (see § 226). Its past participle is भेल *bhēl*, which is conjugated as the same principle as देल *dēl* and लेल *lēl*, that is to say the vowel may always be shortened *ad libitum*, so that we may always have either भेल *bhēl* or भेल *bhel*.

It has for its first verbal noun होइ *hōi* or भै *bhai*, with an oblique form होमै *hōmai*.

The tenses not formed from the past participle may all be regularly formed from हो *hō* , which, as in the case of √दे *dē* and √ले *lē*, may always be shortened to हो *ho*. Moreover, instead of हो *hō* or हो *ho*, we often have a base ह्व *hwa* or ह *ha*, so that the third person of the future may be होएत *hōet* or होएत *hoet* (or contracted होत *hōt* or होत *hot*), or ह्वैत *hwait* or हैत *hait*. There are also the usual varieties of spelling. Thus होएत *hōet* is often found written होयत *hōyat*, होइत *hōit*, or होयित *hōyit*.

The optional shortening of the vowels and these various spellings are not shown in the paradigms, but numerous instances will be found in the examples which follow.

323. (*a*) (1) **Old Present.** 'I become,' 'I am,' &c. (Including Present Conditional, Imperative, and first form of the Future).

PERSON.	SHORT FORM. GROUP I. (Subject: non-honorific. Object: non-honorific.)	SHORT FORM. GROUP II. (Subject: honorific. Object: non-honorific.)	LONG FORM. GROUP I. (Subject: non-honorific. Object: non-honorific.)	LONG FORM. GROUP II. (Subject: honorific. Object: non-honorific.)
1	होइ *hōi*, (Imperat. होउ *hōu*.)		होइऐ *hōiai*, Or (with object in 2nd person.) होइऔ *hōiau*.	
2	होएँ *hōẽ*, हो *hō*.	Same as 1st person.	होअह् *hōah*, होहु *hohᵘ*.	Same as 1st person, but no forms for object in 2nd person.
3	हो *hō* (poetical), होए *hōe*, होअ *hōa*, होय *hōy*	होअथि *hōathⁱ*, (Pros. Cond. and Imperat.) होअथु *hōathᵘ*.	GROUP I. होऐ *hōai*, Or (with object in 2nd person.) होऔ *hōau*.	

324. (*b*) (4) **Future.** 'I shall become,' 'I shall be,' &c. (1st & 2nd persons in 2nd form, and 3rd person in 3rd form).

PERSON.	SHORT FORM. GROUP I. (Subject: non-honorific. Object: non-honorific.)	SHORT FORM. GROUP II. (Subject: honorific. Object: non-honorific.)	LONG FORM. GROUP I. (Subject: non-honorific. Object: non-honorific.)	LONG FORM. GROUP II. (Subject: honorific. Object: non-honorific.)
1	हैब *haib*, होएब *hōeb*, होएबों *hōebõ*, होबों *hōbõ*.		हैबै *haibai*, होएबै *hōebai*, होबै *hōbai*, Or (with obj. in 2nd pers.) हैबौ *haibau*, होएबौ *hōebau*, होबौ *hōbau*.	
2	हैबें *haibẽ*, होएबें *hōebẽ*, होबें *hōbẽ*.	Same as 1st person.	हैबह *haibah*, होबह *hōbah*	Same as 1st person, but no forms for object in 2nd person.
3	हैत *hait*, ह्वैत *hwait*, होएत *hōet*, होत *hōt*.	हैतथि *haitathⁱ*, होएतथि *hōetathⁱ*.	GROUP I. हैतै *haitai*, होएतै *hōetai*, Or (with obj in 2nd pers.) हैतौ *haitau*, होएतौ *hōetau*.	

325. (*c*) (5) **Past Conditional.** '(If) I had become,' &c. | 326. (*d*) (8) **Past Indicative.** 'I became,' &c.

PERSON.	325. SHORT FORM.		325. LONG FORM.		326. SHORT FORM.		326. LONG FORM.	
	GROUP I. (Subject: non-honorific. Object: non-honorific.)	GROUP II. (Subject: honorific. Object: non-honorific.)	GROUP I. (Subject: non-honorific. Object: non-honorific.)	GROUP II. (Subject: honorific. Object: non-honorific.)	GROUP I. (Subject: non-honorific. Object: non-honorific.)	GROUP II. (Subject: honorific. Object: non-honorific.)	GROUP I. (Subject: non-honorific. Object: non-honorific.)	GROUP II. (Subject: honorific. Object: non-honorific.)
1	होइतहुँ *hōitahũ*.		होइतिऐ *hoitiai*.		भेलहुँ *bhēlahũ*.		भेलिऐ *bheliai*.	
2	होइतेँ *hōitẽ*.	Same as 1st person.	होइतह *hōitah*.	Same as 1st person, but no forms for object in 2nd person.	भेलेँ *bhēlẽ*.	Same as 1st person.	भेलाह *bhēlāh*.	Same as 1st person, but no forms for object in 2nd person.
3	होइत *hōit*.	होइतथि *hōitathi*.	GROUP I. होइतै *hōitai*.		भेल *bhēl*.	भेलाह *bhēlāh*.	GROUP I. भेलै *bhēlai*.	

327. **Verbal Nouns.**

(1) होइ *hōi* or भै *bhai* (भए *bhae*. etc.). the state of becoming. Obl. होमै *hōmai.*

(2) होएब *hōeb* (होयब *hōyab*. etc.). or हैब *haib* (हयब *hayab*, etc.), the state of becoming. to become. Obl. होबा *hōbā* or हैबा *haibā*.

(3) भेल *bhēl*, the state of becoming. Obl. भेला *bhēlā*.

328. **Participles.**

Present, होएत *hōet* (होइत *hōit*, होयित *hōyit*. होयत *hōyat*, etc.) or ह्वैत *hwait.*

Past, भेल *bhēl.*

329. NOTE.—In the Southern Maithilī tract we commonly hear the regular form होल *hōl*, or होअल *hōal*, instead of भेल *bhēl* for the past participle (with the tenses formed from it) and for the third verbal noun.

---

330. The following are examples of the use of this verb. Several instances will be noted of spellings different from those given in the paradigms :—

Old Present (and First form of Future).

भनहिं विद्यापति अपरुप नेह। जेहन विरह हो तेहन सिनेह॥

bhanahĩ bidyāpati aparupa nēha । *jehana biraha hō tehana sinēha* ॥

Saith Vidyāpati, 'O wondrous love, according to the length of the separation so (more groweth) the passion' (Vid. lxxx, 7).

अरि मन होए लोप भेल स्रिष्टि, *ari mana hōe lōpa bhela sriṣṭi*, to the enemies the mind becomes (*i.e.*, they imagine) (that) the universe has come to an end (Man. x. 45).

से हरखित मुंह हेरि न होए, *sē harakhita mũha hēri na hōē* (m.c. for *hōe*), therefore joyfully looking at (my) face (in a mirror) does not take place (*i.e.*, I no longer care to look at a mirror) (Vid. lxiii, 8.)

चलु चलु सुंदरि सुभ करि आज।

ततमत करइति नहिं होए काज॥

calu (m.c. for *calū*) *calu sundari subha kari āja* ।
tatamata karaiti nahĩ hoe kāja ॥

Depart, depart, fair one, considering to-day to be propitious. If thou make delay, thine object will not be accomplished (Vid. xxv, 1).

गगन मगन होअ तारा *gagana magana hoa tārā*, the stars have become sunken in the sky (*i.e.*, it is dawn) (Vid. xxvi, 1).

दू पुनि तीनि न होई, *dū puni tīni na hōī*, two, however, cannot become three (Vid. xxix. 7). Here and elsewhere in Vid. *hōī* is m.c. for *hōy*, which is again for *hōe*. See under Imperative.

उपर होअथि तोँ ठामहि ठाम, *upara hoathi tō̃ ṭhāmahi ṭhāma*, as he comes up (*i.e.*, when he came to the surface of the water) then (they were) there as before (Man. viii, 4).

बौरम नदी मेँ पानि पीबि के ऊपर होए, *bauram nadī mẽ pāni pībi ke ūpar hōai*, having drunk water in the Bauram river, he is becoming up (*i.e.*, is ascending the bank).

से सुनि होअए नृपति मन दरद, *sē suni hoae* (for *hōai*) *nripati mana darada*, hearing that (noise) there became in the mind of the king a pain (*i.e.*, he got a headache) (Man. x, 15).

Present Conditional :—

बुध जन हो से कहे बिसेख, *budha jana hō sē kahē bisēkha*, if a man be wise he tells the meaning (Vid. lxvii, 5).

जदि सन्सए होअ जनमक काल ।
बान्हि धरिअ बरु बन्दी साल ॥

jadi sansae hoa janamaka kāla ।
bānhi dharia baru bandī-sāla ॥

If there be doubt, then at the time of the child's birth bind her, yea, cast her into prison (Man. ii, 10).

जोड़हिँ जोड़ लागि गेल जूधि ।
जे ने होए किछु धरम बिरूधि ॥

jōṛahĩ jōṛa lāgi gela jūdhi ।
jē nē hoe kichu dharama birūdhi ॥

Equal with equal began the fight, in order that nothing might be done contrary to fair play (Man. x. 32).

जेहि सौँ ओकर परबरश होइक से अबस्य० कर्तव्य० थीक, *jehi saũ ōkar parªbaraś hōik* (for *hōaik*) *sē abasya kartabya thīk*, in order that there may be support for it (the child), the necessary action must certainly be taken.

Imperative:—

तोँ हेँठ होअह, *tō̃ hēṭh hōah*, do thou become below (*i.e.*, descend from the tree).

हरि कह हलधर होउ समधान, *Hari kaha. ' Haladhara, hou samadhāna.'* Hari says, 'Haladhar, be of good courage' (Man. v, 17).

होऊ परसन हे पुरहु मोर आसे, *hohu parasana he purahu moru āsē*, be gracious, (and) O fulfil my hope (Vid. xlix, 4).

जे छल होअओ सत्रु काँ तेहन, *jē chala, houo satru kā̃ tehana*, what (day) that was,—may such be for my enemies (Man. vii, 60).

पुनु दरसन होअ पुनमति गंगे, *punu darasana hoa punamati Gaṅgē*, Holy Ganges, may I see thee once again (Vid. lxxviii, 2).

मँगि लाएब बित से जदि होय नित ।
अपन करब कोन काजे ॥

māgi lāeba bita, sē jadi hoya nita ।
apana karaba kona kājē ॥

You will get wealth by begging. If that become everlasting, what will you do with that which is your own (Vid. li, 8)?

Hoya is for *hōe*, as explained above.

नन्दी सँ रस रीति बचाओब । गुपुत बेकत नहिँ होई ॥
nandī sā̃ rasa rīti bacāoba । *guputa bekata nahī̃ hōī* ॥

Daily you will conceal the way of love from your sister-in-law, (and therefore see thou that) that which is concealed be not revealed (Vid. xl, 12).

*Future Indicative:—*हम हैब मगन रसातल फेरि, *hama haiba magana rasātala phēri*, I shall again become plunged into the infernal regions (Man. i, 14).

हमहुँ हेँठ होएब तो हमरो धै लेत, *hamahū hẽṭh hōeb, to hamarō dhai lēt*, (if) I also shall descend (*lit.* become below), then he will seize me also.

नहिँ हेँठ होएबौँ *nahĩ hẽṭh hōebõ*, I will not descend.

जिब जाएत परान बचत तैश्रो ने परसा गाछ पर से हेँठ होबौँ, *jib jāet parān bacat taio nē parasā gāch par sē hẽṭh hōbõ*, whether I lose my life or save it, still I will not descend from the *parsā* tree.

परसाक गाछ पर से हेँठ होबहो, *parasāk gāch par sē hẽṭh hobahō* (for *hōbahu*). you will descend (*i.e.*, please descend) from the *parsā* tree.

दौड़-धूप कैला सँ किछु नहिँ हैत, *daur-dhūp kailā sã̄ kichhu nahĩ hait*, from running and fussing nothing will result.

से अब ह्वैत तीनि दिन मध्य, *sē aba hwaita tīni dina madhya*, that will now occur within three days (Man. vii, 32).

ओ बालक घर घालक होएत, *ō bālaka ghara ghālaka hōeta*, that child will become the destroyer of (your) house (Man. vi, 20).

होइत अमोघ मोघ कए जानि, *hoita* (for *hōet*) *amōgha mōgha kae jāni*. knowing that success will be non-success (Man. x. 35).

बनहिँ गमन करु होएति दोसर मति ।
बिसरि जाएब पति मोरा ॥

banahĩ gamana karu (m.c. for *karū*) *hoeti dosara mati* ।
bisari jāeba (m.c. for *jāeb*) *pati mōrā* ॥

Thou wilt make thy way to the forest, and thy mind will become changed ; thou wilt, my Lord, forget me (Vid. lv, 3).

तोहरा सभक केसो टेढ़ नहिँ हैतहु, *toharā sabhak kēs-ō ṭēṛh nahĩ haitahu*, to you not a hair even will become crooked.

एह बेकूफ कैँ कहाँ तक नीक अकिल हैतैक, *eh bēkūph kẽ kahā̃ tak nīk akil haitaik*, how far will there be decent wisdom to this fool.

Past Conditional :—जौहरी एकरा पबैत तँ अत्यन्त खुसी होइत, *jauhari ekarā pabait. tã̄ atyant khusī hōit*, if a jeweller had got this, he would have been extremely happy (*lit.* happiness would have been).

Present Indicative :—किएक सबहु होइछिअ मति मूढ़, *kieka sabahu hoi-chia* (for *chiai*) *mati mūṛha*, why are ye all of foolish mind. Man. v, 22).

कौनो मुसहर ने घर से होइत अछि बाहिर, *kauno musahar nē ghar sē hōit ach*[i] *bāhir*, not one Musahar comes out (*lit.* becomes outside) of his house.

होइछि (*v.l.* ह्वैअछि) उपद्रव बारंबार, *hoich*[i] (v. l., *hwaiachi*) *upadraba bārambāra*, attacks are being continually made (upon us) (Man. iv. 4).

स्वामि-धन वृथा नष्ट होइछ, *swāmi-dhan vṛtha naṣṭ hōich*. (my) master's wealth is being wasted in vain. (*Purush-Parīkṣā*, p. 51).

Imperfect Indicative :—गाछ सबहि में लाही लागि गेलैक । नहिं तँ बहुत होइत छल, *gāch sabah*[i] *mē̃ lāhī lāg*[i] *gelaik. nah*[i] *tã̄ bahut hōit chal*, the trees were attacked by blight, otherwise there would have been much (fruit). (Here the imperfect is, as sometimes occurs, employed in the sense of the past conditional.)

Past Indicative :—कोन तप चुकल भेलहुँ जननी, *kona tapa cukalu bhelahū̃ janani*, what penance was omitted, that I became his mother (Vid. lxxix, 2).

अहाँ सभक कुसल-छेम बूझल मन आनंद भेल, *ahā̃ sabhak kusal-chēm būjhal, man ānand bhēl*, I learned the news of your good health, (and) in my heart there became joy.

संग देव बरह्मा भेल आगु, *saṅga dēba barahmā bhela āgu*. Brahmā became (*i.e.*, stood) in front of the gods who were with him (Man. i, 9).

धरनी भार बेआकुलि भेलि । सुरभि रूप धै सुरपुर गेलि ॥
किछु नहिं ततहुँ काहु सौं भेल । धरनिक संग सबहु जन गेल ॥

dharanī bhār beākuli bhēli । *surabhi rūpa dhai surapura gēli* ॥
kichu nahī tatahū̃ kāhu sō bhēla । *dharanika saṅga sabahu jana gēla* ॥

The earth (fem.) became distressed with the burden, and, taking the form of a cow, went to Indra's paradise; but thence no assistance came to her from any one, and with the earth all its inhabitants went away (to Brahmā) (Man. i, 6).

ओहि अवसर धरनी भेलि आगू, *ohi abasara dharanī bheli āgū*, at that moment the earth came forward (Man. i, 12).

के बेरि काटि बनाओल नव कय ।
तैओ तुलित नहिं भेला ॥

kai beri kāṭi banāola naba kaya ।
taio tulitu nahi bhēlā (m.c. for *bhēla*) ॥

Many times he cut it and fashioned it anew, but still it could not equal (thy beauty) (Vid. vi, 4).

दीना भद्री ठाढ़ भेलाह, *dīnā bhadrī ṭhāṛh bhēlāh*, Dīnā and Bhadrī became erect (*i.e.*, stood up).

भेलिह निसंक, *bheliha nisanku*, she became free from care (Man. iii, 9).

ठाढ़ि भेलिहि धनि आँगो न डोले, *ṭhāṛhi bhelihi dhani ā̃go na ḍōlē*, the lady became motionless. not even do her limbs move (Vid. xxvii, 2).

एक दिन ब्रज मह खेड़ि भल भेलइ, *eka dinu braja mahū kheṛi bhala bhelai*. one day there was an excellent game in Braj (Man. v, 12).

तोहरा सँ ई चूकि भेलह्, *tohᵃrā sā̃ ī cūkⁱ bhēlahᵘ*, from you this mistake has happened (*i.e.*, you have made this mistake).

के मास सँ गाभिनि अछि । भेलैक तँ आठ मास, *kai mās sā̃ gābhinⁱ achⁱ ? bhelaik tā̃ āṭh mās*. from how many months is she in calf? Eight months, indeed. were (*i.e.*, have passed).

फोटरा के देखि अजगुत भेलौक, *phoṭᵃrā kē dēkhⁱ ajᵃgut bhelauk*, the seeing Photrā was wonderful to you.

बहुत दिन भेलैन्हि अहाँ लोकनि तकाजा नहिं करैछिऐन्हि, *bahut din bhelainhⁱ ahā̃ lokᵃni takājā nahⁱ karaichiainhⁱ*, it is a long time since you pressed (him for the money).

Perfect Indicative:—चीज बस्तु सभ अहाँक नोकसान भेल अछि, *cīj bastᵘ sabh ahā̃k nokᵃsān bhēl achⁱ*, your property has been damaged.

Verbal Nouns:—

(1) Obl. होमए लागल अकासक बानि, *hōmae lāgala* (m.c. for *lāgala*) *akāsaku bāni*, there began to be a voice of (*i.e.*, from) the sky (Man. x, 35).

(2) मुर्गीक अंडा सभ सँ पैघ मोती हमरा पेट मेँ हैब कहिआ ध्यान मेँ आबि सकैअछि, *murgīk aṇḍā sabh sa͂ paigh mōtī hamᵃrā pēṭ mē̃ haib kahiā dhyān mē̃ ābⁱ sakai-achⁱ*, can the existence of a pearl bigger than a hen's eggs in my belly come within (the realm of) thought?

अन्धक नेत्र० हयबाक औखध अछि, *andhak nētra hayᵃbāk* (for *haibāk*) *aukhadh achⁱ*, there is a medicine for the becoming of eyes of a blind man (*i.e.*, which gives sight to the blind).

Participles :—

*Present :—*हैत प्रात भेल नय हकार, *hwaita prāta bhela nagra hakāra*, on dawn becoming, there arose a cry in the town (Man. ii, 42).

होइत भिनसरवा भागि चलल, *hōit bhinᵃsarᵃwā bhāgⁱ calal*, as morning dawned he ran away.

जनिका जनम होइत हम गेलहुँ ।
ऐलहुँ तनिकर अंते ॥

janikā janama hoita, hama gēlahũ ।
ailahũ tanikara antē ॥

I returned at the death of him, at whose birth I went out (Vid. xxxix, 2).

मुक्तबन्ध होयित भेलाह, *mukta-bandh hōyit bhēlāh*, he became becoming released from his bonds (*i.e.*, he gradually got free).

Past : See Past Indicative.

*Conjunctive :—*बिमुखि सुतलि धनि सुमुखि न होइ, *bimukhi sutali dhani sumukhi na hōi*, the damsel, not having become sweet-faced (*i.e.*, refusing to smile), slept with her face turned away (Vid. xxx, 2).

व्याकुल भै सभ पहुँचल धाए, *byākula bhai sabha pahũcala dhāe*, all becoming distressed ran up (Man. iv, 32).

भद्रीक आगू सल्हेस भै गेलाह ठाढ़ि, *bhadrīk āgū salhēs bhai gēlāh* (Hindi *hō gayā*) *ṭhāṛhⁱ*, Salhēs became erect (*i.e.*, stood up) before Bhadrī.

एक बेरि ठाढ़ भै के कुस्ती लिअ, *ek bēr[i] ṭhāṛh bhai ke kustī liā*, just once, having stood up, wrestle a fall (with me).

आठम भए हम अपनहिँ आओब, *āṭhama bhae hama apanahĩ āoba*, having become the eighth (child), I shall come myself (Man. i. 32).

CHAPTER VII.

The Passive Voice.

331. As in Hindī, the passive is usually formed by conjugating the past participle with the √जा *jā*, go. The participle is liable to inflection as to gender, in which respect it agrees with the subject of the verb, but in other respects it remains unaltered. Thus देखल जाएब, *dēkhal jāeb*, means 'to be seen' देखल जाइत अछि, *dēkhal jāit ach[i]*, he is being seen; देखल गेल, *dēkhal gēl*, he was seen; देखलि गेलि, *dēkhal[i] gēl[i]*, she was seen. Examples of this form of the passive are the following :—

बड़ सुकुमार हमर स्वामी सलहेस। मारि सहल नहिँ जाइछैन्हि, *baṛ sukumār hamar swāmī sal[a]hēs; mār[i] sahal nahĩ jāichainh[i]*, very tender is my lord Salhēs, a beating is not (*i.e.*, cannot be) borne by him. (Regarding the inanimate feminine मारि *mār[i]*, see § 186.)

भाइ जेठ छलहु से मारल गेल कटैया, *bhāi jēṭh chalah[u], sē māral gēl kaṭaiyā*, he (who) was your elder brother has been killed in Kaṭaiyā.

जखन अपने मन चाही तखन तोड़बा लेल जाय, *jakhan ap[a]ne man cāhī, takhan toṛ[a]bā lēl jāy*, when your soul desires, then having caused (the fruit) to be plucked, let it be taken away.

In old Maithilī poetry we sometimes find the passive participle put into a strong form in आ *ā*, as if we said देखला *dekh[a]lā* for देखल *dēkhal*.

Thus, Man. vii, 12 :—

मुइल असुर गोट छुइला गेल, *muila asura goṭa chuilā gēla*, a dead Asura had been touched (by him, and he was consequently unclean).

332. Another form of the passive is formed by conjugating the first verbal noun with the verb पड़ब *paṛab* or परब *parab*, to

fall. Thus देखि पड़ब *dēkh^{i} paṛab*, to be seen; देखि पड़ल *dēkh^{i} paṛal*, he was seen. The first verbal noun remained unchanged throughout. The whole is an intensive compound (see § 342), and the final इ *i* is often omitted.

Examples of the use of this form of the passive are :—

ई तँ केओ अपूर्ब ढंगक लोक देख पड़ैअछि, *ī tã keo apūrb ḍhaṅgak lōk dēkh paṛai-ach^{i}*, this, indeed, is seen (to be) (*i.e.*, is evidently) a person of some extraordinary kind.

कुमरबैति अछि बा एखन नहिँ। हँ किछु किछु बूझि पड़ैअछि, *kumar^{a}-bait^{i} ach^{i} bā ekhan nah^{ĩ}? hã kich^{u} kich^{u} būjh^{i} paṛai-ach^{i}*, is she showing signs of being in calf or not? Yes, a little is becoming manifested.

333. A **Potential Passive** is formed for some verbs by adding आ *ā* to the root. Thus √देख *dēkh*, see, √देखा *dēkhā*, to be able to be seen, to be visible. This root *dēkhā* is conjugated exactly like any other intransitive root in आ *ā* (see §§ 270 ff). The potential passive indicates not so much that a thing *is* done, as that it *can be* done. Thus ई पोथी पढ़ाइअछि, *ī pōthī paṛhāi-ach^{i}*, this book *can be* read, but ई पोथी पढ़ल जाइअछि, *ī pōthī paṛhal jāi-ach^{i}*, this book *is being* read. Similarly (√मीँझ *mĩjh*, extinguish) we have हमरा पेटक आगि एहि सँ नहिँ मिँझाएत, *ham^{a}rā pēṭak āg^{i} eh^{i} sã nah^{i} mĩjhāet*, the fire of my belly will not be able to be extinguished by this.

———o———

CHAPTER VIII.

The Formation of Transitive and Causal Verbs.

334. As in other Indo-Aryan languages the intransitive verb in Maithili can be made transitive and the transitive verb causal.

The transitive verb is generally formed by adding आब *āb* to the root, and the causal by adding अबाब *^{a}bāb*, but there are many exceptions. The roots thus formed are conjugated like transitive verbs in आब *āb* (see §§ 270 ff). We often find व *w* written instead of ब *b*, as in आव *āw*, अवाव *ᵃwāw*, and this pronunciation is usually heard in Southern Maithili, but in the northern or standard dialect the sound is always that of ब *b*, no matter what is written.

In Hindī grammars we have rules about shortening the root vowel of certain causal verbs. These rules are not necessary in Maithili. The root vowels are shortened according to the regular rule of the short ante-penultimate vowel (see §§ 32 ff).

It thus follows that in forms which consist of only two syllables, the root vowel is not shortened. Thus from √जाग *jāg*, 'be awake,' the transitive root जागाब *jāgāb*, which is also the shortest form of the 2nd person imperative, meaning 'awaken thou.' But the first person future of the transitive is जगाएब *jagāeb*, with the *ā* shortened, as it is now in the ante-penultimate.

335. The following are examples of intransitive verbs becoming transitive, and causal. All verbs are given in the form of the infinitive, so as to show the shortening of the ante-penultimate vowel. It will be remembered that roots in आब *āb* form their infinitives in आएब *āeb* :—

INTRANSITIVE.	TRANSITIVE.	CAUSAL.
गिरब *girab*, to fall.	गिराएब *girāeb*, to fell.	गिरबाएब *girᵃbāeb*, to cause to fell.
चढ़ब *caṛhab*, to ascend,	चढ़ाएब *caṛhāeb*,	चढ़बाएब *caṛhᵃbāeb*.
पिघलब *pighᵃlab*, to melt.	पिघलाएब *pighᵃlāeb*,	पिघलबाएब *pighalᵃbāeb*.
लटकब *laṭᵃkab*, to hang,	लटकाएब *laṭᵃkāeb*,	लटकबाएब *laṭakᵃbāeb*.
जागब *jāgab*, to awake.	जगाएब *jagāeb*,	जगबाएब *jagᵃbāeb*.
पाकब *pākab*, to ripen,	पकाएब *pakāeb*,	पकबाएब *pakᵃbāeb*.
बाजब *bājab*. to speak,	बजाएब *bajāeb*. to call, summon.	बजबाएब *bajᵃbāeb*.
लागब *lāgab*, to be applied, to begin.	लगाएब *lagāeb*,	लगबाएब *lagᵃbāeb*.
भीजब *bhījab*, to be wet,	भिजाएब *bhijāeb*,	भिजबाएब *bhijᵃbāeb*.

INTRANSITIVE.	TRANSITIVE.	CAUSAL.
घूमब *ghūmab*, to go round.	घुमाएब *ghumāeb*,	घुमबाएब *ghum°bāeb*.
डोलब *ḍōlab*, to be shaken.	डोलाएब *ḍolāeb*,	डोलबाएब *ḍol°bāeb*.
लेटब *lēṭab*, to lie down,	लेटाएब *leṭāeb*,	लेटबाएब *leṭ°bāeb*.

In the above, note that the √बाज *bāj*, like the Hindī √बोल *bōl*, is intransitive.

Note also that no verbs insert ल *l* as sometimes occurs in Hindī. Thus:—

INTRANSITIVE.	TRANSITIVE.	CAUSAL.
जीअब *jīab*, to live,	जिआएब *jiāeb*, to make alive.	जिअबाएब *jiabāeb*, to cause to make alive.

336. In the same way transitive verbs form causal and double causals. Thus:—

TRANSITIVE.	CAUSAL.	DOUBLE CAUSAL.
सुनब *sunab*, to hear,	सुनाएब *sunāeb*, to cause to hear.	सुनबाएब *sun°bāeb*, to cause to be heard.
देखब *dēkhab*, to see,	देखाएब *dekhāeb*, to show.	देखबाएब *dekh°bāeb*, to cause to show.
देब *dēb*, to give,	देआएब *dēāeb* or दिआएब *diāeb*, to cause to give.	देअबाएब *deabāeb* or दिअबाएब *diabāeb*, to cause to be given.
धोअब *dhōab*, to wash,	धोआएब *dhōāeb* or धोबाएब *dhōbāeb*.	धोअबाएब *dhoabāeb*.
पीअब *pīab*, to drink,	पीआएब *pīāeb* or पीबाएब *pībāeb*, to give to drink.	पिअबाएब *piabāeb*.
सीखब *sīkhab*, to learn,	सिखाएब *sikhāeb*,	सिखबाएब *sikh°bāeb*.

337. Many intransitive verbs with a short vowel in the root simply lengthen it to form the transitive, and form the causal regularly with अबाब °*bāb*; thus:—

INTRANSITIVE.	TRANSITIVE.	CAUSAL.
कटब *kaṭab*, to be cut,	काटब *kāṭab*, to cut,	कटबाएब *kaṭ^{a}bāeb*.
गड़ब *gaṛab*, to be buried.	गाड़ब *gāṛab*, to bury,	गड़बाएब *gaṛ^{a}bāeb*.
मरब *marab*, to die.	मारब *mārab*, to kill,	मरबाएब *mar^{a}bāeb*.
पलब *palab*, to be reared.	पालब *pālab*, to rear,	पलबाएब *pal^{a}bāeb*.
लदब *ladab*, to be loaded.	लादब *lādab*, to load,	लदबाएब *lad^{a}bāeb*.
निकसब *nikasab*, to come out.	निकासब *nikāsab*, to bring out.	निकसबाएब *nikas^{a}bāeb*.

338. The following are irregular :—

INTRANSITIVE.	TRANSITIVE.	CAUSAL.
खुलब *khulab*, to be open.	खोलब *khōlab*,	खोलबाएब *khol^{a}bāeb*.
छूटब *chūṭab*, to go off,	छाड़ब *chāṛab* or छोड़ब *chōṛab*.	छड़बाएब *chaṛ^{a}bāeb* or छोड़बाएब *choṛ^{a}bāeb*.
टूटब *tūṭab*, to be broken.	तोड़ब *tōṛab* or तोरब *tōrab*.	तोड़बाएब *toṛ^{a}bāeb* or तोरबाएब *tor^{a}bāeb*.
फटब *phaṭab*, to be rent.	फाड़ब *phāṛab*,	फड़बाएब *phaṛ^{a}bāeb*.
अटब *aṭab*, to be stopped.	अड़ाएब *aṛāeb* or आड़ब *āṛab*.	अड़बाएब *aṛ^{a}bāeb*.
बिकब *bikab* or बिकाएब *bikāeb*, to be sold.	बेचब *bēcab*, or बेँचब *bẽcab*.	बेँचबाएब *bec^{a}bāeb*.
रहब *rahab*, to remain,	राखब *rākhab*,	रखबाएब *rakh^{a}bāeb*.
खा *khā*, to eat,	खिआएब *khiāeb*, to feed, give to eat.	खिअबाएब *khiabāeb*.

Amongst others, the following verb takes the causal form, but does not use it in a causal, but only in a transitive sense; the causal form thus becomes an optional form of the transitive.

SIMPLE VERB.	TRANSITIVE.
कहब *kahab*, to say,	कहाएब *kahāeb* or कहबाएब *kah*ᵃ*bāeb*, to say.

339. A few examples of the Transitive and Causal verbs in literature may be given. Many more will be found under verbs in आब *āb* in § 284.

हीरा हीरा मति बाजू, *hīrā hīrā mat*ⁱ *bāju*, say not 'diamonds diamonds.'

एक दिन ओ अपना बेटा सभ कें बजौलकै, *ek din ō ap*ᵃ*nā bēṭā sabh kẽ bajaul*ᵃ*kai*, one day he summoned his sons.

आगि लागल, *āg*ⁱ *lāgal*, fire was attached (to the house, *i.e.*, the house took fire).

स्वामी में लय किए नहिं लगबैछह, *swāmī mẽ lay kiai nah*ⁱ *lag*ᵃ*baichāh*, why do you not apply your mind in (*i.e.*, on the contemplation of) the Lord?

सूपत बेंचि के देली अछि दियाय, *sūpat bẽc*ⁱ *ke dēlī ah*ⁱ *diyāy*, I, having sold, have given the full weight, having caused (him) to give (tobacco in exchange).

अनाथ लोक काँ इच्छा भोजन देआबथि, *anāth lōk kā̃ icchā bhōjan deābath*ⁱ, to the destitute people he causes food to be given (according to) their desires (*Puruṣa Parikṣā*, p. 49).

वस्तु देअबयित छथि, *bast*ᵘ *deabayit chath*ⁱ, he is causing goods to be given (Ib., p. 51).

जाइ पिआबिऐ अधर सुधारस, *jāi piābiai adhara sudhārasa*, having gone, give her the nectar of your lower lip to drink (Vid. x, 10).

हम की की निकासू। आगि लागल झोंपड़ी जे निकसे से लाभ *ham kī kī nikāsū? āg*ⁱ *lāgal jhōp*ᵃ*ṛī, jē nikasē, sē lābh*, what shall we bring out? When a hut is afire, whatever comes out, that is gain.

बहुत ऊपर जाए कँ छाड़ि देलक, *bahut ūpar jāe kā̃ chāṛ*ⁱ *dēlak*, going up very high, he let it go.

धाबाक डारि तोरि माँछी हौंक, *dhābāk ḍār[i] tōr[i] mā̃chī haũk*, having broken off a branch of the *dhābā* tree, drive away the flies.

दुनू भाइ के खिअौलक, *dunū bhāi kē khiaulak*, she fed the two brothers.

CHAPTER IX.

COMPOUND VERBS.

340. Compound verbs may be classed as—(1) those formed with a verbal noun, and (2) those formed with a participle.

I. Those formed with a verbal noun are—

(*a*) Intensives.
(*b*) Potentials.
(*c*) Completives.
(*d*) Permissives.
(*e*) Acquisitives.
(*f*) Inceptives.
(*g*) Desideratives.
(*h*) Frequentatives.

II. Those formed from the participles are—

(*a*) Continuatives.
(*b*) Staticals.

Class I.—**Compounds formed with the Verbal Noun.**

341. As explained in §§ 178 ff., there are three verbal nouns, *viz.* :—

(1) देखि *dēkh[i]* ; obl. देखै *dēkhai* or देखँ *dēkhã*.

(2) देखब *dēkhab* ; obl. देखबा *dekh[a]bā*.

(3) देखल *dēkhal* ; obl. देखला *dekh[a]lā*.

The following are made with the direct form of the first verbal noun :—

(*a*) Intensives.
(*b*) Potentials.
(*c*) Completives.

The following are made with the oblique form of the first verbal noun :—

(*d*) Permissives.

(*e*) Acquisitives.

(*f*) Inceptives.

(*g*) Desideratives are sometimes made with the genitive of the second verbal noun, but more usually with the oblique form of the first verbal noun.

(*h*) Frequentatives are made with the direct form of the third verbal noun.

342. (*a*) **Intensive** compounds intensify, or otherwise modify, the meaning of the verb whose root stands first in the compound. They are made by adding to the direct form of the first verbal noun one of certain auxiliary verbs. The verbal noun remains unchanged, and the auxiliary verb is conjugated throughout as usual. This second auxiliary conjugated member does not, however, retain its separate character and significance, but only modifies, in accordance with the general idea which it embodies, the meaning of the unconjugated verbal noun to which it is attached.

The first verbal noun ends in इ ^{i} (देखि *dēkh*^{i}). This final vowel is only half-pronounced, and, in these compounds, it is often dropped both in writing and in pronunciation ; so that, *in these compounds*, we may have either देखि *dēkh*^{i} or देख *dēkh*. This elision of *i* (or *y*, etc., see § 281) most frequently occurs in the case of verbs whose roots ends in vowels.

The auxiliary verbs usually employed to form intensives are :—

देब *dēb*, to give, implying in these compounds		*intensity*.
डारब *ḍārab*, to throw,	,,	*violence*.
आएब *āeb*, to come, }		
जाएब *jāeb*, to go, }	,,	*completion*.
पड़ब *paṛab* or परब *parab*, to fall.	,,	*chance*.
उठब *uṭhab*, to rise,	,,	*suddenness*.
रहब *rahab*, to remain,	,,	*continuation*.
लेब *lēb*, to take,	,,	*reflexiveness*.

Note that पड़ब *paṛab*, to fall, is also used to make passives. See § 332.

Examples of such intensive compounds are :—

भरब *bharab*, to fill.	भरि देब *bhar*^{i} *dēb*, to fill up.
उड़ाएब *uṛāeb*, to cause to fly.	उड़ाइ or (उड़ा) देब *uṛāi* (or *uṛā*) *dēb*, to squander.
हेड़ाएब *heṛāeb*, to lose.	हेड़ा देब *hēṛā dēb*, to lose out and out.
खसाएब *khasāeb*, to cause to fall.	खसाय देब *khasāy dēb*, to throw down.
काटब *kāṭab*, to cut.	काटि डारब *kāṭ*^{i} *ḍārab*, to cut off.
बनब *banab*, to be made.	बनि आएब *ban*^{i} *āeb* or बनि जाएब *ban*^{i} *jāeb*, to be completely made.
चलब *calab*, to go.	चलि जाएब *cal*^{i} *jāeb*, to go away.
खाएब *khāeb*, to eat.	खा जाएब *khā jāeb*, to eat up.
पीअब *pīab*, to drink.	पी जाएब *pī jāeb* or पिबि जाएब *pib*^{i} *jāeb*, to drink up.
होएब *hōeb*, to be, to become.	हो जाएब *hō jāeb*, भै जाएब *bhai jāeb*, to become (definitely).
जाएब *jāeb*, to go.	जाए पड़ब *jāe paṛab*, to happen to go.
पुकारब *pukārab*, to call out.	पुकारि उठब *pukār*^{i} *uṭhab*, to call out suddenly, give a scream.
होएब *hōeb*, to be, become.	हो रहब *hō rahab*, to be.
सूतब *sūtab*, to sleep.	सूति रहब *sūt*^{i} *rahab*, to sleep on.
पीअब *pīab*, to drink.	पी लेब *pī lēb* or पिबि लेब *pib*^{i} *lēb*, to drink, take to drink.
राखब *rākhab*, to place.	राखि लेब *rākhi lēb*, to lay by (for one's own use).
लेब *lēb*, to take.	लै लेब *lai lēb*, to take for oneself.

343. It will be remembered that the conjunctive participle may be the same in form as the verbal noun. Phrases in which this form of the conjunctive participle occurs are not intensive compounds. Thus लै जाएब *lai jāeb*, 'having taken to go,' 'to take away,' is not an intensive compound. If it were an intensive compound, it would mean 'to take completely,' which it does not

mean. On the other hand दै जाएब *dai jāeb* is an intensive compound and means 'to give out and out.' Again, while बनि आएब *ban*ⁱ *āeb* is an intensive compound, and means 'to be completely made,' निकसि आएब *nikas*ⁱ *āeb* is 'having emerged to come,' *i.e.*, 'to come out,' and is not an intensive compound, but is simply a phrase with the conjunctive participle. The essence of an intensive compound is that the auxiliary verb loses all or some of its proper meaning, which is not in the case in निकसि आएब *nikas*ⁱ *āeb*.

344. These intensive compounds are extremely common in Maithilī. Dozens of instances will be found on every page of any book in the language. The following are a few typical examples :—

काठी सबहि कैं तोड़ि दे, *kāṭhī sabah*ⁱ *kẽ tōṛ*ⁱ *dē*, break the sticks.

हमरा लग पठाय दैह, *ham*ᵃ*rā lag paṭhāy daih*, send (them) to us.

सभ भेँड़हु खाय गेल, *sabh bhẽṛah*ᵘ *khāy gēl*, they ate up all the sheep also.

तीनि से सँ किछु बढ़ि जाएत, *tīn*ⁱ *sai sā̃ kicch*ᵘ *baṛh*ⁱ *jāet*, they somewhat exceed three hundred.

सभ बस्तुजात जरि कँ छाउर भै गेल, *sabh bastujāt jar*ⁱ *kā̃ chāur bhai gēl*, all the property being burnt became ashes.

एक खिखिरि कोनो फुलबारी में जाय पड़लि, *ek khikhir*ⁱ *kōnō phul*ᵃ*bārī mẽ jāy paṛal*ⁱ, a she-fox happened to go into a certain garden.

अम्माक सबद सुनि दीना भद्री उठल चिहाय, *ammāk sabad sun*ⁱ *dīnā bhadrī uṭhal cihāy* (for *cihāy uṭhal*), hearing their mother's words Dīnā and Bhadrī started up.

एक मुर्गा गोबरक ढेरी कैं चाँगुर सँ उकटि रहल छल, *ek murgā gob*ᵃ*rak ḍhērī kẽ cā̃gur sā̃ ukaṭ*ⁱ *rahal chal*, a cock was scratching (going along scratching) a dunghill with his claw.

किछु सीखि लेए, *kicch*ᵘ *sīkh*ⁱ *lēē*, let him learn (for himself).

अपना में बाँटि ली, *ap*ᵃ*nā mẽ bā̃ṭ*ⁱ *lī*, let us divide (it) among ourselves.

आबह बैसह पिबि लह पानि, *ābaha* (m.c. for *ābåh*), *baisaha* (*baisåh*), *pibi laha* (for *låh*) *pāni*, come, sit down, take a drink of water (Vid. lxxx, 4).

In one place Vidyāpati employs a sort of long form of the first verbal noun.

जैतहिँ हार टुटिए गेल ना, *jaitahī hāra ṭuṭie* (for *ṭuṭ*ⁱ) *gela nā*, as I went my necklace broke in pieces (ना *nā* is expletive) (Vid. xxvi, 2). Compare Vidyāpati's conjunctive participle करिए *karie* at the end of § 307.

345. (*b*) **Potential** compounds are formed by conjugating the verb सकब, *sakab*, 'to be able,' with the direct form of the first verbal noun of the principal verb. As in intensives, the final इ *ⁱ* is sometimes omitted. Thus:—

चलि सकब *chal*ⁱ *sakab*, to be able to move.

बाजि सकब *bāj*ⁱ *sakab*, to be able to speak.

लिखि सकब *likh*ⁱ *sakab*, to be able to write.

दै सकब *dai sakab*, to be able to give.

लै सकब *lai sakab*, to be able to take.

जाए सकब *jāe sakab*, to be able to go.

भेट सकब *bhēṭ sakab*, to be able to meet.

Examples from literature are—

ध्यान में आबि सकैअछि, *dhyān mē āb*ⁱ *sakai-ach*ⁱ, it can come into thought, it is conceivable.

पछतौला सँ की भै सकैअछि, *pach*ᵃ*taulā sā̃ kī bhai sakai-ach*ⁱ, from regretting what can happen?

अंगूर सभक गुच्छ लग नहिँ पहुँच सकलि, *ãgūr sabhak gucch lag nahī pahūc sakal*ⁱ, she could not reach the bunch of grapes.

346. (*c*) **Completive** compounds are similarly formed with the verb चुकब *cukab*, to be finished. The इ *ⁱ* is here also sometimes dropped. Thus:—

मारि चुकब, *mārⁱ cukab*, to have finished beating.

खा चुकब, *khā cukab*, to have finished eating.

दै चुकब, *dai cukab*, to have finished giving.

Curiously enough, I have not noted any occurrence of this compound in literature.

347. (*d*) **Permissive** compounds are made by conjugating the verb देब *dēb*, to give, with the oblique form of the first verbal noun. Thus :—

कहै देब, *kahai dēb*, or कहँ देब *kahā̃ dēb*, to allow to speak.

जाए देब, *jāe dēb*, to allow to go.

ओ ओकरा खाए देलकैक, *ō okᵃrā khāe delᵃkaik*, he allowed him to eat.

कालू सदा दीना भद्री के बैसै देलथीन्हि, *kālū sadā dīnā bhadrī kē baisai delᵃthīnhⁱ*, Kālū Sadā allowed Dīnā and Bhadrī to sit down.

नहिँ दूध पीबै देबैँ, *nahⁱ̃ dūdh pībai dēbẽ*, (if) you will not allow us to drink milk.

348. (*e*) **Acquisitive** compounds are similarly formed with the verb पाएब *pāeb*, to get. Thus :—

ओ उठै नहिँ पाबथि, *ō uṭhai nahⁱ̃ pābathⁱ*, let him not get (permission) to rise.

जिबइत जाए एकौ नहिँ पाओत, *jibaita jāe ekau nahĩ pāota*, not one will get leave (*i.e.*, be able) to depart alive (Man. viii, 43).

349. (*f*) **Inceptive** compounds are similarly formed with the verb लागब *lāgab*, to begin. Thus :—

कहँ लागब, *kahā̃ lāgab*, to begin to speak.

दीअँ लागब, *dīā̃ lāgab*, to begin to give.

मारै लागल, *mārai lāgal*, he began to beat.

बाघ खाए लागल, *bāgh khāe lāgal*, the tiger began to eat.

बुढ़िया कहै लागलि, *buṛhiā kahai lāgalⁱ*, the old woman began to say.

चारि जन आलसी पुरुख ततहिं असंक सूतल परस्पर कथा करय लगलाह, *cāri jan ālasī purukh tatahi asaṅk sūtal paraspar kathā karay lagalăh*, four lazy men, lying there without anxiety, began to talk to each other (Puruṣa Parikṣā, p. 51).

In one instance Manbōdh (i, 12) uses the oblique form of the second verbal noun in an inceptive compound, as follows:—

कमलासन किछु कहबाँ लागु, *kamalāsana kichu kahabā̃ lāgu*, (Brahmā) whose seat is on the lotus begins to say something.

350. (*g*) **Desiderative** compounds, as in Hindī, often indicate that something is on the point of occurrence. They are formed in two ways:—

(i) By the phrase इच्छा अछि *icchā achhi*, meaning "there is a desire," following the genitive of the second verbal noun in ब *b*.

(ii) By the accusative, genitive, or simple oblique form of the first or second verbal noun with the verb चाहब *cāhab*, to wish:— Examples—

(i) देखबाक इच्छा अछि, *dekhabāk icchā achhi*, there is a desire of seeing, *i.e.*, I wish to see.

(ii) हम देखँ कँ चहैछी, *ham dekhă kẽ cahai-chī*, I wish to see.

ओ बाजँ चहैअछि, *ō bājă cahai-achi*, he wishes to speak.

मारै चाहलक, *mārai căhalak*, he wanted to kill (him).

धरै चाह फेरि साँपे, *dharai cāha pheri sā̃pē*, a snake again wishes to seize it (Vid. xxii, 6).

घड़ी बाजै चहैछलि, *ghaṛī bājai cahai-chali*, the clock was about to strike.

हमहुँ अपना बालक कँ स्कूल में पठाबै चाहैछी, *hamahũ apanā bālak kẽ skūl mẽ paṭhābai căhai-chī*, I also want to send my boy to school.

ओ जाए चहैछथि, *ō jāe cahai-chathi*, he wishes to go.

ओ मरै (vulgarly मुऐ) चहैत अछि, *ō marai* (vulgarly *muai*) *cahait achi*, he is at the point of death.

धोअल धाएल भेंड़ी पाँका लागै चाहैअछि, *dhōal dhāel bhẽṛī pā̃kā lāgai cāhai-achi*, the sheep washed (for sale) is about to fall into the slough. (Proverb.)

एहि पोथी कैं पढ़क चाही, *ehi pōthī kẽ puṛhåk cāhī*, one should read this book.

तोहरा ओतय जाएक (or जाए or जाए कैं) चाही, *tohᵃrā otay jāek* (or *jāe* or *jāe kẽ*) *cāhī*, you should go there.

बहुत सोच बिचारि कै करैक चाही . . . पछतैबाक नहिं चाही, *bahut sōc bicāri kai karaik cāhī . . . . pachᵃtaibāk nahi cāhī*, one should act after much thought and consideration . . . . one should not regret.

In the above, note the use of चाही *cāhī*, equivalent to the Hindī चाहिये *cāhiyē*.

Class II.—**Compounds formed with Participles.**

351. (*a*). **Continuative** compounds are formed with the direct form of the masculine Present Participle. Thus:—

लिखैत जाएब, *likhait jāeb*. to continue writing.

पढ़ैत जाएब, *paṛhait jāeb*, to continue reading.

बजैत जाएब, *bajait jāeb*, to continue speaking.

जाइत रहब, *jāit rahab*, to continue going

पबैत आएब, *pabait āeb*, to go on finding.

पानि बहैत जाइअछि, *pāni bahait jāi-achi*, the water keeps flowing away.

नदी केर धार बहैत रहैअछि, *nadī kēr dhār bahait rahai-achi*, the stream of the river keeps flowing on.

352. (*b*) **Statical** compounds are similarly made except that the participle agrees in gender with the subject of the verb. Thus:—

कनैत चलब, *kanait calab*, to go along crying.

गबैत आएब, *gabait āeb*, to come singing.

एक स्त्री गबैति अबैछलि, *ek strī gabaiti abai-chali*, a woman was coming singing.

रसायनी ओहि राति कँ कतहुँ चलैत भेल, *rasāy^anī ohⁱ rātⁱ kã̄ katah^ŭ calait bhēl*, the alchemist that night became going somewhere (*i.e.*, took to his heels).

Quasi continuative or statical compounds are also formed with the third verbal noun or past participle, as in :—

पानि बहल जाइत अछि, *pāni bahal jāit achⁱ*, the water keeps flowing away.

एक बाघ पड़ल फिरैछल, *ek bāgh paṛal phirai-chal*, a tiger was prowling about.

हमरा संग लागल चलैह *ham^arā saṅg lāgal calåh*, come along with me.

अढ़ाइ सै तँ बचले रहत। आओर ओहि मेँ सँ जे बाँचल निकसत, ओहि सभक नीक दाम भेँटत, *aṛhāi sai tã̄ bac^alē rahat, āor ohⁱ mẽ sã̄ jē bã̄cal nik^asat, ohⁱ sabhak nīk dām bhẽṭat*, at any rate a hundred will remain over and above, and from those that will remain over and above, I will get a good price for them. Note in this case that the locative of the verbal noun and the direct form of the participle are quite synonymous.

353. The equivalent of the Hindī चला जाना *calā jānā* is the intensive compound चलि जाएब *calⁱ jāeb* or चलि होएब *calⁱ hōeb*. Thus :—

चलि गेल जोगिया जाँजरि, *calⁱ gēl jogiyā-jã̄jarⁱ*, they went away to Jogiyā-Jānjari

हाँथ लेलेँ बाढ़नि चलि भेलि सिंघ दरबाज, *hã̄th lēlẽ bāṛhanⁱ calⁱ bhēlⁱ siṅgh dar^abāj*, taking the broom in her hand she went to the main door of the house.

कुंज भवन सँ चलि भेलि हे, *kuñja bhabana sã̄ cali bheli hē*, (as) she came out of the arbour (Vid. xxi, 1).

चलि जाएब *calⁱ jāeb* means 'to go away,' चलि होएब *calⁱ hōeb* is simply 'to go.'

354. Attention has also been called in § 180 to the use of the instrumental or locative of the third verbal noun or past

participle to indicate continued action, especially to the phrases लेलें जाएब *lēlẽ jāeb*, to take away with one, and लेलें आएब *lēlẽ āeb*, to bring with one, equivalent to the Hindī लिये जाना *liyē jānā* and लिये आना *liyē ānā*, respectively. Equivalent to the Hindī ले आना *lē ānā* or लाना *lānā* is लै आएब *lai āeb*, or लाएब *lāeb*, to bring. Varieties of लै आएब *lai āeb* are लिआएब *liāeb*, लय आएब *lay āeb*, and लऽ आएब *lå āeb*. Equivalent to the Hindī ले जाना *lē jānā* is लै (लय or लऽ) जाएब *lai* (*lay* or *lå*) *jāeb*, to take away. Thus:—

किछु चाँनी हमरा ओतय लै आबँह, *kicchᵘ cā̃nī hamᵃrā otay lai ābåh*, bring some silver to my house.

स्वामी सलहेस लाएब जादू सौं लोभाए, *swāmī salᵃhēs lāeb jādū saũ lobhāe*, I will bring my lord Salhēs, having enticed him by enchantment.

हमरा सौं की लैबै ओजह इनाम, *hamᵃrā saũ kī laibai ojah inām*, what reward or present will you bring from me ?

हम चोरी कै लैलहुँ, *ham cōrī kai lailahũ*, having done theft, I have brought (it).

लै जाह, *lai jāh*, take away, as in § 180.

हमरा सोझा सँ उठा लऽ जाएत, *hamᵃrā sōjhā sã uṭhā lå jāet*, he will take it away from before me.

हमरो रंग रभस लय जैबह ।
लैबह कोन सनेसे ।

hamarō raṅga rabhasa laya jaibaha (for *jaibåh*) ।
laibaha (for *laibåh*) *kōna sanēsē* ॥

Thou wilt also take away also all my joy and passion,
What present will you bring (in return) (Vid. lv, 2).

More usual than लाएब *lāeb* is the verb आनब *ānab*, to bring, as in दुइ सै रुपैआक चाँनी ओहि रसायनी कें आनि देलकै, *dui sai rupaiāk cā̃nī ohⁱ rasāyᵃnī kẽ ānⁱ delᵃkai*, having brought silver (to the value) of two hundred rupees, he gave it to that alchemist.

PART IV.

INDECLINABLES.

A. Adverbs.

355. Henceforth I shall not transliterate.

The following lists have been collected :—

I. ADVERBS OF TIME.

एखन, आब	*Now.*	पहिले	*At first.*
तखन	*Then.*	सबेर	*Early, at dawn.*
तहिआ		सबेरक	
कखन	*When ?*	अत्युख	
कहिआ		भोर	
जखन	*When.*	कदाचित	*Perhaps, sometimes.*
जहिआ		कदापि	
आइ	*To-day.*	कहिओ	
काल्हि	*Yesterday, to-morrow.*	एतबा मेँ	*In the meantime.*
आइ काल्हि	*Now-a-days.*	निदान	*At last.*
परसू	*The day before yesterday, or the day after to-morrow.*	अन्त	
		अन्तकाल	
		बेरिबेरि	*Often.*
		बारंबार	
प्रतिदिन	*Every day.*	सीघ्र	*Quickly.*
अनुदिन		लगले	*Instantly.*
सभदिन		पश्चात्	*Afterwards.*
सदा	*Always.*	पाछा	
सर्वदा		फेरि	*Again.*
नित्ति	*Continually.*	एकबेरि	*Once.*

356. II. Adverbs of Place.

एतय	*Here.*	लगपास	*On all sides.*
ओतय	*There.*	समीप	*Near.*
कतय, कहाँ	*Where?*	एहिकात	*On this side.*
जतय, जहाँ	*Where.*	ओहिकात	*On that side.*
ततय, तहाँ	*There.*	सर्बत्र	*Everywhere.*
एम्हर	*Hither.*	सभठाम	*Everywhere.*
ओम्हर	*Thither.*	उपर	*Above.*
केम्हर	*Whither?*	नीचें	*Below.*
जेम्हर	*Whither.*	पार	*Across.*
तेम्हर	*Thither.*	निकट	*Near.*
कतहुँ	*Somewhere.*	नगीच	*Near.*

357. III. Adverbs of Manner.

अचानक	*Suddenly.*	व्रिथा or वृथा	*In vain.*
अकस्मात्	*Accidentally.*	व्यर्थ	*In vain.*
अचक में	*Accidentally.*	नाहक	*In vain.*
चुप्पे	*Privately.*	एना	*Thus.*
अति	*Very.*	किऐ	*Why?*
पृथक	*Separately.*	किऐक तँ	*Because.*
फराक	*Separately.*	कोना, कोन तरहेँ	*How?*
झटपट	*At once.*	जेना, जँ तरहेँ	*As.*
झटद्	*At once.*	तेना, तँ तरहेँ	*So.*
तथापि	*Nevertheless.*	नीक	*Well.*
तैओ	*Nevertheless.*	सत्य	*Truly.*
यद्यपि	*Although.*	सहज, सहजेँ,	*Gratis.*
जद्यपि	*Although.*	सहज में	*Gratis.*
जैओ	*Although.*	इत्यादि, इत्यादि,	*Etcetera.*

358. IV. ADVERBS OF AFFIRMATION AND NEGATION.

हँ, *Yes.*

निश्चय, *Certainly.*

निस्सन्देह, *Doubtlessly.*

अवश्य, *Necessarily.*

बस, *Enough!*

नहिँ, ने, नै, न, *No, not.*

जनु, मति. *No, do not* (with imperative).

359. The following are further examples of COMPOUND ADVERBS:—

एक बेरि, *Once upon a time.*

कखनो कखनो, *Sometimes.*

नहुँ नहुँ, सुस्ते सुस्ते, *Gently.*

एखन धरि, *Till now, yet.*

कखन धरि, कखन धरि, कहाँ तक, *Till when? How long?*

कखनो नहिँ, *Never.*

दुनू दिस, *On both sides, all round.*

एहन ओहन, *Indifferently.*

जौँ कखनो, *Whenever.*

और कतहुँ, *Elsewhere.*

कतहुँ नहिँ, *Nowhere.*

एतय धरि, *Hitherto.*

नहिँ तँ, *If not, else.*

कखनो न कखनो, *Some time or other.*

कतहुँ न कतहुँ, *Somewhere or other.*

जखन न तखन, *Now and then.*

एना मेँ एना, *Somehow or other.*

360. The following are examples in which adverbs take the signs of cases after them:—

एखनुक बेरि नीक छैक, *Now is the best time.* (Lit. *The time of now is good*).

तखिना सँ आइ भेट भेल अछि, *I have not seen you since then till to-day.* (Lit. *From that time to-day a (first) meeting has occurred*).

निदान कँ ऐलाह, *At last he came.*

अन्तकाल मेँ ग्यान भेलन्हि, *At length he came to his senses.*

ओ आइ कँ काल्हि कहैत छथि, *He puts off from to-day to to-morrow.* (Lit. *He calls to-day to-morrow*).

PARTICLES OF EMPHASIS.

361. These are ई and हि or हिँ, *only, even,* and ओ and हु or हुँ, *also, even.* They are always used enclitically, and when any

of them is added to a word ending in आ, that आ is omitted. Examples: हमरी, *mine only* (हमर + ई), or *me only* (हमरा + ई); एखनहिं, *even now, already*; हमरो or हमरहुँ, *mine also*, or *me also*; उतर, *a reply*, उतरो, *even a reply*; अपनहुँ, *even one's own*.

B. Postpositions.

362. The following is a list of the more usual Postpositions:—

आगू, आगाँ, *Before.*
पीछू, पाछू, पाछाँ, *Behind.*
छाड़ि, *Except.*
ऊपर, *Above.*
नीचाँ, *Beneath.*
पर, पै, *On, upon.*
भीतर, *Within.*
तक, *Up to.*
संमुख, सोझाँ, *Facing.*
साछात, *Before.*
लेल, *For, on account of.*
बिनु, बिना, *Without, except.*
बाहिर, *Out.*
संग, *With.*
बदला, *In exchange (for), instead (of).*
जकाँ, *Like.*

The above all govern either the simple oblique form or else the genitive case, saving छाड़ि, *except*, and बिनु or बिना, *without*. The latter governs either the Instrumental or the Dative, as in:—

बिना पुरुख सौं कोना दिवस गमाएब, *how shall I pass my days without a husband?*

बिना पुरुख कें तिखा एतेक बेरि सूतलि, *did a woman sleep so long without (her) husband.*

छाड़ि takes the accusative. भुँइचा छाड़ि किछु नहिं, *nothing but the husk.*

C. Conjunction.

363. The following are the more useful:—

आओर, औ, or ओ *And.*
के or कि, *That.*
ओ. *Else, even.*
तँ, *Then.*
की...की, *Either...or.*
परंतु, *But.*
जौँ, *If.*

यौँ is often idiomatically omitted. Thus :—

जोहरी एकरा पबैत तँ अत्यंत खुस होइत, *if a jeweller had got this then he would have been much pleased.*

364. D. **Interjections**, see § 93. Others as in Hindī.

ERRATA.

A few of these are important.

Page 5. line 19, *for* see *read* obtain				
,, 6, ,, 7, ,,	देखद् ,, देखद्त			
,, 7, ,, 1 and 3 of footnote, *for* dipthongal *read* diphthongal				
,, 9, ,, 9, *for*	ड		*read*	ड्
,, ,, ,, 17. ,,	ष		,,	ष्
,, 10, ,, 19, ,,	म लीवा		,,	मालीवा
,, 11. ,, 2, ,,	*aū*		,,	*au*
,, 12. ,, 1 of footnote, *for* on			,,	in
,, 13, ,, 10. *for*	~ *ṛh*		,,	~ *ṛh*
,, ,, ,, 15, ,,	खाँभ *bhā̃bh*		,,	खाँभ *khā̃bh*
,, 14. ,, 7, ,,	देखलऊ		,,	देखलहूँ
,, 15, ,, 2, *for* indicate by the sign, *read* indicate by the sign				
,, 16. ,, 13. ,,	ष a		*read*	ष *a*
,, 21, ,, 8, ,,	पोथ		,,	पोथी
,, ,, ,, 12. ,,	*wā̃* or *wē̃*		,,	*wā̃* or वें *wē̃*
,, 25, ,, 5, ,,	*ōnā*		,,	*sōnā*
,, 27, ,, 8, ,,	rower		,,	rower;
,, 29, ,, 5, ,,	§ 10,		,,	(§ 10,
,, ,, ,, 6; ,,	बड		,,	बड़्
,, 36. ,, 10, ,,	करौनी		,,	कँरौनी
,, ,, ,, 14, ,,	डंगौनी		,,	डँगौनी
,, 39, last line, *for* the			,,	by the
,, 44, line 1, *for*	िच		,,	चि
,, 46. ,, 14, ,,	ल		,,	ले
,, ,, 17, ,,	a *a* ब		,,	a ब
,, 49, ,, 9. ,,	बहिरा		,,	बहिरा
,, 52. ,, 7, ,,	al		,,	all
,, ,, last line, ,,	t		,,	it
,, 53. line 16, ,,	कथँ		,,	कथें

Page 55, line 18, *for* o *read* of
„ „ „ 21, „ *carhābai* „ *caṛhābai*
„ 59, „ 2, from bottom, *for* म „ मेँ
„ 60, „ 4, „ „ „ मँ „ मेँ
„ 86, „ 11, *for* एृहि „ प्रहि
„ 90, „ 13, „ क „ केँ
„ 95, „ 23, „ केस... *kēśa* „ कैस... *kesa*
„ 109, „ 3, „ *dekhau* „ *dēkhau*
„ „ „ 4, „ *dekhah*^{u} „ *dēkhah*^{u}.
„ „ „ 6, „ षौ „ षौ *au*
„ 120, „ 2, from bottom, *for* कौ *read* कौ
„ 127, „ 1, and heading. This page should commence with § 197.
„ 133, line 18, *for* कर-गँ *read* करँ-गँ
„ 139, „ 9, „ देव „ देव
„ 155, „ 7, from bottom, for *lagal*^{a} *thīnh*^{i} read *lagal*^{a}*thīnh*^{i}
„ 216, „ 9, *for* sees *read* is visible
„ 270, „ 10, „ two „ two hundred
„ 302, „ 2, from bottom, *for* नौं „ जौं
„ „ last line, *for* नँ „ तँ
„ 303, line 1, „ यौं „ जौं

See § 4 APPENDIX

Table shewing the various alphabets used in Mithilā.

Dēva Nāgarī	Kaithī	Maithilī	English Transliteration	Dēva Nāgarī	Kaithī	Maithilī	English Transliteration
अ	𑂃	𑒁	a	ञ		𑒘	ñ
आ	𑂄	𑒂	ā	ट	𑂗	𑒙	ṭ
इ	𑂅	𑒃	i	ठ	𑂘	𑒚	ṭh
ई	𑂆	𑒄	ī	ड	𑂙	𑒛	ḍ
उ	𑂇	𑒅	u	ढ	𑂛	𑒜	ḍh
ऊ	𑂈	𑒆	ū	ण	𑂝	𑒝	ṇ
ऋ		𑒇	ṛ	त	𑂞	𑒞	t
ॠ		𑒈	ṝ	थ	𑂟	𑒟	th
ऌ		𑒉	ḷ	द	𑂠	𑒠	d
ए	𑂉	𑒋	ē	ध	𑂡	𑒡	dh
ऐ	𑂊	𑒌	ai	न	𑂢	𑒢	n
ओ	𑂋	𑒍	ō	प	𑂣	𑒣	p
औ	𑂌	𑒎	au	फ	𑂤	𑒤	ph
अं	𑂃𑂁	𑒁𑓀	aṁ	ब	𑂥	𑒥	b
अः	𑂃𑂂	𑒁𑓁	aḥ	भ	𑂦	𑒦	bh
क	𑂍	𑒏	k	म	𑂧	𑒧	m
ख	𑂎	𑒐	kh	य		𑒨	y
ग	𑂏	𑒑	g	र	𑂩	𑒩	r
घ	𑂐	𑒒	gh	ल	𑂪	𑒪	l
ङ	𑂑	𑒓	ṅ	व	𑂫	𑒫	v or w
च	𑂒	𑒔	c	श		𑒬	ś
छ	𑂓	𑒕	ch	ष		𑒭	ṣ
ज	𑂔	𑒖	j	स	𑂮	𑒮	s
झ	𑂕	𑒗	jh	ह	𑂯	𑒯	h

The semi-vowel य is not used by Kāyasths in writing Maithilī the vowel इ being substituted for it.

See § 4 APPENDIX

A Sanskrit Slōka written in the three characters of Mithilā.

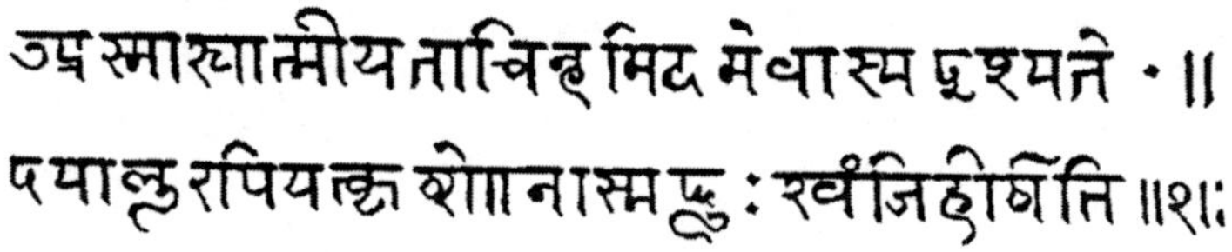

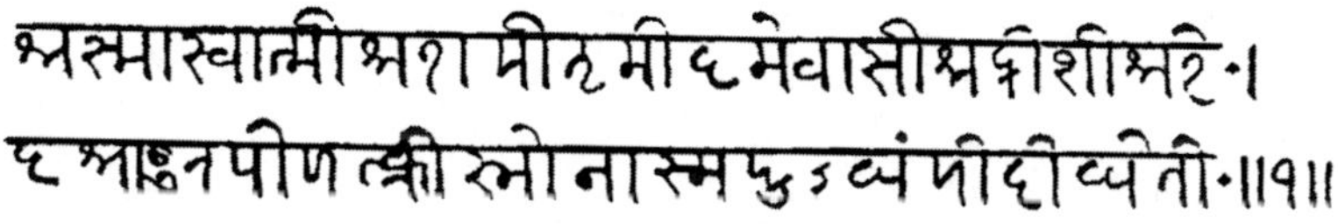

The Kayathī character is not adapted for writing Sanskrit. It has no form for short medial i, and has no semivowel ya.

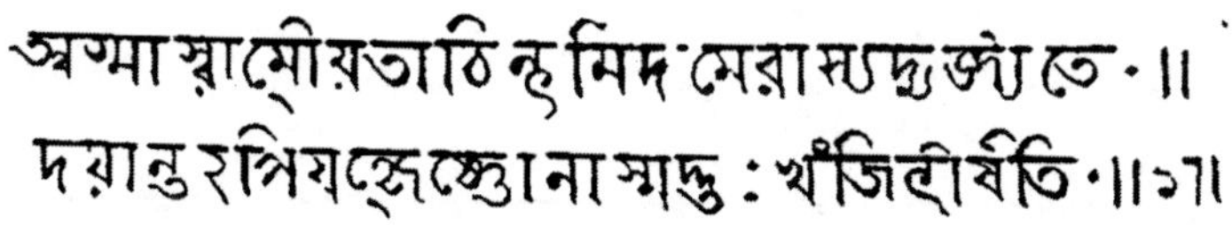